Skills of Management
Sixth Edition

This book is the sixth edition of a highly successful introduction to management. Starting with the transition of employees to a managerial role, it deals with core skills involved in management. These skills include delegation, communication, appraisal, staff development, disciplinary handling, employee relations, negotiation and chairing and conduct in meetings. These are discussed alongside the key themes of prioritisation and the need for thorough identification of objectives and diagnosis of problems before action. In summary, the book is relevant to all those with line management responsibilities, particularly responsibility for people.

This sixth edition of the *Skills of Management* has been thoroughly updated, restructured and given a more international focus. Each chapter includes a statement of learning outcomes and self-assessment questions. Account is taken of the many recent developments in management theory and practice.

The book is accompanied by a website containing over fifty teaching exercises and a separate tutor website containing tutor notes for each case study or exercise. Tutors will also be able to access a series of articles written by the authors exploring key topics within the text in further detail. The case studies on the website have been edited and updated and many new ones have been added. Additions include cases on marketing, finance and those involving issues of national culture.

Real-life examples are offered throughout the book, with the variation in styles of management required by different organisations and national cultures taken into consideration. The authors draw on their wide academic and industrial experience to provide a sound blend of theory and practice which is useful and highly readable.

W. David Rees was a Principal Lecturer in Management at the University of Westminster. He has extensive experience in management consultancy in the UK and abroad in both the private and public sectors and is a member of the ACAS Panel of Independent Arbitrators. He also worked in industry before joining the University of Westminster.

Dr Christine Porter is Head of Human Resource Management Department in the Westminster Business School at the University of Westminster. She worked in industry and consultancy before joining the University and has undertaken several overseas assignments. Her Ed.D thesis was about the cross-cultural issues involved in teaching management.

Skills of Management
Sixth Edition

Skills of Management
Sixth Edition

W. David Rees & Christine Porter

SOUTH-WESTERN
CENGAGE Learning™

Australia • Brazil • Japan • Korea • Mexico • Singapore • Spain • United Kingdom • United States

SOUTH-WESTERN
CENGAGE Learning™

Skills of Management, 6th Edition
W. David Rees and Christine Porter

Publishing Director: John Yates

Publisher: Geraldine Lyons

Development Editor: Leandra Paoli

Production Editor: Leonora Dawson-Bowling

Manufacturing Manager: Helen Mason

Marketing Manager: Rossella Proscia

Senior Production Controller: Maeve Healy

Typesetter: KnowledgeWorks Global Ltd, India

Cover design: Nick Welch, Design Deluxe, Bath, UK

Text design: Design Deluxe, Bath, UK

For product information and technology assistance, contact **emea.info@cengage.com**.

For permission to use material from this text or product, and for permission queries, email **clsuk.permissions@cengage.com**.

Products and services that are referred to in this book may be either trademarks and/or registered trademarks of their respective owners. The publishers and author/s make no claim to these trademarks.

British Library Cataloguing-in-Publication Data
A catalogue record for this book is available from the British Library.

ISBN: 978-1-84480-645-4

Cengage Learning EMEA
High Holborn House, 50-51 Bedford Row
London WC1R 4LR

Cengage Learning products are represented in Canada by Nelson Education Ltd.

For your lifelong learning solutions, visit **www.cengage.co.uk**
Purchase e-books or e-chapters at: **http://estore.bized.co.uk**

Printed by Zrinski dd, Croatia
1 2 3 4 5 6 7 8 9 10 – 10 09 08

Brief contents

Contents

1 Managers and their backgrounds 1

2 Identifying the manager's job 23

3 The manager and the organisation 51

4 Managerial style 87

5 Delegation 115

8 Communication 177

9 Selection 203

10 Appraisal 231

11 Training and development 253

12 Counselling 277

14 The manager and employee relations 321

15 Negotiating skills 347

16   Meetings and chairing 371

List of figures

Preface

Perhaps the best way of explaining the rationale for a new edition is to liken the writing of the book to the production of a car. Car design has to take place within a changing environment – particularly in the technological and market areas. However, if a car is to be produced, at some stage the design has to be frozen so that production can start – even though opportunities for improvement continue to emerge. Note is taken of these opportunities for further improvement, however, so that they can be incorporated into the next model. This is just the process that has taken place with this book. It has been repeated with each new edition. Also – just as with car production – use has been made of the information about the performance of the product after it has been launched. A particularly important source of information in this respect has been discussions about the content of the book with mature students who are in managerial jobs.

The scale of change between the fifth (2001) and sixth editions is considerable. Every chapter has been revised in the light of recent developments and the continuing impact on organisations and managerial jobs of information technology and **globalisation**. There is also an increased emphasis on the impact of national culture on management. Conversely some issues have been found to have diminished in importance, which has created the opportunity to put the concept of prioritisation into practice. The reductions include the amount of detail about employment law. A reduction here has been particularly appropriate as employment law varies from country to country. Such an alteration also fits with the increased international orientation of the book.

The sixth edition also benefits from research by the authors into key topic areas, undertaken since the previous edition. It has long been their contention that most people with managerial responsibility started off as specialists. In a survey they conducted into this issue they found that this was the case in no less than 47 out of the 50 people with managerial responsibility that they surveyed. More detailed information about this survey is included in Chapter 1. Christine Porter's doctoral research into the cultural problems that can be experienced by students studying management has also been very relevant. Consequently, even more attention has been paid to the writing style used, the impact of national culture on management, the examples used in the text and the case studies on the website. A recurring theme is that the concepts and skills involved in management cannot be applied prescriptively regardless of national culture.

The website of case studies and other teaching exercises has been edited and expanded overall. This process will continue after the book has been published. Although the book does not cover the topics of finance and marketing explicitly in the text, it has proved practicable to add cases about marketing and finance issues. This is especially important to indicate the interconnectivity between different areas of management. In addition the range of countries used for case studies has been increased. Throughout the text concepts are illustrated by relevant examples. Where it is possible to reference the source of these examples this has been done. However, where the examples are not identified or referenced, though they are real enough, a certain level of discretion is appropriate.

There are some important issues with regard to writing style. We have dealt with the issue of the use of the personal pronoun 'he' by simply not using it unless it refers to a specific person. Language conventions have changed so that we have followed the practice of some other writers by using the term 'they' in a singular as well as a plural context to avoid sexist connotations. We have preferred to generally stay with the term 'skills' rather than use the term 'competences' (or competencies). This is because the term 'competencies' refers to a particular approach to the identification, development and assessment of skills and we believe the term 'skills' is more generic. This is also in line with our aim to express ourselves as clearly as possible and to avoid using long words if there are shorter alternatives. The slightly narrower concept of 'competencies' is dealt with, however, where appropriate. The consistent feedback we have received about the previous editions has been that they have above all else been readable and we have been determined to try to keep it that way.

W. David Rees
Christine Porter

Acknowledgements

Particular acknowledgement is due to the countless numbers of management students who, in different classes and organisational workshops, have allowed us to test out and develop our ideas and have contributed both ideas of their own and many invaluable illustrative examples that appear in this book. The classes have been on a wide variety of courses – especially at Westminster Business School, University of Westminster and at the University's Diplomatic Academy both in London and in Paris. Particular thanks are due to students on the MA in International Business and Management, the MA in Human Resource Management, the MA in Personnel and Development (and its predecessors), the MA in Diplomatic Studies and the business studies undergraduates on the highly popular 'Role of the Manager' module. They have given us very useful insights about management in a variety of cultural settings. A revelation that has been put to good use is the overlap between the skills needed in diplomacy and management. Further cultural insights were gained from the students on the various management development workshops we have run in Malaysia and Indonesia. Thanks are also due to MBA students who studied at the Faculty of Business at London South Bank University. We have gleaned innumerable valuable ideas from current and former colleagues at the University of Westminster and also by 'in-house' training and consultancy in a wide variety of organisations, especially the former Bass Group and a range of London Borough Councils. We also gratefully acknowledge the University of Chicago Press for permission to reproduce the rectangles diagrams on the website for the Communications Exercise related to Chapter 8 and the magazine Private Eye, for allowing us to reproduce the cartoon that appears in Chapter 9.

We have received direct help in writing the various editions of the book from a wide range of people, including a range of academics and people working in industry, commerce, the public sector and other not-for-profit organisations. Whilst it is perhaps invidious to name just some of them, the list includes Peter Bell, Hywel Davies, Sarah Dowding, Reece Evans, Les Galloway, Denys Groves, Alan Hovell, Bob Lee, Sue Miller, Jonathan Rees, Matthew Rees, Ralph Rees, Angela Rice, John Ring, Gill Sugden, Fraser Tuddenham and Angela Wright. We would also like to thank Simon Marsh, Employment and Communications Director of the Chemical Industries Association for all his support and advice. Thanks are also due to Daniel Rees for his help with data inputting.

List of reviewers

Philip Barbonis, Radboud University Nijmegen
Barbara Dexter, University of Derby
Keith Pond, Loughborough University
Judy Rimmer, Stafforshire University

Introduction

During the time that we have taught management subjects we have become aware of the dearth of books that address a reasonable range of core issues, let alone tackle such topics in an appropriate way. Most books about management are written from the perspective of a particular discipline or function and are intended for a specialist rather than a person with a range of management responsibilities. A further complication has been that the language in many of these books is not particularly user-friendly. Through taking a marketing approach to our teaching and trying to establish the areas those who had management responsibilities actually needed help in, we have built up a fund of relevant material. We have also sought to use clear language and practical illustrations to facilitate learning.

After prompting from some student groups, including one in particular at the Royal College of Nursing, David Rees eventually converted some of his material into a book about practical management skills and, as explained in the Preface to this edition, the book has been systematically developed through various editions, with help throughout from Christine Porter who became joint editor for the fifth edition as well as the sixth. In revising the book once more we have endeavoured to keep to the original idea of writing one that was intended to be of practical benefit to those who had acquired, or who expected to acquire, a range of management responsibilities and which was user-friendly.

Over the years we both became fascinated with the way in which people in widely different organisations and countries seemed to be grappling with similar basic issues and problems. This enabled David Rees to initially identify a core of basic issues that match the syllabus requirements of a wide range of courses, as well as being relevant to the non-student practitioner. We have been able to draw on the contributions made in hundreds of classroom discussions and 'in-house' workshops to provide appropriate practical examples to illustrate and help explain the relevant theoretical concepts and practical skills. Such examples, and continuous contact with those facing management problems on a day-to-day basis, have enabled us to write a book that is relevant, with an appropriate blend of theory and practice.

Providing a blend is critical, as this book is not intended to supply a set of prescriptive remedies. Action needs to be preceded by careful diagnosis. Mary Parker Follett's concept of the 'law of the situation', explained in Chapter 1, is all important. Decisions and action need to take account of the variables in a situation. By providing both a basic theoretical analysis of concepts and an explanation of the skills that are likely to be useful, the intention is to provide readers with the ability to judge when and how to use specific skills and remedies, rather than to apply them as a knee-jerk reaction to problems. Many of the issues dealt with are also crucial 'life-skills'. The need for, for example, accurate problem definition, effective communication, the resolution of conflict, negotiation and the development of practical strategies in these areas are not confined to the workplace. Development of skills in these areas may bring considerable advantages in one's personal life as well as at work.

It is increasingly recognised that people who train as specialists are likely to accumulate considerable managerial responsibilities in the course of their career. As explained in Chapter 1, few people start their careers as managers. Organisations usually have a departmental structure. The normal career progression is for people to start off as a specialist and then progressively acquire responsibility for supervising or managing other specialists. Even business studies graduates usually find they have to be placed initially in a specialist job, despite the general nature of the training they have received. If that is the pattern, it is just as well to prepare people for what is to come. If the specialism requires training, why not also the managerial aspects? The trend to devolution of authority and decision-making within both private and public sector organisations, accompanied by flatter organisational structures, has emphasised this by increasing the range of responsibilities and the speed with which people acquire them. Logically the syllabuses of most professional and specialist courses have now been adapted to include management. Many people, however, do not have the benefit of management training and it is hoped that this book will be of assistance to them as well as those who are engaged in the formal study of management.

We have generally not made a distinction between management and supervision, although we have referred to the role of the first-line supervisor in Chapters 13 and 14. We have used the term 'management' generically to incorporate supervision. Our general scepticism of the value of the distinction has been reinforced when we have run management courses or workshops for people at different levels within the same organisation. On one occasion David Rees was involved in running management courses simultaneously at three different levels in the National Health Service in the UK. These were for ward sisters, middle managers and senior nursing officers. The perhaps heretical conclusion he came to was that many of the basic management problems facing the people employed at these different levels were the same. Status issues required that the programmes be written up in distinctly different ways and there were some genuine differences. However, it was the common nature of the problems rather than the differences that was the more noticeable.

People in senior positions may perceive their management development needs as being very sophisticated by virtue of their position, when the reality often is that they, for whatever reason, can't or don't get the basics right. The general problem is not one of establishing new insights, but of getting people to convert key concepts into effective action. This applies to management syllabuses on formal courses. Any introduction to key concepts is going to have to cover much the same general ground, whether it be on an undergraduate, professional, postgraduate or other vocational course at any level. It is only when the key concepts have been mastered in practice as well as theory that it is appropriate to consider identifying and meeting advanced needs.

The range of topics covered includes general management and the management of people. The text does not specifically extend to finance and marketing. Clearly these are important areas but it has been necessary to place a limit on the range of topics we have covered. We have also had to recognise the limits of our own expertise. Additionally we have taken into account that there are likely to be considerable variations in the marketing and finance content of jobs that readers have, or are likely to have. However, we have included some basic case studies about marketing and finance in this edition.

What we believe we have done, though, is to identify a core range of topics that is of relevance to anyone studying or involved in management. The potential scope of managerial responsibility is so wide that the coverage cannot be exhaustive. However, no-one with managerial responsibilities can escape the need, for example, to consider such issues as the identification of objectives, prioritisation, managerial style, delegation, motivation, remuneration, communication, selection, training and development, disciplinary handling, negotiation, employee relations and chairing and conduct in meetings.

In writing this book we have taken into account the needs of managers and students in a variety of countries. We have for a long time been concerned that teaching and writing should be understandable. The avoidance of long words when short ones will do is very much in keeping with the theme of the chapter on communication. It means that readers do not have to translate unnecessary jargon to understand the contents of the book. The aim is to help, not to impress.

In considering the needs of readers we have been able to capitalise on our experience of teaching and discussing management issues with people from a wide variety of countries. This has particularly included diplomats on the MA in Diplomatic Studies at the University of Westminster, studying both in London and Paris. We have also been able to capitalise on our own overseas working experience. This approach is also of benefit to readers, because of the increasing likelihood of their working or dealing with people from different cultural backgrounds or working in different cultural environments. These issues are particularly addressed in the sections dealing with culture in Chapters 3 and 4. The places where one or often both of us have worked include the University of Guyana; a range of private and public sector organisations in Malaysia, including the Mara Institute of Technology; Ngee Ann Polytechnic in Singapore, where David Rees was external examiner in Business Studies; and Pertamina – the national oil company of Indonesia. We were both also able to gain invaluable insights into the managerial issues involved in former communist countries by our work as policy advisers to the Romanian Economic and Social Council. Our exposure to different cultures and to different nationalities has led us to the conclusion that the bulk of the material in this book is about skills that are needed in a wide range of cultures. Globalisation has increased the international relevance of the material.

How to use the book

The topics that we have chosen are core management skills that most managers are likely to have to confront at some time or other. The writing theme has been to write about what readers need to know about, not what the authors know. What is covered is a range of management issues, particularly relating to the management of people, from the perspective of the line manager. The book may also be of interest to specialists in the human resource management area because of the core issues covered and their user-friendly treatment.

The book is arranged in a logical sequence of topics. The material covered in the first chapter explains the nature of management and the process by which people get involved in management. Subsequent chapters deal with core management skills. The material in the last nine chapters (8–16) all have a particular bearing on communication. Consequently, Chapter 8 on communication skills is a foundation chapter for those that follow.

There could be other ways of sequencing the chapters, but the sequence used is the one that on balance is likely to be most useful to most readers. Each chapter, however, is also written as a free-standing item. Consequently, if readers want to study a particular topic, they will find a comprehensive treatment in the relevant chapter. Where cross-references are needed to other chapters they are given in the text.

Each chapter has a similar structure and contains the following elements:

- Learning outcomes
- Introduction
- Main text
- Summary
- Self-assessment questions (one for each learning outcome)
- General references (with a short statement about the content of key references)

Boxed examples are given throughout the text in order to illustrate the concepts included in the text.

The style of the book is to link theory and practice in a user-friendly way. There is no all-encompassing theory of management. However, there is a range of concepts from a variety of disciplines that can be very useful to readers in analysing management problems and developing problem-solving strategies. The many practical examples are meant to illustrate general issues and to help to show the link between theory and practice. They are also useful for generating interest and helping readers to remember particular issues. The concepts and examples included are also intended to form a link with the problems that readers may have to deal with.

Career management

The book is intended to be of particular importance in helping readers organise their own career management. The first chapter is crucial in explaining how people may accumulate some managerial responsibilities, even if they do not have the title 'manager'. For those who do not yet have managerial responsibilities, or who may not be employed on a regular basis, Chapter 1 explains how they may find that they rapidly acquire some management responsibilities when they are in regular work. The concept of the '**managerial escalator**' explains how the route into management is usually via specialist activity. People are likely to find that they increasingly have to combine specialist and managerial activities. The rest of the book covers key managerial skills that are likely to be necessary for those who have managerial responsibilities.

The career paths of readers may not be as predictable as was historically the case. The ever-increasing pace of organisational and occupational change may mean that organisations and occupational roles are increasingly subject to dramatic change A consequence of this is that readers may find that they need to take increasing responsibility for their own development and career planning. Even if they are working in a stable environment, they may find that they need to view their own training and development as a continuous activity if they are to keep up to date with the job demands placed on them. Ironically the process-type skills involved in management are not so subject to dramatic change, although the context in which process skills are used may alter greatly. This means that the skills covered in the book may continue to be of great value in whatever organisation a person works. As readers rise up the 'managerial escalator' these skills are likely to be increasingly crucial.

Note to tutors

The case studies, exercises and relevant articles written by the authors are available on the companion website: www.cengage.co.uk/rees6. The user name and password for the tutor website are also available from the publishers for tutors who adopt the book. Lecturers should complete the registration form on the website to apply for their password, which will then be sent to them by email.

The case studies and exercises have generally been purpose-written and tested by the authors.

The authors recommend that students read specific chapters of the book either before or after individual teaching sessions. This frees up time in the classroom for the use of participative exercises and discussion. The supporting teaching material is designed to fit with each chapter. There is little point in simply presenting material in class that can easily be read in the book. This is particularly so given the reader-friendly way in which the book is written. The usual pattern is to ask students to read a set case study for discussion in class and read the relevant chapter after it. Classroom discussions can generate considerable interest, enabling people to test out their ideas and share experiences.

The book can be used at a number of different levels of management and the level of discussion adjusted in accordance with the sophistication of the student group. Many of the ideas and examples incorporated in the book are the result of classroom discussions. If groups have a particular orientation the discussion can be centred on their particular needs.

As well as being successfully used on a variety of examination courses, the book has also been used as a manual for in-house courses for organisations wishing to develop key management skills amongst its managers. Discounts can be obtained on bulk orders direct from the publisher.

There are also particular uses to which the book can be put with students who have difficulty with English. Students can discuss the supporting teaching material at their own pace in syndicates, with others helping them with their English when necessary. When teaching students who are all of the same nationality, they can have syndicate discussions, or conduct exercises, in their own language. They can then reinforce classroom work by reading specified material in the book in their own time and at their own pace. One of the advantages of the user-friendly style of the book is that the language needs of those whose first language is not English have been taken into account in writing the book. A glossary is now provided at the end of the book to help readers understand specific management words and phrases.

Supplementary student resources are also available at www.cengage.co.uk/rees6.

Case studies and exercises on the companion website

CHAPTER 1

All that glitters is not gold (television producer fails to adapt to a higher position of Head of Department and is over-reliant on his PA)

Architects of a new era (managerial roles and organisational structure)

Department of Trouble (problems in the identification of managerial roles in a University and lack of prioritisation and delegation)

The employment lawyer (the refusal of a legal partner to undertake the managerial and marketing aspects of his work disrupts the partnership as a whole)

Equal partners? (The unequal distribution of lead roles in an architectural partnership in a developing country and the ineffectiveness and feelings of inequity that this generates)

The fee gatherer (problems of lack of corporate strategy and forward planning in a legal partnership)

The hard sell (a newspaper's survival is threatened by management that is unresponsive to its organisational and management weaknesses)

Streams of trouble (managerial responsibility of academic staff in a college)

The trade commissioner (the problems of a specialist handling managerial responsibilities)

Too many cooks? how confusion about management responsibilities in a new post as Deputy Head in a school leads to avoidable conflict and ineffectiveness

CHAPTER 2

All that glitters is not gold (television producer fails to adapt to a higher position of Head of Department and is over-reliant on his PA)

Department of trouble (problems in the identification of managerial roles in a University and lack of prioritisation and delegation)

The employment lawyer (the refusal of a legal partner to undertake the managerial and marketing aspects of his work disrupts the partnership as a whole)

Equal partners? (the unequal distribution of lead roles in an architectural partnership in a developing country and the ineffectiveness and feelings of inequity that this generates)

The fee gatherer (problems of lack of corporate strategy and forward planning in a legal partnership)

The matrix structure? (poor implementation of a matrix structure in a University)

To be or not to be? (this case demonstrates the precarious financial position of a café and the options open to the owner)

Too many cooks? (how confusion about management responsibilities in a new post as Deputy Head in a school leads to avoidable conflict and ineffectiveness)

Twelve hours in the life of Mr Perry (prioritisation and delegation)

See also briefing sheet for preparing a role set analysis diagram

CHAPTER 3

Architects of a new era (managerial roles and organisational structure)

At your service (TQM)

The employment lawyer (the refusal of a legal partner to undertake the managerial and marketing aspects of his work disrupts the partnership as a whole)

Equal partners? (the unequal distribution of lead roles in an architectural partnership in a developing country and the ineffectiveness and feelings of inequity that this generates)

Faith, hope and charity (organisation structure and staffing costs in a charity)

The hard sell (a newspaper's survival is threatened by a management that is unresponsive to its organisational and management weaknesses)

The High Commission (organisational structure and operation)

In search of sparkle (organisational structure)

Internal diplomacy (power, authority and cost effectiveness in a diplomatic mission and the relationship of a deputy with their boss)

Marriage of convenience (conflict in a charity merger)

The matrix structure? (poor implementation of a matrix structure in a University)

The peninsula bank (the employee relations implications of merging two branches)

A surprise budget (the impact of the budgeting process on the authority of the manager and policy making)

To be or not to be? (this case demonstrates the precarious financial position of a café and the options open to the owner)

CHAPTER 4

All that glitters is not gold (television producer fails to adapt to a higher position of Head of Department and is over-reliant on his PA)

The fee gatherer (problems of lack of corporate strategy and forward planning in a legal partnership)

The hard sell (a newspaper's survival is threatened by a management that is unresponsive to its organisational and management weaknesses)

The High Commission (organisational structure and operation)

The new broom (the impact of restructuring on motivation and staffing needs)

The peninsula bank (the employee relations implications of merging two branches)

Prod.con.breweries (the role of procedures in handling change)

Question of harmony (an attempt to impose Japanese-style working practices in a British manufacturing company)

Trouble abroad (problems with overseas posting)

CHAPTER 5

All that glitters is not gold (television producer fails to adapt to a higher position of Head of Department and is over-reliant on his PA)

Department of trouble (problems in the identification of managerial roles in a University and lack of prioritisation and delegation)

Internal diplomacy (power, authority and cost effectiveness in a diplomatic mission and the relationship of a deputy with their boss)

Too many cooks? (how confusion about management responsibilities in a new post as Deputy Head in a school leads to avoidable conflict and ineffectiveness)

Trouble in store (discipline/delegation, manual worker)

Twelve hours in the life of Mr Perry (prioritisation and delegation)

CHAPTER 6

The hard sell (a newspaper's survival is threatened by a management that is unresponsive to its organisational and management weaknesses)

The new broom (the impact of restructuring on motivation and staffing needs)

Market reality (reconciling labour market reality with managerial demands)

CHAPTER 7

All that glitters is not gold (television producer fails to adapt to a higher position of Head of Department and is over-reliant on his PA)

Availability or activity (job evaluation)

Equal partners? (the unequal distribution of lead roles in an architectural partnership in a developing country and the ineffectivenes and feelings of inequity that this generates)

Grades of trouble (job evaluation)

The hard sell (a newspaper's survival is threatened by a management that is unresponsive to its organisational and management weaknesses)

Incentive for trouble (the organisational impact of an incentive scheme)

Money for value (equal value claim)

The new broom (the impact of restructuring on motivation and staffing needs)

Northern Beers (the unilateral alteration of a production bonus scheme)

Prod.con.breweries (the role of procedures in handling change)

CHAPTER 8

Chairing exercise (process skills)

Process skills: draw a flow chart (or sociogram) of a meeting that you attend. Use the material to analyse the pattern of activity and evaluate the effectiveness of the meeting and the skills of the chair in handling it.

Reference: Chapter 16, *Conduct by the chair during meetings.*

The hard sell (a newspaper's survival is threatened by a management that is unresponsive to its organisational and management weaknesses)

Rectangles exercise (one-way versus two-way communication)

Too many cooks? (the case shows how confusion about management responsibilities in a new post as Deputy Head in a school leads to avoidable conflict and ineffectiveness)

CHAPTER 9

The employment lawyer (the refusal of a legal partner to undertake the managerial and marketing aspects of his work disrupts the partnership as a whole)

Equal partners? (the unequal distribution of lead roles in an architectural partnership in a developing country and the ineffectivenes and feelings of inequity that this generates)

Market reality (reconciling labour market reality with managerial demands)

Practical selection exercise: use one or both of the job descriptions to establish selection criteria. This can be based either on a person specification (required individual characteristics and achievements) or the required job competencies. The job descriptions provided are for a partnership administrator and an international conference secretary

Prod.con.breweries (the role of procedures in handling change)

The new broom (the impact of restructuring on motivation and staffing needs)

Too many cooks? (how confusion about management responsibilities in a new post as Deputy Head in a school leads to avoidable conflict and ineffectiveness)

Trouble abroad (problems with overseas posting)

CHAPTER 10

Ahmad Zainal (appraisal)

CHAPTER 11

Lego assembly exercise (learning curve)

Where do we go from here? (management training and development)

CHAPTER 12

A kitchen-sink drama (grievance handling, manual worker)
Post haste (counselling)
Shelagh Morris (grievance handling, white-collar worker)

CHAPTER 13

Crossfire (evidence in disciplinary situations)
Mission of trouble (discipline/delegation, white-collar worker)
The nursery care incident (managerial accountability)
The peninsula bank (the employee relations implications of merging two branches)
Sickness absence at a nursery (absence control)
Trouble in store (discipline/delegation, manual worker)

CHAPTER 14

Faith, hope and charity (organisation structure and staffing costs in a charity)
Gone to pot (industrial action)
Northern Beers (the unilateral alteration of a production bonus scheme)
The peninsula bank (the employee relations implications of merging two branches)
Prod.con.breweries (the role of procedures in handling change)
Question of harmony (an attempt to impose Japanese-style working practices in a British man-
    ufacturing company)
The research institute (the role of the human resource management function in a research institute)
The salary review (the annual salary claim)
Suggestion of trouble (conflict at a suggestion committee)
White collar recognition (trade union recognition)

CHAPTER 15

The landlord–tenant exercise (a negotiating exercise in which two individuals or teams can
    negotiate with one another)
Northern Beers (the unilateral alteration of a production bonus scheme)
The salary review (the annual salary claim)
Suggestion of trouble (conflict at a suggestion committee)
Negotiating exercise (integrated bargaining)
Negotiating observer's form in PDF

CHAPTER 16

Chairing exercises (process skills)
Practical exercises: draw a flow chart (or sociogram) at a meeting that you attend. Use the material
    to analyse and evaluate the effectiveness of the meeting and the skills of the chair in handling it

Walk Through Tour

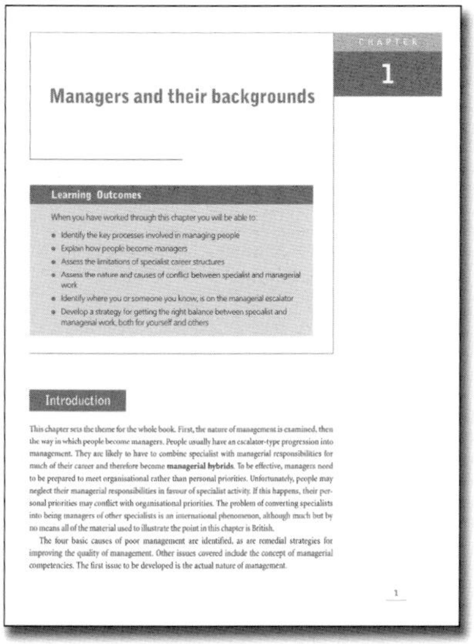

Learning outcomes clearly set out the content and coverage of each chapter

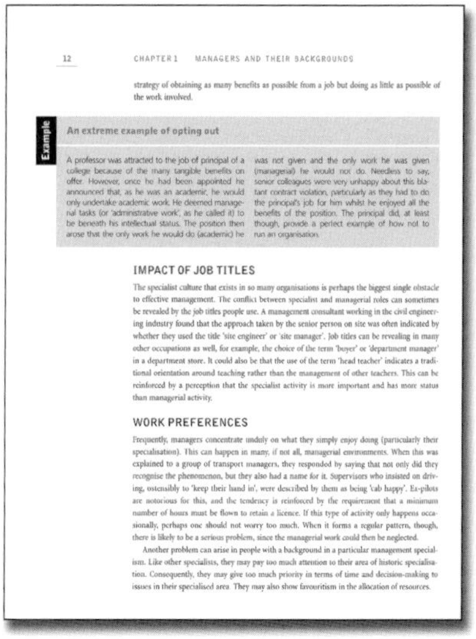

Boxed case **examples** from around the world incorporate and reflect upon issues and problems in management

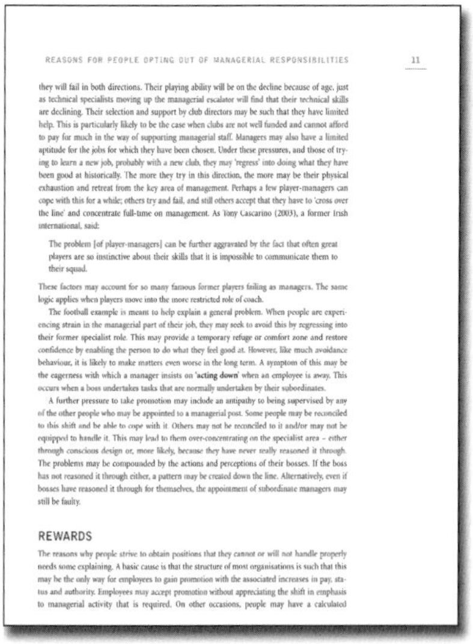

Glossary terms are highlighted in bold throughout the text and a detailed explanation is provided in a Glossary at the end of the book

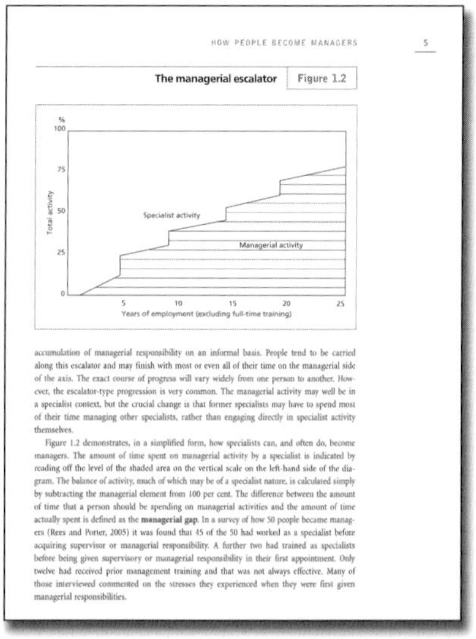

Figures provide a visual representation of key concepts and data

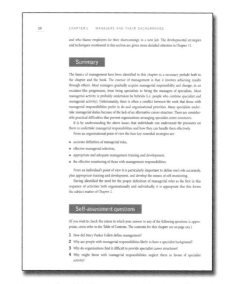

Appendices provide supplementary material for several chapters

Summaries briefly recap and review the main concepts and key points covered

Self-assessment questions are provided at the end of each chapter and help to test your knowledge and understanding through self-analysis

Further reading and references allow you to explore the subject further and act as starting points for projects and assignments

About the website

Visit the Skills of Management sixth edition accompanying website at **www.cengage.co.uk/rees6** to find valuable further learning resources:

For students

- Supplementary case studies and exercises divided per chapter
- A list of weblinks relating to case studies and relevant chapters
- A glossary highlighting key terms and their definitions

For instructors

- Downloadable PowerPoint slides
- Supplementary case studies and exercises divided per chapter with tutor notes
- Key articles written by the authors relating to topics within the text

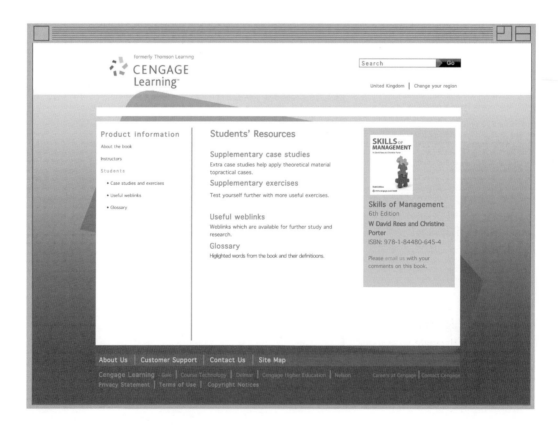

Managers and their backgrounds

Learning outcomes

When you have worked through this chapter you will be able to:

- Identify the key processes involved in managing people
- Explain how people become managers
- Assess the limitations of specialist career structures
- Assess the nature and causes of conflict between specialist and managerial work
- Identify where you, or someone you know, is on the managerial escalator
- Develop a strategy for getting the right balance between specialist and managerial work, both for yourself and others

Introduction

This chapter sets the theme for the whole book. First, the nature of management is examined, then the way in which people become managers. People usually have an escalator-type progression into management. They are likely to have to combine specialist with managerial responsibilities for much of their career and therefore become **managerial hybrids**. To be effective, managers need to be prepared to meet organisational rather than personal priorities. Unfortunately, people may neglect their managerial responsibilities in favour of specialist activity. If this happens, their personal priorities may conflict with organisational priorities. The problem of converting specialists into being managers of other specialists is an international phenomenon, although much but by no means all of the material used to illustrate the point in this chapter is British.

The four basic causes of poor management are identified, as are remedial strategies for improving the quality of management. Other issues covered include the concept of managerial competencies. The first issue to be developed is the actual nature of management.

Figure 1.1	The managerial cycle

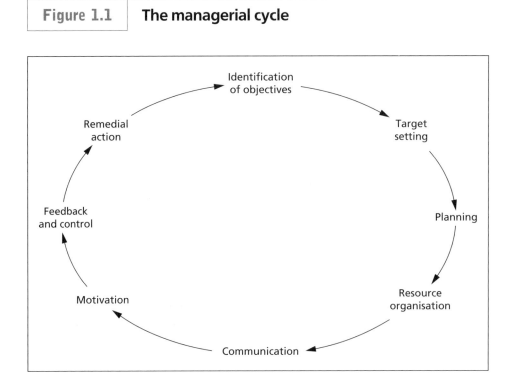

The nature of management

THE MANAGERIAL CYCLE

Management has been defined by Mary Parker Follett as 'the art of getting things done through people' (Graham, 1988). An alternative way of describing the process is that it is 'achieving results through others'.

The elements involved in the process of management were identified by Henri Fayol as 'to forecast and plan, to organise, to command, to coordinate and to control' (Gray 1988). Synthesising Fayol's view with later writers, one can identify the basic elements in terms of the managerial cycle as shown in Figure 1.1.

MANAGEMENT IN PRACTICE

Some writers see the managerial cycle as a simplistic model with too rational a view of the manager. Mintzberg's study of how managers actually operate challenged the concept of the totally rational manager. He observed five American chief executives at work and also reviewed the results of studies of managers at generally lower levels in other Western countries. The overall pattern of managerial work appeared to him to be a hectic and fragmented one with little opportunity for reflective thought. Mintzberg also found that decision-making was often abrupt, intuitive and incremental rather than strategic. It was often influenced by soft information, including internal and external gossip (Mintzberg 1989).

Another writer (Watson 1994) has also spent time observing managers at work. His observations of UK managers in the electronics industry led him to conclude that individuals view the process of management as being interrelated with their identity, values, status, development, self-esteem and material rewards. He also saw these managers' daily activities as particularly concerned with 'feeling one's way in confusing circumstances, struggling to make sense of ambiguous messages, reading signals, looking around, listening all the time, coping with conflicts and struggling to achieve tasks through establishing and maintaining a network of relationships' (Watson 1994, p. 8).

Another recent view of the role and skills of the manager was provided by a study of management in local government in the UK (Local Government Management Board 1993). There is a general relevance in their observation:

> Management is best defined not as a limited number of 'top' or 'leading' positions, but as a set of competencies, attitudes, and qualities broadly distributed throughout the organisation. Management skills are not the property of the few. Effective local authorities will recognise that many jobs which have not conventionally borne the tag 'manager' rely none the less on that bundle of actions – taking charge, securing an outcome, controlling affairs – which amounts to 'managing'.
>
> (Local Government Management Board 1993, p. 8)

How people become managers

RELATIONSHIP WITH ORGANISATIONAL STRUCTURE

The structure of organisations is usually such that most employees are engaged in a specialised activity and managers' entry into organisations is usually into a specialised activity. The number of general managerial jobs involving, for example, the coordination of the work of a number of different specialist departments tends to be very limited. A specialist background is the pedigree of the vast majority of managers. Early on in their careers, they may have been engaged at a lowly level in a specialised department. Alternatively, they may have advanced specialist skills that they have acquired either by experience, training or a combination of both. This can be demonstrated by probing into the background of almost anyone you know who has managerial responsibilities. Engineering managers, for example, come from the ranks of specialist engineers. Ward sisters or nursing officers will inevitably have a professional nursing qualification. A head teacher will normally have a teaching qualification. Football managers are invariably ex-professional players. Small business entrepreneurs are usually running a business based on their initial technical skill, for example in computing, in the building trade or as a motor mechanic.

MANAGERIAL RESPONSIBILITIES OF THE HYBRID

The problems of disentangling specialist and managerial work can be demonstrated by identifying the managerial-type activities in which specialists may need to become involved. Consequently, they may need to act as **managerial hybrids**, being involved in both specialist and managerial activities. Activities that specialists may need to become involved in are:

- Anticipating, planning and allocating work,
- Identification of priorities,
- Establishing and reviewing work methods,
- Quality control,
- Management of budgets,
- Management of physical resources,
- Trouble-shooting,
- Supervision of staff (including selection, on-the-job training, appraisal, counselling, motivation, control and grievance handling),
- Liaison with senior management, colleagues at a similar level and ancillary staff,
- External liaison.

The flattening of many organisational structures has tended to increase the speed at which specialists accumulate managerial responsibilities. Reductions in the numbers of specialist advisers can also lead to a broadening of managerial roles. Conventional specialist and managerial careers and work boundaries are often breaking down so that both specialists and managers have to become multi-skilled. These developments and flexible management structures can also lead to greater lateral movement of employees in organisations.

THE MANAGERIAL ESCALATOR

The concept of the **managerial escalator** seeks to explain how specialists become managers. Initially, a specialist may be employed 100 per cent of the time on a specialist activity. This may well be after professional training as an accountant, engineer or whatever. The competent specialist may gradually acquire minor supervisory responsibilities, perhaps quite informally. For example, this could be helping newcomers with their job. After a certain duration of competent performance (say five years, but it could be as little as one year), it would not be unusual for a specialist to be promoted. Given the structure of organisations, this promotion would usually involve an element of managerial responsibility. An engineer could become a section leader or a sales person a sales manager. The development of the concept of 'team leaders' can lead to specialists acquiring significant management responsibilities despite occupying a junior position.

After a few more years (say five) there could be a further formal promotion, either within the same or another organisation. This may have been preceded by a certain amount of

The managerial escalator | **Figure 1.2**

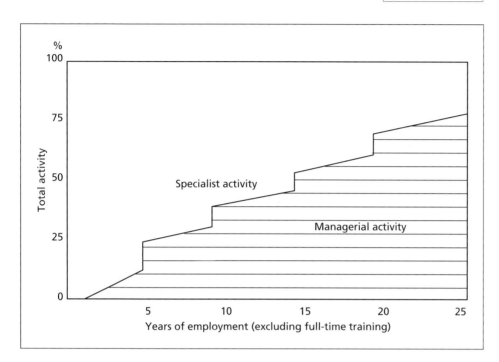

accumulation of managerial responsibility on an informal basis. People tend to be carried along this escalator and may finish with most or even all of their time on the managerial side of the axis. The exact course of progress will vary widely from one person to another. However, the escalator-type progression is very common. The managerial activity may well be in a specialist context, but the crucial change is that former specialists may have to spend most of their time managing other specialists, rather than engaging directly in specialist activity themselves.

Figure 1.2 demonstrates, in a simplified form, how specialists can, and often do, become managers. The amount of time spent on managerial activity by a specialist is indicated by reading off the level of the area on the vertical scale on the left-hand side of the diagram. The balance of activity, much of which may be of a specialist nature, is calculated simply by subtracting the managerial element from 100 per cent. The difference between the amount of time that a person should be spending on managerial activities and the amount of time actually spent is defined as the **managerial gap**. In a survey of how 50 people became managers (Rees and Porter 2005) it was found that 45 of the 50 had worked as a specialist before acquiring supervisory or managerial responsibility. A further two had trained as specialists before being given supervisory or managerial responsibility in their first appointment. Only twelve had received prior management training and that was not always effective. Many of those interviewed commented on the stresses they experienced when they were first given managerial responsibilities.

The conflict between specialist and managerial activity

NATURE OF THE PROBLEM

Management does not take place in a vacuum but in a particular set of circumstances – usually requiring specialist knowledge. This knowledge may be necessary so that instructions are sensible but may also serve to inspire respect in others. The possession of specialist skills is normally an asset and in many cases quite indispensable. If the person who manages in a specialist environment does not understand that environment, they will be under a great, and perhaps insurmountable, handicap. However, the specialist pedigree of most managers is also often at the root of many of the problems that confront them, particularly the danger of getting the wrong balance between specialist and managerial activity.

Some of the problems that are likely to arise may now be obvious. A person may have embarked on a career and acquired specialist skills that they are increasingly less able to use. A person may also have an emotional commitment to their specialist area and a confidence in that area which may be backed up by several years of formal training. Conversely, the commitment to, and training and aptitude for, the managerial side of the job may be low. It would not be unusual for a manager in a specialist environment to have had years of specialist training but only days of management training. This inexorably creates the temptation for managers to adjust the balance of their activity so that they concentrate on what they like doing and what they feel equipped to do at the expense of the managerial aspects of their job.

In seeking to rebut a claim that clinical excellence is enough for senior clinicians in the UK National Health Service, Nigel Edwards (2000), Policy Director of the NHS Confederation, argued that it is no good presuming that management issues are someone else's concern:

> In a world with limited money and in a field where so many complex resources need to be coordinated it is not possible to say that being a world-class surgeon is simply about being good at surgery or research. The truly excellent clinician is also a leader and problem solver and he or she must also take responsibility for the resources that they use and ensure that their services are excellent and continuously improving. Any definition of excellence must include how well clinicians perform in creating a positive culture that sorts out problems and fosters good relationships with other key parts of the healthcare system.
>
> (Letter to *The Times* 2000)

Similar issues have emerged with the appointment of head teachers. A suggestion was made in the UK in 2007 by the consultants, PricewaterhouseCoopers, that 'business leaders with no classroom experience could run schools' (The Times 2007). This was in a report commissioned by the government. However, opposition to this idea was expressed a few days later in a letter to the Guardian by Jo Causon of the Chartered Management Institute.

While the benefits of transferring business leadership and management skills into UK schools is undeniable, surely the more poignant message arising from the PricewaterhouseCooper's research is that teachers are not receiving the correct levels of managerial training early on in their careers.

The development of a supporting environment which encourages all teachers to obtain the skills and competencies needed in areas like accounting and human resources will help support the balance between professional and commercial expertise. Individuals in every sector require skills and competencies to manage people and situations, and education is no exception. While the report is right to identify management deficiencies in UK schools, parachuting individuals from external environments does little to rectify the problem in the long run.

Hopefully the problem of appointing suitably trained head teachers in the UK will be eased by the requirement for all heads to have acquired the National Professional Qualification for Headship.

Specialist career structures and their limitations

THE GENERAL PROBLEM

The dilemma of the specialist who is forced into management is accentuated by the difficulty that organisations have in providing alternative career progressions. In some cases, it may be possible to get around the dilemma by providing the opportunity for specialist career progression, as illustrated in Figure 1.3. However, the extent to which dual career structures can be created seems to be severely limited in practice, as it frequently proves impractical to separate managerial and specialist duties. Managerial responsibility usually flows from specialist expertise. If a person has to run a specialist unit they are unlikely to be able to do this unless they understand what the employees in their department are doing and can give appropriate guidance about working methods and end results.

Ironically, it may be more feasible to have a person without specialist knowledge at the top of an organisation than in less senior positions. A chief executive can rely on a raft of specialist departmental heads and concentrate on coordinating their work. Even then, however, the chief executive would need a good understanding of the environment in which the organisation was operating and of the internal resources and constraints within their organisation.

EMPLOYEE PRESSURES

The pressures for specialist career structures are often employee-driven. Specialists may want to obtain the rewards usually associated with accepting managerial responsibility without actually accepting such responsibilities. Problems that this can cause for the organisation include:

| Figure 1.3 | **Dual career structures** |

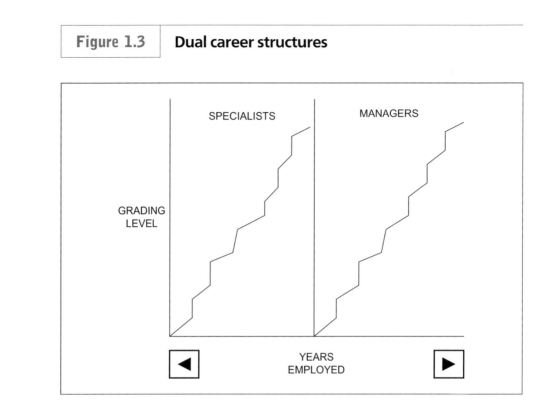

- The demand for highly paid specialist jobs may greatly exceed their availability
- The more highly paid specialists there are, the greater the problems of integrating their work with that of colleagues
- The incentive for and availability of other specialists to accept management responsibilities can be reduced

The above issues have arisen with regard to the nursing profession in particular. In the National Health Service (NHS) in the UK nursing consultants have been introduced into the career structure. However, their role is essentially to undertake medical work hived off from doctors and they have little in the way of supervisory responsibility. This may well have been a useful innovation because of the need to reduce pressure on medical staff, as well as being a popular development within the nursing profession. However, hospitals are still left with the problem of finding enough capable specialists to undertake crucial managerial responsibilities.

IMPACT OF THE LABOUR MARKET

Employers may need to give some attention to how they reward employees and the impact of those rewards on the managerial structure. As explained in Chapter 7, if a particular expertise really is critical to the success of an organisation, it may be necessary to pay accordingly. Workers whose skills are in short supply may, however, be promoted to management in order to provide a suitable level of reward. The worst thing to do is to promote people into managerial jobs while letting them think that they need not take their managerial responsibilities seriously. Care needs to be taken that promotion is not done on spurious grounds and that any advantages gained are greater than the disadvantage of discouraging people from accepting managerial responsibilities.

EXPERIENCE IN THE AREA OF INFORMATION TECHNOLOGY

The area of information technology is one in which organisations do recognise that it is sometimes necessary to retain people with commercially important expertise without forcing them to accept management responsibilities. As with other specialist areas, the person with a high level of technical expertise will not automatically make a good manager or have managerial aspirations. However, even in this area a mix of managerial and technical expertise is often necessary. A partner in a selection consultancy commented:

> Everyone is crying out for project managers, desktop service managers – to keep the system up and running and to talk through problems – and call centre managers ... They are looking for the hybrid manager: someone who has more than just technical skills, but knows how to create a customer-orientated culture within an organisation.
>
> (Coles 1997)

A Swedish manager commented of a colleague who was both young and brilliant at computer work that he had no interest in paperwork and in engaging with colleagues. As a consequence he had to be relieved of his managerial responsibilities.

The problem of getting the right mix of managerial and specialist expertise may be particularly difficult in the information technology area. This is because people may acquire a high level of technical skill at a very early stage in their careers. Management expertise may develop over a much longer timescale. In addition, the patterns of linear thinking that may be the reason for a person's technical ability may be quite different to the often more lateral patterns of thought that are needed in management.

Even when information technologists are hired out to other organisations they still need to have the people skills to interact effectively in client organisations. The essential point is that there are limits to the extent to which specialist and managerial activity can be disentangled. This is not to suggest, though, that there should not be experimentation in this area.

THE ROLE OF ADMINISTRATIVE SUPPORT

Sometimes the response to more explicit management pressures has been to give more administrative support to professionals. A diary study of the work of head teachers interestingly showed that they spend much of their time on boring, irrelevant or trivial tasks which could equally well be undertaken by an administrator (Lever and Blease 1992). An example of administrative support being provided is the introduction of 'partnership administrators' in professional partnerships, e.g. firms of solicitors, general medical practitioners and accountants.

However, partners cannot expect the administrators to determine policy, future strategy and financial priorities, to resolve conflict between partners or to supervise specialists in the professional aspects of their work. More competitive market conditions, including the emergence of more multi-professional partnerships, mean that effective management is bound to become an increasingly important factor in determining success or failure. However, even if appropriate support is given, the dilemma of specialists as managers remains a general problem.

One way of trying to reduce the burden on the person in charge of an organisation is to effectively split their job into two. The Secretary General of the United Nations has the twin tasks of being the senior diplomat and the chief administrative officer of the organisation. A similar dilemma faces the Vice Chancellors of universities. However, even if is practicable to split such jobs into two, the heads of the organisations may not welcome the idea of hiving off so much of their work to a Chief Executive because of the authority, responsibility and power that they would lose. There is though at least one example of where such a division of responsibilities does seem to work. In diplomatic missions, the head of mission (the Ambassador or High Commissioner) traditionally concentrates on external representation, leaving the internal management to be handled by their deputy.

Reasons for people opting out of managerial responsibilities

FAILURE TO IDENTIFY THE MANAGERIAL ELEMENT IN A JOB

One reason why managers sometimes engage in an inappropriate balance of activities may simply be that they have failed to identify that they are doing so. If the general style is for over-concentration on specialist activity, an imbalance may not be easily recognised by others either, far less be the subject of constructive comment and advice.

Example

Finding the right balance of work by accident

Sometimes managers can find the right balance between specialist and managerial activity literally by accident. The player-manager of a football club did this when he broke his leg. He then found that, after a little while, the team actually performed better without him in the side. His enforced absence from the side caused him to concentrate on his managerial responsibilities. This more than compensated for his absence from the team. When his leg healed he refrained from playing again and acted as a full-time manager.

It is easy to see why professional footballers may try to combine the daunting tasks of playing and managing. Their reputations will be as players and, if they step down a division or two, they may find that for a while they can cope with both tasks. However, there is a danger that they will fail in both areas. Their playing ability will be on the decline because of age, just as technical specialists moving up the managerial escalator will find that their technical skills are declining. Their selection and support by club directors may be such that they have limited help. This is particularly likely to be the case when clubs are not well funded and cannot afford to pay for much in the way of supporting managerial staff. Managers may also have a limited aptitude for the jobs for which they have been chosen. Under these pressures, and those of trying to learn a new job, probably with a new club, they may 'regress' into doing what they have been good at historically. The more they try in this direction, the more may be their physical exhaustion and retreat from the key area of management. Perhaps a few player-managers can cope with this for a while; others try and fail, and still others accept that they have to 'cross over the line' and concentrate full-time on management. As Tony Cascarino (2003), a former Irish international, said:

> The problem [of player-managers] can be further aggravated by the fact that often great players are so instinctive about their skills that it is impossible to communicate them to their squad.

These factors may account for so many famous former players failing as managers. The same logic may apply when players move into the more restricted role of coach.

The football example is meant to help explain a general problem. When people are experiencing strain in the managerial part of their job, they may seek to avoid this by regressing into their former specialist role. This may provide a temporary refuge, or comfort zone, and restore confidence by enabling the person to do what they feel good at. However, like much avoidance behaviour, it is likely to make matters even worse in the long term. A symptom of this may be the eagerness with which a manager insists on '**acting down**' when an employee is away. This occurs when a boss undertakes tasks that are normally undertaken by their subordinates.

A further pressure to take promotion may include an antipathy to being supervised by any of the other people who may be appointed to a managerial post. Some people may be reconciled to this shift and be able to cope with it. Others may not be reconciled to it and/or may not be equipped to handle it. This may lead to them over-concentrating on the specialist area – either through conscious design or, more likely, because they have never really reasoned it through. The problems may be compounded by the actions and perceptions of their bosses. If the boss has not reasoned it through either, a pattern may be created down the line. Alternatively, even if bosses have reasoned it through for themselves, the appointment of subordinate managers may still be faulty.

REWARDS

The reasons why people strive to obtain positions that they cannot or will not handle properly needs some explaining. A basic cause is that the structure of most organisations is such that this may be the only way for employees to gain promotion with the associated increases in pay, status and authority. Employees may accept promotion without appreciating the shift in emphasis to managerial activity that is required. On other occasions, people may have a calculated strategy of obtaining as many benefits as possible from a job but doing as little as possible of the work involved.

An extreme example of opting out

A professor was attracted to the job of principal of a college because of the many tangible benefits on offer. However, once he had been appointed he announced that, as he was an academic, he would only undertake academic work. He deemed managerial tasks (or 'administrative work', as he called it) to be beneath his intellectual status. The position then arose that the only work he would do (academic) he was not given and the only work he was given (managerial) he would not do. Needless to say, senior colleagues were very unhappy about this blatant contract violation, particularly as they had to do much of the principal's job for him whilst he enjoyed all the benefits of the position. The principal did, though, at least provide a perfect example of how not to run an organisation.

IMPACT OF JOB TITLES

The specialist culture that exists in so many organisations is perhaps the biggest single obstacle to effective management. The conflict between specialist and managerial roles can sometimes be revealed by the job titles people use. A management consultant working in the civil engineering industry found that the approach taken by the senior person on site was often indicated by whether they used the title 'site engineer' or 'site manager'. Job titles can be revealing in many other occupations as well, for example, the choice of the term 'buyer' or 'department manager' in a department store. It could also be that the use of the term 'head teacher' indicates a traditional orientation around teaching rather than the management of other teachers. This can be reinforced by a perception that the specialist activity is more important and has more status than managerial activity.

WORK PREFERENCES

Frequently, managers concentrate unduly on what they simply enjoy doing (particularly their specialisation). This can happen in many, if not all, managerial environments. When this was explained to a group of transport managers, they responded by saying that not only did they recognise the phenomenon, but they also had a name for it. Supervisors who insisted on driving, ostensibly to 'keep their hand in', were described by them as being 'cab happy'. Ex-pilots are notorious for this, and the tendency is reinforced by the requirement that a minimum number of hours must be flown to retain a licence. If this type of activity only happens occasionally, perhaps one should not worry too much. When it forms a regular pattern, though, there is likely to be a serious problem, since the managerial work could then be neglected.

Another problem can arise in people with a background in a particular management specialism. Like other specialists, they may pay too much attention to their area of historic specialisation. Consequently, they may give too much priority in terms of time and decision-making to issues in their specialised area. They may also show favouritism in the allocation of resources.

Interpreting a job too much through one's specialism

A cost accountant was promoted into a position as a general manager. Unfortunately, instead of taking a broader view in his new job, he still concentrated on cost control. That was the only area where he was disposed to allocate extra resources. He neglected the marketing aspects of his job in particular and was reluctant to authorise expenditure that could have generated significant net income. He should instead have concentrated on optimising the difference between income and expenditure.

PERSONALITY FACTORS

The ability or willingness of people to handle managerial activity can be influenced by powerful psychological factors relating to individual personalities. Some people may strive for the power that managerial authority can give, regardless of whether or not they are competent to exercise that authority wisely. Sometimes people may actually be in flight from their specialism, because they are not very good at it or because they have 'burnt out' in that area.

This does not mean that there are not perfectly valid reasons why people aspire to positions of greater responsibility. One has sympathy for people who are sucked into management but who are concerned that, if for any reason they lose their jobs, they will have difficulty in returning to their specialist sphere unless they have kept up to date. The point being made, however, is that it is necessary at the selection stage to try to identify the real reason why people want a particular job and to distinguish between valid and invalid reasons.

The fundamental nature of some of the personality factors that may discourage people from applying for managerial positions, or regressing when they are in such jobs, needs examination. One basic possibility is that often extroverts prefer the managerial role and introverts the specialist activity. To appoint or not to appoint just on that basis would be somewhat simplistic. However, the value system that specialists develop in their formative occupational years and their self-image may be much more bound up with specialist rather than managerial activity. This, in turn, may conflict with organisational values.

Keenan (1980) points out that several authors have noted how the professional values of engineers and scientists – emphasising technical accomplishment, autonomy and public availability of knowledge – are at a variance with the goals of profitability, marketability of products and safeguarding of knowledge which might be useful to competitors (paraphrased in Blackler and Shimmin 1984). The conflict between these sets of values may be precipitated by promotion and create considerable stress. Blackler and Shimmin comment that promotion to supervisory or management positions of specialists 'may reduce or remove the opportunity to do the work for which they were trained and with which they identify. Professional and skilled manual workers are particularly prone to this type of conflict, for example, nurses whose contact with patients lessens with increasing seniority and engineers for whom advancement means abandoning technical work for management' (1984, p. 23). They add:

The perfectionist, for example, whose self-esteem is tied closely to the idea of a job well done, is likely to be more subject to stress of this kind than someone who is happy-go-lucky in his or her approach.

(1984, p. 25)

As Keenan says of professional engineers, 'the successful accomplishment of meaningful technical work is at the centre of their perception of themselves in their jobs' (1980). Consequently, neither work that underutilises their technical skills nor work that is so demanding that they feel unable to complete it successfully is satisfactory from their point of view.

Those with professional or scientific training may also, according to Pedler and Boydell (1985), have developed norms of carefulness and certainty, and learnt to avoid conflict rather than develop skills to handle it. There may also be little in their specialist culture to equip them to deal with that key variable – people.

Personality factors can, in turn, be reinforced by the uncongenial aspects of many managerial roles. This has led Scase and Goffee to coin the phrase 'reluctant managers', which is also the title of their book (1989). They refer to the 'emotional hardening' that may be necessary to handle managerial roles. They also comment about changing social values and the increasing desire of managers to balance their work and domestic roles. The stereotype of the male manager with the family's interests subordinated to his career is decreasingly representative. What is more common is for managers, as for others, to have significant domestic responsibilities. This can be for a variety of reasons including the career of a partner, dependent elderly relatives and single parenthood. There is also an increasing risk of divorce (Scase and Goffee 1989). Additionally, the actual work may be fragmented, managers can be expected to reconcile a mass of conflicting pressures, be poorly serviced and supported and in some cases even receive a lower salary than their employees. These unenviable aspects are considered further in Chapter 14 under the subheading *supervisory control*.

There are still more reasons why those with managerial responsibilities might wish to shy away from the managerial aspects of their work. Pressure to reduce overall spending is another disincentive. Two further factors to be examined in detail are pressure from employees and inadequate training.

PRESSURE FROM SUBORDINATES

The traditions of a particular occupation may influence a manager's behaviour. In teaching, for example, there may be considerable direct and indirect pressure by junior teachers for senior or head teachers to concentrate on teaching. The person in a supervisory position may have to be prepared to resist the pressures of employees that could lead to them striking the wrong balance. Such a person may also feel that 'they should not give a job to a subordinate that they cannot do themselves' – a popular but dangerous maxim.

There may also be the fear that unless a direct specialist involvement is retained the manager will become out of date and perhaps ultimately unable to manage at all. The problem is that, if a manager responds to these pressures, they may make matters worse. This can happen in two ways: by interfering in the work of employees and also by neglecting the critical managerial aspects of a job.

The pressures by employees for a manager to demonstrate competence and interest in their specialist activity can be real enough. According to research conducted by Adler (1989), quoted in Mead (2005), this is particularly true in certain cultures, especially Asian. As Mead comments:

> In a traditional Asian business, the superior should be able to provide specialist answers
> to technical questions . . . The Asian manager who cannot answer questions loses status.
>
> (Mead 2005, p. 38)

However, employees may quite fail to comprehend the other aspects of a boss's job. Additionally, employees may resent the creaming-off of the more interesting parts of the job by a boss who wants to 'keep their hand in'. This may be particularly annoying if the boss does this on a random basis so that employees never quite know what their job is. Situations where there are 'two cooks in the kitchen' may generate more friction than where one cook leaves the other to get on with it and puts up with any adverse comments about the lack of specialist involvement. In some cases, though, employees will be only too well aware of their boss's managerial shortcomings and the pressure will be for the boss to do their managerial job instead of meddling in what was their former job.

EXPERIENCE IN DEVELOPING COUNTRIES

The problem of imbalance between specialist and managerial roles is not confined to any one country. Many specialists in developing countries enjoy speedy promotion. This can be caused by the shortage of staff with appropriate skills, the speed with which newly independent countries have had to assume responsibility for managing their own affairs, and the tendency for employees in state and parastatal organisations to be obliged to retire when they reach 55. This early retirement age not only reduces the pool of available talent, but also encourages managers to retain their specialist skills for a post-retirement career. As mentioned above, in many Asian countries the respect for specialist qualifications and expertise is even greater than in the UK, and by implication the respect for managerial expertise less (Mead 2005). The following examples, all from developing countries, demonstrate the international nature of the problems identified in this chapter.

Examples of overinvolvement in specialist work and interests in developing countries

Example

In two quite separate countries, medical doctors were appointed as permanent secretaries to the minister of health. There was nothing inherently wrong in that, but there was in their subsequent behaviour. They both spent about 90 per cent of their time on clinical medical work. In both cases they had to be quickly removed from their positions.

The chief executive of a national airline was an ex-pilot. He frequently flew passenger aircraft, particularly if there were prestigious people on board.

A commissioner of police would patrol highways checking unroadworthy vehicles. This left the staff, who should have been doing such work, free to take advantage of the lack of supervision.

An academic was appointed ambassador for his country. However, he continued to write academic books, leaving whatever embassy he was in charge of to run itself.

Often military dictators give high priority to military matters and sanction large defence budgets even if there is no discernible threat to their country's security. This is likely to be partly because they have a military background and this is their 'comfort zone'.

GENERAL CONSEQUENCES OF OPTING-OUT

Managers are likely to be judged ultimately by the results they achieve through constructive management of employees – not by possession of specialist knowledge. The specialist knowledge that managers require is that which enables them to supervise others. If employees can do a particular job better than the manager, the manager's skill is in arranging them to do so. To compete with the subordinate and then fail is hardly recommended.

There is a world of difference between a manager having no specialist competence and having sufficient specialist knowledge to supervise employees. The latter may be quite sufficient. It would be very nice if all managers knew more about every aspect of the subordinate's job than the subordinate, but it is not very realistic, particularly with changing technology. It may also not do a great deal for the esteem of employees. The manager may have to face up to being confronted by a specialist issue with which they cannot deal. Rather than worry about this, it may be that this is simply an instance when the manager reroutes the subordinate to a source where they may get the right information. The emphasis needs to be on seeing that the specialists maintain and develop their skill base rather than on the manager trying to do this.

A whole host of problems can arise if the weaning process, whereby those with managerial responsibilities get the right balance of specialist and managerial activity, is not satisfactorily accomplished. This is the recurrent theme of this chapter.

Remedial strategies

The remedial strategies needed to deal with the problem of poor managerial performance involve dealing with four basic causes of ineffective performance. These issues are so important that they are worth being addressed in detail. They are:

- role definition,
- managerial selection,
- training and development,
- monitoring.

ROLE DEFINITION

When managers are reluctant to accept managerial responsibility, a key remedial strategy is to make such responsibilities crystal clear, for example in a job specification and by paying attention to the job title. Accurate role definition is also necessary if the other remedial strategies of selection, training and development and monitoring are to be effective. This role clarification needs to be an integral part of the basis on which managers are selected. The need to highlight the managerial aspects of a job is necessary for both applicants and those making appointments. This issue is given particular attention in the following section on managerial selection.

MANAGERIAL SELECTION

There are a variety of reasons why the wrong people are given managerial responsibility. Two key mistakes are considered in this section: failure to recognise the managerial element in jobs and general selection incompetence. Intervention strategies need to be based on avoiding such mistakes.

Mistake No. 1: Failure to identify and select on the basis of the managerial element in a job

The easiest way to choose a manager is to look at their historical performance and appoint or reject on that basis. The danger in this approach is, however, that there may be critical differences between the duties that a person has performed in the past and those that they may be expected to perform in the future. Unfortunately, this point may not be properly grasped and, in any case, it is so much easier to assess historical performance rather than speculate about a person's managerial potential. It is, for example, far easier to count the number of international caps that a professional footballer has acquired than judge whether or not they have the appropriate range of skills to manage a football club. Possession or non-possession of a coaching licence may help judge technical ability, but not be that helpful in judging any complementary managerial ability or potential that is required.

The likelihood of selection error is increased if selectors view an appointment as a reward for past specialist achievements instead of a need to choose the right person for the future. In the police service this sometimes led to sergeants being regarded as 'constables with stripes on their arms'.

The dangers of over-reliance on specialist knowledge and interest as job qualifications are illustrated in the case of the Royal Opera House in London. A House of Commons committee called for the resignation of the entire board and the appointment of a new chief executive. They said:

> The administrator must be chosen for his or her business skills . . . We would prefer to see the House run by a philistine with the requisite financial acumen than by the succession of opera and ballet lovers who have brought a great and valuable institution *to its knees*.
>
> (Commons Select Committee Report 1997)

The problems of choosing just on the basis of specialist expertise can arise particularly in university appointments. Staff may be appointed merely on the basis of their record of research and publications. This may bring advantages in terms of prestige and research ratings. However, university departments need to be managed effectively just like any other departments. This applies to research units as well and the real need, even in research units, may be to have someone in charge who can facilitate research in the unit as a whole. The unit activity will need to be judged as a whole, not just on the basis of the performance of the head of such a unit.

Mistake No. 2: Incompetent selectors

The appointment of managers may prove to be a fairly random affair. The competence of the selectors may mean that it is often a question of luck as to whether the people with the right mix of skills and potential are appointed in the first place. However, those who find that they have emerged through the selection system as managers need to address themselves to the behaviour that will be appropriate, even if those appointing them did not. A further obstacle to appointment on the basis of suitability to the job in the UK has, historically at least, been the importance of social class. According to Scase and Goffee (1989):

> The 'skills' that have been traditionally, but perhaps erroneously, associated with leadership may be difficult to acquire, if only because they are derived through particular child-rearing patterns, education and class-based experiences. The persistence of such styles results from the tendency for senior managers to recruit successors with similar personal characteristics. Such processes militate against the career opportunities of those from working-class origins, of women and of others who have been unable to acquire the intangible but real personal attributes of class privilege.
>
> (Scase and Goffee 1989, pp. 185–186)

The problems that can arise as a result of selecting on the basis of historic performance are satirically and amusingly explained in the book *The Peter Principle* by Peter and Hull (1970). Their observations contain more than a germ of truth. The basic concept explained in the book is that if one looks backward in time instead of forward when selecting, people will rise up through organisational hierarchies until they pass their threshold of competence. Only when that has happened will there be no basis for appointment at a higher level of responsibility.

The basic Peter Principle is stated to be that: 'In a hierarchy every employee tends to rise to his (or her) level of incompetence.' Principles that naturally follow on from this will be that:

- in time, every post tends to be occupied by an employee who is incompetent to carry out its duties;
- work is accomplished by those employees who have not yet reached their level of incompetence.

(Peter and Hull 1990, pp. 22–24)

The material on selection in Chapter 9 of this book gives practical guidance on how to appoint on the basis of 'fit' with the job. It is crucial that the managerial ability or potential is included in selection criteria. It is also important that those undertaking the selection are competent in the techniques of selection, which is also explained in Chapter 9.

TRAINING AND DEVELOPMENT OF MANAGERS

Whilst management training is a key intervention area, the quantity and quality of training development has often been neglected. Historically, managers have often received little management training. Charles Handy (1991) maintained that in the UK this had much to do with the amateur tradition:

> Management, after all, was held by the British to be akin to parenting, a role of great importance for which no training, preparation or qualification was required: the implication being that experience is the only possible teacher and character the only possible qualification.

> (Handy 1991, p. 122)

There has been a welcome increasing international attention to management training in recent years. This has increased the scale of both qualification training and 'in-house' courses. However, increases in the quantity of management training are one thing – ensuring that training is effective is another. Management training can often be ineffective for a variety of reasons. These include inaccurate diagnosis of needs, poor selection and unsatisfactory training. A particular problem with management training is the need for those receiving the training to integrate what they have learnt with their personal behaviour. Sometimes the adjustments that managers need to make to manage are effectively beyond them. Also in-house training budgets can be amongst the first casualties in organisations seeking to economise. The problems of providing effective management training are considered further in Chapter 11.

MONITORING

The fourth key intervention is monitoring. This applies whether a manager is managing others or reviewing their own performance. The good work in trying to ensure accurate role definition, selection, and training and development can easily be undone if there is no effective monitoring. A key feature of any strategy for correcting imbalance in the job is for those likely to experience the problem to be made more aware of it. They may do this for themselves by learning, perhaps on a trial and error basis. However, training and monitoring of performance can help to ensure that people do not have to learn everything the hard way – or even not at all. Unfortunately, if an organisation has too much of a specialist culture, it is particularly likely that those with managerial responsibilities will fail to see the need to monitor and then correct the performance of their employees or themselves.

Managers have a responsibility to see that their own training and development and that of their staff fits into an integrated pattern. These are not activities that can be handled just by training departments or by sending people on courses. Performance management, on-the-job learning, appraisal, coaching and formal training need to be integrated. There is a specific responsibility for bosses to see that those who are given managerial responsibilities are also given help through appraisal, counselling and coaching. This is particularly necessary when people make critical moves up the managerial escalator. So often people are 'thrown in at the deep end' by managers who have not handled the transitional problems properly themselves and who blame employees for their shortcomings in a new job. The developmental strategies and techniques mentioned in this section are given more detailed attention in Chapter 11.

Summary

The basics of management have been identified in this chapter as a necessary prelude both to the chapter and the book. The essence of management is that it involves achieving results through others. Most managers gradually acquire managerial responsibility and change, in an escalator-like progression, from being specialists to being the managers of specialists. Most managerial activity is probably undertaken by hybrids (i.e. people who combine specialist and managerial activity). Unfortunately, there is often a conflict between the work that those with managerial responsibilities prefer to do and organisational priorities. Many specialists undertake managerial duties because of the lack of an alternative career structure. There are considerable practical difficulties that prevent organisations arranging specialist career structures.

It is by understanding the above issues that individuals can understand the pressures on them to undertake managerial responsibilities and how they can handle them effectively.

From an organisational point of view the four key remedial strategies are:

● accurate definition of managerial roles,

● effective managerial selection,

● appropriate and adequate management training and development,

● the effective monitoring of those with management responsibilities.

From an individual's point of view it is particularly important to define one's role accurately, plan appropriate training and development, and develop the means of self-monitoring.

Having identified the need for the proper definition of managerial roles as the first in this sequence of activities both organisationally and individually, it is appropriate that this forms the subject matter of Chapter 2.

Self-assessment questions

(If you wish to check the extent to which your answer to any of the following questions is appropriate, cross-refer to the Table of Contents. The contents for this chapter are on pages ix–x.)

1 How did Mary Parker Follett define management?

2 Why are people with managerial responsibilities likely to have a specialist background?

3 Why do organisations find it difficult to provide specialist career structures?

4 Why might those with managerial responsibilities neglect them in favour of specialist activity?

5 Where are you, or someone you know, on the managerial escalator? Where might you be on the escalator in five years?

6 What are the four key areas where attention is needed to ensure that those with managerial responsibilities perform effectively?

References

(Works of particular interest are marked with a star.)

Blackler, Frank and Sylvia Shimmin (1984), *Applying Psychology in Organisations,* Methuen. This paraphrases T. Keenan's (1980) work, which is contained in *Stress and the Professional Engineer,* in C.A. Cooper and J. Marshall (eds), *White-collar and Professional Stress,* Wiley, pp. 23–24.

Cascarino, Tony (10 November 2003), *The Times,* Monday supplement.

Coles, Margaret (1997), *IT skills shortage stumps recruiters* (report of a survey by Theaker, Monro & Newman, Sunday Times appointments section, 16 November).

Commons Select Committee on Culture, Media and the Arts (1997), Chairman Gerald Kaufman, reported in the Evening Standard, London, 3 December.

Edwards, Nigel, letter to *The Times,* 21 November 2000.

Fayol, Henri (1988), *General and Industrial Management,* revised by Irwin Gray Pitman.

Graham, Pauline (1988), *Dynamic Managing – The Follett Way,* Professional Publishing.

Guardian (2007, 23 January).

Handy, Charles (1991), *The Age of Unreason,* Business Studies Books, 2nd ed.

Laurence, Peter and Raymond Hull (1970), *The Peter Principle,* Pan. Alternatively, see the Souvenir Press edition, 1969, reissued in 1992.

Lever, D. and Blease, D. (October 1992), *What Do Primary Headteachers Really Do?,* Educational Studies.

Local Government Management Board (1993), *Managing Tomorrow,* Panel of Inquiry report.

Mintzberg, H. (1989), *Mintzberg on Management,* The Free Press.

*Mead, Richard (2005), *International Management: Cross Cultural Dimensions,* 3rd ed., Blackwell Publishers (an excellent and detailed account explaining the impact of national culture on management practices).

Pedler, Mike and T. Boydell (1985), *Managing Yourself,* Fontana.

*Rees, W. David and Christine Porter (2005) *Results of a survey into how people become managers and the management development implications,* Industrial and Commercial Training, Vol. 37, No. 5 (research evidence indicating strongly that the route into management is via specialist activity – available on *Skills of Management* companion website).

Scase, Richard and Robert Goffee (1989), *Reluctant Managers: Their Work and Lifestyles,* Unwin Hyman.

The Times (2007, 19 January), *Chief Executives with no teaching experience could take over schools.*

Watson, Tony J. (1994), *In Search of Management,* International Thomson Business Press.

Identifying the manager's job

Introduction

It follows from the previous chapter that the first essential requirement for an effective manager is for the manager to define their job carefully and accurately. Effectiveness depends upon the accomplishment of appropriate objectives rather than just being busy. Consequently, the methodology of objective setting is considered in this chapter. The technique of role set analysis is also explained. This can be a very effective way of identifying the priorities in a job, and it enables comparisons between 'model' and 'actual' time allocations. The technique can also be used on a departmental or organisational basis. Careful identification of the job is also a necessary foundation for effective time management. The basic elements of time management are explained.

It is not enough for managers to plan just their own work systematically. If they are to be effective, they also need to help develop a rational framework within which to operate. Consequently, the need for effective strategic planning is also considered. So too are the advantages and disadvantages of setting targets.

Activity versus effectiveness

PROACTIVE VERSUS REACTIVE MANAGERS

Managers can fall into two groups: those who define what has to be done, get on with it and then go home, and those who create a flurry of physical activity and seek to justify their positions by the demonstrable effort they put into a job rather than by the results they achieve. The latter group of managers also tends to be reactive rather than innovative in their responses. The emphasis on effort rather than results tends to combine neatly with a reactive 'management by crisis' approach. There can, perhaps, be some of this in most managers, but it is still useful to make a distinction between the two different approaches.

Sometimes concentrating on effort or activity rather than results can constitute an attempt at self-justification in a combination of humour, pathos and ineffectiveness. This can involve such managerial games as never going home until the chief executive has left, working overtime for the sake of it, and managers seeking to demonstrate to colleagues that they have worked longer and harder than them. This is sometimes done simply by 'presenteeism' – being physically present without actually achieving much. Such stratagems may or may not be useful in the short term. It may even be that in some cases they are necessary political ploys, given that there will be political activity in any organisation. However, the great danger is that, if managers spend too much time simply justifying themselves, they may actually fail to diagnose what they should be doing and therefore fail to do it. Ultimately, managers are much more likely to be judged by results than by anything else. Activity-centred behaviour is in any case much more likely to spring from incompetence and/or insecurity than from adroit political behaviour. Activity-centred behaviour is likely to aggravate the position of the manager in the long run rather than ameliorate it.

WHAT IS WORK?

One point that needs to be established at this stage is just how people define work. One view is that it is synonymous with physical activity. This misconception can have most unfortunate consequences, particularly when considering the job of a manager. An example of this misconception can occur when manual workers apply for white-collar jobs. They may find out too late that the mental activity can be far more demanding than the physical activity to which they have been accustomed. The mental activity of a clerk or supervisor simply may not be perceived by a person used to manual work, because such mental activity is not overt.

Example

What is work: Activity or effectiveness?

A staff nurse working in a hospital noticed that a patient had fallen into a coma. She knew that the patient was on a special diet. Consequently, the staff nurse stopped what she was doing to try to puzzle out if the staff who would administer drip feeding to the patient would be aware of his special dietary needs. However, her mental activity was soon interrupted by the ward sister, who brusquely asked her what she thought she was doing just standing there and told her to get on with her work.

The recurring problem is that it is obvious when people are working at a physical level, but less obvious when they are engaged in what may be more crucial mental activity. This is compounded by the fact that you can have staff just standing around day-dreaming and not engaged in mental problem-solving activity. Also, the tradition of judging manual workers by their rate of physical activity is something that can carry over into judgements about whether managers are working or not. It may be that to some extent managers have to respond to this type of pressure by demonstrating physical activity. It may be crucial to their effectiveness, though, that they do not overreact to such pressure. Managers also need to make this distinction when they are assessing, and perhaps pressurising, their own subordinates.

EFFICIENCY VERSUS EFFECTIVENESS

It is necessary to distinguish between the concepts of efficiency and effectiveness at work. Efficiency can be defined as the extent to which people are working at or near their total capacity. Effectiveness is a different concept. It involves ensuring that people are doing the right things. Ideally employees should be working both efficiently and effectively. However, the two concepts can work against one another.

Efficiency versus effectiveness

The funding authority for higher education colleges and universities in the UK introduced a requirement that all academic hours be accounted for. A consequence of this was the generation of activity by some academic staff to demonstrate that they were working to capacity regardless of how effective that activity was. What was really needed, however, was an emphasis on the overall volume and effectiveness of the teaching.

Example

One source of ineffective activity can be the failure to identify what actually needs to be done. The pressure for activity in some organisations, or for that matter in some people, can be such that activities can be undertaken before the need for them has been properly established. A crucial management skill is the need to diagnose both the nature of problems and their underlying causes before action is contemplated. As will be explained further in Chapter 14, in the context of employee and industrial relations the causes of problems may lie in departments other than the ones in which problems surface. Consequently an integrated approach may be needed to identify problems and devise appropriate solutions. Unfortunately managers all too often adopt prescriptive and often costly solutions before adequate diagnosis has been undertaken. Sometimes prescriptive 'remedies' are imported from other organisations with little thought as to whether or not they will work within the different circumstances of the organisation into which they are imported (Rees and Porter 2002).

The identification of the manager's job

Perhaps the first thing that any manager needs to do is actually to identify their job. This should be seen as a continuous process rather than a one-off activity. Organisations have to change in order to survive, and the jobs of managers need to change accordingly. This is why, if a manager has a job description, it should be seen as a starting point for identifying the job, rather than a definitive unalterable document. Job descriptions, whilst being useful, may leave considerable room for interpretation and will also need updating. They suffer too from the deficiency that they usually do not give a clear indication of the priorities in a job.

There are likely to be other ways in which managers identify and adjust their jobs. They are hardly likely to be left completely to their own devices as there will obviously be instructions from superior managers. In some cases the remit for a manager will be very specific, and the problem will primarily be one of doing the job rather than of identifying what needs to be done. In other cases – perhaps where there is significant internal and external change – the manager may need to spend a considerable amount of time defining and redefining what needs to be done. A further guide may be the way the work was performed by a previous job-holder. It would be folly to ignore the way a previous job-holder had performed a job, but perhaps equally foolish not to review their interpretation of a job nor to allow for changed circumstances.

There can be considerable misunderstanding about just what is done in a job before one gets to the question of what needs to be done. There may be significant surprises when the purpose and content of jobs are actually clarified. Often the job-holder will find that they are undertaking some tasks of which their boss is unaware. It is also likely that there will be some tasks that they are expected to do of which they themselves are unaware. One of the reasons for these misunderstandings is that the boss may have never fully appreciated the demands of the job. Alternatively, they may have appreciated these demands previously, or even have done the job at one stage, but may be basing their view on what was historically done rather than what is now needed.

SHORT-TERM PRESSURES AND LONG-TERM NEEDS

Much of a manager's time will be devoted simply to responding to pressures and demands from other people. The in-tray tends to dominate the daily pattern of activity. Whatever a manager wants to do in the long term is all very well, but often cannot be contemplated until the short-term pressures have been dealt with. However, there are dangers that a manager will simply react to short-term pressures and not think out what they should be doing from a long-term point of view. This problem can be exacerbated by developments in information technology such as email. These developments can make a manager too available, whether at work or at home. Managers are less likely than before to have personal secretaries to act as filters or, if they still do, it may be possible for people to bypass the secretary electronically. Consequently, there may be an even greater need for managers to consciously prioritise. Managers may also fall into a particular pattern of responding to certain short-term pressures and ignoring others. (Key skills involved in using email effectively are considered in Chapter 5.) It is necessary to periodically review such patterns to see if they match the needs of the situation.

Responding to a predetermined selection of short-term issues can become a way of life for some managers. In some cases this may be because of the sheer pressure on a manager, in other cases because they want to avoid certain issues. One problem with this approach is that some of the issues that are left may be important; moreover, if the manager thought things out on a long-term basis, then some of the short-term pressures might be reduced or eliminated. Managers have to react to some, at least, of the short-term pressures. However, it can be very easy to fall into a pattern of only doing this, with possibly disastrous results on long-term effectiveness. Managers need to compare what they are doing with what they should aim to be doing. This issue is one that managers are not always prepared to face. In a study of the way 160 managers actually performed their jobs, Rosemary Stewart observed:

> A fragmented day is often the laziest day; the day that demands the least in terms of mental discipline, though the most in nervous energy. It is easier to pass from one subject to a second when the first requires a difficult or unpalatable decision, or sustained thought. It is easier to respond to each fresh stimulus, to hare after the latest query, than to set an order of priorities and try to keep to it. This, of course, includes knowing when the latest query has priority. It is easier to be a grasshopper jumping from one problem to another, than a beaver chewing away at a tough task.
>
> (Stewart 1988, p. 13)

Stewart's analysis of managerial activity fits with, and influenced the work of, Mintzberg (1989), whose views on the nature of management were examined in Chapter 1. Mintzberg also found that the behaviour of managers in practice was hectic and fragmented. This led him to challenge the concept of the ordered rational manager.

THE IDENTIFICATION OF OBJECTIVES

As has already been indicated, the reverse of the reactive activity-centred approach of managers is one where objectives are carefully identified and then, hopefully, achieved. A consequential benefit can be that the manager's time is allocated in proportion to the priority of a task. Reactive managers may find, assuming they ever think in these terms, that they have failed to match the time available to the key elements in their jobs. Management writers who have made historically important contributions to this issue include Peter Drucker (1955) and John Humble (1979). Drucker appears to be the first person who used the term **'management by objectives'** (MBO). Humble developed the idea into a systematic method of management, not just for the individual manager, but for the total organisation of the concepts on which it was based. The crucial, and still very relevant, question it invited managers to ask was just why they were doing a particular job or task. It is all too easy to say what one is doing rather than why.

Why is a particular job or task necessary?

Example

Answering the question 'why?' can produce surprising results. The following newspaper report, whilst not an example of a managerial job, makes the appropriate point:

Night watchmen at Westminster Council House in Marylebone Road [London] protecting the Council's silver plate cost ratepayers £21,000 last year. Clever economists at the Council now think that the resident caretaker may be able to

►

handle the job alone. They have discovered that the silver was moved elsewhere years ago.

(Evening Standard, 1997)

In a further example, the chief legal officer of a local authority was asked to explain his various activities during an annual appraisal. He described how he sought to minimise payments to claimants against the council. His technique included ignoring claims for liability the first time they were received. He estimated that this would dispose of 20 per cent of claims. If people persisted with their claims he would next send a complicated and threatening letter. He estimated that that would dispose of a further 20 per cent of claims. The remaining 60 per cent of claims would be contested with a view to paying as little as possible as late as possible. The legal officer was then asked by the chief executive why he resisted all claims and responded that it was to meet his objective of minimising payments made by the council. The chief executive then made the point that, as the council had a responsibility to the local public, there was a case for simply accepting liability with regard to valid claims. The chief legal officer's response was this option had never occurred to him.

The identification of the key tasks that are contained in a job does present some advantages over the conventional type of job description. Job descriptions can, by their length and detail, obscure the key elements in a job. Humble (1979) advocated that every manager needed to define the six to eight key tasks that needed to be accomplished if the overall job objective was to be achieved. It was argued that if this was done the residual detail in a job would fall into place. The minimum acceptable standards of performance were also specified. These were accompanied by quantitative and qualitative standards including cost limits and time deadlines. It may still be a useful exercise for managers to go through this type of exercise on an individual basis. Such a methodological approach needs to form the basis of performance management, as the essential first step is to have some criteria for judging what performance should be and then measuring it, either on an individual or collective basis. The concept of performance management and its links with appraisal are dealt with in more detail in Chapter 10.

The management by objectives approach also has relevance, and in some ways broad similarities, to the establishment of organisational performance indicators. These are increasingly used, especially in the public sector. This has special relevance to the public sector because of the absence of the criterion of profit or loss. As is explained in the next chapter, there is much more emphasis now on ensuring that public services are customer-orientated. Consequently, key criteria are measures of customer satisfaction, e.g., with regard to service response times and the achievement of appropriate quality standards. A similar approach is for organisations to produce mission statements. This involves defining the purpose of an organisation, where it plans to go, and the principles that will enable it to achieve its purpose. A statement of the organisational core values that underpin the mission statement may supplement this.

The definition of objectives can present some problems. Key difficulties may be:

- objectives may not be easily defined,

- they may not lend themselves to quantification,

- they can conflict with one another,

- their relative importance to one another can change,
- organisational objectives may conflict with an individual employee's objectives.

Out of all the difficulties outlined above, it is particularly important to recognise the potential for conflict between organisational and individual objectives.

A basic reason why many management by objectives schemes have failed is that they were applied in a simplistic manner. Many managers make the naive assumption that employees will automatically subscribe to the organisational objectives, strategies and priorities that are pronounced by senior management. This is in line with a '**unitarist**' view of organisations, which assumes that what is good for the corporate whole is good for all the constituent parts. Alan Fox (1965) very lucidly explains how, if one takes the pluralistic view of organisations, one can see that this is not necessarily the case: individual employee objectives may differ or even conflict with organisational objectives. If, for example, labour-saving economies can be achieved by making people redundant, then the people who are going to be the subject of those economies may say that it will be all very well for those who remain in an organisation, but what about those who lose their jobs as a consequence? The concepts of **unitary** and **pluralistic frames of reference** are considered in more detail in Chapter 14 in the context of employee relations.

Other conflicts may be less obvious and dramatic, but are nevertheless important. Staff may not, for example, cooperate in reorganising their work to accommodate new organisational priorities if they conflict with individual priorities. This means that attempts to focus organisational activity, so that it is more effective, may be limited by the ability of managers to resolve such conflicts. This is particularly difficult if managers, because of their unitarist philosophy, can't see the potential conflict of interests. There may be some opportunity to coerce employees into accepting change, but organisational initiatives usually need active cooperation, not minimalist grudging acceptance, if they are to succeed.

Attempts to refocus organisational activity may be attempted with little or no regard for how to win the active cooperation of the staff. Consequently, many of the statements relating to organisational purpose may just be the rhetorical expression of what senior management hopes will happen, rather than effective planning tools to ensure that aspirations are actually achieved.

Another technique for identifying the priorities in a job or organisation is that of role set analysis. This technique is explained in the next section. The related concept of strategic planning is explained in the final section of this chapter.

Role set analysis

An alternative or additional technique that may help managers check whether they are using time effectively is **role set analysis**. The definition of role set used in this chapter is that it is those main activities and/or people that take up, or need to take up, most of a person's working time. Role set analysis involves comparing existing activities with current priorities. It can then lead to a consideration or reconsideration of what the end objectives of a job should be.

POTENTIAL ADVANTAGES

The technique of role set analysis has five main advantages. These are:

- it is easy to apply,
- it is easy to update,
- it can enable managers to ask searching questions of themselves about their priorities and objectives,
- it can also be used on a work group basis to see if the activities of colleagues need to be adjusted,
- it can also be used on a departmental or organisational basis to review priorities with regard to resource allocation.

EXPLANATION OF THE TECHNIQUE

Role set analysis involves using a market research approach to one's job. The raw data consist of the expectations of the main individuals and interest groups with whom one has to interact. Instead of identifying one's job by asking 'what should I be doing?' the starting point is to ask 'what do others expect of me?'

In order to do that one first has to identify just what the main elements in the role set are. The process of identifying the expectations of the members in the role set may be undertaken by analysing data already available and, where appropriate, actually consulting with people about what the expectations are. The next stage is to synthesise this raw data, and the often conflicting pressures, into a coherent form. This is done by presenting the information in chart form, as shown in Figure 2.1

The key activities, people and groups with whom a manager has to work must be identified. The chart needs to indicate the volume of work (in percentage terms) that is appropriate for each constituent part and also the priorities. It needs to be remembered that there may be some particularly influential members of the role set with whom contact is infrequent but very important. The diagram should be drawn so that the more important members of the role set are located closer to the person at the centre.

The next step is to see that the time and priority allocated to the elements in the role set are in line with what is actually needed. To do this effectively it is best for the person concerned to keep a diary of how they really spend their time over a few representative days. The actual time allocated to the individuals and groups in the role set can then be compared with what is considered desirable (see specimen figures in Figure 2.1).

Actual time spent is shown as a percentage with the model time given in accompanying brackets. Alternatively, time can be shown in hours and minutes. This enables planned

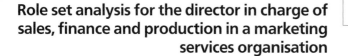

Role set analysis for the director in charge of sales, finance and production in a marketing services organisation | Figure 2.1

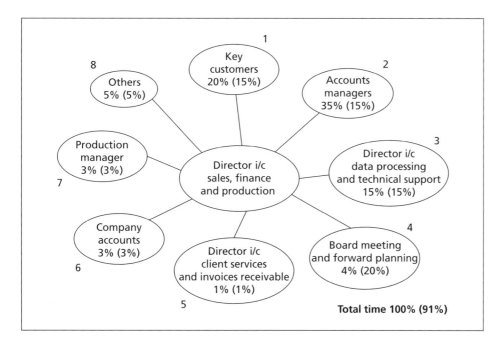

reductions or increases in the total working time to be shown. The other numbers represent the rank order of importance of the individuals, groups or activities.

The marketing and promotions company featured in Figure 2.1 employed 24 full-time and 30 part-time staff. The director concerned allocated the top priority jointly to 'accounts managers' and 'company accounts'. The role set analysis diagram immediately highlighted key issues. One was the lack of time devoted to strategic planning by board members. Another related key issue was the overload of the job-holder.

With regard to strategic planning, it emerged that there were unresolved difficult and controversial policy decisions. However, it was all too easy for the full-time board members in particular to maintain that pressure of work prevented them from addressing these issues. The small size of the board (the three directors in the chart and a non-executive director), and familiarity of the group, also meant that there was a lack of structure and focus for policy discussions when they did occur. This gave rise to the suggestion that the size of the group be widened when strategic planning issues were considered.

With regard to the overload of the job-holder, the role set analysis also demonstrated the dependence of the organisation on the director's skills, health and willingness to stay with the organisation. Immediate plans were made to reduce his workload by promoting one of the accounts managers to supervise the others. Other suggestions were that he use the allocated 9 per cent slack time for emergencies and creative thinking and that he work fewer hours. Long-term plans were made to appoint a director of new business and to promote the production manager to become production director. Another issue addressed by the analysis was the lack of secretarial and administrative staff. The director was satisfied that they were not necessary because of the availability of word processors and other information technology. He was also satisfied that it was inappropriate to engage a full-time accountant as the data processing of accounts, use of accountancy computer packages and occasional use of an outside accountant meant that accounts were cost-effectively handled in-house (Rees 1997).

REASONS FOR POOR TIME ALLOCATION

There are many reasons why managers fail to identify their priorities and time allocations accurately. Role set analysis rapidly reveals how time can be used more effectively. Reasons for poor use of time may be:

- Accessibility: some people may be both physically and psychologically more accessible than others. There is a danger of ignoring the needs of those who are not so easily available. Managers in turn may be too accessible to some who may take up more time with them than they should.

- Congeniality: it is natural for people to want to spend time with those whose company they enjoy and who share the same values. If this is overdone, however, the activities of individual units within an organisation may become lopsided and not integrate well with overall organisational objectives.

- Conflict: people vary in their ability to handle conflict. Most want to avoid it. However, it is often important to air differences of opinion to see if constructive solutions can be found. It may also be important to engage in some maintenance behaviour with colleagues where conflict is particularly likely. This may necessitate talking about non-contentious issues and, if appropriate, social issues, so that the relationship is maintained and, if possible, improved. This may help to preserve the working relationship when it is put under pressure by future conflict.

- Work preferences: people may want to concentrate on what they are good and confident at. The tendency for managers with a specialist background to spend too much time on their former specialism was examined at length in Chapter 1. When students study for exams they may need to concentrate most on the subjects where they are weakest, but where the potential for improvement is greatest, rather than on the subjects they like most.

- Competence: some important tasks may be very demanding. It is important that people are carefully selected and developed to handle managerial responsibilities in particular.

- Changing priorities: sometimes people are locked into historic priorities. Shifts in organisational priorities are not always formally announced. Managers need to examine the external pressures on an organisation in particular and to develop a 'feel' as to when new priorities have emerged. The pace of change in many organisations is such that managers have to cope with an increasing rate of internal change linked to an increasing rate of external change.

Changing priorities?

A dramatic example of an organisation being slow to change from its historic priorities was the failure of the Central Intelligence Agency (CIA) in the USA to give a high enough priority to the threat from Al Qaeda prior to the terrorist attacks on September 11th, 2001.

In estimating the amount of time and attention that other individuals or groups require, it is necessary to remember that one can allocate too much time, as well as too little. Employees can feel over-supervised, and those in senior positions may not want to spend too much time with subordinate managers. However, having said this, it is obviously potentially damaging to spend less time with one's boss than the boss deems to be appropriate. It is also necessary to consider what time one needs for oneself, particularly for reflective thought. Diary analyses by managers usually reveal that it is very difficult for them to arrange periods when they can engage in concentrated work or reflective thought without interruption. Such time may, however, be essential if one is to do long-term planning. Appropriate refinements to the role set diagram would be to allow a percentage of time for oneself as well as for those with whom one occasionally interacts who can be classified in the diagram as 'others'.

JOB STRUCTURE

Amongst the benefits that can be obtained from role set analysis is that it may show whether or not a job is viable as currently structured. There may be so many individuals and groups with whom the manager has to interact that the job may be impossible. Alternatively, the manager may be tackling their job in an inappropriate way. One example of this was the manager who, having used this technique, revealed that he was dealing directly with his subordinate's employees instead of just with his own subordinates! Whether problems are organisational or of the manager's own making, there may also be health implications if the manager has a pattern of interaction which is just too much to cope with.

An overloaded manager

On a management development workshop one participant revealed that he suffered from angina. His role set analysis demonstrated that he was grossly overloaded and that his part of the organisation needed restructuring – a factor which cannot have helped his health problems and may have even precipitated them.

INDIVIDUAL PRIORITIES

A direct way in which individual managers can identify priorities is to ask themselves who is in the position to do them the greatest damage. The leader of an architectural group, when asked to do a role set analysis on this basis, likened it to the theory of damage limitation. The value of doing this is to see that those who can do the greatest damage are on top of the list in getting their share of the time. As will shortly be explained, it is also of value in working out what to do if one comes under conflicting pressures.

Alternatively, the question can be asked 'who can help the manager most?' and time allocated accordingly, though it is to be hoped that this approach is not used too opportunistically.

Establishing the order of importance in the role set is not always that simple. The hierarchy of importance is not always obvious in matrix structures, for agency workers, and with regard to important suppliers or other 'stakeholders'. It may not even be obvious in conventional organisations with a hierarchical structure. It is not the most senior person in an organisation who is necessarily the first in importance in one's role set. The view senior people have of you may well be important, but it is necessary to work out whose word they take into account when forming their opinion of you.

Example

Identifying the wrong key person

One training officer gave an example of how he mistakenly thought the most important member of his role set was the chief executive of a company he was working for. The training officer had numerous differences of opinion with his immediate boss and sought to overcome the bad working relationship by going over the head of his boss, the company secretary, to the chief executive. The company secretary became aware of this and as a countermeasure started giving bad reports about the training officer to the chief executive. Consequently, the more the training officer went to the chief executive the greater the number of bad reports there were made of him. The chief executive, faced with a choice, understandably preferred to accept the view of the more strategically placed company secretary. Ideally, of course, he should not have allowed the training officer to bypass the company secretary, but that is what actually happened. Eventually the training officer, prompted by good advice from other colleagues, came to realise that the most important person in his role set was the company secretary. In the end he did what he should have done in the first place in his particular case, which was to work on improving his relationship with his immediate boss.

It isn't just people of high status who may be in a position to inflict 'damage' on a manager. Often people in low-status positions, but who control important and perhaps scarce services, can do the same. So too may those who control access to important information or who act as 'gatekeepers' to senior managers. Informal members of role sets may also need to be identified, assessed and handled in terms of their importance.

Ignoring a key informal member of the role set

A failure to give sufficient importance to an informal member of the role set allegedly contributed to the enforced resignation of President Reagan's chief of staff, Donald Regan, in 1987. The informal member of the role set was the president's wife, Nancy Reagan, and press reports suggested that on one occasion Donald Regan 'put the phone down on her'. It was also suggested that Donald Regan relied too much on his relationship with the President and not enough on the other powerful political figures in the role set. The other members may not have been individually as important as the President, but collectively their influence was considerable, especially if it was reinforced by the views of Nancy Reagan (Regan 1988). Her influence had steadily increased as the President's health had deteriorated. The extent to which these reports are true or untrue is unimportant as far as the basic point is concerned: the need for careful identification of the role set and appropriate responses based on that analysis.

It is also necessary to distinguish between short- and long-term aims in priorities.

Long-term versus short-term priorities

A freelance TV producer confessed that he only understood the need to identify long-term priorities after conducting a role set analysis in a management development workshop. He explained that on a recent assignment he had let the executive producer have all the contact with the broadcaster on whom his future contracts depended. Partly as a result of that he was now out of work.

ORGANISATIONAL PRIORITIES

The emphasis in this section has so far mainly been about working out appropriate time allocations on an individual basis. Role set analysis can also be used to consider how resources should be allocated on an organisational basis. Managers can also review their budget distribution in this way.

Prioritisation in the Police Service

An interesting example of establishing organisational priorities is the technique of crime-screening. This is a method of allocating resources for criminal investigative work that is sometimes formalised into a 'points system' by police forces. Offences that might realistically lead to successful detection and conviction are allocated resources in preference to cases where success is less likely. The amount of available evidence is considered particularly important in allocating points. Consequently, aspects such as the quality of the description of a person, the noting of a car number or the possibility of forensic evidence could be crucial in determining whether a crime is investigated or not. The severity of the crime is another important criterion, as is the estimate of public priorities. Crimes with a low number of points might just be handled on the phone. The technique can also be used to review the allocation of resources between crime detection and crime prevention. The same type of issue arises with medical work in trying to strike the right balance between health cure and health care.

INFORMATION AND EVALUATION

There are many ways in which information can be collected about role sets. The technique can be a very useful device for getting people to talk about common problems during in-house management workshops. If syndicates of managers doing similar jobs are arranged, they can critically cross-examine one another about the appropriateness of one another's role set analysis. Workshops can provide a climate in which basic issues, which would not otherwise be discussed, are brought out into the open. The technique of role set analysis can have a powerful catalytic effect in this context. Another method of collecting information is for a manager to take a market research approach and ask colleagues just what their expectations are. Care has to be taken, however, about who is approached and the manner of the approach. One of the potential problems is that expectations are aroused which cannot be met. As a minimum, though, one should reflect on just what the expectations of you are by the other individuals and groups in your role set. This may reveal a variety of misunderstandings about what you expect from others and what they expect from you.

What also may be revealed by role set analysis is that some of the expectations are contradictory. This may happen if the manager is given incompatible tasks or if the sheer volume of work they are expected to do is unrealistic. The most practical way of handling such a dilemma is often for managers to try to gauge what the real priorities are amongst the welter of instructions they are given. They also need to be sensitive to changes in organisational priorities. Those senior to a manager may be reluctant to admit that the various expectations are in conflict.

The reality may be that the individual manager has to work out what the real priorities are at a given time. To do this the manager may need to judge just what the priorities are with others in the role set and the ways in which they may be changing. In an ideal world one would only work in organisations where job demands were compatible and all legitimate expectations could be met. However, as we live in an imperfect world, there needs to be a method of resolving contradictory pressures. One should also recognise that when priorities change it is often politically too difficult for policy-makers to say that a certain priority has been abandoned or even downgraded. The most one may get is an admission that a certain objective has been 'put on the back burner'. However, managers ignore these shifts in organisational priority at their peril and need to adjust their pattern of activity to suit the new scale of priorities.

STRESS MANAGEMENT

The pressures for competitiveness in the private sector and for economy in the public sector are putting managers under increasing stress. Consequently, they usually cannot do all that is expected of them and have to develop some basis for deciding how their own time and the resources under their control are allocated. If everything cannot be done, it seems far more logical to consciously and systematically prioritise rather than do things on a random basis. Individual survival and organisational effectiveness are both likely to be served by conscious prioritisation. The best way of coping with managerial stress is to try to reduce it rather than simply deal with the symptoms. Techniques of prioritisation can be enormously useful in this context and also in relieving managers of guilt feelings about not meeting what may be impossible demands.

The issue of managerial stress is dealt with further in Chapter 6, and the organisational problems caused by the mismatch between expectations and resources in the public sector in chapter 3. The issue of individual prioritisation is dealt with further in the next section of this chapter.

INDIVIDUAL INTERPRETATION AND APPLICATION

What has been explained is a progressively more sophisticated method of gathering data and developing insights about how to identify one's job. After all this has been done, it is up to the manager to evaluate and synthesise the material and stamp their own personality on their job. There is more to identifying a job than working out what those in strategic positions want of you, but it is prudent to take that into account before then adding the essential ingredient – one's own personality.

The concept of role set analysis also stresses the interdependence of managers with others. The importance of the manager's role in creating and energising teams is examined in the context of organic structures in Chapter 3, with regard to managerial style in Chapter 4 and in handling meetings in Chapter 16.

Time management

When the overall objectives, key tasks and role set have been clarified it may then be appropriate for a manager to consider how effectively their time is used. One view of the manager's job is that the only real resource is their time. There appear to be enormous variations in the ways in which managers either use their time effectively or waste it. Consequently, this topic deserves specific attention. Issues of particular importance are:

- identification of priorities,
- logical sequencing of work,
- avoidance of fatigue,
- need for managers to avoid wasting other people's time.

IDENTIFYING PRIORITIES

The reactive or 'grasshopper' manager's time management may be ineffective, failing to identify the priorities in the job. Perhaps the worst way of prioritising work is to deal with the last request first, whether it be made in person or be the item just received in the in-tray. Sadly, there are many examples of people who do this regularly. The priorities of a job need to be established quite consciously. To do this it may be necessary to write them down and then either to rank the priorities over a particular time period or to group them into bands of varying urgency. Even well-organised managers find that they have to react to short-term crises and pressures, but they should have as a constant reference point a clear grasp of the priority issues that are accumulating and which merit attention.

Finding the time to think about the job may itself constitute a problem, particularly for managers who are already heavily involved in 'fire-fighting' activities. However, unless they somehow find the time to think their way through to a more rational pattern of activity, managers are unlikely to be effective. One of the problems in organisations is that managers find that they have to cope with so many interruptions that it is difficult to find time to think in a concentrated and systematic way about the job. It may be necessary to do this away from one's normal place of work or to use a secretary or other person as a screen to prevent interruptions. It may also be necessary to have a clear idea of who those people are who make unproductive claims on one's time, with a view to reducing the time spent with them. It is one of the ironies of organisational life that so often the people with the most time to waste are those who insist on spending long periods telling you how busy they are! In such cases it may be particularly necessary to tell people at the start of a discussion how much time you have available for them.

Establishing the priorities in a job may well involve a careful look at the conflict between what a manager prefers to do and what they actually need to do. This is a necessarily recurring issue in this book. The consequences of inappropriate prioritisation can in some cases even threaten the survival of an organisation.

Example

Dramatically wrong priorities

One company was threatened with a hostile takeover. Unfortunately the senior executive responsible for objecting to this failed to turn up at the Government Takeover Panel meeting that could have blocked the change. Consequently, the take-over was approved without opposition!

The personnel policies of organisations unfortunately do not always help people to take a balanced approach in their job.

Example

Training and priorities

In a local authority building department, all the charge-hand manual employees from a range of skills were upgraded to be general trades supervisors. The idea was sound enough in principle – which was to avoid having a charge-hand on every site where employees of that particular trade were working. Unfortunately, the idea was poorly implemented. There was no attempt to select who should be upgraded and who should not. Neither was there any attempt to train the newly appointed general trades supervisors, either in management or in the technical aspects of the new trades that were nominally under their control. Consequently, most of the newly appointed general trades supervisors were too frightened to supervise employees in trades other than their own. This meant that, for example, the person who had previously been a charge-hand bricklayer spent nearly all their time with the bricklayers and rarely tried to supervise the employees in the other groups, such as the electricians, plumbers and carpenters.

SEQUENCING WORK

Two interrelated issues should particularly influence the order in which work is done. One is the priority of importance and the other is the logical sequence. Not all issues need immediate attention. The following checklist may help in identifying the sequence in which work needs to be tackled:

- What needs to be done urgently? This can include minor tasks that have to be completed by an imminent deadline.

- What needs to be done to enable other people to get on with their job?

- What needs to be done when it is convenient, or within a non-urgent time-span?

- What can't be done until activities by others have been completed? Such work may be put in a pending tray, though a follow-up system may be necessary to monitor the progress of other people involved in the task.

- What is simply information received which requires no action?

- Which issues can simply be ignored?

Domestic example of priorities

If time is tight, it is more appropriate for people pressured for time in the morning to get dressed before they eat breakfast. It is much more practicable to run down the road for the train fully clothed but with breakfast unfinished rather than the other way around!

Example

Route planning

The need for careful sequencing is further illustrated by the following case of two delivery drivers working for the same firm. One driver would look at the first address on his list and drive off and then look at the next address and drive to that and so on. In the course of a day he was likely to retrace his route several times. The other driver would spend about an hour each morning planning his route so that, although he started his deliveries later, he covered his route with the minimum mileage.

Example

Some work may need reflective thought before it is finalised. It is not just the speed at which issues are dealt with that is important, but also the quality of any decisions. The thought may not even need to be conscious, as ideas can suddenly fit into place after subconscious mental activity. Students can also find this when answering examination questions. A difficult question that is put on one side, whilst an easier one is tackled, may appear much simpler when it is read for the second time a while later. However, the manager needs to recognise the difference between procrastination and reflecting on difficult issues so that an appropriate decision is eventually taken.

Another issue is whether tasks are undertaken consecutively or simultaneously. The answer to this may depend on both personality and national culture. **Monochronics** may prefer to

| Figure 2.2 | **Critical path analysis: launching a new product** |

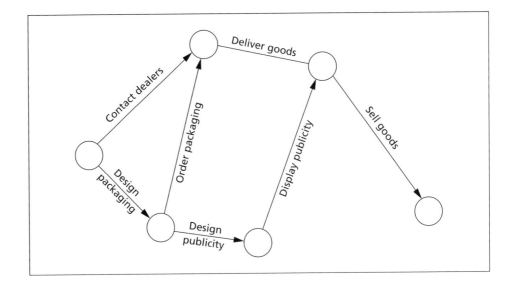

undertake tasks in a linear manner until they are completed. **Polychronics** often prefer to under-take a number of tasks simultaneously. Problems can arise when these two patterns clash, for example, if a monochronic is busily engaged on a task and a polychronic wants something else done immediately. Hall (1987) maintains that these patterns correlate with national culture – for instance, monochronic work patterns are more common in Nordic countries than elsewhere.

CRITICAL PATH ANALYSIS

The concept of logical work sequencing can be developed further by the use of **critical path analysis** (CPA). This is of particular use in planning and controlling tasks where a number of activities need to be carried out simultaneously. The technique has been developed particularly for use on construction projects and in production planning. Its benefits did not live up to early expectations because of unforeseen variables, failures in communication and competing agendas that can affect any project and frustrate mechanistic planning systems. If used carefully, however, critical path analysis often is a powerful planning tool and can also be of value for individual work planning. It is often used intuitively by people who have never heard of the term 'critical path analysis', for example if meat is put to roast whilst the rest of the dinner is prepared. Alternative titles for CPA are 'network planning' and 'network analysis'.

An example of how critical path analysis can be used in launching a new product is shown in Figure 2.2.

In the launch of the new product, one assumes that the market research and design have been undertaken first. The packaging would then be designed and the dealers contacted at the same time to prepare them for the new product. When the packaging is designed it can then be ordered from the supplier. The publicity material can then be designed (not before, as one would want to see the packaged product first). When the packaging is received and orders received from the dealers the product can be delivered. A further step in the planning can be to show the time period during which each step of the process needs to be completed. Although the example is simple, the written explanation is complicated and difficult to follow. In contrast, the diagram (Figure 2.2) is very clear (Lockyer 1991).

FATIGUE

It is necessary for managers to take into account their own physical limitations in planning their workload. Individuals vary considerably in their propensity to fatigue, and fatigue also depends on the commitments a manager has outside the workplace. It can be very tempting to compare oneself to a person with an unusually high degree of energy, but the consequences may be disastrous if the workload is planned on an over-optimistic assessment of what one's physical capabilities really are. If this happens it seems likely that in the long term the quality and rate of work will suffer and the likelihood of illness increase.

RESEARCH EVIDENCE

Research studies demonstrate that long hours of work for manual workers can be counterproductive, and it would seem a common sense step to consider whether the same pattern of work would affect managers eventually. A particular point that needs to be stressed is that recovery time from fatigue tends to increase exponentially with the amount of the fatigue. What this means is that when practicable, one should rest as soon as there are signs of fatigue, otherwise recovery can take much longer. Performance may be unduly affected if one continues working once there are signs of fatigue.

The counter-productive effects of fatigue

Example

Maier (1955a) reports on an interesting British Medical Research Council study of the effects of an increase in the working week in 1940 after the Dunkirk evacuation. Under the pressure of the World War II emergency, Britain increased the hours of its working week. Before Dunkirk, the working week was 56 hours; after Dunkirk it was increased to an average of 69.5 hours in the war industries. The initial effect of this increase was a 1 per cent rise in production, but then production declined, and sickness, absenteeism, and accidents increased. By the end of a couple of months, the average working week was 68.5 hours, but the average amount of time actually worked was only 51 hours, as compared with the period before Dunkirk when the average time was 53 hours. As a result, production was 12 per cent below that preceding Dunkirk. Six months later, the shorter working week was restored, with the result that production steadily rose to a higher point than ever before.

Maier (1955b) also reports on Angela Masso's studies on fatigue. The results of these studies may have considerable implications for the way people, including managers, pace themselves at work.

One study on fatigue concerned the ability of a person to move a 6kg weight attached to a free finger by a length of string. It emerged that if the movement was repeated every two seconds an individual would cease to be able to lift the weight at all after about a minute. However, if the movement was only repeated every 16 seconds the weight could be raised and lowered almost indefinitely.

What is crucial is that people take rest breaks before they get too tired. If they don't, recovery time may be much longer and the pace and quality of work significantly lower when they do resume.

SOCIAL NEEDS

It is necessary to recognise that people may need to meet social as well as work needs when they are doing their job. An over-planned approach to the job may be too inflexible, and it can also make life dreadfully dull. Additionally, it may be necessary to spend some time maintaining working relationships by a certain amount of social conversation. There are obviously limits to the extent to which this should be done, but it could be foolish to ignore this aspect. Managers also need to pace themselves at work, and it may be necessary to have some periods in the working day when they relax a little. However, relaxation needs to be done in such a way that it does not interrupt those who are working effectively. The related issue of monotony at work is considered in Chapter 6 on motivation.

SAVING OTHER PEOPLE'S TIME

Managers need to help others use their time productively, as well as organising their own time management. This can, for example, mean careful preparation for discussions and interviews so that other people's time is not wasted. Prior preparation is particularly important if one has to chair a meeting, as will be explained in more detail in Chapter 16 on meetings and chairing.

Example

The time costs of badly planned meetings

At a local government body 23 people from differ-ent parts of London were called to a meeting that had to be aborted because it had not been properly planned.

Strategic planning

NEED FOR PLANNING

The concepts explained so far in this chapter have focused mainly on how the individual manager can do their own job more effectively over a relatively short-term period. However, managers also need to take a long-term and corporate perspective. This inevitably means cooperating with other managers in order to anticipate and, where appropriate, shape the future. If an individual manager can help develop rational long-term policies, this can make their own job easier to perform and may also lead to improvements in other parts of an organisation that are even more import-ant. It has already been explained how the techniques of setting objectives and role set analysis can be applied on a departmental or organisational basis as well as on an individual basis.

The essence of strategic planning is that it is the broad means of achieving overall objectives. However, it may necessitate careful thought about the nature of the organisational objectives. People in commercial organisations often take the view that they are in business to make a particular product or deliver a particular service when the reality is that their overall aim may need to be to optimise their return on capital investment. Although the literature on this topic is mainly based on the private sector, the concepts can and need to be adapted for use in the public sector and areas such as **non-governmental organisations** (NGOs), or **non-government entities** as they are sometimes described. There the emphasis is likely to be on the need to provide cost-effective services in a changing environment.

PLANNING MECHANISMS

Key concepts and issues involved in strategic planning need to be explained. Even though most managers will not be involved in board level planning, long-term and strategic planning is also needed at a departmental level. For this to be done, it is necessary to involve the key decision-makers.

Experience with strategic planning groups made up of specialists outside the main power structure suggests that they are likely to fail because they do not have the 'clout' or often even the information and expertise with which to fashion long-term policies. The problem that has to be overcome with the key decision-makers is that they are invariably busy people. To complicate matters, such people may be reluctant to commit themselves to long-term strategies, particularly if there are sectional rivalries. Also, even if senior people are given responsibility for strategic planning, if they become distanced from operational reality, their plans may prove to be unrealistic.

The problem of creating time for such strategic planning with key, yet busy, people can be reduced by having a chair who is under less pressure and by the provision of specialist reports for consideration at corporate or long-term planning meetings. It can be inappropriate to include long-term planning with the business discussed at ordinary departmental or board meetings, as this inevitably leads to the short-term issues crowding out the long-term ones. In practice, often the only long-term planning that takes place is that associated with the annual financial budget.

Strategic planning can be a top-down or bottom-up process. In the former, the attempt is made to change the organisation in line with a centrally conceived master plan. With bottom-up planning, information is sought from the grass roots to help shape evolutionary development. In practice, there usually needs to be a fusing of these two approaches. Ideally, a long-term plan will be established and short-term plans integrated with it. This may involve 'gap analysis' to establish what has to be done to bring an organisation's activities into line with that which is planned. Any long-term plan will, however, need continuous adjustment, especially in turbulent environments.

The increasing pace of change has caused a reaction against detailed centralised planning because such a process can be too cumbersome to react quickly and effectively. Now, the emphasis is much more on semi-autonomous business units that can react more quickly. Charles Handy (1994) has argued strongly for this 'federal' concept and for the associated idea of 'subsidiarity' of business in organisation. This involves decisions only being taken at the centre that cannot sensibly be taken lower down. However, it is necessary to guard against fragmentation and the loss of a coherent organisational culture and purpose. Conversely, business units can be set up that are subject to such detailed central control that there is no real delegation. The more strategic planning is pushed downwards, the greater the opportunity for individual managers to get involved in the process and to take initiatives. The impact of **globalisation**, national culture and information technology on organisation structure and the issue of semi-autonomous business units are considered in the next chapter.

FACTORS TO CONSIDER

In considering strategic planning, it is necessary to identify what the potential changes are in both the external and internal environments. Changes may be imposed on an organisation from outside, but opportunities for shaping the future through internal developments, such as product improvement, may also exist. It may be appropriate to establish what degrees of freedom are open to a unit or organisation in planning its future and what will happen if no positive decisions are taken. The lead-time needed to alter activities must also be identified. It may also be useful to identify what an organisation's primary activity should be and to carry out an audit of its main strengths and weaknesses. It is also necessary to beware of imposing rigid structures in conditions of rapid change because it may prevent organisations from adapting to such change quickly enough.

Another issue is the danger of identifying the future simply by extrapolating from the past. To paraphrase Marshall McLuhan (1997), it can be foolish to drive into the future looking in the rear-view mirror. Perhaps Henry Ford had a point when he declared that 'history is bunk' – for him, history had no role to play in the way he revolutionised the car industry.

Example

The danger of looking backwards

The tendency for people to cling to fundamentally wrong assumptions based on experience elsewhere is referred to by Bryson (2000, pp. 29–30). He explains how successive early explorers in Australia dragged boats into the arid interior, in one case for 3 000 miles, on the false assumption that they would encounter vast internal water systems. This was in line with the experience and behaviour of African explorers.

It may be necessary to pay attention to what options are being created by developments in information technology in particular, as well as market changes. A further issue is the need to identify the main ways in which an organisation is, or is likely to become, at risk. According to Porter (1998), the key need is to get the market positioning right and the organisational capacity to sustain competitive advantage. One simple model that incorporates some of these key issues is **SWOT analysis**. The factors to be analysed are:

Internal

- Strengths
- Weaknesses

External

- Opportunities
- Threats

Identification of a key strength

One UK conglomerate, centred on the brewing industry but with interests in many other areas, found that when they analysed the reasons for sometimes quite astonishing turnarounds in the performance of subsidiary companies, they found that the key variable was the managerial talent that had been injected into these companies

Example

'If the SWOT approach is used it is important to ensure that the analysis is rigorous. If it is done in a mechanistic and superficial way . . . it may give a false impression of what the strategic options really are' (Rees and Porter 2006, p. 228). At whatever level strategic planning is undertaken, the process needs to be reasonably broadly based – even if the lesson has been learned that one should avoid centralised prescriptive approaches. Many corporate plans revolve just around the financial and marketing dimensions. The whole move to strategic human resource planning, explained in more detail in Chapter 14, necessitates considering the human resource dimension before and not after strategy is determined. The related interconnections between technical and social factors are considered in Chapter 3.

REALISTIC GOALS

One of the dangers in strategic planning is that unrealistic goals may be set. Although there may be occasions when the circumstances are right to try and bridge the gap between heroic goals and existing resources, this is not always the case. Whilst organisational capability can be developed, structures changed and cultures altered, there are limits to the change that is achievable. Also, competitors can copy technological achievements. What may be key is the web of working relationships within or even outside an organisation and its stock of intellectual capital. Incremental improvement may sometimes be the best option.

Example

Unrealistic goals

One national social work charity embarked on an ambitious programme of expansion by taking over related charitable organisations. They ignored the legal obligations with regard to the employment rights of the employees they acquired and also lacked managerial capability. It was not long before the organisation ran into serious financial difficulties.

Often the difficulties of developing a meaningful and comprehensive corporate plan are so great that it is better to adopt an incremental plan. In a former communist country in Eastern Europe attempts were made to develop a corporate plan in a national consultative body composed of representatives of employers, trade unions and the government.

> There were considerable conflicts of interest not just between the parties but sometimes within the parties. The logical way forward was to identify those areas where reform was acceptable and could be agreed. This was preferable to no change at all.
>
> (Rees and Porter 2006, ICT Part 1)

Another example concerned a rural development authority in south-east Asia:

> It emerged that there was a major difference of opinion within the organisation as to whether its prime function was the prudent development of local industries or the preservation of local communities regardless of cost. Given that there was no immediate prospect of resolving the difference it was necessary to concentrate on areas where organisational reform was practicable.
>
> (Rees and Porter 2006, ICT Part 1)

Sometimes **mission statements** are used as a way of identifying and publicising the overall aims and values of an organisation. This can provide a useful focus both internally and externally. However, there is a danger that such statements degenerate into being 'wish lists' of what organisations believe are acceptable values and realistic aims. For mission statements to be useful they need to be very carefully worked out, with considerable attention being paid to factors such as the amount of control there is about the internal and external environment, the commitment to such documents and the need for its elements to be consistent with one another. Too many mission statements are in practice, to put it kindly, aspirational rather than useful statements of what an organisation is and what it hopes to be.

QUANTIFIABLE VERSUS INTANGIBLE FACTORS

There is a great danger in planning processes that revolve too much around that which is relatively easily quantified. Denis Healey learned this lesson when he was Chancellor of the Exchequer in the UK. Admittedly, he was involved in planning on a macro scale, but his reflections are worth remembering with regard to smaller-scale planning:

Economics has acquired a spurious respectability through the use of numbers, which appear to many people, like my old friend McNamara (Head of the World Bank) much more meaningful than mere adjectives or adverbs, because they appear to be precise and unambiguous. Unfortunately, I soon discovered that the most important numbers were nearly always wrong.

(Healey 1990, pp. 379–380)

Denis Healey was even more forthright in commenting on the dangers of an over-reliance on numbers with regard to defence planning. He felt that people look for what they can measure, which is not necessarily what is important. Referring to an earlier stage in his career when he was Defence Secretary in the UK and Robert McNamara was his counterpart in the USA, and whilst acknowledging what he had learned from McNamara about the control of defence projects, he said:

McNamara, like the whizz-kids who had so much influence on his strategic thinking, demonstrated what I call the 'lamp-post fallacy' in its purest form. Late one night a policeman found a man on his knees under a lamp post. 'What are you doing?' he asked. 'I dropped my keys at the bottom of the street,' was the reply. 'But that is a hundred yards away. Why are you looking here?' 'Because there's no light at the bottom of the street.'

(Healey 1990, p. 307)

It is also necessary to beware of obstacles to rational debate:

An assumption about the development of strategy is that those who need to be involved welcome the prospect of open and 'rational' debate. Personality clashes, rivalries, hidden and even ignoble agendas and sensitive developments are some of the factors that can be obstacles to debate. Account may also need to be taken of human frailties such as personal insecurity and individual 'hang-ups'.

(Rees and Porter 2006, ICT Part 1, p. 227)

TARGETS

The planning and decision-making process in organisations will partly depend on quantitative estimates of what is actually happening, what is expected to happen and what those in charge would like to happen. A problem is that once measures are used as a basis for targets they may get distorted. Distortion is all the more likely if the targets are linked to rewards or penalties. Rewards or penalties may involve the pay of the individuals concerned or future resource allocation to an organisation and may even threaten the very survival of an organisation. These issues can be particularly problematical in the public sector where the measure of commercial profitability is absent, though even that measure is capable of manipulation. What this means is that whilst the use of targets may be necessary, they need to be carefully worked. The danger is that targets are politically convenient rather than realistic. They can distort organisational activity so that other important activities are ignored, and those involved in meeting targets but not involved in the setting of targets may not be committed to their achievement. Such shortcomings can lead to a range of defensive responses that can involve manipulation so there is just the appearance of target achievement or even downright fraud. (A more detailed explanation of the manipulations that can take place with regard to employee incentive payment schemes is given in Chapter 7.)

An example of the type of behaviour that may have been precipitated by target setting concerns the following allegation relating to the British Home Office regarding foreign convicts in British jails. It was claimed that foreign convicts were not considered for deportation:

> . . . so that the [UK] government 'target of driving down the number of applicants for refugee status' could be met. Senior officials knew that most of the prisoners up for deportation would automatically claim asylum. This was one of several 'creative' solutions thought up by senior officials to please ministers.
>
> (Sunday Times 2006)

Another example of the problems that can be caused by target setting concerns the allocation of police resources. Peter Neyroud, chief executive of the National Policing Improvement Agency, said:

> There has been, in the minds of many professionals, including myself, a neglect of the serious . . . Because detecting a stolen milk bottle counts the same as detecting a murder . . . you get your points from, not necessarily milk bottles, but certainly in mid-range, volume crime, rather than serious crime.
>
> (The Times 2007)

Rudolph Giuliani (2002) took a very different approach to achieving improvements in organisational performance when he was mayor of New York City. He understood the danger of targets being manipulated. He also saw the danger of arousing expectations by target setting and feelings of failure if targets were not met, even if there had been significant improvement. Consequently, he adopted a problem-solving approach. Instead of developing grand strategies, he adopted a project problem-solving approach to areas of major concern. Whilst other factors may have been at work as well, the murder rate in New York City fell from 1946 in the year 1993 (the year before he became mayor) to 673 in 2000 (Giuliani 2002, p. 169). Giuliani also developed the 'broken window' theory. This involved dealing with small issues, such as repairing broken windows in public property, to create a better environment and momentum for improvement. Small issues could be linked to larger issues, e.g. to criminal behaviour. This in turn could lead to major strategic benefits (Giuliani 2002, p. 47).

Summary

The importance of identifying realistic job objectives has been stressed in this chapter. Often managers justify themselves by the amount of work they do rather than the results they achieve. Objective setting can be a means of both targeting their activity and assessing their performance. There are many reasons why managers may get the balance of their job wrong.

The technique of role set analysis was explained in detail because of its potential to help people organise their work effectively. It can be an easy and effective way of distinguishing between what managers are doing and what they should be doing. Role set analysis can also help managers prioritise, which will be particularly necessary if they are overworked. If that is the case, it is better that they consciously decide what is done and what is not done rather than engage in random prioritisation, which can lead to important tasks being neglected. Managers also need to distinguish between short-term and long-term objectives. They need to create some time for reflective thought about the future.

Time management was also explained. It includes sequencing work in a logical way. Some account also should be taken of social needs at work. Working too hard can be counterproductive because of the danger of cumulative fatigue.

The need for managers to try and influence the framework in which they operate was explained. Managers should get involved in strategic planning at whatever level possible. This may help prevent their good work being undermined either by non-existent or faulty planning elsewhere. Their involvement may also be able to make overall strategic planning more effective.

Self-assessment questions

(If you are not in a managerial job you may wish to answer some of the questions with regard to whatever activity you are engaged in. If you wish to check the extent to which your answers to any of the following questions are appropriate, cross-refer to the Table of Contents. The contents for this chapter are on page x–xi.)

1 How would you distinguish between managerial activity and managerial effectiveness?

2 Define appropriate work objectives either for yourself or for another person.

3 What are the advantages that role set analysis can have over other methods of identifying work content and priorities?

4 What are the essential elements of effective time management?

5 How would you ensure that you have sequenced your work logically?

6 Why might strategic planning be relevant to you?

References

(Works of particular interest are marked with a star.)

Bryson, Bill (2000), *Down Under*, Doubleday.

Drucker, Peter F. (1955), *Practice of Management*, Heinemann.

Evening Standard (1 January 1977), London.

*Giuliani, Rudolph. W. (2002), *Leadership*, Little Brown. (An interesting and illuminating account of the managerial problems facing the Mayor of New York City and an explanation of how these problems were tackled, which is particularly critical of the use of targets.)

Hall, E.T. (1987), *Hidden Differences*, Anchor Press/Doubleday.

Handy, Charles (1994), *The Empty Raincoat*, Hutchinson.

Healey, Denis (1990), *The Time of My Life*, Penguin.

Humble, John (1979), *Management by Objectives in Action*, McGraw-Hill in association with the British Institute of Management.

Lockyer, Keith and James Gordon (1991), *Critical Path Analysis and Other Project Network Techniques*, 5th ed., Prentice Hall.

McLuhan, Marshall (1997), *Forward Through the Rearview Mirror*, MIT Press.

Maier, Norman, R.F. (1955), *Psychology in Industry*, Harrap, (a) p. 447, (b) pp. 425–428.

Mintzberg, Henry (1989), *Mintzberg on Management*, Hungry Minds.

Porter, Michael (1998), *The Competitive Advantage of Nations*, 2nd ed., The Free Press.

Rees, W. David (1997), *Managerial Stress – Dealing With Causes, Not the Symptoms*, Industrial and Commercial Training, 29 (2): 25–30.

*Rees, W. David and Christine Porter (2002), *Management by panacea – the training implications*, Industrial and Commercial Training, Vol. 34 No. 6. (An explanation of the need for diagnostic skills in management and the further need to identify the nature of and causes of problems before devising solutions – available on the companion website.)

*Rees, W. David and Christine Porter (2006), *Corporate strategy development and related management development: the case for the incremental approach, Part 1 – the development of strategy* and *Part 2 – Implications for Learning and Development*. Industrial and Commercial Training, Vol. 38 No. 5 and Vol. 39 No. 6. (An explanation of why comprehensive strategy development may often be so difficult that the incremental approach may be the only option. This article received a highly commended award by the Emerald Literati Network in 2007. In Part 2 the need for a broad-based approach is explained and also why teaching in the area needs to be multidisciplinary.) (Available on the companion website.)

Regan, Donald T. (1988), *For The Record*, Arrow.

Royal Commission on Trade Unions and Employers' Associations/Alan Fox (1965), *Industrial Sociology and Industrial Relations*, research paper no. 3, HMSO.

Stewart, Rosemary (1988), *Managers and Their Jobs*, 2nd ed., Macmillan.

Sunday Times (30 April 2006), *Criminals not deported 'to avoid asylum claims'* and *Home Office even freed prisoners with deportation orders*.

The Times (13 November 2007), *Targets 'let dangerous criminals escape net'*.

Further reading

Bovaird, Tony and Loffler, E. (2003), *Public Management and Governance*, Routledge.

Grant, R.M. (2005), *Contemporary Strategy Analysis*, 5th ed., Blackwell.

Mallin, Christine A. (2006), *Corporate Governance*, Oxford University Press.

The manager and the organisation

Learning outcomes

By the end of this chapter you will be able to:

- Assess the relevance of developments in organisational theory and practice to your own situation
- Identify and assess the key variables, including information technology, that shape the structure and manner in which organisations operate
- Identify the causes of the lack of effective integration of organisational activity and strategies for dealing with this
- Distinguish between role and personality behaviour
- Identify differences and similarities between the private and not-for-profit sections (including the public sector) and the implications for management

Introduction

In this chapter the organisational context in which those with managerial responsibilities have to work is discussed. Managers need to appreciate this context and the way in which organisations need to establish structures to fit the circumstances in which they have to operate. They may also need help to see that organisational structures and operational methods are adapted to take account of changed circumstances. Historical and recent theories of organisation are explained. Particular attention is paid to the impact of **globalisation** and technology and the development of more flexible organisational structures. Other key variables examined include the size of organisations, the need to identify the critical function and national culture. The increasingly important concepts of **intellectual capital** and **knowledge management** are also examined. The problems of achieving the effective integration of organisational activity are considered and strategies suggested for dealing with this issue. The need to distinguish between role and personality behaviour is also included. General developments in the private sector and the increasing importance of the not-for-profit sector are covered. The similarities and differences between the private and public sectors are given particular attention.

Theories of organisation

SCIENTIFIC AND CLASSICAL MANAGEMENT SCHOOLS

The historical approach to management was that it consisted of a set of principles that were capable of definition and universal application. This was the approach of writers such as F. W. Taylor (1972, first published 1911) and Henri Fayol (1916). Taylor, along with Gantt and the Gilbreths, was a member of the Scientific Management School, which conceptually overlapped with the classical management theorists, including Fayol. Those in the Scientific Management School concentrated on the organisation of manual work, production planning and time and motion study. Taylor advocated the systematic analysis of work, and for management to take over decision-making about which methods of work were used, based on the principle that the average worker preferred a well-defined task and clear-cut standards.

The classical theorists developed the ideas of the scientific management theorists into a framework of organisational principles. The collective view of the classical theorists was that work could be so organised that the objectives of organisations could be accomplished with great efficiency. Organisations were viewed as the product of logical thought concerned largely with coordinating tasks through the use of legitimate authority. Employees were seen as rational beings whose interests coincided with those of the organisations in which they were employed. They were also seen as being capable of working to high levels of efficiency, provided they were properly selected, trained, directed, monitored and supported. Employers would use indoctrination and coercion if necessary to achieve a rational approach. This was presumed to lead to employees behaving exactly as they were told. Great emphasis was also placed on the need for careful and detailed explanation of organisational structure.

Two particularly important concepts that emerged from the scientific and classical management theorists were those of **functional control** and advice and **line and staff relationships**. F.W. Taylor (1911) envisaged organisations based on functional control. To the extent that this was practised, this meant that shop floor supervisors were directly responsible to the various functional departments they interacted with. Specialists such as those responsible for work methods, staff selection and inspection would therefore give instructions and not advice to supervisors – even though this meant that supervisors did not have **unity of command.** In line and staff relationships, however, specialist (or functional) staff only advise line management and the unity of command is preserved. Sometimes, the relationship of specialist staff with line managers is described as a **dotted line relationship**. If a functional specialist feels their advice has been ignored in theory their only recourse is to see that the matter is taken up with their line manager's boss.

Whilst the concepts of functional and line and staff relationships are quite separate, in practice the distinction can be blurred. This is particularly because of the potential repercussions of line managers ignoring specialist advice. Such repercussions can include finding out that the specialist advice was appropriate, having the matter referred to their boss and finding out that they are in breach of the law. In addition line managers may find it convenient to let functional specialists take over some of the administrative duties related to a particular function.

HUMAN RELATIONS SCHOOL

Later, the limitations of the classical writers became apparent, particularly their simplistic approach to people. The Hawthorne experiments conducted at the Western Electric Company in Chicago in the 1920s and 1930s revealed that groups can have a powerful effect on the way organisations work. It was recognised that people did not always do what employers wanted, nor did they always act in a way that employers considered rational (Roethlisberger and Dickson 1939). The existence of informal networks and working relationships was also observed. This led to the evolution of the human relations school of organisational theory with which Elton Mayo in particular was associated. The work of occupational sociologists has subsequently emphasised the need to view organisations as social entities. As explained in the previous chapter, it is also necessary to recognise that there can be considerable conflict between the objectives of the organisation and those of the individuals employed in it. Informal and formal employee organisation, such as organised work groups and trade unions, can also lead to the sharing of power in organisations, so that there are limits to the authority of management.

SYSTEMS THEORY

Another school of thought that has emerged is the systems concept of organisations. This views organisations as dynamic organisms with interconnecting parts. Each part is dependent on integration with related parts if objectives are to be accomplished. Each part, however, has to operate in an environment which influences what the employees in that section want to achieve and are capable of achieving.

Interrelationship of organisational activity

Example

In a local evening newspaper, technological developments made it apparently possible to replace the former full-time print production staff by relatively unskilled part-time staff. Whilst this reduced costs in the production department, it dramatically increased problems in the advertising department. This was particularly because of the loss of accumulated knowledge in the production department of customers' needs ... The consequences of this included the loss of customers and the advertising staff having to spend a significant amount of their time with the remaining customers arranging for rectification work and dealing with customer complaints. This in turn affected the commission payments of advertising staff and caused very high labour turnover in the production and advertising departments, thus aggravating the problems. The newspaper depended on advertising for about 80% of its income.

(Rees and Porter 2006)

The interrelationship of organisational activities is an important issue, particularly for diagnosing the causes of organisational problems. The approach taken in this book is consistent with the **systems theory** of organisations. Viewing the organisation as a system or set of interrelated parts should enable the manager to identify the cause of a problem even if the cause is not within the department where the problem manifests itself. This theme is considered in more detail later in the chapter in the section on the interrelationship of organisational activity.

A concept that overlaps with systems theory is that of **socio-technical systems**. According to socio-technical systems theory, technical systems need to be effectively integrated with the social organisation at work, not simply imposed on it. The concept of socio-technical systems is examined further in Chapter 6, in the context of motivation.

MECHANISTIC AND ORGANIC STRUCTURES

A particularly useful classification of organisational structures is the extent to which they are mechanistic or organic. The ideas of the classical theorists were, and to a large extent still are, particularly appropriate to large-scale organisations operating in stable environments. Burns and Stalker (1972) have since suggested that such circumstances lend themselves to 'mechanistic' systems. This is in contrast to more rapidly changing environments where more adaptive 'organic' systems may be necessary. Although the research conducted by Burns and Stalker took place in the 1950s, it is still of great relevance. Later writers in this area have generally either used Burns and Stalker's work as a foundation or independently confirmed their conclusions even if they have identified further issues.

The features of **mechanistic systems** include:

- a clear hierarchy of control,
- a high degree of specialisation of labour, and
- reference upwards for the reconciliation of differences within the organisation.

This type of arrangement may be entirely appropriate where there is sufficient time to prescribe organisational arrangements and procedures in this type of detail, so that they match the environment in which the organisation operates. Where the technology and market are rapidly changing, however, it could be a recipe for disaster. A mechanistic system is simply not adaptive, or its responses fast enough, to enable an organisation to remain competitive. Hence the need in some situations for **organic systems**. These are characterised particularly by:

- lateral rather than vertical direction of communication throughout the organisation,
- greater room for initiative,
- adjustment and continual redefinition of individual tasks through interaction with others,
- problems dealt with by individuals rather than being posted upwards, downwards or sideways as being 'someone else's responsibility',
- contact, cooperation and decision-making in accordance with the needs of particular situations rather than the formal organisation,

- senior management less likely to be seen as omniscient,
- communication consisting of information and advice rather than instructions and decisions.

Organic and mechanistic forms of organisation represent a polarity, not a dichotomy. There will be organisations that represent intermediate stages between these two extremes with characteristics of both types of organisation.

The work of Burns and Stalker was based on research into certain Scottish companies, particularly the electronics industry during the 1950s. Considerable success had been achieved in the application of scientific research findings within the British Royal Air Force in the Second World War. This had been accomplished by the creation of organic structural arrangements that contrasted sharply with the mechanistic relationships between scientific departments and the Luftwaffe in Germany. The aim of Burns and Stalker's research was to investigate the extent to which organic arrangements needed to and could be introduced into organisations in peacetime.

A particular problem found in the firms in the Burns and Stalker study was that they often had arrangements for coordination between the research and development department and the production department that had more in common with the German wartime procedures than the British. However, it was clear that certain types of technical innovation, where know-how was diffuse and rapidly changing, demanded the reverse type of arrangement.

Unfortunately the lessons learned in wartime in Britain were not always applied afterwards.

Mismatch between organisational design and innovation

Example

A British engine manufacturer unsuccessfully tried to introduce an improved diesel engine. This lack of success led to design and research and development staff blaming the production staff for being technically incompetent. The production staff in turn blamed the design and research and development staff for having been impractical, unrealistic and failing to communicate all their requirements. The company's response was not to create more organic relationships in this area (no-one was aware of this concept) but to establish three competing design teams. The view was that the best design would then be chosen for production. However, as the basic issue of the working relationships between the groups involved was not addressed, this approach did not prove to be very satisfactory either.

Mechanistic and organic approaches should be seen as different ends of a continuum rather than straight alternatives. Few if any organisations will be completely mechanistic or completely organic. However, it is important for the individual manager to be able to recognise the difference between the two. It is also necessary to recognise that market turbulence is likely to increase the need for organic-type structures. Factors particularly causing this include the increasing pace of technological change and the globalisation of markets. The ways in which a mismatch between organisational structure and needs can distort communication, and therefore organisational effectiveness, is examined in Chapter 8 on communication.

INNOVATION AND NETWORKING

Some innovation is likely to occur naturally due to internal discussions and external interactions. The need to structure internal discussions and collaboration has already been considered. There may also be a need to structure external interaction in order to facilitate innovation.

Example

Innovation in Procter and Gamble

Procter and Gamble reviewed their arrangements for product innovation. The background to this was that the company operates in a fiercely competitive international market and its survival depends on regular product innovation. Their wide range of consumer products were normally not that technologically complicated, but adaptations such as having the smell of perfume lingering on clothes after company detergents had been used and having edible pictures on potato crisps could bring significant commercial advantages. Even packaging innovations could be important commercially.

Senior management took the view that there was too much reliance on internal research and development and that half of innovation should come from outside the organisation. The name of this new policy was 'Connect and Develop'. A particular value that senior management wanted to change was the pref-

erence given to internally generated innovation as reflected in the 'not invented here' criticism. Given the international nature of the organisation and developments in information technology, it made sense to exploit new ideas wherever they came from. This particularly involved working with suppliers, customers, business partners and outside specialists and institutions on a world-wide basis. It also increased the need for the company to protect their **intellectual capital** when innovations were planned. It was estimated that for every internal scientist or engineer there were 200 comparable ones potentially available outside the organisation. However, the policy was introduced without making any of the existing 7 500 research and development staff redundant – the primary aim was to increase innovation and related growth.

(Huston and Sakkab 2006)

MATRIX STRUCTURES

The **matrix structure** is a variation of organic arrangements. Essentially, this involves setting up more or less permanent project-type groups to which people are allocated from resource centres. The line, or command, structure is retained on the resource group side but the appropriate mix of specialists can then be allocated, full-time or part-time, to product-type teams. This arrangement is very often found necessary in high-technology organisations. It is also often found in colleges. It can assist in seeing that clients' needs are properly identified and met. If you have resource groupings only, as is often the case in universities, for example, the danger is that activity is focused on the development of the discipline alone without regard to the needs of clients. A feature of behaviour in many organisations, though, is that in any conflict between project groupings and the line structure it is the latter that usually wins. This is because of the power base of the command structure rather than because it necessarily has the better arguments. However, it is still necessary to see that those leading project groups are selected and trained properly to increase their chances of success. This can easily be ignored because project leaders may not be seen as conventional managers, despite the responsibilities that they are likely to have (Rees and Porter 2004).

HANDY'S CLASSIFICATION

A later writer who commented on the various different types of organisational structure was Charles Handy (1993). He identified the following four main organisational cultures:

- Power: this type of organisational culture is said to be frequently found in small entrepreneurial organisations led by a dominant personality.
- Role: this type of culture could be seen as similar to the concept of a mechanistic or bureaucratic structure.
- Task: this could be seen as similar to the concept of an organic structure.
- Person: this type of organisation culture is described as being a loose grouping of individuals who find it convenient to cooperate with one another without sacrificing too much of their independence, e.g., barristers' chambers or architectural practices.

THE FLEXIBLE ORGANISATION

An extension of the concept of the organic organisation is the **flexible organisation** as illustrated by Atkinson (1985). It is particularly evident in Japan, where security of employment is often guaranteed only to a core of permanent employees: other employees are engaged on a temporary basis. Potentially, an organisation is more likely to be able to adapt and survive if the outer core can be shed or replaced easily. This more easily guarantees the security of those in the inner core. Whilst people usually prefer to work in the inner core, those who are unemployed may regard a job in the outer core as better than no job at all. Employment in the periphery may provide opportunities for promotion to the core, and this can be a very useful way for employers to screen potential core employees. The requirement for some specialist skills may not be on a full-time basis, so cost-saving is made by employing some specialists part-time. These arrangements give the organisation numerical flexibility. However, this is at the cost of the job security of those who are only used when needed. Also, some of those with specialist skills may prefer to exploit the new options in the labour market by having non-standard working arrangements, particularly if that gives them tax advantages as well as greater freedom. This may include those who, having taken early retirement, are amenable to the idea of having their skills brought back in, for example, on a consultancy basis. This has led to an increasing number of people having 'work portfolios' rather than working for one employer. Where specialist skills are in short supply, however, employers may prefer to try and lock people with those skills into the organisation by employing them in the core.

Technological developments, such as those in electronic data processing, mean that practices such as working at home and subcontracting are possible in entirely new areas. Teleworking can be another option. Organisations that can predict their likely pattern of activity may also offer annual hours contracts so that employees' work attendance varies with, for example, the seasonal demand for their products. Employers may also want to employ some people at peak periods of the day only. Such arrangements enable banks, for example, to have their counters fully manned at lunchtime, thus overcoming the problem of leaving some counters vacant at a peak time so that staff can have their lunch. Numerical flexibility can also be achieved by employing people on short-term contracts.

Another aspect of the flexible organisation is the benefits that may be derived in terms of functional flexibility. Staff may be contracted to perform a variety of different jobs and even to operate at varying levels of responsibility in accordance with the fluctuating needs of an organisation. Japanese companies in particular place much emphasis on multiskilling and generic job descriptions. Developments such as these are increasing functional flexibility within organisations.

Having explained the greater tendency for numerical and functional flexibility within organisations, it is necessary to say also that if taken too far this can create drawbacks. A sizeable core is needed to retain reasonable continuity and generate organisational **synergy**. Some able people may be discouraged from applying to organisations if, for example, only a fixed-term contract is on offer. Not all activities can be neatly packaged up and subcontracted. It is more difficult to develop an integrated organisational approach with a subcontractor who is only paid for what is strictly defined in the contract. Those in the peripheral workforce also need to be strategically managed. Inadequate attention to their supervision, training and integration can easily lead to the alienation of the customers or clients on which the organisation depends.

In assessing the nature and importance of any trend towards more flexible working arrangements, it is probably best to view it as a series of ad hoc responses to labour market conditions rather than as an attempt to establish a conceptually different structure.

A constraint on the development of the flexible organisation in Europe has been the series of European Union (EU) Directives that have significantly increased the employment protection of employees in countries that are members of the EU. These (and other directives) have created a more level playing field with regard to competition within Europe. However, the directives have had the effect of reducing the cost savings that could be gained by using the distinction between full and temporary and part-time workers. Organisations are generally now not able to treat their part-time workers less favourably than full-time workers, e.g. by paying them a lower hourly rate of pay. Additionally, significant restrictions have been placed on the ability of employers to dismiss employees on short-term contracts, and after employees have been employed in organisations for four years they are generally treated as permanent employees. However, such increased protections are not worldwide and employers that are based in countries that are members of the EU still have to compete with employers in countries that do not have such protections.

A further constraint on flexible working can be the need for management to retain control of the arrangements.

Flexibility and loss of control

British Airways had introduced a considerable element of flexible working. Unfortunately the flexibility that was convenient for the employer was not always convenient for the employees and vice versa. Members of staff were allowed to use 'swipe' cards to clock in and out. Informal arrangements for swapping shifts between staff proliferated. Some weak management compounded the problems that were being generated. Eventually the company lost so much control of who was working when that it had to try and retrieve the situation. This precipitated strike action in 2003 that lost the company £40 million in revenue.

OUTSOURCING

Outsourcing is a concept that is related to that of the flexible organisation. Historically it has been no different from subcontracting. However, developments in information technology and globalisation have greatly increased the opportunity for it to be applied. In addition the option of outsourcing of internal services that were previously regarded as an integral part of organisational activity is increasingly considered. Examples of such activities are payroll administration and copy typing. An overlapping concept is that of **offshoring**. This simply involves outsourcing to another country.

The subcontracting or outsourcing of production components is long established. However, globalisation has increased both the competitive pressures to outsource component production and the opportunities. In the case of motor vehicle production, for example, it is increasingly difficult to attach a national identity to a car, despite its brand name. The financing, design, assembly location and component production may be done in a variety of countries and also involve cooperation between a number of different companies on all these aspects. The development of multi-national and **transnational corporations** is also likely to cause such organisations to keep the location of their various activities continuously under review, with activities being switched from one country to another relatively easily. Developments in transport such as increasing lorry size, the development of motorways and containerisation have particularly assisted, e.g. in the importation of production components.

Offshoring has been given a huge boost by developments in information technology, including developments in satellite phone communication. This has enabled organisations to switch some activities to other countries with lower levels of pay, without incurring significant transport costs or loss of time. In some cases it is even possible to take advantage of different time zones so that work can be sent at the end of the working day in an off-shoring country and be ready by the next morning. Work that has proved particularly suitable for this type of offshoring includes call centre activity, insurance, credit management and 'back office' financial jobs in general. The growing use of English as the language of international commerce has particularly encouraged organisations in English-speaking countries to outsource and also increased the number of countries that can handle offshoring. Countries that have particularly benefited from such offshoring include India, China and increasingly the Philippines, Vietnam, South Africa and some counties that were former members of the Soviet bloc. This trend is likely to continue, although sometimes the process has been reversed because of the lack of local knowledge of those offering advice when they are based in other countries. It has been found that activities such as auditing can be offshored and even some middle management functions.

Whilst outsourcing and offshoring may bring considerable benefits to organisations, it is necessary for managers to be aware of the potential disadvantages, even where there appear to be significant financial advantages. Just as in the case when, for example, a canteen service is contracted out, the relationship has to be actively managed. In this example there may be particular concerns with regard to quality standards, the service provided, reliability of supply and the legitimacy of any charges that are made to the client organisation. When offshoring is considered it may be necessary to consider the impact on organisational capacity and the preservation of intellectual property. A feature that is distinct to offshoring is the need to also take into account currency fluctuations, which can undermine the economic rationale of such an arrangement. An issue that has arisen with some offshoring of call centres is the need for local knowledge about the needs of customers and the communication problems that can arise because of different nuances of languages between customers and call centre workers.

Example

Distance no problem!

A company operating in Scotland included shellfish in its food products. It decided to send the shellfish to China in refrigerated containers for the shells to be removed and then have the fish returned to the UK. This saved the company £1 million a year but led to the loss of 70 jobs in Scotland.

(Scottish Daily News 2006)

There can be a 'Panama type' effect with offshoring. This term is appropriate as it is based on the tradition of merchant ships operating under flags of convenience, such as Panama, in order to avoid protective labour legislation. Whilst this can bring considerable cost advantages, it can also lead to the unacceptable exploitation of labour with regard to health and safety, below-subsistence wages and the use of child labour. Quite apart from the ethical issues involved, this may adversely affect a company's image (Gascoigne 2004).

Another dimension of outsourcing is the impact it can have on organisational structures and patterns of activity. This is considered later in the chapter in the section on the impact of information technology on organisations.

GLOBALISATION

An underlying but recurrent theme in this chapter in particular is that of **globalisation**. This affects organisation structure, patterns of trade and employment and the pace of change. It is taking place in the context of an increasingly interdependent world. Other dimensions of globalisation are political, military, social and religious.

The English Premier Football League

An interesting example of the pace, scale and nature of globalisation concerns the organisation of association football in England. League football used to be arranged just as a domestic competition. However, dramatic changes have occurred in the Premiership League. This league has become an important international brand. The international labour market has developed to such an extent that about 50 per cent of the players in the league are from overseas. There have been occasions when leading teams have fielded sides without a single Englishman in them. There is a distinct trend for financial control of premiership clubs to pass to people in other countries. Coaches are increasingly appointed from abroad. Domestic competitions are not as important as they once were and on one occasion Manchester United did not participate in the domestic cup competition because it was competing in a tournament in South America. European competitions are now the most important inter-club competitions. Revenue is increasingly generated by international television deals, sponsorship and merchandise sales. The naming rights of stadiums can also be a source of income. Premiership football is watched on electronic screens in over 200 different countries. The merchandise is both about the club and its star players. The commercial attraction of a star player to a club can partly be the sales of merchandise they can generate worldwide. There can also be significant revenue from image rights to whoever owns the economic rights of a particular player. This is a far cry from the days when the main level of support and income was from local spectators.

REVIEW OF THEORIES

It can be seen from the discussion so far in this chapter that organisational theory has gradually evolved. The formulation of one school of thought has facilitated the testing of that approach with actual organisational behaviour and the development of further schools of thought. The valid aspects of a particular approach have then been integrated with later views. The approach of the classical writers, in particular, needs to be seen in this light. Apart from its pioneering nature, much of what they had to say about organisations is still worth considering. However, the organisational principles they identified need to be seen as possible guidelines rather than definitive rules. The variety of managerial and organisational situations is such that it is impossible to set down universal principles. In any such list, the principles will appear platitudinous or have clear exceptions.

It is also necessary to have some understanding of the various approaches to management so that one can understand the views that colleagues may have about the way in which organisations should work. Such approaches may be reinforced or caused by an individual's cultural background. People tend to have beliefs and make value judgements about the ways organisations should operate. Even if these are never formally expressed, they may nevertheless be held with considerable conviction. Hopefully, such views will match the situations that arise. However, there are likely to be occasions when they do not match, and it may be as well to recognise when a situation demands particular organisational arrangements that are in conflict with the beliefs of colleagues. It may even be appropriate to reflect on one's own ideology and the extent to which it is appropriate to the current situation.

Factors that determine organisational structure

There are many variables that will affect the structure and operation of an organisation. These may be within the organisation, outside it or a combination of the two. Managers need to determine which factors in their particular situation are likely to be important. These could include the impact of technology (including information technology), the size of their organisation, the identification of the critical function at a given time, and national culture.

TECHNOLOGY

One of the most critical factors in determining organisational structure is that of technology. The importance of information technology is such that a separate section is devoted to it. Organisational structure has probably always been influenced by the technology it deploys. One of the writers who made a historically important contribution to understanding this relationship was Joan Woodward (1965). She reported that organisations with mass-production technologies were found to lend themselves to mechanistic-type systems. Firms with process-type technologies appeared to be at that time best managed by less formal and more **organic systems.** In process type industries, less effort was involved in making items and coordinating thousands of small decisions, characteristic of large-batch and mass-production technology. This meant that managers were left with much more time to initiate and cooperate with others. Consequently, the need for specialisation was found to be reduced in the process-type industries. The organic type of structure was also found to be more appropriate with small firms that were not making standard products. Some small organisations, though, tended to be informal and mechanistic – the routines being so well known that there was no need to formalise them. Technological developments since then, however, such as robotic technology, have enabled some of the traditional mass-production industries to acquire some of the characteristics of the process-type industries. More organic systems have therefore become appropriate for some mass-production systems, with the consequent changes for managers described above.

The important point that emerged from the Woodward studies was the link between organisational structure, organisation behaviour and technology. Related to this was Woodward's observation that many managers had as their model of organisation structure the old classical beliefs (Woodward 1965, p. 256). Her work gave empirical support for the **contingency approach** which emphasises the need for managers to adapt organisation structures and behaviour to the situation in which they find themselves. As explained in the next chapter on managerial style, a mismatch between style and the needs of the situation can have unfortunate consequences. Given the general lack of management training, as explained in Chapter 1, it is still likely that the options in organisational structure and behaviour are not fully understood by many managers.

THE IMPACT OF INFORMATION TECHNOLOGY

The impact of information technology (IT) on organisational structure and behaviour also has to be considered in relation to information technology. The rapid processing and retrieval of data can have a major impact. So too can computer-controlled production and other operational processes. Despite the increasing sophistication of information technology equipment, costs are falling and general levels of computer literacy are rising.

Impact of IT on markets

Rapid information access may increase an organisation's ability and need to respond quickly to market changes. It may also facilitate meeting individual customer requirements. This may necessitate flexibility within the organisational structure, and, especially in commercial organisations, the stakes are rising. The gains to be made by a rapid response may be high, and the penalties for a slow response correspondingly high as well. Many markets are becoming much more 'perfect' as information is more easily obtained and analysed and as the barriers of time and distance are reduced.

This in turn means that product life cycles tend to be shorter, and national and market boundaries less important and more permeable. The greater volatility of markets and knowledge about their behaviour means that customer and brand loyalty is likely to be less. Organisations may find that they have the knowledge and capacity to enter new markets but, conversely, this may mean that they have to face new sources of competition. A particularly important development has been **e-commerce**, which can and does have a dramatic effect on distribution channels by enabling customers to gain direct access to producers or those holding goods, as is the case with Amazon in the book trade. Another example of alternative sources of distribution created by IT is the growing preference customers have for booking holidays via the Internet as opposed to using travel agents.

A related development is the use of software packages to automate processes previously done manually, for example many accountancy procedures and calculations. Such software packages facilitate the organisation of information, use of organisational memories and common databases throughout organisations while reducing internal barriers to communication. Given the increased emphasis on **intellectual capital**, explained later in this chapter, these processes assist in the creation of **added value** to an organisation's intangible assets.

The use of electronic mail (email) enables rapid and simultaneous transmission to any number of colleagues. Linking of email to a wide area network enables messages to be exchanged and material accessed throughout the world. Other external contacts may involve more effective collaboration (as well as competition) with other organisations, shared information with buyers and sellers, and electronic market broking arrangements. Access is also available to an increasing number of public databases, e.g. copies of newspapers, magazines, journals and other archive material. **Electronic data interchange (EDI)** enables ordering to be done on a daily basis. Overnight orders to suppliers may reduce turnaround time. The same system also gives very accurate stock control. Information about organisations can also be made available by information web pages. This can lead to applications for products or services being made 'on line'. An example of this is a facility for people in many countries to apply for travel visas electronically. Another is the facility in some countries for taxpayers to submit their tax returns electronically.

Impact of IT on organisational strategy

The developments described above may enable organisations to use their expertise in information technology to creatively influence strategy rather than simply using technology in a supportive role. A dramatic example of this was how the Italian authorities were able to analyse the previously impenetrable wall surrounding many financial transactions involving the Mafia and then use the evidence obtained to secure criminal convictions. The information now available within the UK National Health Service enables comparisons to be made about the cost and quality of services at different locations. The technology can also be used to identify delays in treatment and the availability of space for those requiring treatment. Surprising spin-offs may be generated by new data.

Example

Unexpected benefits of IT

Details of external phone calls became available in the Social Services directorate of a London local authority when all calls were electronically logged. Analysis of data revealed, amongst other things, the times when home-care workers rang in to liaise with office staff. It emerged that the offices were overstaffed with support staff early in the morning, as the home-care workers generally rang in later than had been realised. This information led to a later starting time being arranged for some of the office staff.

Impact of IT on organisational structure

The changes so far identified may precipitate further internal organisational changes. Potential changes and actual examples are indicated below.

Centralisation

Rapid access to data can have a centralising effect and may enable senior managers to manage more people directly, leading to a flatter organisational pyramid. Sometimes, though, managers may centralise because they can do it more easily, rather than as the result of a considered judgement as to whether decisions are better taken locally or not.

De-layering

Centralisation can also lead to de-layering, particularly by the elimination of tiers of middle managers. The overall scale of the organisational pyramid may also be shrunk in terms of the number of people employed, as many front-line tasks are automated or made easier.

Example

Applications of new technology

Front-line jobs may be eliminated in the police service sector by increasing use of electronic surveillance to deter motorists from speeding and jumping traffic lights, and the possibility of using this method to detect illegal exhaust emissions. In addition such surveillance may be used in the future for charging motorists on a road-pricing basis. It is already used in London to charge motorists who enter the central Congestion Zone in daytime from Mondays to Fridays.

Space savings

De-layering of organisations in turn can generate space savings. However, a host of other factors can also cause space savings. These include:

- computer-controlled production and ordering systems which reduce the level of stock and work in progress;
- the easier storage of and access to data;
- hot-desking: employees may have a reduced need for dedicated office space and may be able to operate effectively by using whatever space and facilities are available at the particular time that they are needed;
- teleworking: employees may choose or be asked to carry out their activities from home or elsewhere. This topic is explained further in the next section of this chapter.

Geographic dispersal of facilities

The use of internal communication systems such as intranets may increase the opportunities for economies by the geographic dispersal of facilities to areas with cheaper costs. This may involve the offshoring of activities, as explained previously in this chapter. Employees may also be able to work more from home or wherever they happen to be by the use of laptop computers and modems. One of the disadvantages of this arrangement for the organisation, however, may be the decrease in face-to-face networking that is important for the coordination of organisational activities, problem-solving and the generation of new ideas. To a certain extent, the lack of formal interaction may be offset by the use of videoconferencing facilities or group decision-support systems (Laudon and Laudon 2000, p. 478). However, these facilities will not replace casual conversations between employees that can result in the priceless exchange of organisational information.

Reduced numbers of employees

Organisations may be able to offer a considerable range of products or services with relatively few employees. The ultimate development is the virtual organisation that simply provides information and services electronically. Whilst there may be relatively few organisations that operate totally on that basis, some large organisations operate with surprisingly few people. Examples include sportswear houses such as Nike and Reebok, whose core employees are designers and who undertake no production themselves.

Organisations can also operate without owning sophisticated information technology systems by hotelling at centres that provide those facilities. A combination of new technology and the reduced number of employees that are needed may also make it possible to start up operations very quickly:

New diplomatic missions established within hours

Example

When the USA granted diplomatic recognition to new countries in the former country of Yugoslavia, new embassies could be set up and operating within a few hours. This was achieved by a government representative using a laptop computer and satellite phone link. This enabled information to be inputted and accessed from the databases in the USA.

Delegating work to the customer

A further way of reducing the numbers employed in organisations is by the delegation of work to customers. In some industries and services, customers are increasingly encouraged to access their files and give telephoned instructions that may require little or no contact with staff of the organisation. This is particularly so with telephone banking. Interest rates and bank charges are manipulated to encourage these developments. This trend is illustrative of the ways in which organisations are changing from face-to-face to electronic contact with their customers or members of the public. Pre-recorded telephone information messages and Internet information pages are also increasingly used. These changes reduce the number of employees needed whilst at the same time increasing the accessibility of the products and services on offer. However, if these arrangements are carried too far, they can cause customer alienation because of the lack of personal contact.

Changes in internal relationships

Power relationships in organisations are likely to be affected by who has and who does not have access to particular data combined with the ability to handle that information. This means that some people in junior positions can acquire considerable influence. This can be an aspect of the **'digital divide'** between those who can handle the new technology and those who cannot. Younger people who are products of a more computer literate generation can undermine the authority and status of some senior managers. Some front-line jobs may be made much easier by developments in information technology. In other cases, ready access to data enables front-line staff to take decisions that would not previously have been thought possible or desirable. The ability of others to maintain power by their control of, and ability to filter, information will be correspondingly reduced. A further impact has been the blurring of traditional distinctions between blue- and white-collar employees, as new skills replace old ones and the shape of an organisation changes. Amongst the jobs that can disappear completely is that of secretary. In one London local authority their employment is not allowed.

Skills development

The importance of developments in information technology makes it essential for organisations to review what new skills need to be acquired by their staff. This involves more than exhortations that everyone become computer literate. A mix of skills is needed, including system design, programming, data inputting and retrieval, the facility to use a keyboard and the ability to make use of the information processes effectively. The acquisition of these skills needs to be matched to individual requirements. The concept of the **learning organisation** (considered in Chapter 11) may be particularly appropriate in this context. Organisations may need to have open systems of learning so that they are able to acquire knowledge about relevant developments on an ongoing basis, particularly in the area of information technology, and be able to apply these new developments as appropriate. However, the changes precipitated by information technology necessitate a range of other skills as well. A particular danger is that computer specialists recognise the need for new skills only in their area and not the range of managerial and other skills that are also necessary if information technology is to be harnessed effectively.

Constraints and dangers

The constraints of information technology also need to be recognised. Whilst there may be general qualitative gains in decision-making and product reliability, the cost and consequence of system and programming errors may be greatly increased.

Other constraints or dangers are:

- Not all important information is readily quantifiable – a point stressed in the previous chapter.
- The consequences of error may be huge, particularly because of the speed with which decisions may be taken and the fact that it may not be possible to reverse them.

Irreversible errors

A South Korean Airlines jumbo jet flying from the USA to Korea was incorrectly programmed to fly close to a sensitive Soviet military installation by Vladivostock in 1983. This caused the Soviets to mistake it for a hostile military plane and shoot it down, killing all 269 people on board.

Example

- Sometimes expensive systems are not integrated and are used on top of existing systems rather than instead of them.
- Systems may be acquired that do not do the job any more effectively than previous arrangements, leading to a low or negative return on the investment.
- Costs and potential difficulties involved in establishing computer systems may not be properly anticipated.

Cost overruns

Examples of major computer design problems and cost overruns are those in the public sector in Britain. The most glaring example has been the cost overrun in the planned computerisation of all patient records in the country – the biggest civilian IT project in the world. The cost estimate in 2006 was £12.4 billion, double the estimate in 2002.

(The Times 2006)

Example

- If the right equipment is acquired, a further adaptation that may be necessary is that of shift-working, so that full use is made of the new facilities.

● The dehumanising impact of IT on certain jobs may also require consideration; for example, the even greater impersonalisation of relationships between staff and customers in supermarkets caused by new technology. Thought should be given to what remedial action can be considered in such cases.

● The security aspects of systems may need considerable attention. Dangers include accidental loss of information, system failures, computer viruses, breach of confidential and statutorily protected information, sabotage and espionage. The scale of potential data security problems was illustrated by the apparent loss in the post of the details of 25 million Britons (as reported in The Times, 2007), the details being on the unencrypted child benefit database.

The general implication of the change precipitated by information technology is that management needs to learn to live not only with continuous change, but also with change that may accelerate in pace. The use of fibre optics to enable massive amounts of information to be transmitted is of particular importance in actually accelerating the rate of technological change. This will facilitate the development of information superhighways. Central to the need to capitalise on these developments is the need for managers, especially in the private sector, to learn to keep abreast of developments in information technology so that they can take advantage of the new applications as they come on stream before their competitors. There is, though, a tendency for technology to race ahead of the ability of organisations to identify areas of application. Even when applications are identified, organisations may lack the ability to use them productively. A key need is for organisations to invest in technical support and in the training of managers and others so that they can make good use of the equipment that is available. A further aspect is that some organisations and countries are technology rich and others technology poor. This can have the effect of increasing the gap between the 'haves' and the 'have nots'. The issue of the impact of developments in information technology on patterns of organisational and individual communication is examined further in Chapter 8 on communication.

SIZE

Another important factor that will affect the structure and operation of an organisation is size. You do not need much formality if you are engaged in constructing a small building, as to a large extent people can see what needs to be done for themselves. The mass production of vehicles, for example, requires much more formality because, amongst other things, people cannot easily grasp what has to be done. The number of variables that has to be coordinated in that situation creates enormous organisational problems. It may well be that these problems increase on an exponential rather than a linear basis. The solution of breaking the units down into manageable sizes may not be an option if the technology adopted dictates that you need a large integrated plant.

Many organisations fail to grow because of their inability to develop a viable structure to cope with increased work. Larger organisations generally need an element of formality, clear reporting lines, delegation, managerial and specialist expertise, and control systems. Small organisations may also actually fail because they do not have the facilities to cope with extra work or the financial resources to wait until payment on large orders is made. A common constraint in family-controlled organisations is the unwillingness of family members to either bring in or make effective use of people with managerial expertise. They may also be very reluctant to bring in outside capital if that threatens their financial control. Very large organisations may need devolved structures so that the centre is not overloaded and too unresponsive to market conditions. This will particularly be the case if they have a wide range of products or services.

INTELLECTUAL CAPITAL

As explained in Chapter 2, organisations can increasingly depend on their **intellectual capital** for survival and development rather than just their physical assets. This is because more organisations are becoming both knowledge-based and amorphous. It can be especially important to attract and retain the right mix of people who have the collective expertise and access to information networks to realise an organisation's potential. This is all the more so given the rapidity of many technological developments and the potential rewards in the private sector for organisations that are the first to exploit new market opportunities. A further aspect is that established national economies are less and less able to compete for work that has a low **added value**. Consequently, such countries need to sustain their economies by an increasing amount of high **added value**. This in turn means that intellectual capital needs to be an increasingly important part of their economies.

Intellectual capital can be divided into 'hard assets' like patents and copyrights, software and databases and 'soft assets'. Soft assets can be described as the expertise of the work force (Stewart 2002). A further distinction is between **explicit knowledge** within the organisation and the less easily identified but still important **tacit knowledge** which is akin to the general 'knowhow' held within the organisation and some of the individuals and groups within it. A related distinction is between the intellectual property that is owned by the organisation and that which is owned by the individual. This is likely to become an increasingly contentious issue as individuals may not be as prepared, as in the past, to let an organisation take over the rights to all their ideas. A factor in this may be the desire of individuals to improve their prospects of getting jobs elsewhere by retaining the rights to what they consider is their own **intellectual property**. This means that both employers and employees may need to pay particular regard to any contract clauses regarding the ownership of intellectual property.

The increased importance of the intellectual capital of organisations can also make them particularly dependent on retaining the goodwill of their staff, because of organisational vulnerability.

Acquiring an empty shell

Example

A Portuguese bank (BCP) acquired an investment management company, despite this being against the wishes of the company's employees. As soon as the merger was completed all the staff handed in their notice in order to set up a rival investment company.

(Brealey and Myers 1996, p. 917)

Organisations may increasingly need to have a clear policy about **knowledge management.** This may need to involve a delicate balance between seeing that knowledge is spread effectively around an organisation whilst not jeopardising the security of commercial secrets. The organic type of organisation, described earlier in the chapter, is more likely to facilitate the distribution of expertise than rigid mechanistic structures.

Human capital management overlaps with the concept of knowledge management, but there are differences between the terms. It does not directly involve the management of hard intellectual assets but is very concerned with the attraction, development and retention of staff with the appropriate expertise to ensure that an organisation retains competitive advantage. 'Recent estimates suggest that 50 to 60 per cent of the value created by a firm comes not from the management of traditional physical assets but from the management of intellectual capital' (ICAEW 1999 – reported in summary of Hartley and Robey 2005, p. 1). This concept is given further consideration in Chapter 11 in the context of the **learning organisation** and in Chapter 14 in relation to human resource management.

IDENTIFYING THE CRITICAL FUNCTION

Another factor that needs to influence the structure of an organisation is the recognition of the critical function at a given time. Joan Woodward (1965) defined commercial success in part as stemming from the ability of those in organisations to identify the area where it was most important to get the correct decisions. If necessary, the views of the management in the critical function need to take precedence over the views of managers in less important areas. The critical function can vary over time, and in mechanistic structures especially such movement of influence from one function to another may be inhibited. The managers in a traditionally powerful function are not likely to take kindly to having a reduced say in major decisions in order to allow a rival function a greater say. The managers in the traditionally powerful function may, in any case, not fully appreciate that the critical focus of decision-making has moved. The success of managers in solving problems may be their very undoing in this respect. If, for example, difficult design problems are overcome, this removes a constraint. The problem then can be how to increase production or sales. However, a 'critical' function is still interdependent with the other functions in an organisation.

The need to recognise the critical function is related to the need for private sector organisations to anticipate market trends and recognise where their future lies, which may not always please those responsible for well-established but declining products and services within an organisation. This also applies to public sector organisations: it would seem that the USA's Central Intelligence Agency (CIA) was too slow to switch resources from old priorities to deal with the rising threat from Al Qaeda and in particular the attacks on American cities on 9/11 in 2001.

NATIONAL CULTURE

Another potentially important variable is national culture. As explained in the next chapter, care has to be used with the term 'national culture', because there are often wide cultural differences within a country. It may be best to refer to the dominant culture within a country and recognise that there may be other important subcultures. However, culture is an increasingly important factor because of globalisation and increasing cultural diversity within countries. Even indigenous organisations need to pay attention to the issue if they are to interact effectively with other societies within and outside their own country. Particular attention needs to be paid to this issue by international organisations. Management structures and practices that appear to work well in a particular country may not be exported easily because the environment in which they operate cannot be transplanted. This also applies to the importation of practices from other countries. Local managers need to be able to adapt the structure, policies and procedures of an organisation in accordance with local conditions.

Historically, Western countries have tended to impose organisational structures on developing countries in particular based on Western rather than local needs. This includes an emphasis on large hospitals in health services, Western-style universities in the education sector and political systems as well as commercial organisations. An example of the difficulties that organisations can encounter in trying to import organisational practices is that of Western companies trying to copy Japanese methods. Much of the industrial Japanese success was because of their highly developed work ethic, cultural homogeneity, outstanding technical achievements, long-term financing, effective and sophisticated system of governmental support for industry and import barriers. The social traditions of conformity and obedience, and the importance of the group or wider organisation compared with the individual, were also relevant. The importing of particular management practices and customs is not going to radically change organisational cultures in the West. That is not to say that some Japanese practices will not work elsewhere – the point is that much of their success stems from more fundamental causes.

Another point that needs to be made is that the Japanese also need to adapt their organisations' structures and style when they have to operate in different cultures. The very success of countries such as Japan is also likely to precipitate social changes in their own societies. A further issue is that some of the apparent strengths in Japan have had built-in problems. The South East Asian economic crisis of the mid and late 1990s demonstrated that if banks have a large stake in the equity of a company, company failure could also jeopardise the banks.

An adaptation that some organisations have made is to become transnational. These organisations are structured so that they do not have their roots in any one country. The related issue of developing a managerial style, as opposed to organisational structure, to fit the local culture is considered in the next chapter on managerial style. The impact of national culture on motivation is considered in Chapter 6 and on communication in Chapter 8.

The interrelationship of organisational activity

DEPARTMENTALISM

As well as considering the nature of the organisation they are in and how appropriate that organisation is to its environment, managers need to consider how they relate to the other functions within their organisation.

Organisations may be arranged on neat departmental lines, but many of the problems that will have to be dealt with will not conveniently correspond to a departmental structure. Such structures, although usually necessary, are artificial. Problems may contain many different interactive dimensions. Managerial approaches to such problems will need to be integrated if they are to succeed. True, some problems may confine themselves to departmental boundaries, but this will not always be the case.

There are often considerable barriers to lateral contact between departments, especially in mechanistic-type organisations. Rivalries, role conflicts, different values and differing types of expertise may all act as impediments. Staff may prefer the security of contact with like-minded people within their own department to the often more hostile encounters with other departments. A lopsided approach to organisational problems may develop as a result. This may have a detrimental effect on the work of departments. It may also lead to problems that straddle departmental boundaries being ignored. It is all too easy for an ostrich-type managerial style to develop in organisations. Managers may keep a low profile and just deal with what is clearly in their own area. This tendency may be reinforced by their initial specialist training, as explained in Chapter 1. Managers may be much more able to identify the problems caused by issues within their specialism than those outside it.

Internal markets can reinforce the inherent problems of effective lateral communication. These markets involve purchaser–provider relationships between departments. Service providers are financially dependent on the income they generate from internal purchasers. Whilst this can focus attention on the real needs of service users, such arrangements can also have severe disadvantages. These include an emphasis on either minimising or maximising internal charges according to whether you are a service provider or service user. This can distract attention from the needs of the organisation as a whole and encourage competitive rather than collaborative internal relationships. Experience in the National Health Service in the UK as well as the railway industry and the BBC in Britain suggests that these arrangements can easily become counterproductive and also generate vast amounts of paperwork and other costly forms of control. Such arrangements may also ignore the costs of running down or closing existing internal activities (Rees and Porter 2002). The same issues need to be faced with subcontracting. Whilst there is a clear logic for subcontracting ancillary services, the process can be carried too far. Hiving off core sections of the human resource function, for example, can ignore the importance of the lateral advisory and developmental links needed between this function and line management. Organisations are not the series of discrete functions that some accountants imagine. Developing an effective organisation is rather more complicated than assembling a permutation of Lego-style building blocks.

The problem of boundary crossing can be particularly acute in the public sector, and it follows that there are many examples. The long-established boundaries which define what is medical work and what is nursing work, for example, do not facilitate organisational change in the Health Services.

The attempt to introduce corporate management in local government has been hampered by the professional orientation of individual departments and officers. The development of a corporate approach necessitates officers at all levels, not just those at the top tier, taking a wider approach. The legal profession provides a particularly glaring example of where well-established professional traditions have led to fierce opposition to suggestions for change in working arrangements. The older and more established the profession, the greater seem to be the problems of altering occupational roles and associated training in line with changing organisational and societal needs.

To understand broader problems – particularly those that fall between different departments – managers need to have some understanding of overall activity in their organisations. Attempts to bring departments together may be frustrated, however, because of the conflict this can generate. The objectives of departments may not always be complementary, nor will they all operate at the same level of performance. Consequently, much time and effort can go into justifying the activity of a particular department to others rather than developing common problem-solving approaches. The hidden agenda at interdepartmental meetings can be that nothing is to be proven wrong about one's own department. However, if everyone takes that approach, the real issues to be discussed simply get lost in smokescreens. One has only to look at the annual report of a company that has made a loss to see the standard smokescreen that can be put out for public, if not internal, consumption. The list of causes for poor performance is likely to include inappropriate legislation, national and international trading conditions, unfair competition, government policy, failures by suppliers, acts of God, bad luck, trade unions and a deterioration in the standards of society. It might include incompetence by previous executives, but is most unlikely to include admissions of failures that were within the current management's control.

The magnitude of the problem of departmentalism is compounded by the fact that often only an interdepartmental group with complementary skills and expertise can identify the very nature of problems. If the current objectives of an organisation, or the major constraints impeding the achievement of those objectives, are to be defined, this may be accomplished only by a pooling of knowledge. Even when the nature of a problem is identified, the causes may be far from obvious. One of the traps that people can fall into is to assume that the problems that emerge in particular departments have their causes in those same departments. Productivity levels may be influenced, for example, by production control, organisation structure, investment policy and human resource management policies. It may be pointless trying to recruit more and more labour to boost production if the production process or planning is inadequate. In some cases, problems, causes and solutions may all exist in the same department, but it is dangerous to assume that this is always the case. That is why the importance of the systems approach to organisations was stressed earlier in this chapter.

THE 'KNOCK-ON' EFFECT OF DECISIONS

A further point of which managers need to be aware is the implications of their decisions for other departments.

Example of the 'knock on' effect

Sales were increased in a soft drinks company when the sales department lowered the limit of the size of orders that could be accepted. Unfortunately, the extra revenue was not sufficient to cover the extra transport costs involved.

Example

The poet John Donne's observation that 'no man is an island' can be applied to managers. They need to see their experience as something to be shared, to help identify and deal with problems facing the whole organisation, rather than simply a means of justifying the activity of their own department. They may not be capable of resolving the problems facing their own department alone anyway. This point is explained further in Chapter 14 and illustrative examples are given from the field of employee relations. This is a function where the root causes of problems very often lie in other areas of management activity. Unfortunately, this is frequently not appreciated. Consequently, attempts to improve matters can erroneously take place entirely within the employee relations function when often the need is to remedy weaknesses elsewhere.

REMEDIAL STRATEGIES

There are preventative strategies which can reduce the problems created by poor inter-departmental liaison. As has previously been indicated, the most important strategy is to have the right fit between organisational structure and purpose. Whatever the formal structure, though, other means can be found to improve cooperation. Broadly based management training may be important. Positive steps can be taken to encourage teamwork by the creation of joint departmental teams or project groups containing staff from a range of departments. Contacts made in this way can help develop informal networks, which are often the glue that holds organisations together and facilitates coherent activity. The geographic arrangement of work can also have an important and constructive impact if this dimension is given attention. Colleagues, especially those who are not in regular contact with one another, may find it very useful to meet in accessible communal areas such as coffee points. Unfortunately, this idea is often missed, with the consequence that work is physically arranged on the 'battery hen' model, with no thought given of the need to promote informal, and sometimes even formal, interaction. Even open-plan offices may be counterproductive in their effect, as relaxed or confidential exchanges may be discouraged by the 'goldfish bowl' atmosphere they can generate.

Whilst informal networks can sometimes work against the objectives of the organisation, they can also be an essential supplement to its activity. In some cases they are mechanisms for coping with deficiencies in the formal organisation. They may also break new ground in demonstrating what organisational mechanisms need to be encouraged and even formalised.

Example

Formalising informal developments

The housing construction department of a local authority in London laid down concrete pathways on new estates. Unfortunately the residents often found shorter and more convenient routes to follow. This led to mud pathways being created that were used to supplement or replace the concrete pathways. Engineers came to the conclusion that it might be best to not lay any pathways when estates were built but instead to concrete over the mud pathways once it became clear which routes the residents preferred.

One could argue that the process of formalising informal arrangements is also evident in the way an increasing number of couples in the Western world live together before formalising their established relationships in marriage.

Role behaviour

PERSONALITY VERSUS ROLE BEHAVIOUR

When interacting with colleagues it is important for managers to be able to distinguish between personality behaviour and role behaviour. Role behaviour occurs when a person acts in accordance with the requirements of the position that they hold. Managers may meet with opposition from colleagues that can be wrongly attributed to personality factors.

It would be foolish to pretend that personality factors never have an influence on people's behaviour, but it can be all too easy to miss the point that a person may feel obliged to behave in a particular way because of the demands of their job. The danger is that the issue can become personalised. Real role conflicts can thus be exacerbated by personality conflicts. Traditions of hostility can develop and spread through whole departments. It is, unfortunately, so much easier, and often more satisfying, to blame a particular dispute on the actual personality of a protagonist. Sometimes this will even be true – a particular person may clumsily or wrongly interpret a role. It can be very difficult, in the heat of the moment, to reflect that there is nothing personal in the perhaps crucial conflict in which you are involved. The basis of the conflict, however, may be entirely to do with roles, and it may be possible to contain the area of conflict by putting one's case assertively, not aggressively. The concept of assertiveness is explained in detail in the next chapter. It is as well to remember, too, that whilst role conflicts can be incorrectly identified as personality clashes, it is rare for the mistake to be made the other way around. The constant danger is that conflict is wrongly attributed to personalities, rather than the reverse.

Failure to recognise that people's behaviour stems from their roles, rather than their personality, is particularly likely when the roles are informal. Often people adopt positions because, for example, they have particular information to hand which is not generally available or of a significance that may not be generally appreciated. This may drive them into conflict with others, even though their formal roles appear to be compatible.

REDUCING CONFLICT

The reason for distinguishing between role and personality behaviour is the need to contain the area of conflict to the minimum. It is also important to get the diagnosis right if one is attempting to resolve the conflict. If one makes the mistake of assuming that a conflict is personality-based when in reality it is because of roles, the false solution may emerge of changing the personalities involved. Thus, an 'awkward' person may be transferred or dismissed, only for the same 'awkward' behaviour to re-emerge with the next job-holder. The original solution, as well as having been wrong from an organisational point of view, may also constitute a grave injustice to the person who is removed. In some cases it may even be that a person is only doing their job correctly if they are being awkward. Traffic wardens (or 'parking attendants' as they are increasingly described), for example, are frequently seen as awkward people. However, the creation of the job of traffic wardens was partly because of the need to avoid giving police the contradictory role of enforcing parking regulations and developing positive relationships with the general public.

In working out whether behaviour is a product of the role or the person, it is important to ensure that people are given viable roles. If people in managerial positions are expected to issue penalties but no rewards to their employees, it is unreasonable to expect them to have an easy working relationship with the same people. There is an inevitable tendency in organisations for there to be competition for the handing out of rewards – such as wage rises, good news and special privileges – and a great reluctance to get embroiled in, for example, disciplinary matters. A way of making it easier for a manager or supervisor to handle the disciplinary aspects of their job is to allow them also to take the credit for distributing rewards when these are available.

The task of distinguishing between role and personality behaviour can demand considerable intellectual effort and emotional discipline. However, the rewards can be considerable, starting with the more accurate diagnosis of organisational problems. This can in many situations lead to real instead of false solutions. The amount of personal injustice can be reduced and, last but not least, the amount of personal aggravation for oneself diminished.

General organisational developments

It is appropriate at this stage to review some of the major recent developments in organisations. In order to do this it is necessary to distinguish between the public and private sectors, as well as the not-for-profit sector. The distinctions are, though, sometimes blurred. An example of this blurring has occurred as a result of the trend in Britain for greater contracting out of work by the public to the private sector. It is also not clear in some cases, such as universities, whether they should be classified as part of the public or not-for-profit sectors. In addition, some not-for-profit organisations may receive a significant part of their income from public funds. It is also necessary to consider how the public sector is influenced by private sector practices. There is also often an international dimension, as in the case of multi-national corporations and international non-governmental organisations. However, there are some general trends in the various sectors that merit consideration. It is also necessary to consider the issue of corporate governance and how it affects all three sectors.

THE PRIVATE SECTOR

Developments relating to long-term and corporate strategy, including the relationship between operational units and the centre, were covered at the end of the previous chapter. Competitive pressures have caused many private sector organisations to downsize and sometimes the concept of being 'lean and mean' has been carried to such an extreme that organisations have become 'anorexic'. There has been a general tendency to move towards semi-autonomous business units with financial performance targets. This has reduced the potential for cross-subsidisation within organisations. However, the move to semi-autonomous business units sometimes is contradicted by demands for detailed control information and prior approval on a range of matters large and small.

The concept of added value has been prominent, with units and individuals expected to justify themselves more in terms of their profitability. These developments in turn have led to a trend to much smaller head offices. There has been a reaction, too, to the Taylorist scientific management approach of division of labour, functional control and non-involvement of the workforce. This has partly been a consequence of more volatile markets. There is more emphasis now on flexibility, multitasking and workforce involvement in process, product and service improvement. This in turn has necessitated more emphasis on training and creative human resource management. The search for new markets and cost reduction opportunities is also causing more collaborative ventures. Another development has been for companies to plan international marketing strategies. As markets have become globalised, so it has become more possible and appropriate to market global or regional, as opposed to national, products.

THE PUBLIC SECTOR

A recurring theme in the section on the public sector is how changes in its framework and operation are creating a much more managerial, as opposed to administrative, culture. This is with a view to getting better 'value for money' with the resources available.

In many countries there has been a systematic attempt to redraw the boundaries between the public and private sectors so that many of the activities that were previously in the public sector could be run privately instead. As is so often the case, the shift in emphasis away from direct state spending and control seems to have started in the USA. Many of the interventionist and regulatory policies of the 1960s and before in America and elsewhere were seen not to have worked and had often become prohibitively expensive. Rising public expectations and reduced economic growth were further factors forcing a rethink of the role of the state, including an attempt to reduce the expectations of what the state should do for individuals. One development of deregulation or divestment tended to lead to another until it became a flood. Associated developments were the opportunities this created for private business and the revenue generated by the sale of state assets, by way of privatisation and tax cuts. This is a route many countries in both the West and the developing world have followed. Some of these changes have also been introduced in the former Soviet bloc after the collapse of communism, where there has also been a general reduction in the boundaries of the state activity. However, in collaborating more with the private sector, those in the public sector need to be able match their private sector counterparts in commercial acumen so that they do not enter into contracts that unduly favour private sector collaborators.

Part of the rationale for reducing the level of state involvement in many economies has been a desire to further increase the 'enterprise', as opposed to a 'dependency' culture. A political advantage for governments in devolving authority within the public sector is that sensitive decisions about prioritisation and resource allocation can be removed from central government.

At one stage in the UK a massive shift in activity was envisaged by opening up work from the civil service and local government in particular to competitive tendering. Whilst there has been a significant increase in the amount of public sector work that has been subcontracted, a constraint has been the European Union Acquired Rights Directive. This means that those who win contracts may assume responsibility for the workforce previously undertaking the work at their existing terms and conditions of employment. There is ongoing uncertainty, however, about the circumstances under which the directive applies. A rough guide is to distinguish between the disposal of an economic entity (which may involve acquired rights obligations) and an activity (which may not).

COMPARISONS WITH THE PRIVATE SECTOR

As a corollary of reducing state ownership and control there has been a strong trend to the more effective use of those activities still financed or run by the state. There have been attempts to make the public sector operate more like the private sector. Whilst the public sector has undoubtedly had lessons to learn from the private sector, it would be a mistake to imagine that the differences between the two sectors can be ignored. It would also be a mistake to ignore the considerable variations within the private and public sectors. Public bodies are democratically accountable, have statutory obligations and often have to operate in a sensitive political environment. The process of decision-making may be slower, more complicated and more risk averse than the private sector. The aims of public sector bodies often cannot be easily defined and quantified. Often public sector organisations are very large. Much of the private sector, by contrast, is in small units with clear commercial goals. These differences enable private sector organisations often to behave in a way that would be quite inappropriate in the public sector, particularly with regard to risk-taking. The overall need in the public sector can perhaps best be described as for the various elements of that sector to become more businesslike without trying to operate as businesses.

Having defined the distinctive nature of the public sector, it is appropriate to examine the way in which it is adopting a more commercial approach. One way of explaining this is to examine the historic differences between management and administration. This has been done by a British civil servant associated with the Treasury Centre for Administrative Services. The emphasis, with management, is on results and on taking calculated risks; with administration it is on procedures, accountability and risk avoidance. These are not complete opposites but rather the ends of a continuum. The general thrust in the public sector has been to shift it more to the managerial end of the continuum. The full list is included as an appendix to this chapter.

Another basic change is that policy and budgeting is now much more finance-led instead of being on a needs or demand basis in the public sector. This in turn has meant that managers have to make the best use of a given level of funding, which may necessitate making conscious priorities, as explained in the previous chapter. Often the level of funding is geared to performance indicators. In Britain at least there has been a substantial move to use private sector cash to boost investment in the public sector, for example with major transport projects and hospitals, under **private finance initiatives (PFIs)**. Publicly funded organisations are now expected to take less of a custodial approach to their assets and more of a market orientation of matching resources with demand. This is in keeping with greater customer orientation and focus on service delivery. A number of organisations have been required to produce citizens' charters guaranteeing standards of service to the public, and in some cases being obliged to make penalty payments if the standards are not met.

An increasing amount of work is organised on a contract basis, with public sector bodies being partly or totally financially dependent on the winning and retention of contracts, sometimes in competition with the private sector. The practice has now come to be known as 'market testing'. This concept is sometimes applied to employment contracts, especially for senior positions. Renewal is logically likely to depend on performance. Amongst the effects of the structural and operational changes in the public sector is the identification of much more explicit managerial roles than before. This means that there is a much clearer need for those in positions of authority to develop managerial skills.

The evaluation of performance in the public sector has increasingly been on the basis of performance as measured by **key performance indicators** (KPIs). Whilst the use of such measures may be necessary, it is also necessary to beware of the ways in which they can be manipulated. This issue was discussed with regard to organisational targets in Chapter 2. The issue of the danger of manipulation of measures and targets is also covered in Chapter 10 in the context of **performance-related pay**. Whilst there has been a move to performance-related pay in the public sector, the results have often been disappointing.

NOT-FOR-PROFIT ORGANISATIONS

The not-for-profit sector includes charities and this in turn can be said to include organisations such as churches and trade unions. They can also be described as **non-governmental organisations** (or entities)(NGOs). The activities of international not-for-profit organisations (INGOs) are increasing and examples of increasingly active international not-for-profit organisations are Amnesty International and OXFAM. As economies become richer, and less is controlled by the state, more income becomes available for the activity of not-for-profit organisations. In turn this may mean that developed countries are more easily able to finance activities abroad either directly or via INGOs.

Decision-making may be convoluted in not-for-profit organisations, particularly where a number of countries are involved. This will be all the more so if a consensus is needed for major decisions. This may mean that policy can only be agreed on a lowest common denominator basis. However, one way of facilitating decision-making can be the use of qualified majority voting on some issues, as happens in the European Union. The problems of operating on a consensus basis are considered further in Chapter 15, in the context of negotiating.

There are other problems that are particularly likely to occur in not-for-profit organisations. One is that those in charge may be chosen for their commitment to a particular cause rather than their ability to run an organisation. It may also be the case that a professional management structure is not developed. As those in charge may give up a lot of time on a voluntary basis they may fail to pay their staff appropriately, feeling that they too should make financial sacrifices in the interests of the organisation. If a not-for-profit organisation is dependent on a volunteer element to achieve its aims and objectives, they may have to accept volunteer labour on the basis on which it is offered and have relatively little in the way of sanctions if volunteers do not do quite what is expected or required of them.

CORPORATE GOVERNANCE

Increasing attention has been paid to the concept of **corporate governance**. This has been particularly in the private sector and also with some national governments. There are also issues that merit attention in the public and not-for-profit sectors.

The directors of a company have a general duty of care to their shareholders as well as a need to operate within the framework of the law. Dramatic cases of fraud in the USA have focused attention on the duty of care and also the severe penalties that can be imposed if that care is breached.

Example

Corporate fraud and individual liability

The world's two biggest corporate bankruptcies to date have been the American energy giant Enron and the communications company WorldCom. Because of suspected fraud, prosecutions were initiated in the USA against both companies. The former chief executive of WorldCom was given a 25-year jail sentence.

The former chairman of Enron died in 2006 after being found guilty but before he was sentenced. His former Chief Executive Officer received a jail sentence of 24 years. Other former senior officers of Enron also received significant jail sentences.

Some companies are also paying increasing attention to stakeholders in their organisation other than shareholders and employees. This may be either because of genuine concern or because of enlightened self-interest or a combination of the two. The growing sensitivity of customers is likely to create a commercial pressure on an increasing number of private organisations to demonstrate that they have ethical business practices and that they are behaving responsibly with regard to the local community and the environment. An example of this is the way in which consumer resistance to buying genetically modified food in the UK caused supermarkets to withdraw such goods from sale. The Fairtrade movement is an example of customer pressure for goods where producers in developing countries are paid a reasonable price. The food chain Waitrose has featured a series of adverts with the slogan 'Quality goods, honestly priced'. As was explained earlier in this chapter, offshoring can lead to exploitative labour practices, and, apart from the ethical issues involved, this can lead to negative publicity for the companies concerned. Developments such as these have led some companies to develop formal policies of **corporate and social responsibility**.

There are also pressures on public bodies to behave as responsible employers. An interesting development in the USA concerns the use of government purchasing power to influence business behaviour. The federal government has increasingly sought to impose ethical business practices on government contractors.

Problems of corporate governance may arise when too much authority is vested in the hands of the Chief Executive. A check against this can be to ensure that the Chief Executive does not also act as Chairman of the Board. However, even then Chief Executives can and sometimes do accumulate enormous power. This can be done by the control and manipulation of information, control over other executives, influencing appointments to the Board and patronage. Also the fact that the Chief Executive is likely to be a person of ability and is, unlike outside Board members, employed full-time can further increase their potential power. Such factors can apply even more so in the public and not-for-profit sectors. Sometimes a high concentration of power leads to abuse, as in the following example:

Failure to control the full-time head of an organisation

The Head of a sixth form college in London was convicted in 2003 of misappropriating £5 million of school funds and engaging in a lavish personal lifestyle. She was sentenced to five years in prison.

(Sunday Times 2003)

Example

One of the problems in trying to control a wayward Chief Executive is that the Board members may not have the information, expertise, time, energy or even inclination to act as an effective check. This can particularly be the case in the not-for-profit sectors where the governors are not even allowed to be paid. It can also prove difficult to control the activities of an active governor who undertakes tasks that others do not have the time or inclination to do.

The issue of corporate governance in developing countries arises particularly when they want aid. Increasingly aid is only given if certain conditions are met. These are likely to include the country's record with regard to democracy, human rights and good governance. As explained in Chapter 10, in the context of appraisal, some countries may arrange a peer audit, by another developing country, of their corporate governance in order to demonstrate their eligibility to receive aid. In 2006 Romania and Bulgaria were told that their applications to join the European Union were approved but subject to both countries making significant progress in dealing with corruption.

Summary

This chapter has attempted to set the scene within which those with managerial responsibilities have to operate. Key organisational theories have been examined. Organisational types that have been described and analysed include mechanistic and organic structures, matrix arrangements and the **flexible organisation**. Managers need to examine the fit between what is appropriate in terms of organisational design and operation and what actually exists. The factors that shape organisational structure have been identified. These include the impact of technology, particularly information technology; size; the extent to which the organisation is dependent on its intellectual capital; the nature of the critical function; and national culture. The importance of the market, and the way it needs to influence organisational structure, was stressed in the examination of key organisational theories.

The dangers of sectional goals conflicting with broad organisational objectives has been examined and suggestions made as to how such conflicts may be handled. These particularly include developing lateral organisation links and broadening the base of training so that people can have a broader view of the organisation. The need for managers to distinguish between personality and role behaviour has also been covered. This is because of the unnecessary aggravation that can occur if managers fail to analyse the behaviour of colleagues in terms of their role.

There are distinct differences in the nature of the private and public sectors. However, some trends have been common to both sectors. These include pressure for more market- or client-orientated structures with a generally greater devolution of authority for decisions in financial and other matters. Governments are under pressure to secure value for money in the public sector and often find it convenient to devolve authority for sensitive decisions about resource allocation. Whilst public sector organisations need to be run in a business-like way it is important to remember that they are not businesses, as they have constraints such as democratic accountability that businesses do not. The rising importance of the not-for-profit sector has meant that managerial issues in this area have also been considered. Finally the issue of corporate governance has been considered and its relevance and practice in all sectors. The chapter is an essential prelude to considering the topic covered in the next chapter, managerial style.

Self-assessment questions

(If you wish to check the extent to which your answer to any of the following questions is appropriate, cross-refer to the Table of Contents. The contents for this chapter are on pages xi–xii.)

1 Why is it important for managers to have an understanding of the options in organisational design?

2 What are the main factors shaping the structure and operation of an organisation with which you are familiar?

3 Why might units within an organisation pursue sectional rather than corporate aims? What can realistically be done to deal with this problem?

4 Why might role behaviour be mistaken for personality behaviour?

5 In what ways might managers need to behave differently in the private sector as compared with not-for-profit organisations?

References

(Works of particular interest are marked with a star.)

Atkinson, J. (1985), *Flexibility, Uncertainty and Manpower Management*, IMS report No. 89, Institute of Manpower Studies.

Brealey and Myers (1996), *Principles of Corporate Finance,* 5th ed., McGraw-Hill.

Burns, T. and G. M. Stalker (1972), *Management of Innovation*, Tavistock Publications, first published 1961. For a summary of this work, see Honor Croome (1970), *Human Problems of Innovation*, Ministry of Technology pamphlet.

Fayol, Henri (1967), *General and Industrial Management*, transl. Constance Storrs, Pitman; first French edition published 1916; Storrs' translation first published 1949.

Gascoigne, Clare (4 September 2004), *Don't park problems on distant shores,* Sunday Times, pp. 14–15.

Handy, Charles (1993), *Understanding Organisations*, 4th ed., Penguin.

*Hartley, V. and D. Robey, Institute of Employment Studies (2005), *Human Capital Management –* for summary refer to www.employmentstudies.co.uk.

Huston, Larry and Nabbil Sakkab (March 2006), *Connect and Develop – Inside Procter and Gamble's New Model for Innovation,* Harvard Business Review.

Laudon, Kenneth C. and Jane P. Laudon (2000), *Management Information Systems – Organisation and Technology in the Networked Enterprise,* Prentice Hall, New Jersey.

*Rees, W. David and Christine Porter (2002), *Management by Panacea – the Training Implications*, Industrial and Commercial Training, Vol. 34 No. 6 (available on the book's companion website).

*Rees, W. David and Christine Porter (2004), *Matrix Structures and the Training Implications,* Industrial and Commercial Training, Vol. 36 No. 5. (An explanation of the nature of matrix structures, the dual reporting relationship and how they can be made to work effectively – available on the book's companion website.)

*Rees, W. David and Christine Porter (2006), *Corporate Strategy Development and Related Management Development – the Case for the Incremental Approach, Part 2 – Implications for Learning and Development,* Industrial and Commercial Training, Vol. 38 No. 6. (Includes an explanation of the dangers of corporate decision-making based on too narrow a range of variables – available on the book's companion website.)

Roethlisberger, F. J. and W. J. Dickson (1939), *Management and the Worker*, Harvard University Press. For one of several abridged accounts see John Sheldrake (1996), *Management Theories: From Taylorism to Japanization*, Chapter 11, Elton Mayo and the Hawthorne Experiments, International Thomson Business Press. (See Sheldrake's book also for a very clear and useful account of the thoughts of key earlier management writers.)

Scottish Daily News (on Sunday), 24 September 2006.

Sunday Times (7 September 2003), *The School cowed by Saddam in a skirt.*

Taylor, F. W. (1972), *The Principles of Scientific Management*, Greenwood Press, first published 1911.

The Times (21 November 2007), *25 million exposed to risk of 1D fraud.*

Woodward, Joan (1965) *Industrial Organisation: Theory and Practice*, Oxford University Press. For a summary of this work see Joan Woodward, *Management and Technology* (Ministry of Technology pamphlet, 1970), reprint.

Further reading

Bovaird, Tony and Elle Loffler (2003), *Public Management and Governance,* Routledge.

Chaffey, David and Steve Wood (2005), *Business Information Management – Improving Performance Using Information Systems,* Financial Times/Prentice Hall.

*Flynn, Norman (2007), *Public Sector Management,* Sage, 5th ed. (A useful analytical and up-to-date account of public-sector management including developments such as public private partnerships.)

Hudson, Mike (1995), *Managing Without Profit – the Art of Managing Third-Sector Organisations,* Penguin.

*Kennedy, Carol (1998), *Guide to the Management Gurus: Shortcuts to the Ideas of Leading Management Thinkers*, Century Business, 2nd ed. (A useful guide to the thoughts of later management writers.)

Luo, Yadong (2006), *Global Dimensions of Corporate Governance*, Blackwell Journal of Knowledge Management, http://emeraldinsight.com/uhournals/jkm/jourinfo.htm (Metropolitan University Press [MCB]). (A peer-reviewed quarterly publication dedicated to the exchange of the latest research and practical information on all aspects of managing knowledge in organisations.)

Mallin, Christine A. (2007), *Corporate Governance*, Oxford University Press, 2nd ed.

Mayle, David (ed.) (2006), *Managing Innovation and Change,* Open University, Sage, 3rd ed.

*Stewart, Thomas A. (2002), *The Wealth of Knowledge,* Nicolas Brealy. (A thorough account of the concept of intellectual capital by one of the leading writers in the field.)

Appendix to Chapter 3

THE DIFFERENT CHARACTERISTICS OF ADMINISTRATION AND MANAGEMENT

	Administration	Management
Objectives	stated in general terms and reviewed or changed infrequently	stated as broad strategic aims
		supported by more detailed short-term goals and targets reviewed frequently
Success criteria	mistake-avoiding	success-seeking
	performance difficult to measure	performance mostly measurable
Resource use	secondary task	primary task
Decision-making	has to make few decisions but affecting many and can take time over it	has to make decisions affecting few and has to make them quickly
Structure	roles defined in terms of areas of responsibility	shorter hierarchies
	long hierarchies, limited delegation	maximum delegation
Roles	arbitrator	protagonist
Attitudes	passive: workload determined outside the system; best people used to solve problems	active: seeking to influence the environment; best people used to find and exploit opportunities
	time insensitive	time sensitive
	risk-avoiding	risk accepting, but minimising it
	emphasis on procedure	emphasis on results
	doing things right	doing the right things
	conformity	local experiments: need for conformity to be proved
	uniformity	independence
Skills	literacy (reports, notes)	numeracy, statistics, figures

Managerial style

Learning outcomes

By the end of the chapter you will be able to:

- Understand the concept of managerial style and current trends
- Identify and evaluate the range of managerial styles that are commonly practised and the associated relevant theories
- Appreciate the need to adapt managerial style according to the needs of a situation
- Identify and assess the organisational factors that influence managerial style
- Evaluate the impact of national culture on managerial style
- Apply key skills involved in assertiveness
- Assess the key variables in planning effective change
- Evaluate the effectiveness of managerial style
- Identify and evaluate your own preferred managerial style

Introduction

Managerial style can be defined as 'the way in which a manager achieves results'. It overlaps with the concept of leadership. The range of commonly practised managerial styles is examined in this chapter. People need to be aware of their own preferred style but also of the need to adapt their style to the needs of the situation. Trends in management style are examined, as are key factors such as organisational pressures and national culture, that can influence it. A style that is often required is the ability to behave assertively as opposed to being aggressive or non-assertive. This concept is examined, as are the key skills in assertive behaviour.

The topic of handling change is a recurrent one in this book. The opportunity is taken in this chapter to review the key variables and to cross-refer to other parts of the book where the variables are examined in more detail. Finally the effectiveness of managers is considered. Managerial style is a means to an end and not an end itself. Whatever style or styles a manager uses, they will ultimately by judged by results. A questionnaire is included as an appendix to the chapter so that readers can identify their own preferred managerial style.

Trends in managerial style

THE CONCEPT OF MANAGERIAL STYLE

Managerial style was defined in the introduction to this chapter as 'the way in which managers achieve results'. Management overlaps with the concept of leadership. However, not all leaders are managers. While managers can provide leadership, those in a range of other roles can also be leaders. Managers are appointed and are responsible to those who appoint them. In contrast, leaders are not always appointed. In representative structures, for example, leaders are responsible to those who have allowed them to become their leader, which may or may not involve a formal election. Leaders in such situations need to demonstrate that they represent the needs of the group they represent, while the objectives of managers can sometimes conflict with those objectives of the groups they have to manage.

Some writers (beginning with Drucker 1955) see business leaders as heroic figures who devise overall objectives and strategy and drive organisations forward, with managers simply being there to implement their vision. Limitations with this approach include identifying too sharp a distinction between the roles of leaders and managers. The notion of business leaders as heroic figures also suggests that their personal characteristics will be appropriate to any organisational situation, regardless of the match between the individual's strengths and situational requirements.

The concepts of effective management and leadership are often confused with **charisma**. While charismatic leadership can be appropriate in some situations, this is not always the case. Sometimes charismatic leadership can be the reverse of what is needed, particularly if the person concerned needs to be primarily a facilitator and conciliator.

Example

A successful non-charismatic leader

The former Australian Prime Minister, John Howard, won four successive general elections despite not having a charismatic image. His success may have been in part because of his image as an ordinary person to whom the voters could relate.

An understanding of the concept of leadership may help people develop leadership skills in the workplace. What may be more important, however, is for managers to develop the confidence that comes from correctly identifying their role and developing the managerial skills that are necessary to fulfil such a role effectively.

THE AUTHORITY OF THE MANAGER

Managers will normally have a certain amount of formal authority to do their job. This will usually have been delegated to them by a higher level of management, enabling them to take decisions and commit organisational resources. They will also need to have some authority over their staff in the way of rewards and penalties. The extent of a manager's authority will vary considerably according to their seniority and from organisation to organisation. However, a number of factors have tended to limit the authority of individual managers. These are identified below.

ORGANISATIONAL DEVELOPMENTS

Organisations are often becoming more complex. This is because of factors such as accelerating change, technological development (particularly in the area of information technology) and **globalisation**. Levels of uncertainty are generally rising and knowledge within organisations is often becoming diffuse. Also, the process of management is increasingly becoming the management of **intellectual capital** rather than that of physical resources. The ability of managers to control the flow of information is often greatly reduced. The cumulative effect of these changes is to make the manager more of a facilitator rather than a traditional authority figure.

LEGAL CONSTRAINTS

Increasingly managers are constrained in what they can do by the law. This is particularly so in the area of employment rights, e.g. unfair dismissal and anti-discrimination law. The ability of managers to hire and fire at will has been considerably curtailed, in Western countries in particular.

SOCIAL DEVELOPMENTS

Social trends, such as rising levels of education, have created pressures for people to manage in a more acceptable way. Managers are often also dependent on the information and expertise of their employees. Younger employees, for example, may be able to access and manipulate new information systems more easily than their bosses.

While there are discernible general trends, the extent to which they have impacted on individual organisations and managers will vary widely. Some managers still rely significantly on their formal authority. Even managers who do not rely too much on their formal authority may need to use it when all else fails. Feelings of insecurity amongst employees may depend very much on their personal prospects of alternative employment.

SAPIENTIAL AUTHORITY

As organisations change so managers may be more dependent on their sapiential rather than their formal authority. **Sapiential authority** is that which derives from a person's expertise. The sapiential authority of a manager may lie in their specialist area, their organisational facilitating skills, or both. This concept is similar to that of expert power, which is considered below.

POWER AND INFLUENCE

Whereas authority (the right to get something done) is officially sanctioned by the organisation, power is distributed throughout the organisation and may be invested in people at any level and not just managers. The determinants of power are also not only at the disposal of the organisation in the way in which authority is. Power can be defined as 'the ability to marshal human, informational, or material resources to get something done' (Lewis et al. 1995, p. 425). It can be used effectively even if the manager does not actually possess power but the party whom the manager is seeking to influence believes that they do. Power can be prescribed by a person's position in the organisation or as a result of their personal attributes.

Positional power can derive from the following four factors in particular:

- Legitimacy: this exists when employees feel that the manager has the right to ask for particular tasks to be undertaken.
- Coercion: this is the ability to discipline or penalise by withholding rewards. This type of power is more effective if used as a perceived threat rather than if penalties have to be imposed.
- Rewards: these are the tangible benefits that a manager has at their disposal and will include not only salary increases but also other benefits that the employee values. These could include improved work schedules, promotion and formal recognition of a job well done.
- Information: managers and others, by virtue of their position, often have access to information that people need in order to carry out their jobs. This information may be acquired in a variety of ways and not just by formal channels.

Personal power also derives from several sources:

- Expert power is similar to sapiential authority. This type of power stems from expertise in solving problems and performing important tasks. If a person is perceived as having expertise in a situation then they will exert more influence than someone who is not perceived in this way.
- Persuasive power is the use of logical arguments and factual evidence to convince others to agree to a course of action.
- **Referent power** is the ability to influence others based on personal liking, charisma or reputation. If an employee feels a deep personal loyalty to someone, then the employee may be influenced to do something that they might not otherwise have done. This is the basis on which high-profile personalities are recruited to advertise products (French and Raven 1968).
- Changes in the environment can affect the power balance. For example, in times of skills shortages particular employees may possess more power than they do when their skills are available in abundance. This change in power is determined by the state of the labour market and may not be within the organisation's control. The factors that determine the labour market are identified and examined in Chapter 14.

LATERAL RELATIONSHIPS

Managers may need considerable political skills in negotiating their working arrangements with other departments. General organisational developments are such that fewer organisations have a traditional bureaucratic structure. The trend is to have more flexible and organic (as opposed to mechanistic) structures. In organic structures there will be a need for, and a pattern of, relatively open access to people in other parts of the organisation. This in turn can generate a greater need for work arrangements such as project teams and matrix structures. Managers and other employees may find that they often report to more than one boss.

MANAGERS AS FACILITATORS

Organisational trends are such that managers are increasingly likely to be the focal points for assembling the right mix of financial, physical and human resources to undertake specific tasks. This is particularly so in organisations with a high level of intellectual capital, as described in the previous chapter. These developments in turn affect managerial style. In explaining the concept of the **triple 'I' organisation**, based on the effective use of intelligence, ideas and information, Handy said:

> It is this type of organisation which has given rise to what has been called the post-heroic leader. Whereas the heroic manager of the past knew all, could do all and could solve every problem, the post-heroic manager asks how every problem can be solved in a way that develops other people's capacity to handle it.
>
> (Handy 1991, p. 132)

The increasing need for managers to act as facilitators demonstrates that the charismatic approach to managing can have a downside as well as being a potentially effective way of managing. Working for a charismatic manager can be reassuring and exciting but it is heavily dependent on the judgement of the leader and the results can be disastrous if that judgement is flawed. The gap between followers and leader can become too great, rendering upward communication difficult and encouraging subordinates to surrender responsibility and independent thought. This in turn may create further opportunities or pressure on the charismatic leader to behave as though they are omniscient, thus further increasing the likelihood of failure. These views of the manager as facilitator fit with those expressed by the UK's Local Government Management Training Board:

> Among future management roles are those of the honest broker and negotiator, requiring qualities of peacemaking and peacekeeping between conflicting interests, and a temperament which maximises agreement and mutual benefits. Vital management skills, in short, include dealing with leading, motivating, handling people. Good management will more and more be seen as unlocking barriers to performance by colleagues and subordinates, enhancing their contribution and releasing their potential. Management involves simultaneously playing as a team member while pushing the team forward – not least in conveying a sense of direction, by successfully painting a picture of the future
>
> (Local Government Management Board 1993, p. 15)

Options in managerial style

A number of writers have identified options in managerial style. Concepts such as Fox's (1965) **unitary** and **pluralistic frames of reference** also are relevant to this topic. Styles are generally viewed as being neutral: what matters is that the style used matches the situation. Trait theories are examined in the work by McGregor (1969), as are the concepts of the managerial grid, contingency and management team mix.

TRAIT THEORIES

A traditional way of examining the broader concept of leadership is to identify the personality characteristics that are required by a leader. If this approach is used, one can quickly generate a long list of personality traits. This may include characteristics such as honesty, intelligence, consistency, integrity, firmness, ruthlessness, flexibility, vision, charisma and so on. It would be very difficult to find a person who possessed all these characteristics. Furthermore, many of the characteristics can be the opposite of one another, such as consistency and flexibility.

If any value is to be made of trait theories it is necessary to identify what traits are important in a given situation. The traits that are important in one situation may not be important in another or may even be a handicap. A matching exercise needs to be undertaken when selecting managers to try and ensure that the person appointed has those few critical traits required for a particular job. If the demands of the job change, the person appointed may no longer match the changed requirements. Consequently, it may be necessary to consider how a manager would be able to adapt to changed circumstances.

There are many examples from the world of politics of leaders not being able to adapt to changed circumstances. Great leaders can be thrown up in times of revolution or war who might otherwise have remained in relative obscurity. This is in keeping with the adage 'cometh the hour, cometh the man'. However, when the revolution or war is over a different style of leadership may be required. Often great revolutionary or war leaders have been unable to adapt to the demands of peacetime. This may because the very qualities that made them great revolutionary leaders may be the opposite of what is required in peacetime. One of many examples is that of Mao Zedong, the revolutionary communist Chinese leader.

Many successful business people have failed in the political world. Conversely, many politicians have failed in business adventures. A reason for this may be that business people operate in a hierarchical environment with an executive chain of command. Politicians need the skills to develop and retain grassroots support. Successful business people may particularly require financial acumen and politicians the power to impress an audience.

Example

Serial entrepreneurs

An interesting way in which some entrepreneurs have coped with the change in behaviour that might be required when they have successfully created a business is to simply continue what they are particularly good at doing, and that is to create another business. A particularly good example of the **serial entrepreneur** is the businessman Sir Richard Branson. His series of Virgin enterprises includes retail, radio, air travel, rail travel and finance.

MCGREGOR'S THEORIES X AND Y

McGregor (1969) distinguishes between managers who manage in a Theory X style and those who manage in a Theory Y style. Assumptions that Theory X managers make about employees were said to include:

- employees need and respond to close direction and control;
- people prefer to avoid work if they can;
- employees do not want to accept responsibility;
- employees have to be coerced to achieve organisational objectives.

The assumptions made by Theory Y managers about employees were said to include:

- individual and organisational goals can be integrated;
- work is a natural activity;
- employees will respond positively to objectives to which they are committed;
- emotional satisfaction can be achieved at work;
- employees will, under the right conditions, accept responsibility.

The value of this classification is to identify the assumptions of other managers and yourself. On the face of it, the Theory Y style is more enlightened, but the basic point is that the style adopted needs to fit the situation. The danger is that managers may have fairly fixed assumptions and consequently have difficulty in adapting their style to a situation that requires an approach different to their natural one. It is also necessary to distinguish between genuine Theory Y styles and ones which are only superficial. Critics of Japanese techniques of employee involvement, which could be interpreted as Theory Y style simply see these techniques as attempts to create a coerced consensus (Garrahan and Stewart 1992). The relationship between managerial assumptions about why people work and motivation is examined further in Chapter 6.

TANNENBAUM AND SCHMIDT'S CONTINUUM OF LEADERSHIP STYLES

Tannenbaum and Schmidt (1957, p. 96) developed a model of leadership styles based on the concept of a continuum ranging from authoritarian behaviour at one end to democratic at the other. One can extrapolate a third style at the democratic end of the continuum, which is the laissez-faire leader who exercises little or no control and who may be a leader in name only. Leaders, or managers, can be at any point in the continuum. Their style can, and will need to, vary over time and according to situational requirements. See Figure 4.1

BLAKE AND MOUTON'S MANAGERIAL GRID

The **managerial grid** is based on the concept of managers having two potentially conflicting centres of attention: employee needs, and task needs. Blake and Mouton (1978) designed a questionnaire so that managers could identify where they were located on a grid. This would show the extent to which they were orientated around employee needs, task needs, or both. The effective manager was viewed as one who set out to reconcile these two sets of needs, rather than concentrating on meeting just one or the other.

Figure 4.1	A continuum of leadership styles

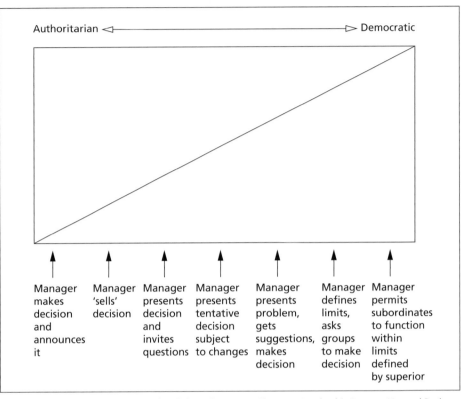

Source: Tannenbaum R. and W. H. Schmidt (1957), *How to Choose a Leadership Pattern*, Harvard Business Review, 36 (2).

CONTINGENCY THEORIES

Several theorists have examined the idea that the leadership style needs to be contingent on key factors in whatever situation requires leadership. This is consistent with Mary Parker Follett's concept of 'the law of the situation', explained in Chapter 1. John Adair (1982) identifies three key factors that he believes are important in determining an appropriate leadership style: task, group and individual needs. He suggests that the effective manager will be the one who gives priority to one of these three overlapping interests according to the needs of the situation. If, for example, there were an emergency, task needs would predominate: there would be no point in having a period of consultation if it was imperative that a task was completed in a short period of time. See Figure 4.2.

BELBIN'S MANAGEMENT TEAM MIX

Meredith Belbin's work (2006) focuses on the relationship between the membership of management teams and their effectiveness. He identifies the right 'mix' in a group as a key requirement

John Adair's action-centred model of leadership | Figure 4.2

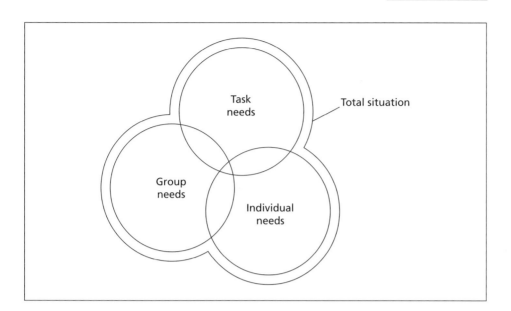

for effectiveness. Belbin suggests that it is necessary for a management team to contain people prepared to play the various complementary roles. A group of talented individuals could fail because there could be too much competition to play some roles with no one prepared to play important but possibly less glamorous ones. The roles that he identifies as being likely to be necessary are:

- Plant (creative, intelligent, introverted),
- Resource investigator,
- Coordinator,
- Shaper,
- Monitor/evaluator,
- Team worker,
- Implementer,
- Completer, finisher,
- Specialist.

This list needs to be viewed as a set of guidelines for group membership, as not all groups will require the exact permutation identified by Belbin. Also, people may need and be able to play different roles according to the needs of a situation. People may also need and be able to switch from one role to another within a group. This is particularly important as managers may have to work with groups where they have little or no control over the membership.

A particularly important aspect of group activity is their potential creativity. Managers sometimes make the mistake of believing that they must be the ones who come up with the creative ideas and ignore the potential creativity of the rest of the team. This may be because they have concepts of managerial leadership that are old-fashioned and egocentric. It can actually be counterproductive to have the senior manager also trying to play the role of creative thinker as this may detract from the effective organisation of the group. Groups also have to beware of unbalanced 'groupthink'.

Example

The need for a balanced team mix

The importance of having the right mix of people in a group and the potentially disastrous consequences of unbalanced 'groupthink' were sadly illustrated by a climbing disaster in 1995. Six climbers were blown to their death while trying to descend from the summit of the second highest peak in the world, K2 in the Himalayas. A seventh member of the team, who did not reach the top, died of pneumonia. The team included the British mountaineer, Alison Hargreaves, who had recently climbed Mount Everest without oxygen. The lack of a person who was prepared to play the role of monitor/evaluator may have been crucial. Peter Hillary (1995) – another mountaineer and the son of Sir Edmund Hillary, one of the pair who first scaled Mount Everest – had abandoned his simultaneous attempt to climb K2. He commented:

> Summit fever had developed in that group. There was a chemistry in there that meant that they were going for the summit no matter what. They were all driving each other on ... These people came together and, because of the place and the atmosphere and their personalities, they became blinkered and simply focused on the top ... There was no careful awareness in the group and the most dangerous thing about groups is that people hand over responsibility for themselves to someone else ... It means that no one is taking responsibility. There can be a false sense of security in numbers.

There can be occasions when managers and just one other colleague need to have complementary styles.

Example

Two examples of necessary complementary styles

- A former British Royal Air Force officer commented about the relationship between the commanding officer of a unit and their adjutant. In his view it was necessary for the one to take a hard disciplinary line and for the other a much softer line and be psychologically available, so that they could find out what people really felt as well as soothe any hurt feelings. He also maintained that it did not matter who took the hard line and who the soft line as long as each took one and that they worked as a team. That way, effective control, based on reliable information and reasonable morale, could be exercised. If both the commanding officer and the adjutant adopted the same style he argued that either there would be an excess of control and lack of reliable information or the reverse.

- The doctor or dentist will usually leave the potentially embarrassing business of payment to the receptionist, so that it does not interfere with the relationship between the professional and their client.

FRAMES OF REFERENCE

The ability of managers to handle internal organisational conflict may be largely determined by whether they have a unitary or pluralistic frame of reference (Fox 1965). Unitarists may be ill-equipped to handle such conflict because of their assumption that sectional interests will or should always be subordinated to overall organisational objectives. In the event of this not happening, they may operate in an authoritarian manner. If this does not work they are likely to be both frustrated and ineffective. Those with a pluralistic frame of reference will be conceptually equipped both to recognise conflicts of interest and, when appropriate, to negotiate about them. This is in keeping with the view that the manager often needs to be a facilitator rather than simply an authority figure. This issue is examined in more detail in Chapter 14 in the context of employee relations. The role of the first-line supervisor is also examined in the same chapter. They often have to deal with significant conflicts of interest between the workforce and the organisation. Strategies are suggested as to how this can be constructively handled.

If you want to check on your own managerial style, complete the questionnaire in the appendix to this chapter.

Organisational factors

While managerial style will be influenced by the individual personality of a manager, a number of external factors are also likely to influence their style and are outlined below.

NATURE OF THE WORK

The nature of the work may influence the managerial style. Of particular importance will be the knowledge gap between the manager and employees. The nature of the work will largely determine the level of skill needed in employees. The knowledge gap may be high if the work is predictable and routine. It may be small if the work is demanding and varied. The greater the gap, the more appropriate it may be for the manager to behave in an authoritarian way. If there is a small, or even reverse gap, the more consultative the manager will need to be.

The time pressures affecting the work are also likely to influence managerial style. Organisations that are capital intensive, for example process-based plants such as oil refineries, may be able to have reasonable staffing ratios. This will reduce the time pressures on managers and enable them to consult more. Organisations in which labour costs are high may have to keep staff to a minimum, which in turn can mean that there is less time for consultation. The consequences of error may also be a factor. If the consequences are small, an authoritarian style may be appropriate. Conversely, if the consequences are high, managers will need to investigate and consult more fully. In emergencies, however, managers may need to behave in an authoritarian way.

ORGANISATIONAL VALUES

Organisations will have certain expectations of the way in which their managers behave. Managers may be selected and trained in such a way that these values are reinforced. They may also be rewarded or punished according to whether they conform or not to organisational values.

The values of organisations are sometimes enshrined in documents such as **mission statements**. These can be genuine statements about organisational values or statements of how the organisation would like to be viewed. In the latter case, managers need to be careful not to confuse the stated values with the real value system that may operate in an organisation. It is particularly important that prospective or new managers try and identify the real values in an organisation before they commit themselves to joining it or, if they have joined it, to see what adaptations in behaviour they may need to consider. Key questions are:

- Attitudes to innovation: are you likely be rewarded or punished if you take initiatives?
- Organisational protocol: how important is it to observe organisational protocol about approaching other employees?
- Attitudes to risk: are you likely to earn disapproval for making mistakes, however small, or is a certain amount of risk-taking encouraged because of the need for commercial enterprise?
- Ethical values: is the organisation one in which only success matters, or is this constrained by a need to behave ethically?
- Constraints: to what extent is the organisation constrained in its actions by factors such as the law, image and public accountability?
- Level of conformity: to what extent are nonconformity and dissent tolerated?
- Customer/client orientation: do clients or customers really come first?
- Developmental needs: to what extent will you be able to develop yourself in the organisation?
- Values: what are the values of your immediate superior?

STYLE OF THE BOSS

Managers need to take into account the values of their boss as well as those of the organisation at large. The boss is usually in a powerful position to put pressure on a employee. While some can see the value of having employees with complementary skills, many expect them to behave as 'clones'. Consequently, employees will need to work out the values and style of their boss and the extent to which they are expected to model themselves on it. One of the problems that organisations can have is that the 'cloning' process can go on throughout the managerial hierarchy. This may not necessarily be of benefit to the organisation, but it can reinforce the pressure on a employee to conform to established values and patterns of behaviour.

The managerial style of a boss can greatly influence the way in which issues entrusted to them are handled. A study of the former Wales Gas Board (cited in the next example) showed how attempts to change managerial style were frustrated by the very style that was meant to be changed.

The overriding impact of managerial style

Example

The former Wales Gas Board had been statutorily obliged to consult with representatives of employees. Seventeen consultative committees were established, but eight of them collapsed. Ostensibly, this was because the employees stopped nominating representatives to serve on these eight committees. Detailed analysis of consultative committee minutes showed, however, that the managers who had chaired the eight defunct committees had taken a very reactive approach to discussions. They had also often ignored those issues raised by the employee representatives. This contrasted with the productive discussions at the nine other committees. These prospered because the managers who chaired them generally prepared for the meetings, actually raised more items for discussion than the employee representatives, and took the issues raised by the representatives seriously. Ironically, the committees were most successful at those well-run establishments where they seemed to be least needed and vice versa.

(Rees and Porter 1998, pp. 165–170)

The impact of national culture

National culture was identified in the previous chapter as one of the factors that determine organisational structure. It was also explained that it was best to qualify the concept of national culture as the dominant culture in a country because of the potential range of subcultures. It is now necessary to examine the impact of national culture on managerial style. The term is used instead of 'societal culture' because it is much more generally used and broadly understood. Care has to be used throughout in using the term 'national culture' because of the danger of stereotyping. This is all the more so because stereotypes tend to emphasise negative rather than positive characteristics. Culture is defined as:

> The collective programming of the mind which distinguishes the members of one human group from another ... Culture in this sense includes systems of values: and values in this sense are the building blocks of culture.

> (Hofstede 1984, p. 21)

Managers need to pay an increasing amount of attention to the impact of national culture. This is because of growing cultural diversity within countries and **globalisation**. Managers are also more likely to have to work abroad, even if only for short periods, which may require considerable adjustment on their part. It is important that managers avoid taking an **ethnocentric** approach and adapt appropriately to other cultures. The growth of international organisations in both the private and public sectors means that managers may have to deal with a number of different nationalities simultaneously.

KEY VARIABLES

Key variables that can affect the way in which managers need to work include:

- Climate and geography,
- Language,
- Religion and general societal values,
- Systems of government,
- Attitudes to gender and age,
- Patterns of doing business,
- Attitude to time,
- Level of technology,
- Costs, particularly of labour,
- Local law,
- Work ethic,
- Relationships with the manager's country,
- Facilities for family members,
- History.

HOFSTEDE'S MODEL

The most important study to date on the impact of national culture on work was conducted in 1984 by Hofstede (2001). His research was based on 116 000 IBM employees in 53 countries. Hofstede found that there were wide variations in values and behaviour between countries. Originally, he identified four dimensions for classifying key national differences that affected work behaviour.

- **Power distance**: the lengths of hierarchies vary considerably. Low power distances encourage individualism and high ones conformity. This is because the fewer the levels in the hierarchy there are, normally the greater the opportunity and need for decision-making at the levels that do exist. High power distances are also associated with authoritarian managerial styles.

- **Uncertainty avoidance**: some cultures encourage acceptance of ambiguity and uncertainty while others do not. A high need to avoid uncertainty can generate anxiety and a need to plan to reduce uncertainty levels. Low needs for uncertainty avoidance, such as in Sweden, can lead to low anxiety and a willingness to take risks.

- Individualism versus collectivism: there are large variations in the extent to which the focus of work and society is the individual, as in the USA, or the group, as in Japan. This has major implications for the way work is organised. Initiatives such as **total quality management** (TQM) which are dependent on group cooperation are more likely to work in societies such as

Japan but are more likely to fail if transplanted into more individualistic cultures. The nature of the culture also has implications for payment arrangements, social control and attitudes to innovation. Attempts at social control may be relatively ineffective in individualistic countries, but individual merit schemes are more likely to be successful and innovation is likely to be higher.

- Masculinity versus femininity: masculine cultures are characterised by strong gender distinctions and an emphasis on individual achievement and material possessions. Feminine cultures have greater equality between the sexes and a greater concern for people. In feminine cultures, collaboration is also valued more highly in comparison with competition.

Great Britain was classified by 2001 as having the following cultural characteristics:

- Relatively small power distance,
- Weak uncertainty avoidance,
- Highly individualistic,
- Moderately masculine.

Japan in contrast was classified as exhibiting:

- Relatively large power distance,
- Strong uncertainty avoidance,
- Moderately collectivist,
- Highly masculine.

Hofstede later identified a fifth factor – Confucianism. He, in common with other scholars, saw religious and philosophical values as helping explain economic success in many South East Asian countries. Key factors identified by Hofstede (1991, p. 165) were:

- The social stability that can be created by high power distance,
- The family as a role model for the rest of society,
- Respect for others,
- A high work ethic accompanied by patience and perseverance.

Care has to be taken in assessing this factor, however, because of the variation of the success in the economies of South East Asia – even those with Confucian values. Also some of the factors identified are also common to other religions, particularly Protestantism.

There are dangers in using any model too prescriptively. Hofstede's research work was undertaken in the 1970s and only on IBM employees. There are also the obvious dangers of assuming that everyone will conform to a pattern of national characteristics. In addition, Hofstede did not take account of factors such as organisational and industry subcultures. However, the model is, arguably, the most useful one currently available. If nothing else, it can give managers a checklist of the factors they may need to take into account when working with people from different national cultures.

Example

The impact of national culture on work-related values

An example of the insights that can be generated by work such as Hofstede's is the ambivalence of the UK's attitude to the European Union. In many ways the UK has stronger ties and cultural similarities with the USA than with much of Europe. These include language, kinship, legal tradition, high individualism, low uncertainty avoidance and small power distance.

These in turn are reinforced by a generally Protestant individualistic tradition compared with the generally more Catholic tradition in many other parts of Europe. Such differences may also help explain the Nordic versus Mediterranean division within the European Union.

LOCAL CULTURE

As well as needing to adapt to national culture, managers may need to adapt to regional or local culture within their own or another country. Sometimes the cultural variations and mutual antagonisms within countries are very high. A related issue is that managers may also have to deal with 'third country nationals', i.e. employees who have been imported to work from countries other than the manager's. Managers may also need to beware of being too closely associated with a particular cultural group within a country.

Example

The impact of local culture

A national brewing company in the UK decided to build its biggest brewery on a greenfield site in a development area. A reason for doing this was the government funding available for generating work in an area of high unemployment. Managers from the company's plant at Burton-on-Trent were transferred to help build and commission the new brewery. Initially, they concentrated on the technical aspects of their work. However, it soon became apparent that employee relations were of a much higher priority than was the case in Burton. This was because of the different regional culture in the development area. A key

difference was the traditional local antagonisms between management and employees. The more amicable working relationships at Burton had not prepared the managers who had been transferred for this key aspect of their jobs. Attempts were made to strengthen the management at the new brewery and a number of expensive concessions were made to the trade unions. However, when the firm needed to rationalise its production it was this new and most modern brewery that was closed. Labour relations and labour costs were partly the reason for this.

MANAGING DIVERSITY

Workforces are increasingly culturally diverse and managers will need to respond to the characteristics of such workforces whether they are working at home or abroad if they are to both achieve organisational objectives as well as some element of social justice. Benefits of managing diversity from the organisation's point of view include better utilisation of talent as well as increased market understanding. Cross-cultural teams may present certain problems in terms of creating a shared understanding of a situation, including language differences and utilising different systems of communication, but they can also be more creative. In order to manage diversity effectively, the manager will find it necessary to develop cross-cultural knowledge and understanding. In addition, it will be necessary to develop an organisational climate that focuses on valuing diversity and an organisational culture that is tolerant of some of the differences in values and behaviour.

An organisation can be seen as having a moral obligation towards members of all ethnic groups. At the same time, the benefits of managing diversity effectively from the organisation's point of view can include reduced labour turnover and absenteeism, improved problem solving and innovation, greater appeal to minority ethnic groups, improved marketability of goods and services, and a better public image. A recent feature of globalisation is the development of a growing international group of workers who move from country to country and no longer have their roots in any particular one. Another major issue, though, is that while there are some strong trends towards cultural convergence there are other factors, such as the increased importance of Islam, and in some cases its radicalisation, that are leading to increased cultural divergence. The issue of cultural diversity is considered further in Chapter 9 on selection as well as the related concept of equal opportunities.

WORKING ABROAD

The problems of cultural adjustment are likely to be magnified if a manager has to work abroad. The natural temptation is for managers working abroad to rely on their own national culture as a model and to judge all other cultures by that. Depending on the country in which they are working, they will find that the responses of employees vary according to the culture of the country and the different industrial context.

Ideally, managers should receive some cultural briefing (and a preliminary visit if that is possible) before they go on an international assignment of some length. However, even with good initial briefing, there will be much to learn once the manager starts to work in another country.

Speedy expatriate failure

Example

An engineering manager was sent to Singapore on a three-year appointment. He paid no attention to how he might adjust to the habits, beliefs and expectations of local colleagues. Instead he plunged straight into the technical aspects of his work. After three weeks he was sent back to the UK.

A further danger for managers working abroad is that they may live and socialise in an 'expatriate ghetto'. If managers restrict their social contacts to other expatriates this may reinforce existing prejudices about the local community and inhibit learning about and appreciating the local culture. It may also not be very good public relations to do this. If managers do try and adapt, however, even if they make mistakes, people from the host community may well be understanding of a person who is at least trying to get it right.

Expatriate failure can be costly for both the organisations involved and the individuals concerned. The main cost to the organisation may be the **opportunity cost.** This is the loss incurred by missing the opportunity to have an employee in place who could have moved the organisation in an appropriate way. The chances of failure are likely to be considerably reduced if one accounts for the following factors:

● Selection: managers need to be carefully selected for overseas missions. As well as having the appropriate job expertise, managers crucially need to have the ability to adapt to working in a different environment. A precondition for selection is to have an accurate understanding of the job that needs doing.

Example

The wrong job being identified

Expatriate engineers were recruited for a major internationally funded public sector transport project in the Philippines. However, it emerged that there were plenty of local engineers who could have handled the technical work. The need instead had been for expatriates with financial expertise and an ability to understand the local politics, who could effectively monitor the financial progress of the project.

● Training: as well as needing induction training, managers may need to have training to prepare them for new job responsibilities. As managers often get promoted when they go abroad, this preparation may need to include management training.

● Domestic arrangements: if a manager plans to take other family members with them, thought needs to be given to how well they are likely to be able to adapt. Key issues will include the career opportunities for any partner and education facilities for any children. Children may suffer from loss of cultural identity if they spend too much time away from their own country.

● Length of assignment: the longer a manager works abroad, the more successful they are likely to be in adapting to local conditions. However, the more they do this, the more out of touch they may get with what is happening elsewhere in their organisation.

● Organisational adaptability: organisations need to adapt their structure, policies and procedures to meet local conditions. It may help in making appropriate adaptations if local people are considered for senior positions. Unfortunately, many organisations seek to rigidly impose their own arrangements in cultures where actual variation is needed.

● Repatriation: organisations often fail to consider the issue of the repatriation of a person sent to work abroad. Expatriates can find that it has been a case of 'out of sight and out of mind'. They may also suffer from reverse culture shock when they return to their own country.

The adjustments necessitated by **inward investment** are considered in Chapter 14. These are considered from the point of view of both the employer and local employees.

NATIONAL CULTURE AND ETHICS

When working abroad, managers may find that there will be differences in the criteria applied in situations where ethical issues have to be considered before decisions are made. What may be seen as unethical in one culture may be acceptable and even necessary in another culture. A common problem is what attitude to take towards questionable payments. In some societies it will be common practice for bribes of some description to be paid when awarding contracts or when securing other people's services. Difficult moral and business decisions may have to be taken about the extent to which one adjusts to apparent local customs. The consequences of decisions may also be difficult to predict.

Jumping to conclusions about local customs

Two Western companies were operating in the same market in Indonesia. One took the policy decision that it would not pay bribes. The other took the opposite decision and tried to bribe its way into the market. The first company found that virtue was rewarded as it found it was able to operate perfectly satisfactorily without paying bribes. The second company found that once it had become known that it would pay bribes the numbers of people soliciting them proliferated. Also, although a considerable amount was paid in bribes, it brought no apparent benefits. While concepts of 'honesty' (according to Western definitions) may unfortunately not always be the best policy, this example shows the dangers of jumping to conclusions about what is appropriate local practice.

Example

This discussion relating to selecting and organisational support of managers who are to work overseas needs to be integrated with the discussion on selection in Chapter 9 and on management and employee development in Chapter 11.

Assertiveness

Although managerial style needs to fit the situation, there is a strong case for managers developing the skills of behaving assertively. This is in contrast to being non-assertive or aggressive. While there may be occasions when managers may need to be non-assertive or aggressive, in general being assertive is likely to achieve better results. In any case, managers need to know how to be assertive so that they have the option of using this style.

AGGRESSIVE, NON-ASSERTIVE AND ASSERTIVE BEHAVIOUR

Assertiveness training was originally particularly associated with developing the confidence and skills of women. However, the skills are equally relevant to both genders and are appropriate for use in work as well as in personal situations (Back and Back 1999). These skills involve consideration of the rights of the parties involved in a situation. The patterns of behaviour associated with aggressive, non-assertive and assertive behaviour are outlined below.

Aggressive behaviour

If a manager behaves aggressively they may be standing up for their own rights but behaving in such a way that the rights of others are violated. The assumption behind their behaviour is that their needs are more important than those of others, and that only they have something to contribute.

The consequences of aggressive behaviour may be that the manager concerned gets their way and is able to vent their feelings. However, this may be at the expense of worsening working relationships, as well as generating stress in the person who is being aggressive. Aggressive behaviour will sometimes generate aggressive responses. It can also lead to a pattern of employees concealing bad news, which can lead to managers taking decisions on inadequate information. (See also Chapter 8 on communications.)

Aggressive behaviour is often an emotional response to a situation and not one calculated to be effective. Managers may need to find ways of diffusing their anger before dealing with people who are the object of it. One way of doing this is to write something down and then rip it up with a view to writing, or doing, something that is more rational. If a manager is having to cope with aggressive behaviour by someone else, they will probably need to let them dissipate their anger and only then try and have a rational dialogue. To do this they will need to curb their own anger and remember not to descend to the level of the person behaving aggressively.

Non-assertive behaviour

Non-assertive behaviour is based on the opposite assumption to that involved in aggressive behaviour. It implies that other people's rights are more important than your own. It also implies that the manager has nothing to contribute. Non-assertive behaviour is a way of dealing with situations in the short-term to avoid initial or further conflict. It may also create short-term popularity. However, in the long term, employees may become frustrated because of the lack of direction. Also, while non-assertiveness may sometimes be appropriate, it may be a form of escapism. Managers normally need to face up to problems, whatever they may be. If they do not, they may internalise their anger, which may not do their health or job performance much good. Non-assertiveness can also cause a manager to overreact on subsequent occasions and behave aggressively.

Assertive behaviour

Assertive behaviour involves recognising both your own rights and those of whoever else is involved. It also involves recognising the right of all the parties involved to speak in a direct, honest and open way. Employees are therefore encouraged to behave assertively. This enables the identification of issues that need to be addressed. It also has the potential to enable issues to be addressed in a way that is satisfactory to all the parties involved and which develops constructive working relationships between them. Another potential advantage is that it may take much less emotional energy to deal with issues this way.

THE SKILLS OF BEHAVING ASSERTIVELY

Key aspects of behaving assertively are:

- Concentrating on facts and not feelings.

- Concentrating on issues and not personalities.

- Questioning technique and the choice of language can be important.

- Phrasing statements and questions in a neutral way.

- Avoiding leading statements or questions that may discourage people from raising points that are necessary both for themselves and the manager.

Managers also need to consider their tone of voice and body language.

How to be assertive

If a conscientious and heavily loaded employee is simply told to undertake a new urgent task they may behave in a non-assertive way and simply get on with it. This, however, may generate feelings of resentment on the part of the employee and lead to other important work being delayed. An over-loaded employee may also eventually suffer ill-health, causing a problem for themselves and also for the organisation. Even though it might be inconvenient for the manager to be told by the employee of the practical problems, they may well need to know of them before deciding to give the work to that particular person.

To obtain necessary information from the employee it will be necessary to approach them in such a way that they can explain their situation. This does not mean that the manager can't insist on them doing the work. However, it would give the manager the opportunity to explain why, having taken everything into account, the employee needs to do this task as well. It may also cause the manager to consider if there was another employee who would be better placed to handle the work.

If managers need to present a case, whether in writing or orally, they also need to consider the option of presenting assertively. Aggressive presentations can lead to aggressive responses, while non-assertive presentations can simply be ignored. Attempts to sway the minds of those who take a different stance or who are uncommitted are more likely to be successful if the would-be persuaders adopt assertive behaviour.

How to protest effectively

A practical illustration of presenting assertively, as opposed to aggressively, concerns attempts to prevent the rundown of services at St Bartholomew's Hospital in London. The secretary of state for health at the time of the proposed closure of the hospital was Virginia Bottomley. She said that she 'had paid no special attention to "noisy lobbies"' and had listened at least as much to those who had made cases 'calmly and quietly'.

Handling change

NATURE OF ORGANISATIONAL CHANGE

A recurring theme in this book is the increasing pace of change. Given this theme, it is particularly important to consider how organisational change can be handled constructively. The handling of change is considered a number of times throughout the book but it is appropriate to pull the threads together in one section, even if this involves a number of cross-references. It is also necessary to distinguish between specific (or 'set piece') change – for example, the introduction of a new operational method – and erratic and continuous change. It is also necessary to make the point that 'set piece' change is likely to be taking place within the context of a greater or lesser amount of continuous change. A particular type of continuous change is that envisaged by the process of **kaizen**. This involves discussion groups designed to secure improvements in organisational quality and efficiency particularly found in Japanese businesses. Although individual improvements may be small their cumulative effect may be considerable.

NEED FOR EFFECTIVE PLANNING

A key aspect of change is to ensure that management planning is properly thought out. Unfortunately this is not always the case. Initiatives can be taken which deal, for example, with the symptoms of problems rather than the root causes. This crucial issue was previously considered in the section on strategic planning in Chapter 2, in the section on the interrelationship of organisational activity in Chapter 3 and is considered further in the section on diagnostic skills in Chapter 14 (see also Rees and Porter 2002 and 2006, Parts 1 and 2). Organisational change can have many dimensions and unexpected consequences. This means that whoever seeks to initiate major change needs to grasp the scale of what they are planning. This may necessitate opening up the planning process so that there can be inputs from a range of people who can comment on the appropriateness of the change, anticipate the likely effects, and undertake a realistic cost-benefit analysis. Too often it is assumed that there will be only winners and that everyone will be as committed to change as the person who is initiating it. An understanding of the concepts of **unitary** and **pluralistic frames of reference**, first explained in Chapter 2, can be vital in identifying whether there will be losers as well as winners and how the manager might handle prospective losers. As also explained in Chapter 2, resistance to change can be attributed too often to simply being because of inertia. Whilst inertia can be a factor, if staff's genuine interests are threatened by change it is appropriate to identify the nature of the threat to see what, if anything, can be done to reduce or even avoid such threats.

A major factor causing change, or being used as an agent of change, is information technology. The impact of changes in this area was considered in some detail in Chapter 2. A further key concept is that of **socio-technical systems**, explained in Chapter 6 in the context of motivation. The introduction of a new technical system may disrupt complementary social systems. Again the impact of this needs to be anticipated and potentially allowed for in planning rather than viewed as an unexpected fallout of change. Other key issues that may need to be taken into account in planning organisational change include national culture (Chapter 4) and the training and development implications (Chapter 11).

IMPORTANCE OF APPROPRIATE ORGANISATIONAL CHANGE

To point out that planning change may be more complicated than is perhaps initially realised might suggest that change should be avoided. On the contrary, the pace of change is such that adaptation will be increasingly essential if an organisation is to survive. The case being made here is that it is increasingly essential to see that planned change is effective. As explained in Chapter 3, organisations may actually need to structure themselves so that they can embrace necessary innovation. A feature of this may be to adopt the philosophy of a **learning organisation**, as explained in Chapter 11. An option that can sometimes take the risk out of planned change is to see what can be learned by piloted change, so that appropriate adaptations can be made to any major change that is subsequently introduced. (The theme of handling change is the core issue in a number of the case studies contained in the list for Chapter 4 and available on the accompanying website.) Adopting a style appropriate to the situation will be a key dimension to consider in handling organisational change.

Evaluation of managerial style

Managerial style is not an end in itself but a means to an end. Ultimately, managers are judged by results. Different managers may achieve the same results by using different means. The key to effective management is matching the style to the situation. Despite the differences between management and leadership, evidence about who is likely to emerge as the informal leader of a group may nevertheless help in judging the effectiveness of the style that managers adopt. In analysing research findings of group behaviour, Homans identified six factors that were strongly associated with who would emerge as the informal leader (1975, Ch. 8). These can provide a rough and ready way of evaluating the effectiveness of managerial style. Although this seems to be suggesting that there is a standard effective style, the factors do take into account the requirements of the situation in which leadership is exercised.

Assessment exercise

As a way of assessing managers and the appropriateness of their style, identify one or more managers and rank them on the following six-point scale.

1 Excellent
2 Very good

3 Good

4 Meets the minimum standards

5 Does not meet the minimum standards

6 Should be dismissed

The next stage is to compare the rating or ratings on the above scale with the six points identified by Homans as being characteristic of the behaviour of informal group leaders (Homans 1975). Answer yes or no to the following questions:

1 Do they represent what the group finds to be most important in a person at that time?

2 Do they make decisions that turn out, by and large, to be correct?

3 Do they keep their word?

4 Do they settle differences between members in a way the group believes to be fair?

5 Do they allow followers to go to them for advice and keep them informed about what is going on?

6 Do they give information to the group in the form of advice, orders, etc. and maintain two-way communication?

When the second part of the assessment is completed it is necessary to compare the number of 'no' responses with the initial rating of managerial effectiveness. Usually this correlates so that the fewer the 'no' responses to Homans' six points, the more likely it is that the manager or managers would have received a high rating in terms of managerial effectiveness. For example, a person who received six 'yes' responses, and therefore zero 'no' responses, would have received a rating of 1 (excellent). Conversely, a person who was given 'no' six times would be rated as 6 (should be dismissed).

This method of assessment can act as a means of identifying the reasons for managerial ineffectiveness as well as a means of assessing the level of performance. It can also be used as a method of self-assessment.

Summary

In this chapter the concept of managerial style has been explained, as have the differences between the overlapping concepts of management and leadership. Managers are appointed but leaders often emerge as popular choices, particularly in representative structures. Managerial style is not an end in itself but a means to an end.

The range of managerial styles has been examined. A key distinction is the level of direction that the manager gives. Examination of the various theories has shown that it is largely determined by the assumptions the managers make about why other people work and other variables in the situation. These variables are likely to include the organisational culture, the level of skill of employees and the extent to which their objectives converge with organisational ones. For managerial styles to be effective they need to match the situation. This may involve selecting people whose style fits a situation or in people adjusting their style to the circumstances.

National culture also does, or needs to, affect managerial style. This is an increasingly important issue because of globalisation and cultural diversity within countries. The work of Hofstede has been examined in this chapter and in particular the four key dimensions he used to differentiate between managerial styles in different countries.

Whatever style is adopted, there is usually a case for managers behaving assertively rather than aggressively or non-assertively. Assertiveness involves respecting other people's rights to state their case but being prepared to firmly yet politely state one's own case. The associated skills in doing this have also been explained.

A key activity for managers is the effective handling of change. This is ever more important because of the increasing pace of change. Consequently, the way in which significant organisational change needs to be planned was examined and reference made to other parts of the book where relevant concepts are examined in more detail.

Ultimately, managers have to be judged by effectiveness and not, for example, by their popularity. An exercise was included within the chapter so that readers can assess the managerial effectiveness of other people. Much depends on their relationship with their employees. A further exercise has been included as an appendix so that readers can examine their own managerial style and see if there is any need for adjustment.

Self-assessment questions

(If you wish to check the extent to which your answer to any of he following questions is appropriate, cross-refer to the Table of Contents. The contents for this chapter are on pages xii–xiii.)

1 How would you define the concept of managerial style?

2 Identify the main different types of managerial style.

3 Why does managerial style need to match the circumstances in which it is used?

4 What organisational factors can influence managerial style?

5 Identify key ways in which national culture can affect managerial style.

6 Explain the differences between assertive, aggressive and non-assertive behaviour.

7 How would you ensure that a change you are involved in is properly planned?

8 How would you evaluate the effectiveness of a particular managerial style?

9 What is your own preferred managerial style? If you have managerial or other responsibilities, assess its effectiveness.

References

(Works of particular interest are marked with a star.)

Adair, John (1982), *Action-Centred Leadership*, Gower Publishing.

*Back, Ken and Kate Back (1999), *Assertiveness at Work: A Practical Guide to Handling Awkward Situations,* 3rd ed., McGraw-Hill.

Belbin, R. Meredith (2006), *Team Role Descriptions,* http://www.belbin.co.uk/downloads/Belbin_Team_Role_Summary_Descriptions.pdf, accessed 29.10.06. See also Belbin, R. Meredith (2006), *The Evolution of Human Behaviour and its Bearing on the Future,* Belbin Associates.

Blake, R. and J. S. Mouton (1978), *The New Management Grid*, Gulf Publishing.

Bottomley, Virginia (1993), *Bart's Seeks Merger and Drops Fight*, The Guardian, 18 February.

Drucker, Peter F. (1955), *Practice of Management*, Heinemann.

Fox, Alan (1965), *Industrial Society and Industrial Relations,* Research paper no. 3, Royal Commission on Trade Unions and Employer's Associations, HMSO.

French, J. R. P. and B. H. Raven (1968), *The bases of social power,* in D. Cartwright (eds) *Group Dynamics, Research and Theory,* pp. 607–623, Harper & Row.

Garrahan, Philip and Paul Stewart (1992), *The Nissan Enigma – Flexibility at Work in a Local Economy,* Thomson Learning.

Handy, Charles (1991) *The Age of Unreason*, 2nd ed., Business Books.

Hofstede, G. (1984), *Culture's Consequences – International Differences in Work-Related Values*, Sage.

Hofstede, G. (1991), *Cultures and organisations: Software of the Mind,* McGraw-Hill.

Hofstede G. (2001), *Culture's Consequences*, 2nd ed., Sage.

Homans, George (1975), *The Human Group*, Routledge and Kegan Paul.

Hillary, Peter (1995), comments reported in Evening Standard (London), 23 August.

Lewis, Pamela S., Stephen W. Goodman and Patricia M. Fandt (1995), *Management Challenges in the 21st Century* – Annotated Instructor's Edition, West Publishing Co., USA.

Local Government Management Board (1993), *Managing Tomorrow, Panel of Inquiry Report*, Local Government Management Board.

McGregor, Douglas (1969), *The Human Side of Enterprise*, McGraw-Hill.

*Rees, W. David and Christine Porter (1998), *Employee Participation and Managerial Style (The Key Variable)*, Industrial and Commercial Training, MCB University Press, 30 (5). (Available on the book's companion website.)

*Rees, W. David and Christine Porter (2002), *Management by Panacea – the Training Implications.* Industrial and Commercial Training, Vol. 34 No. 6. (An explanation of the diagnostic skills in management and the need to identify the real nature and causes of problems before devising solutions.)(Available on the book's companion website.)

*Rees, W. David and Christine Porter (2006), *Corporate Strategy Development and Related Management Development: the Case for the Incremental Approach, Part 1 – The Development of Strategy,* Industrial and Commercial Training, Vol. 38 No. 5 and Vol. 39 No. 6. (An explanation of why comprehensive strategy development may often be so difficult that the incremental approach may be the only option. This article received a highly commended award by the Emerald Literati

Network in 2007. (Available on the book's companion website.) *Part 2 – Implications for learning and development,* Industrial and Commercial Training, Vol. 38 No. 6. (Includes an explanation of the dangers of corporate decision-making based on too narrow a range of variables.)(Available on the book's companion website.)

Tannenbaum, R. and W. H. Schmidt (1957), *How to Choose a Leadership Pattern,* Harvard Business Review, 36(2).

Further reading

Belbin, R. Meredith (2000), *Beyond The Team,* Butterworth-Heinemann.

Chen, Min (2004), *Asian Management Systems,* 2nd Edition, Thomson Learning.

*Golzen, Godfrey and Jonathan Reuvid (2004), *Working Abroad,* Kogan Page, 26th ed. (for a wealth of information on the practical issues concerning working overseas).

Hall, E. T. (1987), *Hidden Differences,* Anchor Press/Doubleday.

Hughes, Mark (2006), *Change Management,* CIPD.

*Mead, Richard (2005), *International Management – Cross-Cultural Dimensions,* 3rd ed., Blackwell. (A thorough, well-written account of the impact of national culture on management. The main theories are explained and evaluated.)

Storey J. (ed.) (2004), *Leadership in Organizations,* Routledge.

Trompenaars, Fons (1997), *Riding the Waves of Culture: Understanding Cultural Diversity in Business,* 2nd ed., Nicholas Brealey.

Appendix to chapter 4

SELF-ASSESSMENT QUESTIONNAIRE FOR PERSONAL DEVELOPMENT PLANNING

1 Do you vary your style to match the situation?

2 Do you naturally adopt a Theory X or Theory Y style in the assumptions that you make about employees?

3 Where do you fit on the leadership continuum?

4 Is your managerial style people-centred, task-centred or both?

5 Do your assumptions about conflict in organisations fit with those with a unitary or pluralistic frame of reference?

6 Are you generally non-assertive, assertive or aggressive?

7 Are you reactive or proactive in your managerial style? (See Chapter 2 on identifying the manager's job.)

8 Is your orientation primarily managerial or specialist? (See Chapter 1 on managers and their background.)

9 Do you generally get on with tasks yourself or do you generally see that they are done by others?

10 When you chair meetings, is your orientation towards process management or substantive contribution? (See Chapter 16 on meetings and chairing.)

11 How effective is your style?

12 In the light of your answers to the above questions do you need to alter any of your managerial behaviour in order to improve your effectiveness?

Delegation

Introduction

Management has already been described in Chapter 1 as 'getting things done through people'. It therefore follows that delegation is a part of every manager's job. Delegation involves giving others the authority to act on your behalf. Criteria are given in this chapter for deciding what might be delegated and what should not be. The managerial skills needed to delegate effectively are identified. These skills include risk assessment, consideration of the strengths and weaknesses of employees, and the establishment of appropriate control mechanisms. As well as developing these skills, managers also need to be prepared to spend time training their employees so that they are able to handle delegated authority.

Unfortunately, although the concepts involved in delegation are relatively easily explained, many managers are very bad at delegating. Consequently, the barriers to effective delegation are examined here. Whilst some of these managerial omissions are because of a lack of understanding of the nature of delegation, others may be of a more deep-seated nature. A particularly difficult barrier is psychological insecurity on the part of some managers. This can make it very difficult for them to give employees reasonable freedom to act on their behalf.

The overlapping concept of **empowerment** is also examined in this chapter. It is important to try and identify what people mean by this term. Sometimes it is used interchangeably with delegation. However, empowerment often focuses on groups rather than individuals. Historically, it was a 'bottom-up' process whereby community groups in the USA took more control over their lives. Latterly, it has become more used in a managerial context as a 'top-down' process. These aspects of empowerment and others are discussed in more detail in this chapter.

The nature of delegation

DEFINITION

Delegation may be defined as 'a person giving authority to someone to act on their behalf'. It should not be confused with simply giving instructions to employees. Although the manager remains accountable for the actions of the employee, the essence of delegation is the conferring of authority on the employee. Thus, delegation is much more than just passing a task over to be executed. Like all management techniques delegation is neutral: it can be used to good or bad effect. What matters is that it is used appropriately.

ACCOUNTABILITY

When managers delegate they still remain accountable for the actions of their staff. Delegation does not involve abdication of responsibility. This has been illustrated by a number of important and well-publicised cases.

Example

Accountability cannot be delegated

The owner and chief executive of the bankrupt Fire, Auto and Marine Insurance Company, Dr Emil Savundra, was cross-examined in a fraud trial in Britain in 1967 about the contrast between his personal wealth and the state of his former company. He responded by saying that he had practised modern management techniques – including delegation – and that such questions should be addressed instead to his former financial controller. The judge understood management better than that though, and when sentencing Dr Savundra to a lengthy term of imprisonment, commented that whilst authority can be delegated, accountability remained.

ACCOUNTABILITY IN THE PUBLIC SECTOR

There is an extra dimension to the general concept of accountability in the public sector because of the issue of ultimate democratic control. At one stage in the UK it was the practice for government ministers to accept responsibility and resign if there was a serious enough error by one of their employees – regardless of whether the minister even knew of the action beforehand. The following examples explain how the concept has developed in the public sector:

> In 1955 it was found that land on Crichel Down, in the UK, which had been compulsorily purchased by the government for military use during the Second World War, had been later used for agricultural purposes and then sold to a private buyer. This was despite an earlier assurance to give the original owner the first option of buying the land back. The minister was obliged to resign, even though he had not been personally involved in the decision and had no reason to believe that his officials had acted in other than good faith.

Example

This convention of public sector resignation, regardless of personal blame was, however, later modified, as demonstrated in the following example:

> The Aberfan disaster of 1966 occurred when a large slag heap of waste coal was dislodged by a swollen underground stream after heavy rain. It engulfed part of the village of Aberfan in South Wales, including a school just after the children had arrived in the morning. A total of 144 people died, including 116 children. The owner of the slag heap was the National Coal Board, and its chairman, Lord Robens, offered his resignation. This was not accepted, however, on the basis that there had been no prior knowledge about the danger at Board level. This was in spite of a tribunal of enquiry report that was highly critical of the Coal Board. The report concluded, in 1967, that 'blame for the disaster rests upon the National Coal Board' (McLean 1999, p. 12). Critics of the Coal Board maintained that it had been the Board's responsibility to ensure that there had been a safe slag tipping policy throughout the industry, which would have prevented the tragedy.

Example

The Aberfan precedent, in the previous example, was not enough, however, to save a British foreign secretary from resignation:

> Both the British Foreign Secretary, Lord Carrington, and the Defence Secretary, John Nott (later Sir), offered their resignations after the Argentinan occupation of the Falklands Islands, a British colony, in 1982. In the event, the Foreign Secretary's resignation was accepted, despite his illustrious record, but not the Defence Secretary's. Presumably this was because it was judged that the Argentinian invasion should have been anticipated and preventative action initiated. It was also possible that it was politically necessary for someone to resign.

Example

> A dramatic reinforcement of the concept of accountability occurred with regard to the political responsibility of the members of the European Union Commission.
>
> An investigation by independent experts into fraud and mismanagement within the European Union Commission concluded that the president of the European Commission, Jacques Santer, and his team of 20 commissioners:
>
> > 'has to bear responsibility for fraud, irregularities and mismanagement'. It also concluded that political responsibility 'cannot be a vague idea, a concept which in practice proves unrealistic ... It is becoming difficult to find anyone that has even the slightest sense of responsibility.'
> > (Castle and Grice 1999, pp. 1–2)
>
> Despite the vigorous protests of Jacques Santer, the European Parliament also demonstrated their disapproval by passing a 'no confidence' motion in the work of the commission in 1999. Consequently all the commissioners, including the president, were obliged to resign. Only four commissioners were subsequently reappointed.

Example

The cumulative effect of these cases and others is that, particularly in the public sector, policy-makers are accountable for reasonably foreseeable and important failures. Failures of this nature may force their resignation. Consequently, it is important for them to set up effective control procedures so that they can either avoid major failures or take prompt action to limit their effect. However, a distinction may need to be made between operational and strategic failures.

The need for delegation

One of the main reasons for delegation is that it is a means whereby a manager can, having decided their priorities, concentrate on the work of greatest importance, leaving the work of lesser importance to be done by others. If delegation is set up effectively, the delegated work may, in time, actually be performed better by the employees. This also has the advantages of motivating and developing employees.

EFFECTIVE USE OF TIME

The time of managers is limited, thus it is important for them to tackle their work in some order of priority so that the most important tasks get the appropriate attention. If at the end of the day some work has not been completed, or has had to be passed on to others, this should be the work of lowest priority. Even if the work of lesser importance is not done, or is not done so well, this is appropriate behaviour for the person in charge. It would not be sensible for a manager to do their own clerical work because they thought they could do it better than their secretary or clerk. Running the risk of a slightly lower level of performance by a employee is a small price to pay for creating time to concentrate on the more important aspects of a job. Ironically though, delegation is initially time-consuming. Managers somehow have to find the time to establish delegation effectively, even though the need for it in the first place is that they are short of time. Like other investments, the return will be in the future rather than immediately.

The lower the level at which a task is performed, the lower the cost of performing that task is likely to be. Cost needs to be considered not just in terms of the salary of the person undertaking a particular task but also in terms of **opportunity cost**, i.e. the opportunity that is denied or created for the manager to do other work.

EFFECTIVE USE OF EMPLOYEES

Many managers fail to make effective use of their employees. This can both reduce their own effectiveness and demotivate their employees. In some cases there would be a blatant disregard of the specialist expertise of a employee if the boss tried to do the employee's job. What would be the point and the results if, for example, a managing director tried to run the accounts department if they had a finance manager?

Arising out of this is the need for managers to seek to dovetail their activity with that of their employees. Everybody has relative strengths and weaknesses in their work. If a employee has particular strengths it may be appropriate to make use of those strengths rather than compete in that area or simply ignore those strengths. What matters is the effectiveness of the team as a whole rather than the direct performance of just the manager.

Further possible advantages of delegation are that the employee often has more time and readier access to the appropriate information than the boss. Also, what is routine work to the boss may be challenging to the employee, as well as carrying prestige. The more that employees are developed, the more they are likely to be able to undertake in the future.

Managers have to think carefully about the balance between managing by systems and through people. Detailed control procedures tend to be statements of lack of trust and can be unnecessary as well as demotivating if there are capable employees. Such systems may also inhibit healthy evolution and act as an organisational straitjacket. In any case, systems tend to be as good or bad as the people who operate them. A director of one British civil service agency commented that the best legacy he could leave the agency was to see that the six key jobs under him were manned by capable people.

Here is an example of the failure to use employees effectively.

Developing managers to do less

Example

The chief executive of an organisation invested in the management training of those with managerial responsibilities. Jobs that were mainly supervisory or managerial were given the designation 'manager'. Remuneration was also improved for those with managerial responsibilities. However, simultaneously, more detailed central control was introduced and the number of senior managers at the head office was doubled. The newly designated managers became increasingly frustrated with their work. This was because the clarification of their managerial responsibilities and their management development coincided with a considerable reduction in their delegated authority. Their management training made them all the more aware of this contradiction.

DEVELOPMENT OF EMPLOYEES

A further advantage of effective delegation may be that a manager is setting the pattern for their employees to delegate in turn down the line. One adage about managerial assessment is that you judge a manager by the quality of their employees. Delegation can also be important to enable employees to develop the skills to deal with any emergencies that may arise.

Extreme example of failure to delegate

Example

King Philip II of Spain was not a believer in delegation. He governed Spain in the sixteenth century in a manner which created 'apoplexy at the nucleus and paralysis at the periphery'. All state mail was sent to him and his conscientious attention to detail included sending personal letters to each of the families who lost relatives in the unsuccessful Armada attack on England in 1588.

Effective delegation can also help prepare employees for promotion. However, it is important that employees take advantage of the opportunities that may be presented to them. It may seem that promotion decisions are taken by the manager responsible for making the appointments. In reality, though, it may be much more the case that it is the managers being considered for promotion who decide for themselves whether or not they get it. Managers responsible for appointments do not make decisions in a vacuum. The existing pattern of behaviour of a manager is likely to influence any decision about their promotion. If a manager has got their pattern of delegation right, and because of that gets promotion, the onus may then be upon them to establish a new pattern so that they prepare themselves for even further promotion. The same reasoning can apply to people running small businesses. The expansion or non-expansion of a small business may depend less on external factors than is often imagined. Much may depend on the ability of the person running the business to identify and concentrate on the key tasks, leaving the less critical, even if more enjoyable, tasks to others.

Example

The self-perpetuating nature of a failure to delegate

Two small hospital groups had been merged, partly because of the ineffective management style of the chief executive of one of the groups, who was prematurely retired. He had operated on the classic Theory X assumptions about his staff, explained in the previous chapter. The chief executive of the other group now had to administer both groups. He was much more prepared to delegate and, interestingly, had attracted around him a much more capable group of managers than had his retired colleague, despite a common salary structure.

Initially, the chief executive of the merged group tried to cope with his own increased workload by increasing the delegated authority of the managers in the group which he had taken over. One of the unit managers tried to cope with his extra responsibility by doing all the extra work as well as the work he had traditionally undertaken. However, this was too much for him and the work he left undone was most of the extra and important work which had been delegated to him. He was quite unable to identify his new priorities and to delegate down the line, as his new boss had delegated to him. Consequently, the chief executive had to take back most of the delegated authority, recognising that the unit manager had reached his limit as far as his capacity to assume responsibility was concerned. Ironically, the chief executive was then able to delegate even more authority to the managers in the other part of the group, as they were used to coping with increased responsibility. The unit manager, who had been relieved of part of his authority, had imposed his own limit. By demonstrating his inability to cope with increased authority and responsibility, he had not only restricted his own job but ruled himself out of consideration for future promotion. In ways such as this, people can set limits on their career without necessarily realising it.

The skills of delegation

The case for delegation is easy to make. However, people may rush into delegating without effective planning. The delegated work may then be mishandled, causing the boss to withdraw the delegated authority without realising that the problem lay in the lack of planning rather than the basic idea. The factors critical to effective planning of delegation need identification and explanation. As part of this process managers may need to have established a structure within their area of responsibility so that they do not have too many people reporting directly to them. This will involve them looking at their immediate **span of control**. A historic convention was that a chief executive would have no more than six (senior) executives reporting to them, but the growing complexity of organisations is such that often managers will deal directly with more than that number. Tom Peters (1987, p. 359) envisaged a future where organisations would have a decentralised structure with front-line supervisors being directly in charge of from 25 to 75 staff. A recent factor affecting the span of control has been the ability of managers and supervisors to communicate with, and be communicated with by, employees using information technology. This seems likely to have increased the potential span of control, if not necessarily to the range Peters envisaged.

DISCRETIONARY AUTHORITY

The first critical factor is the need for clarity about just what has been delegated. A useful concept in this respect is Wilfred (later Lord) Brown's distinction between the **prescribed** and **discretionary content** of a manager's job (1965, p. 123). Prescribed work is that which must be performed in a predetermined manner. The discretionary element of a manager's job is where they are expected to use their own judgement. For example, a human resources officer could be told that they had authority to determine at what point on a given salary scale a recruit to an organisation would start. The salary range to be used, however, would be prescribed. Time and care need to be taken in defining a person's job in this way, particularly when a person has just started.

The use of discretion by employees must be tolerated, within reasonable limits. An employee cannot always be expected to perform in exactly the same way as their manager would. If that is the expectation, then the work concerned is prescribed content not discretionary content. If there is discretion, and it is used sensibly, it can be very demoralising for a employee to be told 'I wouldn't have done it quite that way'. If the discretion has been used unwisely, this may well reveal a weakness in the way the delegation was set up originally.

The appropriate use of discretionary powers may well involve considerable discussion between manager and employee. The access of the employee to the manager needs to be determined. If people are unsure of how to use their delegated powers, they may well act inappropriately or pass things back up to the manager. When items are passed up to managers, they need to consider whether they should do them or pass them back to the employee with a reminder about the employee's **discretionary authority**. When an appropriate discretionary area has been established, it is up to the manager to see that the employee gets on with their job and does not seek to over-involve them. It is important to clarify what the boss does and does not need to know.

SUBSIDIARITY

A concept that is important in the context of the European Union in particular, that has relevance to delegation, is that of **subsidiarity**. This concept involves not taking decisions at a higher level than is necessary. In the case of the EU the argument is that decisions should not be taken at EU level if they are more appropriately taken at the level of individual member countries. Similarly with regard to delegation, there is no point in having decisions taken at a higher level than is necessary. This can be particularly so if decisions can be taken just as well, or even more effectively, at a lower level and more quickly.

WHAT TO DELEGATE?

Managers need to develop criteria for judging what they do themselves and what they delegate. Useful criteria are:

- Existing arrangements for the allocation of work.
- Confidentiality.
- Complexity.
- Managers' strengths and weaknesses relative to those of their employees.
- Speed of response required.
- Availability of people to do a particular task.
- Reversibility: if a decision can be reversed quickly and easily then it may be appropriate to delegate it. The consequences of error will not be great.
- Repetition: if an issue or problem arises frequently it may be sensible to delegate it. There will be scale economies in investing time in setting up such a delegation.
- Consequences: if the impact of a decision is small, the risks involved in delegating it will be small. The case for delegation will be stronger if no important precedents are being set.
- Future commitment: future commitments can vary in resource implications and the timescale involved. The smaller the commitment and the smaller the timescale the greater the case for delegation.
- Values and image: the impact of decision-making on the image of an organisation needs to be considered. Representatives of an organisation may, for example, need to be much more carefully briefed about how they handle clients or customers, compared with their dealings with colleagues.
- Authority can only be delegated to people who, in the long run, are going to be able to cope with the delegated powers. This may in turn become a criterion in selection, so that one chooses staff who will be able to integrate effectively with the work pattern of their boss.

The use of the above criteria may also help managers to avoid rationalising about why they need to undertake a particular task. It is all too easy to pretend that a particular task has to be carried out by oneself when that may not really be the case.

ROUTING OF WORK

Care has to be taken with work that is routed to the manager but which should be done by employees. In some cases colleagues and clients will need to have it explained to them that they should go to the employees directly. On other occasions it will be entirely appropriate that the work should be routed to a manager so that the chain of command is not bypassed. If a manager's boss routes something to them, it does not automatically follow that the manager must do the job themselves: the decision as to who does it is one for the manager. In some cases, especially in high power distance cultures, offence could be caused by a manager refusing to handle a request from a colleague or client themselves. In such situations it is probably appropriate for the manager to pass the request 'down the line' themselves for action. They may then want a report back on what has happened or, if necessary, be able to report back directly to the colleague or client concerned with the outcome.

The real pattern of delegation is likely to be set by the way a manager handles routing decisions such as these. The critical question to be asked, before any work is undertaken, is 'whose job is this?' If managers fail to ask this question they can (and frequently do) get sucked into a counter-productive **micromanagement** of their area of responsibility.

The danger of established chains of command being short-circuited have been greatly increased by the development of email. This has greatly increased both the temptation for people to involve senior staff inappropriately and for senior staff to get involved in issues in a counterproductive way. This is such an important issue that a section is devoted to it in Chapter 8 on communication.

CONTROL MECHANISMS

All delegated authority needs to be accompanied by effective control mechanisms, particularly in view of the accountability of the person doing the delegating. It is difficult to envisage managers being given plenipotentiary powers, i.e. being allowed to decide crucial issues without reference to anyone. Control mechanisms can take many forms. These include:

- getting approval on specified issues before taking action;
- reporting back on issues after action has been taken;
- activity sampling by the boss;
- reporting by the employee on exceptional issues;
- appraisal systems, both informal and formal;
- visual observation;
- monitoring of results;
- inspection procedures by the boss, a separate inspection function or both;
- internal and/or external auditing;
- peer observation;
- internal and external complaints procedures.

Performance indicators are increasingly used in the public sector, in particular to monitor the progress of whole organisations.

The potential cost of lack of effective control mechanisms

Nick Leeson was a market derivatives trader employed by Barings Bank at their Singapore branch. The derivatives market is highly speculative. Nick Leeson generated dramatic profits for the group which earned both him and his superiors large bonuses. Few questions were asked about his success and there was no effective check on his activities. Unfortunately, he generated his large profits by hiding his losses in a secret account. In an attempt to cover these hidden and mounting losses he speculated increasingly large amounts of the bank's money. Eventually the scale of the losses became unsupportable. The bank collapsed in 1995 with debts of approximately £900 million. Nick Leeson was sentenced to six and a half years in prison in Singapore following his breaches of local stock exchange regulations. In upholding one of the applications in Britain by the Department of Trade and Industry for the disqualification of the directors of Barings, the judge described their lack of control as 'crass' and 'absolute'. (Evening Standard 1998, p. 4)

CONTROL OF PROFESSIONALLY QUALIFIED STAFF

There can be particular difficulties in trying to set up control systems for professionally qualified employees. This is sometimes because such employees see this as a slight on their professional independence. However, if they are funded by an organisation, they are accountable for the use of those funds. Their activity needs to be integrated with the rest of the organisation. The employment relationship is quite different from a professional working in practice on their own. The dangers of specialists indulging in meeting their objectives, which may not necessarily be the same as the organisation's, were explained in detail in Chapter 1.

A useful distinction is to hold professional employees accountable for end results but to leave it to them as to how they achieve the results. In some cases, it is necessary to set up systems for monitoring the quality of professional work. This is an issue that is of particular concern in hospitals because of the issues of public and legal liability and the potential seriousness of poor quality work. It has led to the concept of 'clinical governance'. The need for this was underlined following a report in 1998 of an investigation into the deaths of 29 babies after heart surgery at Bristol Royal Infirmary. The need for further controls over the way general medical practitioners operate, in the UK at least, was dramatically emphasised when, in 2000, Dr Harold Shipman was convicted of murdering 15 of his patients. The total estimate of the patients he killed was a minimum of 250 (Smith 2005). These and other medical scandals led doctors themselves to pass a motion of no confidence in the work of the body responsible for monitoring medical standards, the General Medical Council, at the annual conference of the British Medical Association in 2000. The system of **peer audit** has been developed in both medical and university teaching as one way of increasing the quality control of professionals working in these areas. This technique is considered further in Chapter 10.

USE OF DEPUTIES

Delegation can be achieved by the appointment of a deputy or deputies. However, such arrangements need thinking through or they can be counterproductive. If a person is appointed as a full-time deputy, it begs the question of what the person does whilst the boss is available. It can be something of a luxury to have a permanent understudy available but not necessarily used. Such an arrangement would also be very frustrating for a deputy of any ability. If the arrangement of routing everything through a deputy is used, it raises the question of just what is the value of such a duplication of activity. This can generate rivalry and competition for what may really be only one job.

Normally deputies would carry ongoing responsibilities as well as being asked to 'act up' when the boss is not available. However, there needs to be a very clear understanding between the boss and the deputy about the demarcation between their jobs. Other employees also need to know these arrangements so that they are able to route issues to the correct person.

There is a case for avoiding the title of deputy because of the confusion it can cause. Instead, a manager may designate who is to act as deputy when they are not available. It may be appropriate to ask just one person to **act up** or to have employees act up according to defined areas of responsibility.

Sometimes deputies are used to support a manager who is under pressure. However, before such an arrangement is used, thought needs to be given as to whether there are better solutions or not. This may involve other forms of work reorganisation or a review of the abilities of the manager under pressure. If the boss is replaced by a more capable person, there may no longer be any need for a deputy. However, the continuing need for a deputy may be a question people forget to ask in such a situation.

Failure to use a deputy and other senior staff

Example

The chief executive of a large hospital was overworked and a deputy was appointed to ease his workload. However, the deputy was not given enough work to do and soon left. Another deputy was appointed. He had turned down the chance of running a small hospital to gain experience in a large one. However, he also found that he was not given enough to do. The chief executive encouraged people to come to him directly. Most mail was routed to him, even though it might take a day for him to look at it. He also sometimes countermanded the orders of employees, including those given by his 'deputy'. To compound these problems, the chief executive sometimes criticised his deputy to others because of his lack of experience and because he maintained that he was not prepared to work as hard as he did.

The pattern of activity continued, and little long-term planning or strategic thinking took place. The newly appointed deputy began to look around for another job. Heads of department were generally either frustrated by their lack of delegated authority or were content to let much of their work be handled by the chief executive. He was sent on a four-week management-training course. This, however, did not lead to any change in his behaviour. He came into the hospital on Saturdays during this period to check what was happening and to deal with urgent business.

TRAINING AND DELEGATION

Delegating authority to others may well be accompanied by a need to train them in the way in which that authority is to be used. It is no good delegating authority to a subordinate unless they know what to do. All too often this stage is omitted and managers exclaim that people won't assume authority. There may be a need to start training well in advance of the delegation. Training needs to combine the substantive knowledge and skills required by the employee in their job with a careful definition of just what constitutes their job.

Training can be formal, informal or both. A useful convention is that when people with managerial responsibilities are absent their employees act up. This is as opposed to the manager in charge of the person absent acting down. Acting up can leave managers free to concentrate on high priority work, develop employees and help identify promotion potential. Unfortunately, sometimes managers are only too keen to **act down** because it enables them to engage in their historic and preferred specialist activity.

Obstacles to effective delegation

Even when people recognise the advantages of delegation and are aware of the skills involved in planning it effectively, they may still not delegate to the extent to which they should. There are a number of barriers to effective delegation – usually these are a lot easier to recognise in others than in oneself. Also, these are sometimes not so much barriers as genuine constraints. Sometimes it can be very difficult to disentangle imagined from real constraints.

TIME

Paradoxically, and as previously explained, delegation may initially be time-consuming. In particular, significant time may need to be spent in:

- identifying what is to be delegated,
- establishing appropriate control procedures,
- briefing and training employees.

Delegation is like a capital investment: time spent setting it up may achieve substantial dividends – but only in the future. If the manager does not carefully think through the pattern of delegation, it may backfire and discourage them from further attempts.

LACK OF TRAINING

Many managers are not trained in how to manage. They may either lack formal training or the ability to learn and develop on the job under the guidance of managers. Even those managers who have received formal training may not have been trained in delegation. Despite its importance, it is often quite wrongly assumed that delegation does not need to feature in management training programmes.

FACTORS OUTSIDE THE MANAGER'S CONTROL

There can be a number of genuine constraints preventing or limiting the ability of managers to delegate. These include:

- lack of resources, particularly of employee staff – shortages of staff can be in terms of quantity, quality or both;
- an organisational climate that discourages delegation;
- their own lack of authority;
- lack of work to do anyway;
- jealousy between employees;
- over-ambitious employees;
- pressures to do particular tasks themselves that it would be counterproductive to resist;
- confidentiality.

MANAGERIAL INSECURITY

Although there can be genuine limits on the extent to which delegation can be implemented, some managers simply do not want to delegate. Often the greatest obstacle to delegation is the psychological insecurity of a manager. If this is the case, attempts to train a manager to delegate, or exhortations to delegate, may simply fail. One of the problems with management training generally is that managers have to integrate good management practice with their own personality.

Example of false alibi of staff not taking responsibility

Example

A college principal had all the college mail addressed to him personally. He would open the envelopes and, when rerouting mail to subordinate staff, instruct them on what action to take. This enabled him to complain that no-one else in the college worked as hard as he did or was prepared to assume responsibility. The fact was, of course, that he would not permit anyone else to take responsibility. One of the psychological payoffs in this game was that if one starts with the assumption that one's employees are no good, this can then become a self-fulfilling prophecy – as good staff will be driven away. However, there was some progress in the case of the college principal. Eventually, his secretary was allowed to open the envelopes before the principal himself took out the enclosures!

THE INDISPENSABLE EMPLOYEE

Sometimes people can deliberately seek to make themselves indispensable. This may be a means of managers dealing with their feelings of personal insecurity. A rough guide to the competence of a manager is to see how well things work when they are absent. The effective manager should have developed systems and staff abilities so that people can cope in their absence. This may not be the case with the ineffective manager. The poor manager may even be glad that things have not gone well in their absence and even publicise that fact. The creation of a state of indispensability may be subconscious or carefully planned.

Example

Contrived indispensability

An engineer in a local authority set out to make himself indispensable. Some of the maps of the local underground drainage system had been destroyed and he was the only person who knew the exact location of all the drains. He consistently refused to commit his knowledge to paper on the basis that as long as only he knew the complete layout the council would not dismiss him. When it was put to him that if he suddenly fell ill or died the lack of a full record would cause obvious problems, he responded by saying that that would not be his problem!

Example

Accidental indispensability

The head of the avionics division of an electronics company managed his division very effectively for 27 years. Unfortunately he became so good at his job that when he retired nobody could be found who could replace him. Ironically, had he been less good at his job a management system might have evolved that could have survived his retirement. As it was the division had to be closed down.

Empowerment

BACKGROUND

The concept of **empowerment** has become increasingly fashionable in recent years. The term seems to have originated in the USA when Democratic administrations in the 1960s were seeking to build 'The Great Society'. It was a response by government to the need for disadvantaged groups to have more control over their lives with a view to improving them. These groups particularly included ethnic minorities and the physically and mentally challenged. It was a bottom-up process.

Subsequently, the term 'empowerment' was increasingly used in the business world. Authority was often devolved to lower levels of management to help achieve business objectives. However, this was a top-down process. It coincided with many other trends, which included delayering, downsizing, and loss of faith in centralised planning. These trends were associated with an increased pace of change because of **globalisation** and the increasing use of new technology. The practice spread to the public sector, partly as a means of devolving the difficult prioritisation that was necessary when expectations outstripped available funds.

DEFINITION

A problem with the term 'empowerment' is what people actually mean when they use it. Michael Armstrong (1991) defines it as:

> Ensuring that people are able to use and develop their skills and knowledge in ways that help to achieve both their own goals and those of the organisation. Empowerment is achieved by organisation and job design approaches which place responsibility fairly on individuals and teams, by recognising the contribution people can make, by providing mechanisms such as improvement groups to enable them to make this contribution and by training and development programmes which increase both competence and confidence.
>
> (Armstrong 1991, p. 123)

EMPOWERMENT IN PRACTICE

Even if people are clear what they mean by empowerment, it may be implemented poorly or applied in situations where it is inappropriate. Unfortunately, the term is often used very loosely or applied with a messianic zeal as though it were an end in itself, instead of a means of helping to achieve organisational objectives. It is not a concept that should be applied regardless of circumstances. A particular danger is that those seeking to apply it may ignore the potential for conflict between individual or sectional objectives and those of the rest of the organisation. This fundamental issue is explained under the heading **unitary** and **pluralistic frames of reference** in Chapters 4 and 14.

In many organisations that have introduced greater employee empowerment there is a strong internal social and cultural control to ensure that, for example, semi-autonomous work groups perform in a way that is congruent with organisational goals. Empowering people without thinking through the implications, however, could be disastrous. The example, given earlier in this chapter, of the lack of control of the derivatives market trader Nick Leeson dramatically illustrates this point. The tendency of specialists with managerial responsibility to go their own way has been documented in Chapter 1. It is perhaps also worth making a point about the dangers of self-regulation by referring to groups such as doctors, lawyers, newspaper editors and stockbrokers. It is arguable that the interests of these groups have sometimes been allowed to have a higher priority than that of other interest groups, including the public, by virtue of their self-regulatory arrangements.

Another aspect of empowerment is that it is sometimes associated with organisational downsizing. This can create genuine opportunities for empowerment for the remaining managers. However, if the downsizing is badly thought out, it can mean managers having to try and pick up the pieces of a restructuring exercise without the necessary resources, direction, or extra remuneration to handle their new responsibilities adequately.

KEY QUESTIONS

Key questions to ask to see if people are clear about actual or proposed empowerment arrangements are:

- Is it seen as an end in itself or as a means of helping to achieve organisational objectives?
- Are management control procedures still required?
- Exactly what authority is being delegated and to whom?
- What resources are being allocated to the person or unit that is empowered to enable them to achieve their objectives?
- How does the empowered unit or person interrelate with existing authority structures?
- What happens if there are conflicts of objectives between the person or unit empowered and the overall organisation?

Summary

Delegation has been defined as 'a person giving authority to someone to act on their behalf'. However, whilst authority can be delegated, the person who delegates remains accountable for the actions of the person to whom they delegate. Delegation frees up time for the manager to concentrate on the key aspects of their job. It can also be used as a means of developing employees. Key skills that have been identified include:

- the need to clarify the discretionary authority of employees,
- identifying what to delegate,
- routing work to the right people,
- establishing appropriate control mechanisms,
- selection and training of employees.

Initially, implementing delegation takes time, and so it is time-consuming. As with all investments, the potential rewards are not immediate but will be evident in the future. The many obstacles to delegation have been examined. Some of them may be legitimate, such as a lack of staff. Unfortunately, the biggest obstacle can be the personal insecurity of some managers.

Delegation overlaps with the concept of empowerment. A key difference between the two concepts can be that it involves conferring authority on groups of people. However, the term 'empowerment' is often used very loosely and it is often necessary to find out exactly what people mean when they use the term. It is also necessary to recognise the potential for conflict between empowered groups or individuals and overall organisational objectives.

Self-assessment questions

(If you wish to check the extent to which your answer to any of the following questions is appropriate, cross-refer to the Table of Contents. The contents for this chapter are on pages xiii–xiv.)

1 How would you define delegation?

2 Why is delegation a core management skill?

3 How would you decide whether a particular activity should be delegated or not?

4 What are the main obstacles in practice to effective delegation?

5 Identify the differences between the concepts of delegation and empowerment.

References

Armstrong, Michael (1991), *A Handbook of Personnel Management Practice*, 4th ed., Kogan Page.

Brown, Wilfred (1965), *Exploration in Management*, Pelican.

Castle, C. and A. Grice (1999), articles in The Independent, 17 March.

Evening Standard (1998), *Business ban on bungling Barings chiefs*, London, 1 December.

McLean, I. (1999), *Heartless bully who added to the agony of Aberfan*, The Observer, 5 January.

Peters, Thomas (1987), *Thriving on Chaos*, Pan.

Smith, Dame Janet (27 January 2005), *The Sixth and Final Report*, Published by the Shipman Inquiry.

Motivation

Introduction

In this chapter the variety of reasons why people work are examined. It is important to consider the range of reasons because it is all too easy for incorrect assumptions to be made. If the diagnosis of reasons for poor performance is inappropriate corrective action may be taken. Behavioural theories concerning motivation and the practical uses that can be made of these theories are considered. The potential impact of national culture on motivation is also covered. The motivational implications of job design are examined, as is the concept of **job distortion**. A key issue is the extent to which job demands and individual needs can be reconciled.

Increasing market turbulence is causing some employers to introduce flexible employment policies. This can cause employer commitment to reduce whilst expecting an increase in employee commitment. The accelerating pace of change may be one factor causing increasing stress at work. Managers need to protect both themselves and their subordinates from undue stress. Whilst some attention is given to the role of money as a motivator, it is considered in more detail in Chapter 7.

Work performance

Maximising work performance can be defined as 'providing the right conditions for people to work effectively'. One aspect of maximising work performance will involve motivation. Motivation overlaps with the concept of morale, which is a measure of the extent to which employees feel positively or negatively about their work. While levels of performance and morale are usually positively correlated this is not always the case. There can be cases of people performing well under authoritarian but competent managers, perhaps out of fear, but who feel badly about their work. Similarly you can have instances of people doing as they please and enjoying it but not meeting organisational objectives. Ideally what is needed is a good match between the person and the job. Also, what most people may want is to have a comfortable amount of challenge, a good boss, good pay and security. Unfortunately, this is not always possible. However, often a better match is possible between individual needs and organisational requirements than is actually achieved.

DIAGNOSIS OF REASONS FOR POOR PERFORMANCE

If people are not working effectively, or in some cases not working at all, it may be the match between job and person that needs to be examined, not just one of those factors. Some people may never work effectively under any circumstances. Some jobs will always pose motivational problems whoever is supposed to be doing them. However, it is also likely that there are circumstances under which most people will work effectively, just as there are circumstances under which the same people will not work effectively. Similarly, with many jobs there may be people who will perform effectively and other people who will perform ineffectively. If there is a problem of ineffective performance it is necessary to establish if it is the person, the job or the matching of the two. Remedial action depends on the diagnosis. It may be that, in the short-term, neither can be changed. If that is so, attention will need to be paid to either the type of person selected in the future, the job structure or both, according to the diagnosis of the reasons for poor performance.

The need for accurate diagnosis has been stressed because it is all too easy for the diagnosis of reasons for poor performance to be faulty. It is a subjective area. The very criteria for judging effective work performance may be difficult to establish, as was demonstrated in the section on the definition of work objectives in Chapter 2. It can be vital to analyse situations in role and not personality terms, as was explained in Chapter 3. If the blame is put on the person working ineffectively, then that absolves the boss, who may then fail to see the connection if the next person in the job also performs badly. In some cases the fault will be with the person doing the job.

However, it is important not to automatically assume that this is the case. When the fault is not with the job-holder, there may be uncomfortable implications for the boss. The onus may then be on them to examine the job structure or the support given to the job-holder.

The following checklist may be useful in establishing the reasons for poor performance:

- Job design;
- Work organisation: this can cover a wide range of factors, including lack of appropriate equipment, shortage of raw materials, poor work flow, inadequate support and incompetent management;
- Selection: it may be necessary to examine the match between people's abilities and needs with job requirements;
- Training; this may be inadequate.
- Expectations: the expectations of both employer and employee may need reviewing and also the extent to which promises have been kept;
- Pay.

ASSUMPTIONS ABOUT WHY PEOPLE WORK

Alternative sets of assumptions that managers may have about why people work were identified in Chapter 4 in the explanation of Douglas McGregor's concepts of Theory X and Theory Y. The implicit assumptions that managers make may or may not be appropriate in relation to particular situations. As well as not necessarily knowing why other people work, managers may generalise on the basis of bad examples with particular individuals which may not even be very representative of the individuals concerned. The faulty generalisations made by managers can result in them either assuming the worst of their employees, or in other circumstances assuming that work is being done when more direction and control is actually needed.

QUESTIONNAIRE

To check your assumptions about why people work, complete the following questionnaire. Rank the reasons for why you think staff who work, or have worked, for you actually do work. If that is not possible, choose another group of people whom you know. You may need to do some averaging to choose your rankings:

Reasons why people work

- Chance to use initiative at work
- Good working conditions
- Good working companions
- Good boss
- Steady, safe employment

- Money
- Good hours
- Interest in the work itself
- Opportunity for advancement
- Getting credit and recognition

When you have completed the questionnaire redo it, but this time identify the reasons why you work, also ranked in order of importance. When you have done this, compare the two rankings.

What usually happens is that managers rank three factors more highly for themselves than for their staff. The factors that managers rank highly for themselves are: the chance to use initiative at work, interest in the work itself and the opportunity for advancement. What also usually happens is that managers rank three factors more highly for their staff than for themselves. These are money, steady, safe employment and security. It may be that your responses do not conform to this general pattern. Even if they do, this may be for perfectly valid reasons. When managers examine their own reasons for working they are in a position to make informed judgements because of their self-knowledge. This may not be the case when they make assumptions about why other people work, and they may consequently make uncharitable assumptions about the reasons for others working or not working.

Even if they are accurate, other managers may make inaccurate assumptions, and this may affect motivational strategies. Sometimes, however, managers may make the reverse mistake. This can easily happen in small businesses. Proprietors may almost completely identify with their business and assume that their employees do, or should do, the same. The point may be missed that whilst the proprietor may make many sacrifices for the business, it is also the proprietor who will reap most of the financial and psychological rewards if the business prospers. It is also necessary to take into account the concept of **job instrumentality**. This can involve employers or employees carefully calculating the least they need to do to secure their objectives and then behaving accordingly.

Example

An example of job instrumentality

A firm making car components in the UK recruited a significant number of immigrants for production work. The employees that they recruited were often of a high calibre and performed well. Many of the recruits had high educational standards and the firm, knowingly or unknowingly, had 'over-selected' in terms of ability to do the job. After a while a serious and increasing problem of absenteeism emerged. Investigation revealed that many of the employees had understandable ambitions to better themselves in their new country. When they had accumulated some capital some of them took increasing amounts of time off in order to develop their own small commercial enterprises. This was with a view to developing their businesses sufficiently to work in them full-time. The more their businesses developed, the more risks they were prepared to take with their full-time job.

It may be possible to classify managerial strategies for motivation into one of the four following categories:

- coercion;
- calculated compliance;
- cooperation: this is likely to include a problem-solving approach and some involvement in decision-making;
- commitment: this can overlap substantially with a cooperative strategy.

Which strategy is used will depend on managerial assumptions about why people work, organisational circumstances or a combination of both.

Theories of motivation

It is necessary to have an understanding of some of the more important theories relating to motivation. Although the theories that will be examined are not particularly new, nor beyond methodological criticism, they are important and do have relevance to current problems and initiatives.

MASLOW

Abraham Maslow (1970) provides a very useful theory for examining individual motivation. He suggests that individual needs are arranged in a hierarchy. The lower-level needs must be satisfied before people concern themselves with higher-level needs. Hunger is seen as a basic need, even more important than safety. When one need is met, people proceed to try and meet their next need. The third level of needs is social, followed by status. The highest level of need is self-actualisation, which involves self-development by successfully responding to challenges. It is the next factor that can be satisfied that acts as a motivator, like a carrot being held in front of a donkey. If threats emerge to a lower-level need that has previously been satisfied, individuals will refocus their activity to protect the lower-level need.

Figure 6.1 illustrates the theory in a very simplified form. The actual pattern of needs will vary from person to person. There may be trade-offs between meeting needs at different levels. For example, some people may be prepared to take some risks with their safety in order to meet higher-levels needs, such as self-actualisation. The level of need can vary from person to person, e.g. the amount of status satisfaction that is desired. Also, needs are likely to vary over time and according to situational requirements. A person with considerable domestic commitments may not be too concerned with self-actualisation in their job. However, if their domestic commitments are met, they may then wish to achieve self-actualisation and to accept greater work responsibilities in an attempt to meet that need.

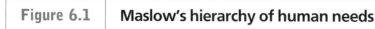

| Figure 6.1 | **Maslow's hierarchy of human needs** |

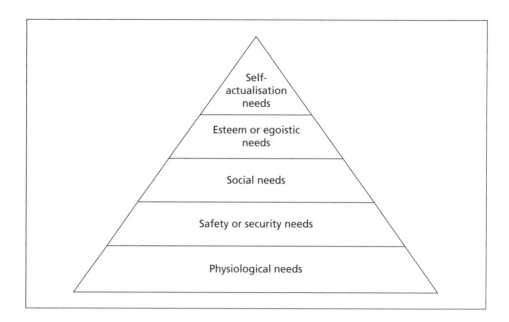

According to McClelland (1961), the need to achieve self-actualisation may critically depend on social conditioning during childhood.

Despite the qualifications inherent in Maslow's hierarchy, his ideas lend themselves to practical application. It can help to see that people's needs are matched to job requirements. Ways in which this can be done are job design, selection, training and promotion.

HERZBERG

The work of Frederick Herzberg (1960) complements that of Maslow. He conducted research into the motivational factors affecting engineers and accountants working in the USA. Herzberg grouped the responses into the factors that caused dissatisfaction. The factors that were found most likely to cause negative feelings (dissatisfiers) were generally external to the job. These are:

- company policy and administration,
- supervision,
- interpersonal relations,
- status,
- salary,

- security,
- impact of the job on personal life.

In contrast, the factors most likely to cause positive feelings about the job (satisfiers) were intrinsic to the job. These are:

- achievement,
- recognition of achievement,
- responsibility,
- advancement,
- interesting work,
- possibility of growth.

The absence of dissatisfiers was not enough to cause positive satisfaction. These tend to only operate in a negative way. For example, if office facilities are poor, that could cause strong negative feelings about the job. If the facilities were improved, that could remove a cause of irritation but would not normally be enough to cause positive feelings about the job. Herzberg termed the potential dissatisfiers 'hygiene factors', related to the context in which a job was done. He argued that it is important to pay attention to these issues, but the opportunity for a measure of self-actualisation generally needs to be built into the content of a job if positive feelings are to be created. These 'motivators' require people to have the opportunity to be stretched in their jobs, through overcoming challenges. However, if the challenges are too high, this could cause negative feelings because of failure. Also, there is the danger that challenges that are too demanding may interfere with domestic life.

The opportunity for success or failure can arise out of the same set of circumstances, and the dividing line between the two can be very small.

The thin line between success and failure

Example

The Indonesian captain of an oil tanker said that his most positive feelings about his job were when he had successfully and very skilfully navigated his ship through a typhoon off Hong King when many ships had been sunk. His most negative feelings about the job were experienced shortly afterwards when the ship's agent came on board and carefully checked all the damage but neglected to enquire or comment about the risks that had been experienced by the captain and his crew.

The role of money, according to Herzberg, is that it is primarily a hygiene factor. Inadequate salary could generate strong negative feelings and cause a person to leave their job. However, a good salary was found not generally to lead to strong positive feelings about a job. Paying people more money won't increase performance if organisational obstacles prevent them working more effectively. Also, there is a danger that paying people more money will increase frustration levels by increasing the difference between ability levels and job demands. This issue is examined further in the section on job design later in this chapter. Account needs to be taken of variations in people's desire for money, their circumstances and the fact that some jobs may lend themselves to, or require, financial inducements more than others.

The practical implications of Herzberg's work are considerable. The basic message is: don't ignore the hygiene factors but don't stop there. People may want considerable involvement in their job for their own self-development. Employers may find that this is a source of considerable energy that is available. Conversely, underutilised employees may engage in potentially destructive activity.

Example

The devil finds work for idle hands

Before the general introduction of speed cameras to detect speeding offences some traffic police in the UK allegedly booked vehicles in the same colour sequence as though as they were playing a game of snooker in order to relieve their boredom.

It is necessary to be cautious in generalising about the relevance of Herzberg's work. There have been methodological criticisms of it, particularly because of his reliance on the critical incident technique, which only established the highs and lows in the attitudes of employees to their jobs. Also his research was conducted some time ago and only with professional-level employees working in the USA. Furthermore, not everyone wants to, or is able to, concentrate on meeting the higher-level need of self-actualisation. This can be for a number of reasons, including preoccupation with meeting lower-level needs. National culture can also be important, and the potential importance of this factor is examined in greater detail later in this chapter.

Herzberg's work, however, can provide a very useful framework for trying to match individual needs to job requirements. The distinction between intrinsic job factors relating to the job content, which can cause positive satisfaction, and external factors relating to the job context, which can cause negative job attitudes, is important and can be put to practical effect.

If people want the opportunity for self-development, the most important thing for managers to do may be to set up their work so that it provides a challenge, then help see that the challenge is met. Excessive help may be counterproductive. The main payoff with human relations skills may to avoid unnecessarily upsetting employees. The control of the manager over work content will vary, but it is something that usually demands close attention. It may be one of the few important factors that managers can influence. Factors such as organisation policy, pay and working conditions may be outside their control. One of the problems for the prospective employee is that it is much easier to judge job context – for example salary, fringe benefits and working conditions – rather than more elusive factors such as independence within the job.

Consequently, recruits may only find out after they have started whether a job really has positive motivational features or not.

EXPECTANCY THEORIES

Another perspective that needs to be integrated with the previously explained theories is that provided by the expectancy school of motivational theorists. The expectancy approach attempts to overcome one of the criticisms of other motivational theories by accounting for individual differences. The expectancy model of Nadler and Lawler (1977, p. 27) has three major components. These are:

- Performance-outcome: this concerns the outcome that individual employees expect from certain behaviour.
- Valence: this is the value that employees put on the outcome which they are expecting from particular behaviour – this will determine the motivating strength of a particular reward.
- Effort-performance expectancy: these are the expectations of how difficult it will be to perform successfully, which will affect people's reaction to a particular incentive. The logic is that employees will select the level of performance that seems to have the best chance of achieving an outcome they value.

It follows that it is necessary to check whether the reward system in an organisation actually works in the way that it is intended to work. It is no good, for example, expecting to motivate people by offering incremental salary increases or promotion on the basis of merit if the reality is that such rewards are based on seniority or some other factor not connected with merit. Employees are likely to make judgements about what reward system really operates by what they believe is actually happening, rather than by statements of organisational policy. Even if rewards are based significantly on merit it is necessary to convince people of that, as motivation is likely to depend on what people perceive to be happening. It is also necessary to review how equitably rewards are distributed. Even if people are inclined to respond to a particular incentive, they may be discouraged from doing so by perceived unfairness in the way in which rewards are distributed. The relationships between the rewards given to different people may therefore need to be examined, as well as the size of the rewards. The gap between intended and actual reward systems can be alarmingly high. As is explained in the next chapter, some can degenerate into arrangements for restricting rather than increasing performance.

SOCIO-TECHNICAL SYSTEMS THEORY

This topic was given some attention in Chapter 3 in the context of organisational design but needs further consideration in the context of motivation. A number of writers have described the **socio-technical systems** that exist in workplaces. They have also commented about the disruptive effect that changes in work methods can have on social systems at work. Such changes can, in turn, affect motivation and levels of work performance. Seminal work in this area was done by Trist and Bamforth (1951, pp. 3–38). (See also Trist et al. 1963.)

The negative impact of technological change on team working

Trist and Bamforth (1951) examined the impact of the new longwall mechanised method of coal mining. This was far superior technically to the old board and pillar system. However, the new system involved people working in relative isolation from one another along a conveyor belt. The work was also made more special-ised and repetitive. This was far less socially satisfying than the teams of two or three who had previously hand-cut coal in recesses in the seams and who had carried out a wider range of activities. The previous arrangement had also involved a high acceptance of responsibility for the safety of one another. Adjust-ments were successfully made in the new system to try and deal with the problems of production, absen-teeism and safety that had risen.

The compromise solution involved forming small groups along the conveyor belt and was known as the 'shortwall method'. However, the partial restoration of semi-autonomous work groups had to be a practical option both technically and economically. Change in itself is neutral and can have positive or negative effects or a combination of the two. Sometimes the technical advantages of systems, such as vehicle as-sembly lines, outweigh the social disadvantages. Sometimes, though, as in the example given, it is pos-sible to modify the technical system to take into account social and psychological needs. They key to doing this is to recognise the social dimension of tech-nical changes.

IMPACT OF NATIONAL CULTURE

When considering theories of motivation and seeking to improve employee motivation via reward structures or redesigned jobs, the potential impact of national culture needs to be taken into account. Most theories of motivation are based on experience in the United States. These theories are usually based on the assumption that employees have the same values as those in American society – high levels of individualism, low power distances, relatively high masculin-ity and a consequent emphasis on material values. Using Hofstede's (2001) terminology, those working in an individualist culture may value opportunities for individual promotion and growth, while more collectivist cultures value opportunities to belong to an influential group. Employees in collectivist cultures may not be highly motivated by reward systems based on individual effort which undermine the importance of the group. In Western societies there is also much more opportunity for self-actualisation than in developing countries where, for those struggling for survival, concepts such as self-actualisation may be meaningless.

Examples of cultural norms and their impact on pay

At Beijing Jeep, a joint venture between AMC and Bei-jing Automative Works, some workers willingly gave up their pay rises in order to appease the resentment of less productive colleagues. (Mead 2005, p. 127)

In Thailand, the introduction of an individual merit bonus plan, which runs counter to the societal norm

of group cooperation, may result in a decline rather than an increase in productivity from employees who openly refuse to compete with one another.

(Rieger and Wong-Rieger 1990, p. 1, reported in Mead 2005, p. 123)

Mead points out (2005) that as national cultures change, due perhaps to economic advancement, so value systems may alter. He gives the example of changes in Chinese society where it was apparent that it had become acceptable to make money for one's own gratification rather than just in the service of society.

Job Design

One of the major implications of the theoretical perspectives discussed in this chapter, particularly Herzberg's, is that considerable attention needs to be given to human needs in job design. The tradition set by the advocates of scientific management, such as F. W. Taylor was, however, to simplify work as much as possible. This enabled employees to be selected and trained to undertake repetitive tasks. This approach later became known as **Fordism**. It did, though, ignore factors such as boredom and social needs. The Hawthorne experiments of 1927–32 demonstrated that social factors could play an important part in motivating employees to achieve high performance (Sheldrake 1996, Ch. 11). (See also Chapter 3 of this book.) Later approaches are taken into account in the rest of this chapter, particularly the need to reconcile individual needs with job demands to the extent that that is possible.

ERGONOMICS

Ergonomics involves looking at the job and person in relation to one another as a combined unit. This is in contrast to designing a job and then expecting to find someone who will be both willing and able to adapt to its requirements.

Making the worker fit the job!

Procrustes was a legendary figure in Greek mythology who had a special bed. He was obsessive about guests fitting his bed exactly. If they were too long for the bed, he cut off their feet; if they were too small, he stretched them on a rack until they fitted. Allegedly the Procrustean approach was used in the engineering industry in the design of some capstan lathe machines. This was because some were best operated by people who were 4 feet 6 inches in height but with the arm span of a gorilla!

Example

The use of the concept of ergonomics can be particularly important in the design of capital equipment so that, for example, instrument panels and other signals are arranged so as to minimise the risk of misreading. It can also be of vital importance in the design of high-performance military equipment. Good design can make all the difference in the achievement or non-achievement of objectives. It can also mean the difference between life and death for the personnel using the equipment on operational or even training missions.

Figure 6.2	The skill pyramid

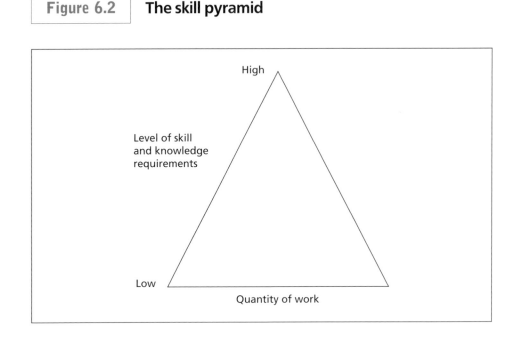

MARKETING OF JOBS

A useful concept to apply to job design is that of marketing. Companies would soon get into financial difficulties if they designed products without regard for customer needs. Similarly with jobs, it is necessary to consider who would want to do them, or do them well. If jobs are particularly boring, for example, there may be problems in recruiting, motivating and retaining staff. Options may be to consider if jobs can either be made less boring, or automated out of existence. Jobs also need to have internal coherence and viability. They need to be assessed as a whole and the questions asked as to who would be able to and want to do such a job. Consideration may also need to be given to how long a job will stay in its present form. If it is likely to change significantly, that may affect the required range of skills and adaptability of applicants. The problem of contradictory job demands also needs to be taken into account. This issue is considered in detail in the next section.

BASIC JOB STRUCTURE

Basic issues in job design include the range of skills required and the compatibility of the tasks. Many jobs contain a large element of routine activity but some demanding work as well. This is true in jobs as diverse as skilled manual workers and general medical practitioners. This issue is illustrated in Figure 6.2.

A motivational problem for jobs that have a large element of routine work and a small amount of complicated work is that the capable person may get bored with the routine work. It may also may be unnecessarily expensive in terms of their salary level. The capable person may

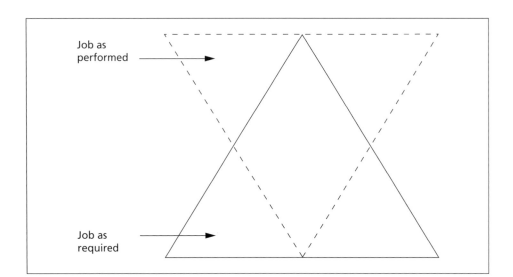

Job distortion | **Figure 6.3**

Job as performed

Job as required

also spend too much time on the work they find interesting. Conversely, the person who finds the routine work satisfying may not be very good at the complicated work. Unfortunately, some jobs need to be designed like this for safety reasons. Airline pilots, for example, have to be able to cope with emergencies that it is hoped will never happen. A way of reducing the boredom in skilled jobs can be to hive off aspects of the work so that auxiliary staff can undertake them under proper supervision. Examples of this are the use of practice nurses in general medical practices and dental hygienists in dental surgeries.

A related concept is that of skill mix. This involves comparing the skills actually needed to perform a job and those that job-holders actually have. There needs to be an accurate match so that people on the one hand have the skills to do their jobs, but on the other hand are not performing work that could more cheaply and more satisfyingly be performed by others.

JOB DISTORTION

Job distortion can occur when a job is rearranged in a way that satisfies the needs of the organisation but not the individual. If, for example, a graduate is recruited to perform routine clerical work they may be initially glad to have the job. However, the graduate may rapidly get bored because of the lack of intellectual stimulation. They may then expand the more interesting parts of the job and ignore the less demanding parts. The greater the gap between the demands of the job and the ability level of the job-holder, the more the temptation to try and alter the job. This process is illustrated in Figure 6.3. The continuous lines represent the boundaries of the job that the organisation requires to be performed, whilst the broken lines represent the boundaries of the job as it actually is performed.

Example

Inappropriate job enlargement

The process and dangers of job distortion are particularly well illustrated by the example of a young man employed to collect and distribute the post in a local authority directorate. The mail in the directorate kept on being distributed later and later. Officers found that if they had to leave their offices before lunchtime, it might be the following day before they got their morning mail. Investigation revealed that the job-holder had been doing the job for five years and had got very bored with it. Consequently, he had taken to reading the mail before he distributed it. He also used the mail round as an opportunity to talk to friends and organise social events. Because of his reputation for being slow with the mail, no one had been prepared to give him a more demanding job.

The mismatch between individual and organisational needs should have been addressed long before. This could have been by restructuring the job so that it was combined with other work, limiting the time that a person spent doing that work, or employing someone who would have been less frustrated with the work. A further approach would have been to eliminate the job by requiring departments to organise the collection and distribution of their own mail.

Another pressure which can create job distortion can be the frustration of a person who considers that they should have a job more in line with their ability level within the same organisation. This can particularly happen if a person feels that they have outgrown their job.

Too many cooks

Some of the directors in an organisation concerned with the distribution of public grants were concerned about the lack of career opportunities for capable secretaries. It was proposed to upgrade some of them to positions as personal assistants (PA) to the directors. Juniors were to be recruited to undertake the more routine aspects of their work. However, it emerged that there was not enough of the more demanding work to justify the PA's having full-time junior assistants. The real solution was to encourage the more capable secretaries to undertake specialist or professional training so that they could apply for genuinely more demanding jobs, either in the organisation or elsewhere.

A further cause of job distortion can be differing views on what needs doing in a job. The danger of managers spending too much time on their historic specialism and ignoring important managerial responsibilities was dealt with at length in Chapter 1. People may even find that the organisation of activities that are clearly against their employer's interests provides both psychological and material rewards. The adrenaline can run for a person perpetrating a fraud just as it can for honest employees who develop themselves in their employer's interests instead of attempting to outwit the employer.

JOB ENLARGEMENT, JOB ROTATION AND JOB ENRICHMENT

Job enlargement

Job enlargement is a generic term used to indicate an increase in the number of tasks within a job. This can be achieved by increasing the range of activities, increasing the responsibility level or both. Job rotation and job enrichment can be aspects of job enlargement.

Job rotation

Job rotation involves a horizontal broadening of the job without increasing the level of responsibility. It can be useful in reducing the monotony factor. One example is the rotation of staff working at leisure centres who may move from supervising one sporting activity to another every few hours. A potential disadvantage is when this is disruptive of social relationships at work. Also, it does not make jobs inherently more interesting.

Job enrichment

Job enrichment involves a vertical increase in the level of responsibility within a job. Sometimes this can be accomplished informally, for example, by a manager delegating more. The practice of having someone act up whilst the boss is away is an example of a temporary form of job enrichment. The ability of managers to delegate varies considerably and this factor is likely to influence the motivation and development of subordinates significantly. The concept of delegation was examined in detail in Chapter 5.

SELECTION, TRAINING AND PAY

When jobs have been sensibly designed it is then necessary to consider how people are selected, trained and paid for them. The danger of over-selection is a recurring issue. Ideally what is needed is a good match between the demands of the job and the abilities and motivation of the job-holder. Sometimes, however, organisations over-recruit on the basis of status instead of trying to get a good match between person and job

Appointments based on status

The newly appointed head of an engineering company's research department announced that he was only prepared to engage research staff who had good and relevant honours degrees. Investigation revealed, however, that much of the work that needed to be done was routine and would more appropriately be undertaken by technicians operating under the guidance of more qualified staff.

Example

When people have been selected it is necessary to consider their training needs. It can be highly demotivating for a person not to be able to perform effectively because they have not been trained adequately. This is also likely to be costly to the organisation. Adequate training is not only likely to improve performance and reduce labour turnover, but also enhance the status of a job.

Sometimes employers respond to the problems of retaining staff on boring work by increasing their pay. However, a danger of doing this is that they attract more able staff who get even more bored with the job even more quickly. This can also happen when employees use their bargaining strength to force up their wages.

Example

How bargaining power can increase boredom

Train drivers in the UK are well-paid. They are one of the few groups of workers who still have considerable industrial power. This is because of the damage they can inflict by interrupting or closing down train services. However, as signalling systems develop and an increasing number of fail-safe systems are introduced, the job may become less demanding. This can significantly increase job boredom. This is because of the increasing gap between the abilities of the job-holders and the demands placed upon them.

Vulnerability and stress

CORPORATE INVOLVEMENT AND CORPORATE LOYALTY

Increasing emphasis has been placed by some organisations (and writers) on treating the workforce as a valuable asset whose potential should be fully exploited rather than simply seen as a cost. This idea is in line with the concepts of **intellectual capital** and **knowledge management** covered in Chapter 3. Such initiatives may be reinforced by the social pressures that may be deliberately engineered by employers to obtain compliance with and commitment to organisational goals. The concept of the quality of working life is also relevant here. The treatment of the workforce as a valuable asset has the broad aim of bringing together and satisfying both the goals and development of organisations and the needs and development of all their employees. It emphasises the need to release human potential – which is all the more important given the economic pressures on organisations and rising educational standards within workforces.

THE PSYCHOLOGICAL CONTRACT

The concept of the **psychological contract** is being used more and more to reflect the day-to-day behaviour that management and employees expect from one another. Research shows that where employees believe that management has broken promises or failed to deliver on certain commitments then this has a negative impact on job satisfaction and commitment and, therefore, on the state of the psychological contract (Marchington M. et al. 2001).

Management behaviour can have a highly diverse impact on employees where promises appear to have been broken or where particular changes to work methods or work organisation appear to have been badly handled. Once management is suspected of having broken the psychological contract it can be very difficult to repair the relationship.

IMPACT ON CORPORATE MORALE

Given the pressures that there are, well intentioned and otherwise, to increase organisational commitment, it is important to recognise the pressures that there are for employees to set limits on their organisational commitment, or even reduce it. A major complication is that the increased psychological commitment by the workforce may be expected at a time when organisations have reduced their commitment to their employees in ways that will now be discussed.

Black (1993) referred to the concepts of **just-in-time employment** and the **disposable workforce** (both aspects of the flexible workforce) in the USA and the impact this has on corporate morale. Consequently, one needs to examine the impact of the flexible workforce on motivation and in particular the use of fixed-term contracts, especially for senior employees. A further complication can arise because of the actual generosity with which employers often treat those who are being made redundant.

The reappraisals of commitment to the organisation caused by restructuring may be in tune with a general trend. Scase and Goffee (1999, p. 13) comment that:

> If, in earlier decades, managers were committed to their jobs to the extent that all other interests were subordinated to their work-related goals, they may now be developing more instrumental and calculative attitudes towards their employing organisations (Hearn 1977). Indeed, by deliberately cultivating personal identities that are separate and removed from organisational demands, they could be better equipped to cope with work-related stresses and to withstand the psychological challenges that can be posed by threats of redundancy and unexpected career changes. Accordingly, managers may cease to be psychologically immersed in their work roles and become less committed to their employing organisations. To do otherwise, in the light of increasing uncertainties, would be to make themselves more emotionally and psychologically vulnerable.

Social trends, including changes in the role of women both in the family and in society generally, also have an impact on the work relationship. The custom of family commitments needing to be subordinated to the primary aim of promoting the career of the man in the home has long been under challenge. In many developed economies the size of the female workforce is approaching half of the total workforce. The pattern of female careers is also changing – women are tending to have children later and to have shorter maternity leave. The growing number of dual-career couples also imposes constraints upon both partners and lessens the dependency on the primary income. Also a significant number of employees are single parents. However, rising property prices, repayment of student loans and the need for increased pension contributions can force staff to earn whatever they can in order to meet a scale of liabilities that their parents did not have to meet.

Having explained the constraints that may exist with regard to attempts to improve employee involvement and develop corporate loyalty, it would be foolish to suggest that all attempts are doomed to failure. It is more logical to argue that, given the organisational turbulence that is often inevitable, it is even more important to consider how to try and get the best out of the workforce despite the difficulties. This is more likely to be done effectively if the nature of the difficulties is clearly recognised. It is necessary to consider the human dimension at the time that organisations are being restructured and to build in the direct and intangible costs of change before decisions are finalised. It is also important to have positive and integrated human resource strategies, and the nature of these are considered in Chapter 11 (in relation to training) and generally in Chapter 14 (in the context of employee relations).

STRESS

The general point has been made that organisations tend to underutilise and underinvolve the human resources available to them but that there is an increasing recognition of the need to correct this. The point has also been made that a variety of factors are causing an increasing number of employees to try and set limits to their work involvement. Consequently, it is probably appropriate for both organisations and employees to consider the optimum level of involvement. This may be particularly necessary given the increasing potential intrusion of work into the home because of developments in information technology. Individuals may need to look carefully at their work in relation to their general lifestyle and periodically conduct an audit on their work–life balance. Whilst the emphasis in the literature on motivation is on underinvolvement, overinvolvement may present risks for the employer as well as the employee. The dangers of workaholicism may include problems of employee replacement, damage to health and the loss of a sense of perspective and good judgement that comes from having other interests as a counterbalance. Workaholics may also seek to establish themselves as role models when they are really self-indulging or engaging in compensatory behaviour.

There is a distinction between pressure and stress. Some managers enjoy high levels of pressure and may perform more effectively when they are put under a certain amount of pressure. The pressure may relate to the volume or responsibility level of work or both. Other managers may react in a different way, and their inability to cope with pressure may result in stress. One could therefore define managerial stress as a symptom of being unable to cope with the workload. Unfortunately, this can precipitate a counter-productive chain reaction with those managers experiencing stress amplifying and transmitting it to those in their immediate circle. Stress may be caused by the problems inherent in a particular job, the mismatch between the abilities of an individual and the requirements of a job, or a combination of the two. It is important to diagnose the causes of stress in particular situations because it is only when that is done that one can work out whether the appropriate remedy is to change an individual's behaviour, the pressures they are put under, or both.

It is also important to recognise that work stress is probably on the increase. This is because of the increasing impact of key factors which generate stress. These factors include the rate of change, pressures for cost-effective performance and job insecurity generated by change.

Managers also have responsibility for monitoring the stress under which subordinates are placed. There is also likely to be an increasing need to ensure that pressure to ensure that managerial styles do not degenerate into harassment and bullying. This is because of rising expectations of the duty of care owed by employers to employees (ACAS 2007).

Example of employer liability for employee stress

In 1994, John Walker, a senior social worker in the UK, won a High Court action against Northumberland County Council (IRLR 1994), because of its negligence in not doing enough to prevent him having further nervous breakdowns because of work overload. The council agreed to pay him £175 000 because of their breach of duty of care to him.

Alan Barber, the head of the maths department in a comprehensive school, complained about stress because of his workload late in 1995. His workload was not adjusted and he was signed off sick with stress the following May. He was told to prioritise his work but suffered a mental breakdown in 1996. In the subsequent court action he was awarded £101 000 damages, payable by Somerset County Council, because the school had not responded positively enough to his condition. This decision was confirmed in a House of Lords judgement in 2004.

Whether managers are being submitted or submitting themselves to too much pressure or experiencing stress, the consequent work style may generate an excessive flow of adrenalin within the body. Dependence on physical stimulants such as nicotine and alcohol can prevent an individual from having an appropriate diet and sufficient physical exercise and rest. If the stress is self-induced, it is perhaps just as well to face up to the medical implications in case there is any scope for personal adjustment. There is also the potential benefit that if stress is reduced for oneself, it may also be reduced for those around you.

Doctors and stress consultants may be able to measure stress and advise on how the symptoms are treated, e.g. by relaxation techniques. However, managerial skills are likely to be needed to deal with the basic causes of managerial stress. The aim of this book is to do just that, by helping managers to define their role and develop the key skills to carry it out effectively.

Summary

The difference between motivation and morale and the wide variety of causes of underperformance have been explained. For effective action to be taken to improve performance, it is necessary to accurately diagnosis the reasons. If this is not done, corrective action may be ineffective or even counterproductive. One of the mistakes that can be made is for managers to make wrong assumptions about why their subordinates work. Even if there is a problem of low motivation among employees, it is necessary to consider what can be done to improve it. Relevant theories have been examined, particularly the work of Maslow, Herzberg, expectancy theory and socio-technical systems theory. According to Herzberg, money is an important hygiene factor but not necessarily an important positive motivator. However, some care has to be taken in generalising on the basis of Herzberg's research. The impact of national culture on motivation was also considered.

It is important to try and match individual needs and job demands as far as is practicable. This is an issue that needs to be considered when jobs are designed and marketed. One of the consequence of not doing this can be job distortion. Market turbulence and trends towards flexible employment policies can generate job insecurity and this may conflict with employer demands for greater employee commitment. Such factors can also increase the amount of job-related stress. Social trends also often aggravate the conflict between work and domestic commitments. The judgement, effectiveness and health of managers will be at risk if they experience too much stress. They also have a responsibility to see that their employees are not subjected to unreasonable amounts of stress. The development of managerial skills such as prioritisation can be an effective way of dealing with the causes of stress. The issue of pay is considered further in the next chapter, which is devoted to that topic.

Self-assessment questions

(If you wish to check the extent to which your answer to any of the following questions is appropriate, cross-refer to the Table of Contents. The contents for this chapter are on page xiv.)

1 Think of a group of workers you judge to be performing poorly. Identify the reasons for their poor performance.

2 Using the same group as you have used in answer to the first question, what assumptions have you made about why these people work? How accurate are they?

3 Explain any one theory of motivation.

4 What do you believe is the role of money in motivating people?

5 How can a good match be made between individual needs and job demands?

6 Why is it important to take human needs into account when designing jobs?

7 Examine the potential for conflict between employers wishing to increase managerial commitment and managers wishing to redress their work–life balance.

8 How can you try to reduce or avoid work-related stress both for yourself and others?

References

(Works of particular interest are marked with a star.)

ACAS (2007), *Bullying and harassment at work. guidance for employees*, London: ACAS. Available at http://www.acas.org.uk/index.aspx?articleid=797.

Black, Larry (1993), *Downsizing Towards a Disposable Workforce – a View from New York*, The Independent, 22 March.

Herzberg, F. Mausner and B. Snyderman (1960), *The Motivation to Work*, Wiley.

Hofstede, G. (2001), *Culture's Consequences*, 2nd ed., Sage.

Marchington, M., A. Wilkinson and P. Ackers (2001) *Management choice and employee voice*. Research report, London CIPD.

Maslow, A. H. (1970), *Motivation and Personality*, 2nd ed., Harper and Row.

McClelland D. C. (1961), *The Achieving Society*, Van Nostrand.

*Mead, Richard (2005), *International Management – Cross Cultural Dimensions*, 3rd ed., Blackwell (Ch. 6 – *Needs and Incentives*, is particularly useful in examining the impact of national culture on motivation).

Rieger, F. and D. Wong-Rieger (1990), *A Configuration Module of National Influence Applied to Southeast Asian Organisations*, Proceedings, Research Conference on Business in Southeast Asia: Southeast Asia Business Program, University of Michigan, pp. 1–31.

Scase, Richard and Robert Goffee (1989), *Reluctant Managers*, Unwin Hyman.

Trist, E. L. and K. W. Bamforth (1951), *Some Sociological and Psychological Consequences of the Longwall Method of Coal-Getting*, Human Relations, No. 4.

Trist, E., G. Higgin, H. Murray and A. Pollock (1963), *Organisational Choice: Capabilities of Groups at the Coal Face under Changing Technologies: The Loss, Re-discovery and Transformation of a Work Tradition*, London, Tavistock.

Cases cited

Barber versus Somerset County Council (2004), House of Lords (http://www.lawreports.co.uk).

Walker versus Northumberland County Council (1994), IRLR 35, QBD.

Further reading

Nadler, David and Edward E. Lawler III (1977), *Motivation: a Diagnostic Approach*, in Hackman, R. and E. Lawler (eds), *Perspectives on Behaviour in Organisations*, McGraw-Hill.

Sheldrake, John (1996), *Management Theory from Taylorism to Japanization* in *Elton Mayo and the Hawthorne Experiments*, International Thomson Business Press.

Truss, Katie, Emma Soane, Christone Yvonne L. Edwards, Karen Wisdom, Andrew Croll and Jamie Burnett (2006) *Working Life: Employee Attitudes and Engagement*, CIPD.

Payment systems

Learning outcomes

By the end of this chapter you will be able to:

- Identify the objectives of payment systems and assess the main pressures causing change in the way organisations remunerate their employees
- Assess the objectives of job evaluation schemes and the potential contribution of such schemes to setting fair and equitable payment structures
- Assess how job evaluation schemes operate in practice
- Identify and assess the circumstances under which financial incentive schemes may improve performance
- Evaluate the potential long-term effects of financial incentive schemes

Introduction

Having considered the relevance of various behavioural theories of motivation in the previous chapter, it is now necessary to look more explicitly at payment systems. The pressures for change in the way job evaluation operates and its changing role are examined. These include trends towards smaller and more flexible organisations and a greater emphasis on rewarding on the basis of individual performance. General trends are examined including the use of incremental salary scales and cafeteria-style fringe benefits are also considered.

The issue of internal relativities is examined, as is the way in which job evaluation may assist in establishing and maintaining a rational pay structure. The various types of job evaluation schemes are explained and the ways in which they need to be chosen, operated and maintained if they are to be effective. Consideration is given to the European **equal pay** and **equal value** legislation which stipulate that employees do not suffer pay discrimination on the basis of sex. The advantages and disadvantages of financial incentive schemes and profit-sharing arrangements are also considered in this chapter.

The issue of individual merit payment, especially performance-related pay (PRP) is deferred until Chapter 10 so that it can be considered in the context of appraisal.

Objectives of payment systems

Payment systems need careful consideration since, to be effective, they need to meet a number of different and sometimes conflicting objectives. The main objectives of payment systems are likely to be:

- Attracting, retaining and motivating staff who are competent in the jobs they are given.
- Not paying over-generously, for reasons of cost.
- Establishing internal relativities that minimise feelings of discontent about what other employees are getting.
- Establishing differentials that encourage appropriate employees to apply for promotion.
- Encouraging geographical and functional flexibility for employees where appropriate.
- Reflecting power realities in the organisation so that the pay structure is not likely to be easily overturned by groups with strong bargaining power.
- Compliance with the law, particularly minimum pay legislation, regulations regarding hours of work, and legislation and regulations regarding equal pay and equal pay for work of equal value.
- Establishing a structure that is manageable, adaptive and cost effective in administrative expense.

Trade-offs may be necessary in determining which objectives have higher priority. Payment systems need to be synchronised with other organisational processes such as human resource planning and budgetary control. Such integration is necessary if overall organisational objectives are to be achieved.

Job evaluation

Job evaluation schemes can provide a useful framework for creating an effective pay structure by establishing a basis for the relationship between the various different types of job in an organisation. The determination of wage and salary levels is a process that will take place after such relativities have been established. Job evaluation may also help with the process of salary surveys.

Job evaluation has historically been associated with the determination of administrative and professional pay structures in particular. However, occupational changes, the generally reduced bargaining power of trade unions and, in Europe, equal pay and equal value legislation have all been factors leading to the greater use of job evaluation schemes for manual workers.

Even if employees are paid well in comparison with similar work in other organisations, there can often be considerable dissatisfaction about perceived internal inequities. Job evaluation can be particularly useful in reducing discontent about this. Even if individuals do not always agree with the results of job evaluation schemes, they may at least accept that the employer has tried to resolve pay issues in a fair and systematic way.

TYPES OF SCHEMES

In considering the different types of job evaluation schemes, particular attention is paid to important practical problems that are often overlooked in explanations of how schemes are supposed to work as opposed to the way they may work in practice. Few people argue that the process of job evaluation is scientific – it is essentially a systematic way of making a series of judgements about relativities. The use of scientific method is in making those subjective judgements, not replacing that judgemental process.

A basic distinction between the various types of schemes is between the non-analytical and the analytical ones. Examples of non-analytical schemes are job classification, job ranking and paired comparisons. A recent development has been to evaluate jobs in terms of competencies required or deployed by the person doing a job. This approach may be a factor in an analytical scheme or the basis of a complete scheme.

NON-ANALYTICAL SCHEMES
Job classification

Using the job classification technique, jobs are looked at as a whole and then grouped into families to which a grade is then allocated. Definitions are sometimes given of the basic characteristics of a classification or grade to help judge where particular jobs should go. Job classification can be a relatively cheap form of job evaluation to install. It also facilities flexibility in the allocation of tasks, particularly if the range of tasks within a job grade is wide.

Job ranking

Job ranking involves arranging jobs in a hierarchy, and the vertical rank order can be split up into various job grades. This can also be a relatively cheap form of job evaluation.

Paired comparisons

The technique of paired comparisons is a more sophisticated way of arriving at a rank order. It involves comparing each job with every other job to identify the correct rank order. However, the greater the number of jobs, the greater the problem in making valid comparisons between jobs. Whilst the arithmetic may be handled by use of a computer, there remains the problem of people knowing enough about all the other jobs in the organisation to make informed judgements.

The basic feature of all three of these non-analytical approaches is that the ultimate grading is achieved by comparison with other jobs rather than by systematically identifying the component elements in each job. They tend to be relatively cheap and easy to operate. However, it can be difficult to defend sex discrimination claims based on European-wide equal value legislation with a non-analytical scheme. This is because it can be argued that the overall judgements contain an element of sex discrimination. Equal pay and equal value legislation is explained later in this chapter.

ANALYTICAL SCHEMES

The main analytical schemes, including many of the proprietary schemes offered by consultancy organisations, often involve points rating. Points rating involves identifying the common factors in jobs (or job demands) and then allocating points to these factors according to the specific demands in each job. The points allocation, or weight, for each factor is established after systematic internal discussion about the relative importance of the factor to the organisation. Each factor in a job is then assessed and a total points score for the job obtained. The total points score indicates what job grade is appropriate. Proprietary schemes are often sophisticated versions of this points rating approach.

The job competence approach

Organisations may use competencies as a basis for part, or even all, of a job evaluation scheme, particularly if **job competencies** are also used for selection and training. The job competence approach is analytical in terms of the processes adopted. It involves a detailed examination of the range and varying levels of skills that can be brought to bear in a job. The job competence approach compares with more traditional approaches where the focus of the evaluation is the job requirements. With job competencies the minimum competencies required in a person to do a job are specified but it is acknowledged that people may perform at a higher level than the minimum. This blurs the more traditional distinction usually made in job evaluation between assessing the needs of the job as opposed to the performance of the individual. The approach recognises that some individuals can interpret and develop a job more productively than others. The level of competence displayed by a person doing a job can be used to determine the pay grade that they are given.

Advantages of using the job competence approach in job evaluation are:

- It can link in with competencies developed for selection and training.
- Employees can be encouraged to develop relevant skills.
- Employees can be rewarded for showing initiative in their job, developing it and adding value to the work of the organisation.

Disadvantages of the job competence approach are:

- It focuses on skills, not outcomes. If this approach is used, the extent to which objectives are achieved may also need to be considered.
- Mundane but essential tasks may be ignored in favour of building up the more interesting parts of a job.

- It is a top-down process with little scope for employee or union involvement in the design of the scheme. This may affect the extent to which a scheme is felt to be fair.

- Consistency of ratings may be hard to achieve, especially if the approach involves significant devolution of authority to line management.

- If a scheme is based completely on job competencies, it may be extremely complicated.

Choice of scheme

The dilemma for the individual employers is what, if any, scheme to adopt. No one scheme or approach is superior to all others; it is basically a question of choosing the most appropriate for the situation and then operating whatever scheme is chosen in a sensible manner. However refined and sophisticated schemes may appear to be, it must always be remembered that any statistical calculation is built on a basis of subjective judgements of, for example, what factors should be chosen and what weights they should be given. Consequently, one should beware of spurious accuracy and of claims that everything is near perfect because ratings are very consistent. Raters may be consistent in applying a scheme, but as schemes rest on subjective judgements this can lead to consistent error.

Assessing the merits of rival proprietary schemes

Example

The complexity of some of the proprietary schemes designed by consultants can make them particularly difficult to understand. This can make it difficult to identify potential disadvantages. One ingenious human resources officer, however, discovered a way of finding out the potential weaknesses of proprietary schemes – by inviting comment from rival consultants!

KEY FACTORS IN DECIDING WHAT TYPE OF SCHEME TO HAVE
Coverage within the organisation

Whilst it may seem convenient and fair to have one scheme for the whole of an organisation, this is not always practicable. There can be so little in common between, for example, manual, technical and managerial grades that one may have to develop different schemes so that the jobs being compared and evaluated have a reasonable amount in common. There is not much point in having an overall scheme that seeks to assess a chief executive's job in terms of factors such as physical strength, monotony and boredom. However, a counter-argument that has emerged in favour of schemes covering all employees is that it may help in defending cases brought under the equal value legislation where comparisons are made between different parts of an employer's pay structure.

Cost

The costs of installing and maintaining a scheme need to be considered. The more sophisticated the scheme, the greater such costs are likely to be. Another critical cost is the uplift in pay that usually results from the introduction of a scheme. Job evaluation is unlikely to leave the existing pay structure undisturbed, and the holders of jobs that are downgraded normally have their own salary protected. Consequently, an immediate effect of job evaluation is that as no-one has less pay and some will get more pay, so the total wage and salary bill will increase. A rule of thumb for major restructuring exercises is that such an uplift will be in the order of 3 per cent of the total wage bill. However, sometimes the introduction of a job evaluation scheme can get out of hand and the cost increase can be much greater.

Example

Examples of schemes running out of control

In 2006 a job evaluation scheme was introduced in the National Health Service in Britain. This was part of a policy of significantly greater investment in the health service. General practitioners and hospital doctors, as well as other staff, were required to write up the details of their activities so that they could be evaluated against a preset scheme. The range, level and volume of activities undertaken by doctors had not been anticipated when the scheme was introduced. The consequent uplift in the remuneration of doctors meant that much of the increased investment was used in paying doctors more for much the same work that they had been doing before the scheme was introduced. Under the new scheme average pay for GPs 'has soared 30% to £106 000 a year' (The Times, 20 Jan. 2007). The Secretary of State for Health commented that, in retrospect, there should have been a limit to the increases that doctors could receive under the new scheme. Having agreed and implemented such increases, though, there was obvious difficulty in trying to impose such a ceiling

retrospectively. In addition it was estimated by the National Audit Office (The Times, 19 April 2007), that a three-year pay deal covering hospital consultants agreed in 2003 gave them a salary increase of 25% for doing *less* work. This resulted in an expenditure of £150 million more than had been anticipated.

Also in 2006 a national job evaluation scheme was introduced in British universities under a national framework agreement. Implementation was at the level of individual universities. In some cases, there were no management representatives on the job evaluation panels. In addition, the job descriptions submitted by staff were not always properly verified by their academic managers. This meant that in some cases exaggerated accounts of the work of those being evaluated were accepted. This meant that some individuals were over-graded – often to the great annoyance of colleagues who had not been upgraded but who were working at the same level of responsibility, as those who had been upgraded.

Size of organisation

The investment in a costly scheme for a small group of employees may simply be too great. Also it may be much easier to operate simpler schemes in small organisations because of the knowledge that people have about one another's jobs.

Rate of change

An important factor that often is ignored is the expected rate of change in an organisation. Job evaluation schemes are usually introduced on the assumption that the organisational arrangements are fixed. However, the pace of change is such now that one has to evaluate how well schemes will cope with projected change. There is not much point in having an expensive and sophisticated scheme that is soon going to be out of date. This question also needs asking, in a slightly modified form, of existing schemes. It may be that existing schemes, which may historically have been sound, have become irrelevant through not being adjusted, or not being capable of adjustment, in line with organisational change.

Dangers of obsolescence

A comprehensive proprietary job evaluation scheme was installed at an engineering factory in London. Unfortun- ately it became obsolete within four months because of the rapidity of technical and organisational change.

Example

Employee involvement

Trade unions are likely to take more than a passing interest in job evaluation and their involvement in schemes has to be considered. They are likely to see job evaluation as a framework for bargaining. In any case, regardless of whether there is a trade union or not, one needs to consider the issue of employee involvement. If schemes are supposed to incorporate internal views about equity and fairness there needs to be some mechanism for taking employees' views into account with regard to the design and operation of schemes. The need to do this has been reinforced by developments in European law.

An almost inevitable consequence of job evaluation is that some jobs will be downgraded. Even if a person's salary is 'red-circled', i.e. protected, it is arguable that such a change necessitates consultation with union or employee representatives if more than 20 employees are involved. This is a requirement under European law because the requirement for statutory redundancy consultation has been widened to cover changes in contractual terms. The remedies for a breach of these requirements are just in relation to lack of consultation and not those for redundancy or unfair dismissal.

If anyone ever did design a perfect system, representatives would still feel obliged to try and bargain about the matter, as what trade union could countenance being told that it had no bargaining role? Unions also often rightly query the basis on which schemes are based and the results they give. Unions may have to distance themselves a little from schemes, however, as otherwise they may seem to be implementing managerial policies. Once a scheme has been established they tend to acknowledge it, and use the right to represent anyone who feels that they have a case for upgrading.

IMPLEMENTATION AND OPERATION
Job versus person

One of the basic issues is to remember is that unless job-holders' competencies are being assessed, it is the job and not the person that is being evaluated. If a job-holder has outgrown a job, the real answer is for them to be encouraged to seek promotion rather than to distort the pay structure by giving an upgrade that temporarily meets their needs but not the organisation's. One must also beware of the danger, explained in the previous chapter, that employees may distort a job to justify an upgrade. In contrast, if a person is not up to a job, it can sometimes be that this is because the job is not graded highly enough to attract people of the right calibre.

Choice of factors

Factors in analytical schemes have to be chosen carefully so that they don't overlap. Otherwise a job-holder can benefit twice under such factors as job complexity and education required, which may be different ways of measuring the same requirement. Another complication can arise from the establishment of 'weights' for factors. Apart from the judgemental problems of doing this anyway, there is the statistical problem that the real weights depend not just on, for example, the points allocated for a particular factor, but also on the extent to which those making judgements use the full extent of the scale.

Example

Inappropriate weights

There was once an attempt to introduce a new job evaluation scheme for nursing officers in the health service in Britain. It rapidly became apparent that for some jobs the only factors on which the scores differed were those related to the level of the unit in which a person was employed. The reality was that in practice the scheme for some jobs was based on a single factor – the one that was easiest to measure.

A further explanation of these statistical problems is given in the section on recording and rating in Chapter 10.

Upgrading claims

There can be misconceptions about the extent to which employees can be expected to change their duties without receiving any extra remuneration. Changes in the range of work at a given level do not normally constitute a case for upgrading. Work at a higher level of responsibility may provide a valid basis for upgrading, but even in this case it has to be remembered that job grades normally embrace a range of jobs and a person's increase in, for example, responsibility level may not be sufficient to lift them into the next grade. There is a common law requirement for employees to accept reasonable changes in job content and the prudent employer will reinforce this by the use of generic job titles and a flexibility clause in any job description.

Claims for upgrading can also be made on what may turn out to be basic job requirements rather than additional demands. Schemes need to be operated on the basis that there are minimum performance requirements which justify retention in a given job as opposed to justifying an upgrading. However, one cannot but admire the ingenuity with which some cases are argued.

Examples of spurious claims

One forklift truck driver applied for an upgrading at an oil refinery. His case rested on his responsibility for expensive plant and equipment as evidenced by the fact that he had recently fractured a fuel line and caused a fire (causing over £1 million worth of damage!). This was the basis of his argument for an upgrading.

Another such case involved a receptionist who was asked to elaborate on the decision-making elements in her job – which consisted mainly of routing telephone calls and visitors. She beamed and said she had to decide whether to come in each day or not. The argument advanced was that she had to decide if she was fit enough for work or not, as if she was not it would be bad for the external image of the firm if she came in and was in a bad mood.

Appeals

Irrespective of whether there is employee involvement in the design of a scheme or not, some sort of appeals mechanism is necessary. Appeals criteria need to be specified, such as a change in duties, and appeals bodies established. These may be managerial panels, joint management–union panels or involve the use of an outside arbitrator – either sitting alone or chairing a joint panel.

The knock-on effect

A crucial issue in establishing the grading of any job is its effect on the overall equilibrium of the pay structure. Serious inequities obviously should be corrected, but not insubstantial cases for locating jobs in a higher grade. The key issue is not the extra direct costs this would involve but the **knock-on effect**. The danger is that by solving one person's perceived grievance you can create a host of repercussive claims.

External job market

Another key issue in evaluating jobs concerns the relationship of pay to the external job market. It is no good having pay levels that are out of line with the market. However, markets do not always operate so clearly and systematically that you can dispense with job evaluation. In making comparisons with pay in other organisations, care has to be taken to ensure that you are comparing like with like. The use of job titles alone may be dangerous – for example a title such as 'fitter' can cover a wide range of different jobs in terms of actual duties and responsibility level. Sometimes there can be a marked conflict between internal relativities and the market rate for particular groups for whom there is a strong demand.

The realistic answer in cases like this is not to have a spurious re-evaluation of the staff concerned, but to openly recognise and deal with the problem. It may be necessary to pay a market supplement for such staff or even take them out of the evaluation scheme altogether. This way at least the rest of the pay structure can remain consistent.

Using standard schemes

A further issue concerns the transferability of evaluation schemes to different organisations, countries and cultures. It may seem a short cut to copy someone else's scheme or use one's own in an overseas subsidiary. The usual rationale for job evaluation schemes is that they reflect the attitudes within an organisation about what is a fair set of relativities. However, the attitudes towards what is fair may be quite different in an organisation or country in which there is a different set of values. Consequently, such transfer of schemes may be an extremely hit-and-miss affair. This also applies to the use of schemes designed by consultants that are not sufficiently adapted to the needs of a particular organisation.

EQUAL PAY

A further dimension of pay structures and job evaluation is the law regarding equal pay and pay for work of equal value. Employees in Europe have a broad right not to be discriminated against in terms of pay and conditions of employment on grounds of sex if their work is similar or of equal value to someone of the opposite sex in the same organisation. This is a consequence in European Union (EU) member countries of governments being obliged to comply with the requirements of the Treaty of Rome and the Equal Pay Directive of 1975. The right to equal pay is for those engaged on similar or broadly similar work, or on work rated as equivalent under a job evaluation scheme. The right to claim pay of equal value, like the right to claim equal pay, excludes comparisons with employees of the same sex. Claims are usually made by women rather than men, but they could be made by men if they can argue that their work is valued less than that of female comparators.

The right to equal pay for work of equal value exists where the job demands are the same in categories such as 'effort, skill and decision-making'. This implies a need for some sort of analytical job evaluation if the employer is to try and defend their position. Employers need to be able to provide 'objective' justification for differences in pay between the sexes. If an individual claim succeeds. this may reveal that there is the basis for further claims and if any of these succeed the process may continue. The 'knock-on' effect can lead to the undermining of the whole of an existing pay structure.

For an employer to have a defensible case it may be necessary to review not just a pay structure but the processes by which pay rates and differentials are established. The implications of this for the operation of job evaluation schemes include ensuring that there is a fair cross-representation of any benchmark jobs and that there is adequate representation of both sexes on panels. If a points-rating scheme is used, it is necessary to ensure that the factors and weights used are not discriminatory. This may be all against a background where the internal 'felt fair' values represent, for example, dominant male values which may be in conflict with the legal requirement to avoid sex discrimination. Analytical job evaluation fairly applied will help avoid discrimination but not necessarily put a stop to argument. People sometimes think that the use of, for example, sophisticated statistical techniques enables scientifically objective decisions to be made about pay grades. However, what such techniques do is to provide elaborate means of establishing systematic opinions about job relationships. The judgements about how dissimilar factors, or whole jobs, should relate to one another can be carried out systematically, but the judgements are subjective. It is nevertheless such subjective judgements that may have to be offered as a defence in law as being an 'objective' justification for pay differences.

The case law arising out of equal value claims is proving to be a guide as to how the law operates in practice. The following important issues have been decided by case law. Case law established in one country is binding on other member countries of the EU. The final judicial authority is the European Court of Justice.

- Claims have to involve comparisons with another job where employees are predominantly of the other sex (Pickstone versus Freeman, 1988).

- Equal value law may be a powerful pressure for the harmonisation of the conditions of employment of manual and white-collar employees. Otherwise applicants may be able to point to just one element of the remuneration package where they think there is an unjustified difference and argue the case for parity (Hayward versus Cammell Laird Shipbuilders, 1988).

- The practice of slotting-in jobs to outline structures without analysis of the jobs slotted in seems to be inadequate (Bromley versus H. J. Quick, 1988).

- The existence of a separate collective bargaining structure is not an acceptable defence (Enderby versus Frenchay Health Authority, 1993).

- The defence of a genuine material factor difference may include market rates, but only if that accounts for the whole difference (Enderby versus Frenchay Health Authority, 1993).

Employers have strong financial reasons for appealing against adverse judgements (as do unions). Consequently, it can be years before a case is decided. The lessons for employers include taking the basic steps already suggested to avoid obvious discrimination and hoping that they are not targeted for an important test case. If the pay structure is adjusted to take account of possible sex discrimination, the extra pay costs need to be taken into account when any general increase is considered. The response by the National Health Service in the UK to the loss of a number of cases has been to introduce a national system of job evaluation. One of many examples which shows the huge potential implications of equal pay and/or equal value claims is as follows:

> The [British] prison service could face a £50 million bill after losing its [Employment Appeal Tribunal] claim against 2,504 equal pay cases [in 2005] . . . The Public and Commercial Services Union (PCS) brought the claim that there were pay gaps between women working in support, administrative and managerial roles and prison officer and governor grades. The gaps – of up to £5000 – were in spite of job evaluation exercises that scored the support jobs favourably with prison officer colleagues.
>
> (People Management 2005, p. 12)

One of the huge practical problems involved in establishing non-gender discriminatory pay structures is that male colleagues are not often likely to be sympathetic to having their pay frozen to enable gender inequalities to be financed. However, any such lack of sympathy seems unlikely to prevent cases being pursued at tribunals, if necessary by lawyers on a 'no win, no fee' basis. One estimate puts the potential cost of backdated equal value compensation claims across the whole of the public sector in the UK as over £10 billion (The Times, 12 March 2007). The former chair of the former Equal Opportunities Commission in the UK also commented that:

> The private sector was just as vulnerable to legal action. Companies with opaque mechanisms for handing out bonuses and which do not have performance reviews were particularly at risk
>
> (The Times 2007)

Commenting in a UK government report, the Women and Work Commission (2007) indicated that they believed that low pay amongst women was due to the narrow range of occupations that women in the UK occupy, together with the fact that many women work part-time whilst caring for dependents. Whilst they believed that equal pay reviews 'provide clear incentive schemes and reduce the cost of litigation', the Equal Pay Act could work better (Women and Work Commission 2007, p. 95). In addition, the commission reported that women in the UK did not receive very good careers advice and as a consequence, did not make the best use of their skills. It was estimated that this poor use of resources cost the UK economy £23 billion a year.

PRESSURES FOR CHANGE

The major changes that so many organisations have experienced, and which have been previously described particularly in Chapter 3, are having a major impact on the way job evaluation is operated. The trend to less labour-intensive, more flexible organisations has been particularly important. Also, changes in job evaluation have been necessary in some cases to help bring about such organisational changes. Generally there has been a move to fewer job grades, with less-detailed job descriptions and an emphasis on flexible working. In the case of Nissan, in Sunderland, for example, this has involved the compression of manual jobs into just two different job titles with no job descriptions. The trend to multi-skilling, as an aid to greater labour flexibility, also puts more emphasis on the personal attributes of the job-holder. This may include payment for additional competencies that the job-holder has acquired. These developments reduce the distinctiveness of individual jobs and encourage the concept of job families. Simpler schemes are more adaptive, more easily controlled in terms of pay drift, and less expensive in terms of administrative costs, including the use of managerial time. Such costs savings are a particularly important pressure for change given the ongoing pressure to reduce costs in the private and public sectors. Computer-assisted schemes help reduce the costs of operating schemes further, provided that managerial politics are such that the results are viable.

The decline in union power has tended to give management more freedom with regard to job evaluation, and this has often been reinforced by more devolved patterns of organisational decision-making. The decline in union power has also facilitated more of an individual and less of a collectivist approach. This trend has tended to emphasise the link between pay and individual performance and to reduce the importance of grade levels. The traditional approach to job evaluation was that individual performance was discounted, but there is more acceptance now that the nature of the job may be shaped by the individual performing it. The concept of **added value** is important in this respect. All this has tended to reduce the need for complex schemes and high levels of accuracy, particularly as grade level is a less dominant factor in determining overall pay. The one contrary pressure arises from equal value legislation, which may cause organisations to consider retaining or introducing analytical schemes. Organisations may also have to respond to claims during pay bargaining that their job evaluation schemes are sex-discriminatory. Other trends include less emphasis on hierarchies and more use of overlapping pay scales.

A related development has been that of cafeteria-style benefits so that employees can have some choice in matching their benefits to their needs. However, this can generate significant administrative problems, particularly as a change in the level of one benefit can affect the relative worth of all the other benefits. This may be so even if computer programmes are used to help maintain consistency with the overall benefits package.

INTERNATIONAL DIMENSION

A further complication with pay structures is the international dimension. Organisations increasingly are sited in more than one country. Also, the search for executive talent in particular is increasingly globalised. However, accommodating people from other countries in pay structures can cause many complications. These include the differences between tax, employment law and social security systems between countries, overseas allowances, differences in living costs and differences in national labour markets. Too rigid an approach to offering competitive terms to overseas talent may make the job unattractive. Conversely, too loose an approach may mean that the knock-on effects may make the appointment of a person from another country counterproductive (see Shortland 2007 for a fuller explanation of rewarding employees working overseas).

Financial incentives

Probably the ideal arrangement for most jobs is that people have an interesting job, good supervision and an appropriate basic wage or salary. If the theories of Maslow and Herzberg mean anything at all, such arrangements should lead to effective work performance and satisfied employees. Unfortunately, the achievement of such a happy state of affairs is, needless to say, not always possible. When this cannot be achieved, financial incentives may be appropriate. However, it is most important for managers to ensure that their diagnosis of the reasons for underachievement is correct before they try to improve work performance by the use of financial incentives. As part of this analysis they may need to consider the extent to which different individuals respond to financial rewards. There can be dangers in building systems around individuals, as they and their needs may change.

DIAGNOSIS OF NEED

As has previously been explained, problems of work performance may be due to factors outside the control of the employee. Even when it would seem that employees could increase output by reasonable increases in effort, it is necessary to ask why the effort is not forthcoming. The structure of jobs and the matching of individuals to jobs should be examined. If poor performance is because of poor supervision, it may be that it is the supervision that should be changed and not the arrangements for payment.

It is particularly necessary to examine the standard of supervision as the long-term effect of incentive schemes can be to diminish the role of the supervisor. Employees operating under incentive schemes may see themselves akin to independent subcontractors, with the supervisor as an external figure who is likely to come into conflict with them over a range of issues concerning the operation of the incentive scheme. This can lead to the exclusion of the supervisor from the work group because of attempts by them to monitor schemes in the interest of the employer rather than of the employee. Alternatively, the supervisor may be 'captured' by the work group so that, for example, they do not report on manipulations to the incentive scheme or show excessive concern about safety and quality standards. Unfortunately, these developments can lead to the continued erosion of first-line supervisors' authority to a point, sometimes, where they act as little more than a conduit for messages between management and the workforce.

FINANCIAL INCENTIVES AND CORPORATE STRATEGY

There are jobs in which the ideal arrangements identified above will simply not always be attainable. There will, for example, be situations in which the structure of jobs is such that they are inherently boring and that, in the short-term at least, output will be best achieved by the use of financial incentive schemes. The introduction of incentive schemes may be part of a new corporate strategy, as is illustrated by the following example.

Example

Impact on corporate strategy

A large clearing bank in the UK changed its recruitment and staff development policies so that sales and marketing potential largely replaced banking knowledge and commitment to the organisation. This new profile was adopted throughout the organisation and was reinforced by a bonus scheme based on sales of financial services. In addition, front-line staff were obliged to work in small teams, even though their bonuses were paid on an individual basis. This was accompanied by massive redundancies, mainly because of the introduction of new technology, including automatic telling machines (ATMs). Many talented and experienced employees who did not like the new working arrangements were only too pleased to take redundancy packages. Unfortunately for the bank they soon found that they had a major qualitative and quantitative gap in their workforce which substantially affected their ability to compete in the marketplace.

(Porter and Spear 2007)

The point that it is necessary to stress is that all the potential disadvantages of incentive schemes need to be taken into account before they are adopted. The trouble is that the short-term tangible benefits may be much more obvious than many of the long-term intangible, but nevertheless important, consequences. A policy of choosing 'horses for courses' is appropriate rather than any dogmatic assertion that one should always use incentive schemes or never use them. The matching of pay arrangements to situations can, however, be ill-conceived, or the circumstances in which schemes operate can alter and make them invalid. A common example is when automatic production processes are introduced which predetermine the rate of production, which had previously been determined by operators. If the speed at which the now-reactive operators work consequently becomes an effect and not a cause of some other variable, it becomes pointless to reward them for something over which they no longer have control. The achievement of high levels of production may be related instead, for example, to ensuring that automatic process equipment is properly maintained and does not break down or operate in such a way that there are quality defects.

The ramifications of incentive schemes are such that considerable thought has to be given, not only as to whether they should be used or not, but also as to how they should be managed if they are used. If incentive schemes are used, they may require just as much, or even more, managerial effort to see that performance targets are met, compared with the managerial effort involved when people are paid just a basic wage or salary.

APPROPRIATE CONDITIONS FOR OUTPUT-BASED SCHEMES

The circumstances under which payment by results schemes might be appropriate are identified in a checklist drawn up by the former National Board for Prices and Incomes as part of one of their investigations (NBPI 1968a, p. 11). Despite the length of time since this study was undertaken, their observations are still relevant. The four necessary conditions for the introduction of payment by results (still relevant) are where:

- the work can be measured and directly attributed to the individual or group; in practice this generally means highly repetitive manual work, as found in mass-production manufacturing;
- the pace of work is substantially controlled by the worker rather than by the machine or process they are tending;
- management is capable of maintaining a steady flow of work;
- the tasks are not subjected to frequent changes in method, materials or equipment.

Even under the above conditions and with proper monitoring, the NBPI commented on the inevitable slackening that occurs in schemes because of factors such as technological change. They found that, even under ideal conditions, there is likely to be an unavoidable wholly unproductive wage drift of at least 1 per cent a year (NPBI 1968b, p. 50). It is to be regretted that there are so few independent studies on the effects of incentive schemes to warn employers of the ways in which they can be counterproductive. Much of the information available is either in textbooks explaining how schemes are supposed to operate in theory or in literature provided by consultants who make their money from selling and installing incentive packages.

LONG-TERM EFFECTS

Proposals for introducing incentive schemes and their short-term benefits can seem very convincing. However, managers need to review carefully their diagnosis of the real reasons for poor performance and the possible long-term effects of incentive schemes before committing themselves to this route to higher output. Figure 7.1 shows what can happen in both the short and long term if, for example, a payment by results scheme is introduced.

Output may well increase by about one-third after the introduction of a scheme, with earnings going up in relation to output. However, as time goes on even in relatively static production situations there are likely to be improvements in work methods that are not entirely clawed back by the employer in terms of consequential reductions in time allowances. There may also be errors in initial time allowances, and employees can be remarkably ingenious in manipulating schemes to their advantage. The most sophisticated manipulations involve capturing the supervisor and other potential enemies so that the higher levels of management are not aware that ultimately effort may decline whilst output and earnings increase. Schemes can degenerate to such an extent that they actually become arrangements for restricting production – for fear that, if normal effort is resumed, the output achieved would give the whole game away.

| Figure 7.1 | **The long-term pattern of incentive schemes** |

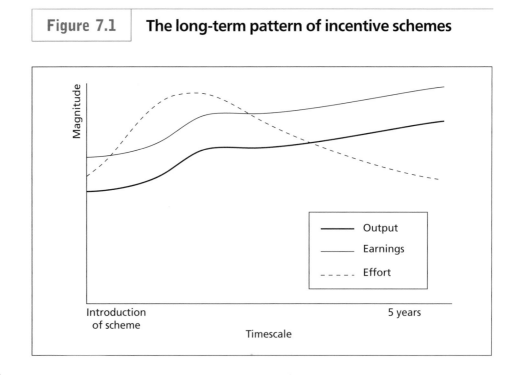

Another problem can be the distorting effect that incentive schemes can have on pay structures. If, for whatever reason, the incentive earnings of one group rise, this can create stresses with regard to pay relativities. Sometimes these can be acute and lead to a negative differential on the part of those, for example, who are supposed to supervise them. The introduction of new working methods may be accompanied by fear about the impact of this on earnings and may lead to resistance to the changes or haggling about any consequential adjustments to the incentive scheme. Another problem can be resistance to moving from jobs with slack times to those with tight times. The impact on quality of production or service also has to be examined. The need for this is illustrated by the following two newspaper reports:

> Parking attendants ... are developing a thirst for issuing tickets for minor offences to earn 'productivity' bonuses. The poorly paid officials are taught tricks and ruses to enable them to earn extra money if they meet targets. An undercover investigation by The Sunday Times (2002) has confirmed what many motorists suspect: parking tickets are not issued to ensure a smooth flow of traffic but are slapped on windscreens in a frenzied race to make money and exert power. ... Parking attendants are an enormous asset to the council [Westminster], which made £31.3 million from enforcement notices and penalty charges last year.

> When the telephone number enquiry service was opened up for competition in Britain there was a scramble by private companies to capture as much of the market as they could. In one case a company introduced individual incentive payment schemes for employees, with unfortunate results.

> However, workers [were] so keen to get a bonus for completing enquiries in under 40 seconds, that they [were] said to be getting rid of calls as quickly as possible and by any means possible. One operator at a call centre in Plymouth told an undercover reporter 'Loads of people just give the first number they find to keep their call time down.' Another worker referred every single enquiry to a Pizza Hut in order to get the bonus, which [could] amount to a 15 percent increase on salary.

> (Daily Express 2003)

In fairness it must be added that thirty staff were dismissed by the call centre concerned shortly afterwards for giving out wrong numbers and a further thirty faced disciplinary proceedings as reported in The Times (2003).

The impact on safety also needs to be examined in case employees are actually rewarded for working dangerously. One of the many ways in which this can and does happen concerns some of the 'job and finish' arrangements for lorry drivers. Such schemes may enable drivers to be paid at premium rates for trips done over and above their daily target. As well as encouraging unsafe driving this may also lead to excessive vehicle wear and fuel consumption.

GROUP SCHEMES

Most of the comments already made about financial incentive schemes also apply to group schemes. However, there are some specific aspects relating to group schemes that also need to be considered. Group schemes seem to work best when the group is no bigger than eight to

12 people, and the task is inherently a group rather than an individual task. If a plant-wide scheme is used, the relationship between individual effort and reward may be too weak for there to be an obvious causal relationship between the effort of the individual and overall output. Individual earnings may move in parallel with total output, but that does not prove that people are working harder because of a group incentive scheme. Employees may perceive that their earnings will be very much the same, however hard or little they work. They may also perceive that many factors other than their effort, or even the effort of themselves and their fellow workers, may affect total output – for example workflow and technological change.

PROFIT SHARING

There are two main types of profit-sharing arrangements – profit-related pay and employee-share option plans. The same issues concerning the weakness of the link between reward and individual performance emerge as with group bonus schemes. A fallacy about distributing profits in the form of shares is the assumption that once employees have a shareholder role they will forget about the far more important wage-earner role and simply behave in the best interests of the shareholders. It is when 'weights' are attached to these two roles that it becomes apparent that any link between group performance and group profits may not actually be caused by a profit-sharing incentive. If the roles come into conflict employees may behave in such a way that they protect their wage-earner role and subordinate any shareholder interests to this much greater primary role. Admittedly, often the roles will not be in conflict and there may be a general value in exposing employees to the shareholder perspective. However, variations in profits may in fact have little to do with the supposed motivating effect of a profit-sharing scheme regardless of whether the rewards are in the form of direct payments or shares. Much may depend on market factors over which employees have little or no control.

Example

Potential impact of profit-sharing on business survival

In extreme circumstances such arrangements can threaten the survival of a business. Another lesson from the collapse of Barings Bank in 1995 (see Chapter 5) was that the reckless and uncontrolled pursuit of profits and bonuses can destroy an organisation. An estimated £80 million was paid out in bonuses based on the false profits reported by Nick Leeson (Fay 2004). These high profits may well have encouraged those responsible for supervising Nick Leeson to fail to examine his activities closely enough.

Sometimes the remuneration of company directors includes share option schemes. This may enable them to purchase shares in the company they work for at preferential prices. Whilst this may bring positive results, there is the danger that company results are manipulated in the short term in order that directors improve their own capital gains by the purchase and resale of shares acquired in this way.

Summary

Employers need to bear in mind the often conflicting objectives of the payment systems that are installed in their organisations. The conflicting pressures on organisational pay arrangements include the need to pay certain employees more because of market conditions and the need for a payment system that is, internally, felt to be fair. Two main frameworks which employers may consider for remunerating their employees, and which may complement one another, are the use of financial incentive schemes and job evaluation.

Job evaluation is a technique that may provide the basis for establishing a rational organisational pay structure. It may also be particularly useful in establishing viable internal pay relativities. However, schemes have to be carefully chosen, operated and monitored. The two main types of job evaluation schemes are non-analytical and the generally more complicated analytical schemes. A relatively recent innovation has been to grade jobs in part, or even sometimes completely, on the basis of the relevant job competencies that people need and/or display in a job.

Despite the European Equal Value regulations, there are strong cost and organisational pressures for schemes to be simpler. The pressures for simpler schemes include the increased rate of organisational change, the desire for broader job banding to achieve greater job flexibility and more emphasis on individual performance in determining pay.

Care needs to be taken before embarking on the use of financial incentive schemes. There are many potential reasons for poor performance and lack of financial incentive may be only one of them. Even if there is a lack of financial incentive, schemes that link pay to productivity or profitability don't always work. The basic conditions that have to be met for schemes to succeed were identified. Even when the conditions are right for the use of a financial incentive scheme, the right scheme has to be chosen and carefully implemented and operated.

Schemes that are inappropriate or badly run may not only fail to improve performance but can be counterproductive and have damaging long-term consequences for an organisation. The main types of financial incentive are individual and group schemes related to output or performance, and profit-sharing. The issue of performance-related pay is considered in Chapter 10 in the context of appraisal generally.

Self-assessment questions

(If you wish to check the extent to which your answer to any of the following questions is appropriate, cross-refer to the Table of Contents. The contents for this chapter are on pages xiv–xv.)

1 What are the main labour market and organisational changes causing employers to review the way in which they financially reward their employees?

2 What are the purposes of job evaluation schemes?

3 What are the main operational problems in ensuring that job evaluation schemes remain effective?

4 Under what circumstances might financial incentive schemes be effective?

5 Identify the potential long-term effects of employee financial incentive schemes.

References

(Works of particular interest are marked with a star.)

Daily Express, 29 September 2003.

Fay, Stephen (2004), *The Collapse of Barings*, Diana Publishing Co.

National Board for Prices and Incomes (1968a), *Payment by Results Systems, Report No. 65*, Cmnd. 3627, HMSO, p. 11 of pamphlet summarising the above report.

National Board for Prices and Incomes (1968b), *Statistical Supplement to Payment by Results report*, para. 22.

Porter, C. and B. Spear (2008), *Strategic Human Resource Management*, Ch. 3 in C. Porter, C. Bingham and D. Simmonds (Eds), *Exploring Human Resource Management*, McGraw-Hill.

People Management (2005), Journal of the Institute of Personnel and Development (UK), August.

Shortland, Sue (2008), *Managing Internationally Mobile Personnel*, in Christine Porter, Cecilie Bingham and David Simmonds (Eds) *Exploring Human Resource Management*, pp. 408–412, McGraw-Hill.

The Times, Business Section, 30 September, 2003.

The Times, 20 January 2007, *Doctors' anger over plan to limit pay*.

The Times, 12 March 2007, *Thousands face pay cut under new equality law*.

The Times, 19 April 2007, *Consultants given 25% pay rise for fewer hours*.

The Times, 21 September 2007, *Equal Pay Tribunals 'not fit for purpose'*.

Women and Work Commission (2007), *Shaping A Fairer Future*, HMSO.

Cases cited

Bromley versus H. J. Quick Ltd. (1988), IRLR, no. 249, CA.

Enderby versus Frenchay Health Authority (1993), TLR, 12 November, ECJ.

Hayward versus Cammell Laird Shipbuilders Ltd (1988), ICR 464, IRLR 257. HL.

Pickstone versus Freemans plc (1988), IRLR 267, HL.

Further reading

*Armstrong, Michael and Helen Murlis (2004), *Reward Management – A Handbook of Remuneration Strategy and Practice*, Kogan Page. (A comprehensive and highly practical account and evaluation of reward strategies, including salary administration.)

*Hastings, Sue, Willie Wood, Michael Armstrong and Ann Cummins (2004), *Job Evaluation – A Guide to Achieving Equal Pay*, Kogan Page. (A very useful guide about job evaluation, particularly on the increasingly important issue of establishing schemes that are not gender biased.)

*Wright, Angela (2007), *Reward Management in Context*, CIPD. (A sound analytical and critical account of reward strategies giving a good balance between theory and practice.)

Communication

Introduction

This chapter is probably the most important in the whole book. The topic, as well as needing to be covered in its own right, serves as a foundation for much of the rest of the book. It also links back with material covered in previous chapters. This includes the link between organisational structure and the effectiveness of communication, and the growing importance of electronic communication, both covered in Chapter 3. Other phenomena that interrelate with communication are managerial style and culture, topics that are covered in Chapter 4.

The chapter starts with an explanation of why communication is such an important topic. Managers spend most of their time trying to communicate with others. This can be in a variety of ways, particularly talking, listening, writing, reading, attending meetings and sometimes by use of the media. Consequently, if readers are able to develop their communication skills as a result of reading this chapter, they can benefit time and time again. If the communication process is ineffective, the basis on which managers or others try and take decisions is likely to be faulty. Unfortunately, managers are often over-optimistic about the effectiveness of the communication process.

Over-optimism is one obstacle to effective communication. Other obstacles to effective communication are also examined. An understanding of these obstacles is a way of identifying the skills needed for effective communication. A key skill is active listening. Attention is also paid to presentational and written skills, including the effective use of email. Emphasis is placed on the importance of managers letting other people communicate with them, as much of the time this is what is needed. As organisational structure can facilitate or hinder effective communication, attention is paid to this issue. The problems in communicating between different national cultures are also considered. The growing importance of electronic communication and also some of the problems that it can create are examined. The final topic is the role of the mass media. This involves both the interpretation of media messages and presentational skills.

The importance of communication

Managers are likely to spend most of their time engaged directly in some form of communication process. Even when they are working alone – for example, studying or preparing reports – they are relying on other people's attempts to communicate with them or they are preparing to communicate with others. Accuracy in decision-making depends, in particular, on effective communication. If the communication process is faulty, then everything else can be affected.

Experiments, research and sheer personal observation show that most people are far too optimistic about the accuracy of the communication process. This applies not just to communication processes within employing organisations, but to life in general. Even when errors are identified it may be too late, or the inherent faults in the process that will lead to further errors may not be recognised. The effective communication of factual information can be difficult enough, but often attitudes and feelings need to be communicated, and that can be far more complicated. The number and nature of the barriers are such that there is a strong case for communication skills training being given as part of the standard school curriculum. This is not yet generally the case, and in this chapter the attempt is made to give managers practical guidance on how to identify the communication processes in their organisations with a view to evaluating their effectiveness. This evaluation can then provide the basis for the development of the manager's own practical skills of communication.

In Rosemary Stewart's study of how managers spend their time, referred to in Chapter 2, it was established that on average the 160 managers in the sample spent two-thirds of their time working with other people (Stewart 1988, p. 50). It seems reasonable to assume that most managers spend the bulk of their working day in some type of communication activity. Even the 33 managers in backroom-type jobs in Stewart's survey sample spent about half of their time working with other people. This may be through attendance at meetings, the giving and receiving of instructions, discussions with colleagues and contact with customers or suppliers. Such contact may be electronic, face to face, over the telephone or a combination of all three. Much of the remainder of the time is likely to be concerned with the assimilation or preparation of written information. If managers are to make the correct substantive decisions in their jobs, it follows that they need to be able to handle the communication process effectively. A problem of communication within organisations is that if it is faulty, everyone else in the communication chain can be misinformed. Also, the longer the chain, the greater the chance of further error creeping in.

It follows that the need to develop skills for effective communication may be a critical priority for many managers. Regrettably, this need is often not perceived, and managers may neglect the importance of, and the opportunity for, development in this critical area. Communication skills tend to be taken for granted and lack of skill far more easily recognised in others than in oneself. A consequence of blaming others is that people do not see the need to improve their own skills. The process of communication is often far more complex than people realise, and this is a further reason why skills development in this area tends to be neglected. It is only when people realise the subtleties concerning effective communication that they may become communication-conscious and start to develop their own skills. The complexities are such that those who are good at communication are likely to become even better if they systematically evaluate and consider their own effectiveness in this area.

Obstacles to effective communication

Having stressed the importance of the communication process, it is appropriate to develop further the hypothesis that communication in organisations is a great deal worse than most people realise. Explaining the nature of communication processes and the potential for breakdown will do this. Case examples are given to illustrate some of the major points.

TIME

Communication can be time-intensive. This can be either because of the need for prior preparation, giving people time to ask questions and the amount of listening that may be required. Time will also be needed to identify potential problems and ways of overcoming them. As managers are usually short of time, and often not as skilled as they think they are in communicating, insufficient time may be allowed.

LANGUAGE

Those involved in the communication process may not have a common language. Language differences can occur because of variations in technical understanding, general vocabulary levels and the use of in-house terms that are not familiar to others. This can be aggravated if there are significant differences in ability levels. The complications involved in communicating between different nationalities are dealt with later in this chapter in the section on national culture.

LISTENING PROBLEMS

It is appropriate to explain one major misconception about communication at this stage. This point is not only important in its own right, but develops the argument that the approach of many managers to communication may not be sufficiently sophisticated.

Communication is usually seen as the need to brief other people. The reality is that most of a manager's time needs to be concerned with *receiving* rather than the imparting of information and views. The reason for this is simple – in any conversation between two people there is a need to alternate between talking and listening. There is not much point in anyone talking if the intended recipient is not prepared to listen. If the two people involved in a discussion take equal turns talking and listening, they will obviously spend half of their time in the listening role.

As much of the communication in organisations involves face-to-face discussion between more than two people, it follows as a mathematical fact that most managers will need to spend more time listening than talking. There will be exceptions to this, but the very existence of exceptions reduces the time available for others to do the talking. Admittedly, managers may often need to take the lead in explaining things to their subordinates, but a statistically unequal share of talk in this direction may easily be counterbalanced by the time they have to spend in discussions and meetings involving a number of people when they talk only for a minority of the time. The basic point of this argument is that managers may fail to see that they will normally need to spend more time listening than talking.

Effective listening does not come naturally to all managers, particularly if they do not recognise the importance of it. People who set out to improve the quality of communication in organisations often assume that good communication is synonymous with the imparting of information. House magazines, letters from the chief executive, briefing meetings and training in public speaking are based mainly on the assumption that the problem is in disseminating information. The reality may be that it is more important to unblock the obstructions to information and views flowing in to the key decision-makers. The problem may be that, until such time as communication is effective, managers may not realise that the obstructions are there. In any case, if everyone concentrates on imparting information and views, just who will be left to receive all these messages? It is also easy for people to be distracted from effective listening. They may have other problems on their mind, be physically distracted or simply lack the motivation to listen carefully.

BOGUS FEEDBACK

When communication is initiated it is necessary for the initiator to consider both what the evidence is for assuming that the communication has been effective and the consequences of communication being defective. People can be very aware of their lack of understanding when they are on the receiving end of an instruction. It can be very tempting, however, to create an impression of understanding through silence. The problem is that the initiator may be left with quite a false impression of their effectiveness. If a message is particularly important it is up to the initiator to search for more positive corroboration that communication has been effective than mere silence. They will need to consider other forms of feedback and to distinguish between accurate and bogus feedback.

Silence is not the only way in which people give false impressions about having understood explanations. There are occasions when people actually say they have understood when they have not. This commonly occurs, for instance, when someone asks for directions somewhere but are so confused by the instructions that they may say that they have understood when they have not. This type of breakdown can happen within organisations and for a variety of reasons. These include fear of embarrassment, inability to understand the person trying to help, politeness and impatience. Often people do not like to show their ignorance to people in positions of authority.

Miscommunication

A student nurse was asked to give a patient an air ring. She apparently was not quite sure what to do but guessed that the appropriate interpretation was to move the patient's bed on to the veranda and remove the bedclothes. In actual fact, the nurse had been expected to get an inflatable rubber air ring so that the patient could sit on it and receive a blanket bath. Another student nurse was given the same instruction but with slightly different phraseology – she was told to go and get an air ring. She returned three-quarters of an hour later saying how much she had enjoyed her walk!

A further student nurse was expected to give a patient a warm drink of potassium citrate. As is so often the case, an abbreviation was used and she was asked to give the patient a 'hot pot cit'. Unfortunately her interpretation of this instruction led to the patient being sat upon a bedpan of boiling water!

In the above cases the students' guesswork fortunately just led to comic results. That will not always be the case and such errors in the communication process may be picked up too late or not at all. The errors in the previous examples may be seen as stupidity or feebleness on the part of the student nurses, but such an interpretation is to miss the point. The fault really lies with the person who gave the instruction not ensuring that they had made themselves properly understood. Either they needed to make a positive check that the instruction was understood, or they needed to have created a working relationship with the student nurse such that queries would be raised if necessary. The objective with communication needs to be to see that it is effective rather than being able to lay the blame on someone else if things go wrong.

Nursing examples have been given to illustrate the need to get accurate feedback. However, such problems are likely in almost any organisation, particularly if the culture is authoritarian. Sometimes those in authority may go through the motions of obtaining feedback when in fact what they want is simply the pretence and alibi that people have had a fair opportunity to raise queries. Rhetorical questions may be used – such as 'Is that clear?' – which do not really invite responses. The technique can be observed with lecturers and after-dinner speakers who leave the opportunity for questions until an impossibly late stage in the proceedings.

A military example

When military orderly officers had to go through the routine of asking if there were complaints about the food some mastered the technique of asking if there were any queries in such a way that anyone who did complain deserved a medal. This enabled the orderly officer to maintain the fiction that people had been given an opportunity to complain about the food if they were dissatisfied.

Should subordinates nevertheless voice criticisms in situations like those described above they may have the blame put back on them, however unjustly, to discourage further criticism. However, employees can also misperceive the response to their comments or questions. Sometimes it may be necessary and possible for them to raise sensitive issues. In doing this it may be as well to remember the skills of assertiveness explained in Chapter 4.

RESISTANCE TO CRITICISM AND BAD NEWS

It is important to recognise that any manager is going to prefer to hear good news rather than bad news, and the temptation for colleagues and subordinates is to tell people what they want to hear. In the long term this can be disastrous, and managers and political leaders alike need consciously to recognise the distortion that can occur in channels of communication and beware of succumbing to it.

The chances of blocking out critical or unfavourable news can be greatly reduced if the temptation to do this is consciously recognised and if modern-day equivalents of the ancient Greek tradition of slaying the messenger who brings news of defeat in battle is avoided. Another classical example concerns the Greek Mathematician Pythagoras:

Extreme example of resistance to criticism

A student of Pythagoras, Hippasus, grasped the concept of irrational numbers, contrary to Pythagoras's view that all numbers were rational. 'However, Pythagoras was unwilling to accept that he was wrong . . . To his eternal shame he sentenced Hippasus to death by drowning'.

(Singh 1998, p. 54)

Withholding bad news

On 21st July 2005 the London Metropolitan Police were involved in a hunt for people who had attempted to become suicide bombers on the underground network and on a bus. Unfortunately an innocent person was mistaken for a suicide bomber and was shot and killed by the police at an underground station. Some senior police officers then began to real-ise that a tragic mistake probably had been made, but did not warn the Commissioner of the Metropolitan Police, Sir Ian Blair, before he went on television the next day to assert that the person who had been shot, Jean Charles de Menezes, had been a would-be suicide bomber.

(Sunday Times 2007)

It is often necessary to make independent checks to evaluate the information that is received. It was comprehension of this point which led some generals at the time of the First World War to say, 'If you want to know what's going on you have to go to the trenches.' Having said this, it is necessary also to make the point that there are few people, if any, who can cope with the whole truth all the time. Total exposure could be destructive to the individual concerned. What is needed is a realisation that the information fed to one in organisations needs careful evaluation, and other information may be needed but not passed on. Managers may need to seek out the bad news to the extent that it is necessary and to the extent that they can cope with it. An adage concerning delegation is that managers get the subordinates they deserve. The same adage can be used with regard to communication: managers get the communication they deserve.

SELECTIVE PERCEPTION AND BIAS

In considering barriers to communication, it is also necessary to deal specifically with the prob-lems caused by selective perception and bias. The sheer volume of data that is available means that one has to have some basis for deciding what to look for and what to react to. However, careful judgement is needed in making these decisions. A totally open mind can simply mean that a person is swamped with data. A closed mind can mean that a person doesn't respond to what is under their nose. Particular dangers are seeing only what you want to see, making the 'facts' fit what has already been decided, and suppressing unpleasant facts.

A military example of selective perception

Example

Norman Dixon (1976), a former Army psychiatrist, explains a number of Western military disasters in terms of selective perception on the part of the military leaders concerned. Three of the many examples he documents concern the Japanese attack on Pearl Harbour, the fall of Singapore and the failure of the Arnhem offensive in the Netherlands. The pattern according to Dixon is clear and recurrent – the warning signs were there but, because they did not fit into the established thinking, they were ignored until too late. The extent to which people can be misled or even coerced into believing things, which are untrue, can be alarming.

Impact of group pressure

Example

In one experiment conducted with American students by S. E. Asch it was found that a quarter of students could be coerced into stating that straight lines were of identical length when one was 25 per cent shorter than the other (Secord and Backman 1964, pp. 304–307). This effect was achieved by priming the seven students in an experimental group to say that the lines were identical in length.

One must be careful not to overgeneralise about the amount of social coercion possible from the results of a series of experiments in America with a particular group and at a particular time. However, if social pressure can have this effect on such obvious matters of fact, what is the scope for social pressure on matters that are more subjective or where people's self-interest is involved?

As well as having to cope with one's own subjectivity, it must also be recognised that much of the data which is available within organisations is subjective or actually misleading. In Chapter 3 some of the reasons were given as to why department managers might be more concerned with protecting their reputations than with supplying objective data about their performance. Most people working in organisations are likely to be concerned with the pursuit of truth, but people in organisations, as in life generally, are under a variety of pressures to highlight some things and not others. There are also pressures to view events in a particular way. This means that managers need to evaluate carefully the information that is being fed to them. One of the themes of the British TV comedy series 'Yes, Minister' (later 'Yes, Prime Minister') was that information was fed to the Cabinet minister by his permanent secretary in such a way that the minister thought that he was taking the decisions himself. One stratagem was that the options were put so that the minister was bound to choose the one preferred by his permanent secretary. This is why politicians at both national and local government level sometimes have political advisers and support staff to provide them with alternative viewpoints and other information.

Selective perception may be particularly likely if the parties involved in the communication process have different objectives. The greater the amount of the conflict, the more likely that there are emotional blockages to effective communication. A major problem can be created by the frames of reference of the parties concerned. Managers with a unitary frame of reference may have difficulty in understanding that what is in the interests of an organisation as a whole may not necessarily be in the interests of all sections of the organisation. This concept is dealt with in detail in Chapter 14 on employee relations.

GENDER DIFFERENCES

There may be obstacles of communication when a person is trying to communicate with a member of the opposite sex. It would seem reasonable to assume that just as cultures vary in their masculinity and femininity (Hofstede 2001) so also there are likely to be variations in the way that members of different sexes communicate, both with one another and with members of the opposite sex. The existence of different national conventions of communication between people of different genders is referred to in the later section in this chapter on national culture. The extent of the difference is likely to vary according to how much sex equality there is within a particular culture. Whilst there is an obvious danger of stereotyping, the implication of Hofstede's work is that men may tend to be more aggressive and individualistic than women. They may also tend to operate on a low-context basis whilst women may tend to rely more on non-verbal cues, which are high-context (Hall 1997). Particular difficulties may arise when a person of one sex fails to adapt their style of communication, where appropriate, when communicating with a member of the opposite sex. For example, there may be a lower tolerance level for aggression in communication on the part of many women compared with men. Also the body language and body contact acceptable in communication between men may not always be acceptable in their communication with women. The dress code adopted by both may also give an indication of the expected pattern of communication between the sexes.

Skills of effective oral communication

Much of the skill in effective communication lies in recognising the problem areas that have just been identified. Effective communication is achieved as much as anything by avoiding these traps. One also has to beware of relying on information that is not in the form of original evidence. Groups such as research scientists, historians, medical doctors and lawyers are amongst those who are particularly aware of the danger of distortion – whether deliberate, subconscious or accidental – through relying on evidence that is not received first-hand. It won't always be possible as a manager to rely on direct evidence, but at least the dangers of relying on secondary sources can be recognised. Also, the quality of original or secondary source material provided by managers can be improved by the positive approaches explained in the rest of this section.

COAXING INFORMATION

It may be necessary for managers to work hard at coaxing information, particularly if people feel inhibited about discussing a particular issue. The lament, 'Why didn't someone tell me?' can be as much a condemnation of a manager's lack of skill in developing effective channels of communication as a condemnation of others for keeping them in the dark. It can be very hard for those in authority roles to realise the difficulty that others may have in communicating with them. The authority figure may feel totally relaxed and uninhibited and not appreciate that perhaps the very factors which create their security also create difficulties for others. The proprietor of a business may feel totally self-confident and secure and be amazed to find out, if they ever do, that people who are very dependent on them are reluctant to tell them anything unpleasant. Parents can encounter the same problem with their children. They may forget what it was like to be a child and be unaware of many of the thoughts and anxieties that their own children have and see any suggestion to the contrary as quite preposterous.

ACTIVE LISTENING

Adopting a listening role can be harder than taking the lead by talking. The problem with this can be that the more an authority figure talks, the less others may be inclined to talk. There can be a critical moment when people in the subordinate role might just start saying what they really feel, if only the authority figure stays quiet long enough. Once the subordinate has started talking, things may come out with a rush, to the amazement of the authority figure. One useful technique in any such situation can be to count silently to ten before breaking the silence after you have asked a particularly important question.

Once a person has started to talk it can be relatively easy to get them to continue and for any others to join in. The problem is likely to be how to get them started. The authority figure needs to be aware of letting their ignorance, impatience or even their own nervousness prevent such a process starting. Care has to be taken with the timing of invitations for people to open up – it is not only the time and the place that can be important but also the stage in a discussion. It may be necessary to build up rapport gently before the invitation is given.

Thought also needs to be given to the way in which questions are put. Questions can be leading in nature, giving the impression that all that is required is confirmation of the questioner's obvious views, such as 'Don't you think this is a good idea?'. Alternatively they can be probing and phrased in such a way as to encourage the respondents to state their own views. One useful distinction, especially important in selection interviewing, is between open questions, which encourage people to talk, and closed questions which limit responses to, for example, 'yes or 'no'. These issues are examined further in Chapter 9 on selection and Chapter 12 on counselling.

SCENE SETTING

The choice of time and place to invite people to talk can be critical. There are circumstances in which people may be prepared to 'open up' and circumstances in which they will not. One of the skills of communication is picking up the cues as to whether a person is or is not prepared to talk about a sensitive matter. Even if the place cannot always be chosen, sometimes the geography of a room can be arranged to encourage, or for that matter to discourage, a person from talking. The more status symbols surrounding the authority figure, the less likely a subordinate is to feel free to talk.

Example

Scene setting

A Human Resources officer, who was over six feet tall, always made a point of seeing that he and the works superintendent were both seated if anything of consequence was to be discussed. The HR officer had learned from experience that the superintendent was self-conscious about being short so he did his best not to emphasise it.

A related issue is the use of open-plan offices. Originally these were found to be particularly useful in drawing offices and were meant to facilitate both monitoring of work and communication. However, the very openness can discourage people from speaking about confidential issues because of the fear of being overheard, or just being seen talking to a particular person. Consequently, open-plan layouts can actually create barriers to effective communication.

CHOICE OF LANGUAGE

Language difficulties can obviously hamper communication between people who have different national languages. Regional dialects can also complicate matters. However, there can be many other and more subtle language problems even between people who are from the same country, region and class. Technical language, which is beyond the comprehension of some of the participants, may be used in discussion. In any organisation there are likely to be abbreviations, words with special connotations, and 'in-terms' whose meaning is taken for granted by those inside the organisation. Even when communication is between professionals of the same organisation there can be confusion about the meaning of words.

Words with more than one meaning

Two nurses were talking about sterilisation policies in their respective parts of the health service. One was a midwife and the other a community nurse. It took a quarter of an hour before they realised that one was talking about sterilisation as a means of birth control and the other about sterilisation of feeding bottles as a means of protecting babies from infection!

The recurring problem with language in communication is that the person who is trying to explain something may understandably use the language that is most convenient to them without perhaps realising that there is a choice of language. The person receiving the explanation may also, understandably, be reluctant to admit that they cannot understand the language that is used. The skill is in recognising that even when ordinary language is used there may be problems of comprehension. The initiator of any communication needs to get positive confirmation that the language they are using is one that can be understood.

In identifying the appropriate language for communication, attention needs to be given to the possibility of ambiguity. The more important the consequences of error, the more attention needs to be devoted to avoiding ambiguity. If stress is needed on this point, it can be provided by the ambiguous use of words which contributed to the world's worst air disaster at Tenerife in the Canary Islands in 1977.

Potential consequences of word ambiguity

The Dutch pilot of a KLM jumbo jet, who was ironically also the head of their flight training department, was preparing to take off at Tenerife. He explained that he was ready to the air traffic controllers and in response was told 'OK. (pause) Stand by for take-off. I will call you.' In the pause after the word 'OK' there was radio interference because of a radio query by the captain of a Pan Am jumbo about the intentions of the KLM captain. It seems likely that this caused the KLM captain to assume that the word 'OK' was the complete message. In any event, the KLM captain then took off and collided with the Pan Am Jumbo, killing a total of 583 people. The investigators commissioned by the American Airline Pilots Association concluded that this was the most likely explanation of events. They also commented on the ambiguous use of the term

Example

Example

'take-off'. Their comments on the use of the term 'OK' were as follows:

The word (or letters) 'OK' can be ambiguous also; to the controller it was either a word of acknowledgement or a delaying term to allow a moment to think. It can also mean a host of other things, such as a state of well-being, a check-off of a task accomplished, or a statement of approval. It could have had the latter meaning for the KLM crew.

(American Airline Pilots Association 1978, pp. 22–24)

BODY LANGUAGE – GENERAL

The expressions, gestures and other body language that people may use without necessarily realising it can be important cues as to what they really think. Communication is not just imparting information; it often involves, or needs to involve, understanding people's attitudes and feelings, which are not always clearly expressed in words. In some cases people may even feel obliged to say the opposite of what they really think. It is not uncommon, for example, for people to say 'how interesting' in a tone of voice which indicates that they are in fact bored. An adage which makes the point that people sometimes accidentally misrepresent themselves is, 'Listen to what I mean, not what I say.'

As words can be an inadequate or a misleading guide to what people really think, it can be important to look for other cues to people's thoughts. A catalogue could be prepared of what particular physical cues could mean: fidgeting, that a person has other things on their mind; a glazed expression, that a person doesn't understand, and so on. Given that such a list could be very long and only be a guide anyway, the point that needs to be stressed is simply to watch for physical cues to a person's real thoughts, especially when it is likely that a person is not able to be, or does not want to be, frank about a particular topic. It can be very tempting to rely just on the words that a person uses, particularly if they give the answer that one wants to hear. To rely on words alone can be quite insufficient.

Example

Contradiction between body language and other behaviour

An intriguing example of what might be learnt by studying a person's bodily behaviour concerns an allegation about Nikita Khrushchev's conduct during a famous debate at the General Assembly of the United Nations. Khrushchev interrupted proceedings by banging on the table with his shoe. This was part of his protest about American reconnaissance flights over the USSR in their U2 spy planes, which came to light when the American pilot Gary Powers was cap-tured in 1960. The allegation is that TV cameras revealed Khrushchev had shoes on both feet and that the one he banged on the table just before he left the platform was a third shoe brought into the conference chamber expressly for that purpose. If the allegation is true, it reveals that the demonstration was a calculated piece of histrionics and not a spontaneous burst of anger.

The topic of body language is examined again later in this chapter in the context of national culture and also in Chapter 15 in the context of negotiation.

Oral presentation skills

LIMITATIONS OF DOWNWARD COMMUNICATION

Having emphasised the obstacles to effective communication and in particular the importance of upward communication, it is appropriate to say something about the presentational skills involved in downward communication. At the risk of being repetitious, it is first of all necessary to be aware of the limitations of downward communication, particularly in terms of volume, accuracy and commitment to that which is being communicated. There can be a role for devices such as mission statements and team briefings, but only in the context of the appropriate organisational culture and structure, and only if such devices are carefully thought out and competently implemented.

SPECIFIC SKILLS

Having commented on the limitations that downward communication can have, it is also necessary to emphasise how it can be very important. Managers have a responsibility to impart information and they need to do this effectively. They need to use time to optimum effect so that they influence the audience in the way they want to without wasting their time. The larger the audience, the greater the potential for wasted time. If the time available is limited, it is particularly important that the presenter makes good use of it. Crucial decisions can be made as a result of formal presentations, e.g. whether or not important business proposals are accepted or not. The reputations of managers may also depend on how effective their presentation skills are, particularly because people will be able to judge how good these skills are. As with teaching, it is no good a person being technically competent if they cannot explain their ideas in such a way that others are motivated to listen and able to understand. Whatever level of oral presentation skills a person has, it is usually possible to improve it by analysis, preparation and practice. The following checklist may be useful with regard to formal or informal oral presentations.

- Clarify objectives
- Identify the target audience
- Consider what prior publicity may be necessary
- Geographical and acoustic arrangements
- Consider structure
- Will the opening attract interest?
- To what extent can the audience be involved?
- Motivation and comprehension of the audience
- Timing (e.g. for dramatic effect), pace and duration
- Time control (taking into account length of time slot available)

- Beware of reading from notes, as this reduces spontaneity and eye contact – prompt cards or an aide-memoir may be much better
- Visual aids, e.g. PowerPoint, overhead projector slides, prepared flip chart material, exhibits (PowerPoint should be used as a supplement to presentation and not degenerate to the presenter simply repeating what is on the screen)
- Clarity of expression and choice of language
- Eye contact and body language
- Volume of information – not too little, but beware of presenting too much and losing the audience in the detail
- Use of humour and dramatic pauses
- Pitch and variety of voice
- Use of examples
- Rehearsal
- Opportunity for feedback
- Back-up notes and sources of further information
- Evaluation of presentation
- Modifications for the future

Written communication

Written communication is a form of one-way communication. Forms of written communication can range from a memorandum to one person to a formal report that will be distributed to a large readership. Because of the lack of opportunity for immediate feedback, it is important that writers express themselves clearly, concisely and without ambiguity. Time invested in doing this can avoid error, inappropriate responses, reduce queries and save the time of the reader. If a document is going to a number of people, organisational time can be saved if the distribution list is accurately targeted. The need to invest time in writing was emphasised by the French writer Pascal (1657) when he wrote to a friend: 'I have made this letter longer than usual only because I have not had the time to make it shorter.'

USE OF LANGUAGE

The language used when writing needs to be convenient to the reader. There are a variety of reasons why writers may use inappropriate language. They may simply use the language that is most convenient to them. However, if this is too full of technical jargon or is unnecessarily complicated, the content may not be understood. However, if the writer wants to communicate and understands their subject, it should generally be possible to explain issues clearly. Written communication that is difficult to follow is often caused more by deficiencies of the writer than the lack of ability of the reader.

Sometimes matters have to be expressed in a precise technical way, and the use of particular language is unavoidable. This can be the case with legal documents, where the only way of achieving the necessary clarity is to use precise legal expressions. However, even when technical language is used there is good and bad practice. There is no benefit in explaining matters in a more complicated way than is necessary. All too often sophisticated terms can be used unnecessarily because of a desire by the writer to impress, clumsy expression, or lack of clarity in the actual thinking. The use of many sociological terms, in particular, can be for these reasons. Increasingly correspondence is by email. The skills involved in using this effectively are considered later in this chapter in the section on electronic communication.

HELPLINES

A growing practice with manufacturers and providers of some services is to provide a helpline telephone number. This enables clients to engage in two-way communication about the use of the product or service. It may be an important selling point. It may also give the provider of the product or service useful feedback about the quality of any written instructions. Furthermore, it may provide important market research data about customer responses to the product or service itself.

HOUSE MAGAZINES

Many organisations keep staff informed by way of house magazines or newsletters. This can be very useful, but it has to be remembered that it is an exercise in one-way communication. It is important to devise complementary ways of checking on staff opinion, such as employee representative structures. Readership surveys are a way of judging the reaction to the actual magazines and newsletters. Care, however, needs to taken about the content of magazines and newsletters. Employees may have a quite different perspective of the organisation to that of senior managers. It may also be necessary to check that the messages don't have unintended consequences.

In one national brewing company a copy of the house magazine was produced at a negotiating meeting. The employee representatives wanted to know why the company was only offering a low wage increase when the magazine included details of its healthy profits and major expenditure programme.

Example

Organisational structure

The need for organisational structures to facilitate the accomplishment of organisational objectives was considered in Chapter 3. As part of that process organisations need to be structured so that the right information gets to the necessary people at the right time so that any appropriate action can be taken. Unfortunately, the structure of many organisations does not facilitate communication and therefore is, or has become, no longer 'fit for purpose'.

There is no one correct model of an organisation. Structures need to fit the needs of particular situations. Even if the fit between the need for information flows and organisational structure is right, the way in which the organisation actually operates may obstruct necessary information flows. Even if the structure is right, though, the style of individual managers may not be appropriate for the job they are doing. The options in managerial style were considered in Chapter 4. As a general rule authoritarian styles do not encourage accurate upward communication.

Example

An example of the problems that can be caused by not finding out what subordinates really think concerns President Saddam Hussain's invasion of Kuwait in 1990. It was difficult and dangerous for his advisers to warn the President of the risk of a Western military response. Consequently, although his military advisers are likely to have had a more realistic assessment of the consequences of invasion, they were unwilling or unable to warn him of the likely consequences.

(Simpson 1991, pp. 431–442)

National culture

Culture has many dimensions, including class, organisational, regional and national. The impact of culture on organisations was necessarily given attention in Chapter 3. The impact of national culture on communications is potentially so great that it is examined separately in this section. That impact is also growing for a number of reasons. **Globalisation**, ease of international travel and developments in information technology are making international collaboration in both the private and public sectors much more common. Managers are much more likely to have to deal with people of other nationalities, whether it be in their home country or working abroad.

Some potential obstacles to communication, such as language, are obvious. A feature of language developments is the ever-increasing importance of English as a means of international communication, including between people neither of whom speak English as their first language. There can, however, even be communication differences between those who apparently both speak English as their first language.

Example

Misunderstanding within a common language

In 1951, during the Korean war, the British brigadier in charge of the Gloucestershire Regiment needed reinforcements because he was outnumbered by Chinese soldiers by a ratio of eight to one and encircled. This was in one of the most famous battles of the war. Unfortunately, he used classic British understatement in reporting his predicament and told his American allies that 'things are a bit sticky'. This was interpreted as simply being a little difficult but not serious enough to need American help. The outcome was that only 39 of the 600 troops in the regiment escaped.

(The *Guardian* 2001)

It may be important to use what has become known as 'offshore English' when communicating with people from other countries. This form of English can be defined as that spoken by people whose first language is not English and who have learned the language as adults from a practical rather than academic perspective (Guy and Mattock 1991). Other potential obstacles to effective communication may be less obvious but nevertheless important. The very fact that they are not obvious can make them harder to deal with. These obstacles include cultural values and the varying use of body language in different cultures.

National culture can be shaped by many factors. These include history, religion, geography and climate. These in turn shape the behaviour of people, including the way they communicate with one another. The most important study to date of the impact of national culture on organisations was carried out by Hofstede (2001). This study was examined in some detail in Chapter 4. In high **power distance** cultures communication is hampered by long hierarchies and associated levels of high social inequality. It may be particularly difficult in such cultures to express views that are contrary to those of people in authority. In cultures where there is high **uncertainty avoidance** there is an emphasis on formality and on rules and regulations. In collectivist cultures it is difficult for people to express views contrary to the group or organisation at large. Feminine cultures are in contrast to macho cultures and are characterised by high levels of mutual respect for one another's opinions.

HIGH AND LOW CONTEXT CULTURES

A related concept is the distinction between high context and low context communication (Hall 1987). Some low context cultures, particularly the USA, are characterised by direct and specific expression, often reinforced by written contracts. Other cultures, particularly in Asia, are high context and much more depends on the context in which communication takes place. People in high context cultures will be much more used to interpreting meaning in accordance with factors such as personality, rank and body language. Language itself may be deliberately ambiguous. Demands for greater clarity may be seen as insulting and imply that a person is not to be trusted. The homogeneity, size and social control in a country may be important in determining whether the dominant culture is high or low context. A large country with relatively low social homogeneity and social control will be more likely to be low context. This may be why the annual output of lawyers in the USA is equal to the total stock of lawyers in Japan.

LEVEL OF FEEDBACK

In high power distance and high context cultures, managers may get little genuine feedback on their performance from their employees, particularly if they are not very effective. In such cultures local managers may realise this, but managers originating from other cultures may not.

Example

Danger of perceived lack of feedback

A British manager was anxious to impose his ideas on a group of Indonesian managers. Unfortunately he mistook silence for agreement with his suggestions and this led to him pressing his points harder and harder. He had not appreciated the need to carefully evaluate the meaning of silence or the problems the managers would have had in directly confronting him. The longer he went on, the greater the resistance he created and the greater the barriers between him and his audience

BUILDING AND MAINTAINING RELATIONSHIPS

It may take considerable time to develop working relationships between people of other cultures. It may not be realistic to discuss serious issues until an adequate level of trust is established. The distinction between roles and personalities is not as clear in some cultures as in others. When this is the case, much time may be needed to develop acceptance as a person. Particularly in Asian cultures, considerable care may need to be taken to save people's face as a way of maintaining relationships.

Example

Preserving the dignity of others

At a meeting of Indonesian and British managers one of the Indonesians made an inappropriate suggestion and everybody, including the person who made the suggestion, realised its weaknesses. However, so that the standing of this person was not damaged in the eyes of his colleagues, great efforts were made by all those present to let him gracefully retreat from the idea and to thank him for his initiative. This process took far longer than it would have in many other cultures but was necessary in the local situation.

BODY LANGUAGE – CULTURAL

The importance of body language has already been considered because of its general potential importance in communication. However, it is also necessary to specifically consider the cultural aspects. Managers need to pay attention to this, particularly in high context communication cultures. It is also important that they do not assume that particular body language signals have the same meaning in all countries. The range of body language signals, conscious or otherwise, is very great. Illustrative examples of what they might mean are explained below.

Body contact

Conventions about body contact may vary considerably between cultures. Germans, for example, are renowned for shaking hands as a form of greeting. However, Indians traditionally clasp their hands together and bow. In France and Russia a traditional greeting is to kiss one another on the cheeks. As well as needing to understand these different conventions, it may be particularly important in certain cultures to take into account potential problems about body contact between people of opposite sex.

Avoidance of inappropriate body contact

The Chinese Head of State visited Iran at a time when revolutionary Islamic fervour was particularly high. A protocol problem arose because of the presence of a woman in the Iranian reception party. Unlike the men, and because of religious conventions in Iran, she could not be seen to be shaking hands with the Chinese leader, particularly in public and on national television. However, it was also essential for her graciously to acknowledge the visitor. The problem of how she should handle her greeting was resolved by her presenting the Chinese leader with a red rose, which was handed over in such a way that each touched different parts of the stem. He was delighted with this gesture.

Eye contact

In low power distance cultures there will be an expectation that people will look you in the eye when you are talking to them. In high power distance cultures this could be seen as disrespectful on the part of the subordinate.

Facial expressions

In high context cultures more of the message may be transmitted by way of facial expression. Conventions in the permitted facial expressions that are demonstrated to members of the opposite sex can be strict in some cultures.

Misinterpretation of facial expressions

There was ill feeling amongst the female canteen workers in a West London factory because of the unappreciative way in which the Asian male production workers responded when they were served with their food. In particular, it was commented that the Asian men never smiled. When the Asian men became aware of this criticism they were bewildered. This was because, in their culture, it was seen as being unacceptable for men to smile at women they did not know. Far from trying to cause offence, they had been trying to avoid it by their impassive expressions. When this story was told to a college receptionist in London she said she could now understand why she received such few smiles from Asian visitors when she often received very broad smiles from other visitors.

Cultural differences in smiling are commented on by Platt (1998, pp. 23–29). She maintains that in the USA, for example, people generally smile when greeting someone. This is in contrast to the French, who generally only smile for more specific purposes – to do otherwise would be seen as hypocritical and devalue the role of a smile. She refers to 13 different types of smiles, each for a specific purpose.

Spatial relationships

People may have a preferred physical distance between them and the person they are talking to. Swedes and Scots tend to prefer a long distance; Arabs and Latin Americans usually prefer to be much closer (Argyle 1994).

Example

Cultural differences with spatial relationships

Americans and Europeans have been seen retreating backwards and gyrating in circles at international conferences while pursued by Latin Americans trying to establish their habitual degree of proximity (Argyle 1994). This phenomenon has led to the story, apocryphal or otherwise, of the Latin American diplomat, frustrated at not being able to get close enough to British diplomats, saying that these British diplomats are very good – if only you can catch them!

Dress

People may not always be aware of the signals they send out by the way they dress or appear.

Example

A negative dress signal

Mr Shevardnadze, who later became the President of Georgia, used to be the Communist party boss of the country when it was part of the Soviet Union. He made a name for himself by campaigning against corruption. In a famous incident he 'demanded a show of hands from members of his central committee ... and dismissed those wearing expensive wristwatches'.

(The Times 2003)

Example

Appearance

British troops serving in the RAF regiment were advised to grow beards before going to serve in Afghanistan. This was because of the respect given by local people to men who wore beards.

(The Sun 2007)

Electronic communication

The impacts of developments in information technology on organisations were examined in Chapter 3. However, the overlapping impact on communication processes also needs to be examined in this chapter. A key skill is that of using email effectively.

EMAIL

The volume of email traffic is such that people can be so swamped by information that they are prevented from getting on with the key aspects of their job. The overuse of email, in particular, can lead to managers having to spend much time sifting the important from the unimportant. This also means that managers need to ensure that they in turn do not send out unnecessary emails or unnecessary copies. The whole issue is potentially so important and relatively undocumented that it is appropriate to highlight key features of effective email communication:

- Beware of letting emails sent to you short-circuit existing organisation channels. Giving out your email address indiscriminately can encourage this.

- Only copy emails to people who really need to be involved. Beware of 'antagonistic' copying in particular, e.g. copying critical comments to a colleague's boss.

- Take time to compose an email so that it is to the point. Note too that poor grammar and typing errors betray the fact that you have not spent much time on an issue, which will not endear you to the recipient.

- Controversial, sensitive and confidential issues may be best handled by face-to-face discussion and not by email. 'Screaming' emails are generally to be avoided, e.g. where some of the content is in block capitals or underlined. Beware of getting involved in email wars or 'flame mail'. It is also necessary to beware of potential data protection liability when sending confidential information.

Speed can be a disadvantage as well as an advantage. Email does not give the opportunity for second thoughts. They can also be sent to the wrong person in error or forwarded to others without your knowledge or authority.

The potential cost of error

Example

In 2005 the president, managing director and head of technology of the Tokyo Stock Exchange (TSE) all resigned when an inputting error by a dealer of Mizuho Securities caused that bank to lose an estimated £185 million. 610 shares were offered for sale at one yen each instead of one share worth 610 yen (£3, 000). Many investment houses took advantage of the artificially depressed price of the stock. 'The TSE has been blamed for failing to respond to repeated cancellation orders placed by Mizuho within seconds of making the blunder'.

(The Times 2005 and 2006)

Media communication

The amount of time that people spend watching television, other electronic images and listening to the radio justifies a section on the media. Whilst this fits with a general consideration of communication, there may well be specific issues presented on the media that involve people in their role as managers. The material presented often needs to be carefully evaluated. Managers may also need to use the media to present their views, so consideration is also given to the basic skills of media presentation.

SPEED OF REPORTING

The impact of the media can be extremely powerful and pervasive. Strong visual images of dramatic events and human suffering can be brought quickly into the living room. Viewers can see events during wars either as they happen or shortly afterwards. People around the world saw the destruction of the twin towers in New York on 9th September 2001 as it happened.

Technological media developments mean that it is generally much more likely that important issues are handled in public than in an unobserved or unrecorded manner. There can be great benefit in this, but there are also certain dangers. Those involved in publicly conducted events have to bear in mind the simultaneous impact of their statements and actions on those with whom they may be negotiating, those they represent and the general public. This may limit their room for manoeuvre and make it much more difficult for them to retrieve mistakes and errors of judgement. Also some developments have made both open and secret recording more likely. These include the miniaturisation of equipment, its reduced cost and its easier handling.

EVALUATION OF DATA

A further issue is the evaluation of material that is presented in the media. Issues of bias or misrepresentation are often easy to spot in advertisements. However, there are other causes of distortion that may be much more difficult to recognise. This distortion may include editing of material previously recorded. In live presentations the balance of presentation, the advantages gained by a skilled presenter and the juxtaposition of items that are reported can all have a strong influence on the overall message. A trade union official, for example, may, rightly or wrongly, have a hard time explaining the reasons for industrial action just after a film showing vivid examples of the inconvenience that action may be causing.

There is an inherent conflict between the responsibility of media reporters and producers to present a fair and balanced programme and the pressure on them to attain high viewing or listening figures. The need for speedy reporting can also reduce its accuracy. All this can lead to sensationalised reporting, emphasis on the unusual and the camera bias of dramatic visual images. Such problems led John Birt and Peter Jay to comment when they worked together at Independent Television's 'Weekend Word' about the 'bias against understanding' with regard to television reporting of news and current affairs (Billen 2000, p. 29).

Presentation on the radio can be more balanced because it does not suffer from camera bias. Newspapers often have clear political affiliations but also offer readers the choice of which sections to read and the pace at which they read them. Although people can decide what programmes they watch on the television or listen to on the radio, the content has to be heavily filtered because the material has to be compressed and contained within a standard format. There cannot be the flexible use that there is with a newspaper.

The implication of the complexities of media presentation and the opportunity for distortion, deliberate or accidental, mean that it is important to evaluate critically what is being presented rather than passively accept it. This is particularly important for managers if the information they receive from the media is likely to influence the managerial decisions they make. It is as well to remember also that a whole range of interest groups are concerned in providing information to the media in order to put over a particular point of view.

At times distortion can degenerate into 'fakery'. Examples of this emerged in 2007 in Britain such as bogus winners being used in TV and radio premium phone line quiz competitions. A number of quiz shows were also withdrawn after it emerged that a significant number of viewers were being invited to contribute via premium phone lines after the winners had already been chosen. Disciplinary action by the BBC included the dismissal of some producers (The Times 2007a and 2007b). Similar problems at the Independent Television Company (ITV) caused a 'zero-tolerance' policy to be announced for such practices. The television company GMTV was also fined £2 million by the industry regulator OFCOM because of the acceptance of premium phone calls when the potential winners had already been accepted (The Times 2007c). A related issue was the 'creative' changing of the sequence of a film commissioned by the BBC. In a trade preview, a film of a 'photo-shoot' of the Queen was edited in such a way that it had the effect of showing her in an unsympathetic light and leaving the photo-shoot in a bad mood. This lead to the resignation of the controller of BBC1 and of the Chief Creative Officer of the production company involved (The Times 2007d).

MEDIA PRESENTATION SKILLS
Pitfalls

Given the potential importance of the media it is important that managers know how to present themselves on it effectively if the need arises. The earlier section in this chapter on oral presentation skills may be particularly relevant. However, managers also need to beware of the potential dangers in dealing with the media. They may have to face unexpected and hostile questions by a person well practised in the art of media interviewing. There is the possibility that they may be confronted by people with an opposing point of view without warning. Prerecorded interviews can be selectively edited to the organisation's disadvantage and/or placed in an unfavourable juxtaposition with other issues and images. Managers may also be misquoted, or have injudicious statements quoted out of context.

Countermeasures

Countermeasures that managers may wish to consider in dealing with aggressive or unfair media interviewing include:

- Insisting on a live interview to prevent selective editing.
- Only saying what you want to say – there are no penalties, as in exams, for not answering questions exactly as an interviewer wishes, apart from whatever conclusions may be drawn by the audience. Politicians can be particularly adept at not answering embarrassing questions.

- Ensuring that when answering questions you use your own words and not ones suggested to you by an interviewer.

- Before answering a question, considering saying whatever it is you want to say first of all before answering it.

- Recognising who your real audience is. It will be the viewers and not those participating in a programme. This may mean that you have to be very clear about your agenda. You may also need to use very clear language, which may differ from that wanted by other people involved in a programme.

- If provoked, not losing your temper. The person who is the most aggressive is the one most likely to lose the sympathy of the audience.

- If you do not want to give an interview, it may be much better to issue a prepared statement rather than simply state 'no comment'.

Managers engaged in potentially newsworthy activities may need to be able to react quickly to put over their point of view. Organisations may need to consider what in-house skills, policies, procedures and facilities they need to handle the media.

Summary

Managers normally spend most of their time trying to communicate with other people. Although the ability to communicate with others is important, it can be even more important to ensure that others can communicate with you. This is particularly so as managers usually need to spend more time receiving than imparting information. Accurate communication is necessary if decision-making is to be appropriate and implementation effective. Unfortunately, communication is often much less accurate than is appreciated. This lack of awareness not only leads to error, but means that people do not pay sufficient attention to the need to develop their skills in this area. However, communication skills are often easily developed and can lead to important recurring benefits.

Identification of the potential obstacles to effective communication provides a foundation for developing skills in this area. Important obstacles can be poor listening skills, lack of time, lack of a common vocabulary, poor or false feedback and resistance to criticism. A key skill is that of active listening. The way in which oral presentation skills can be improved has also been examined; however, written communication is also important. The ways in which organisational structures can facilitate or hinder communication have been considered. It is also necessary to take into account the problems of communication caused by differences in national culture.

Attention has been paid to the growing importance of electronic communication as well as some of the problems it creates. It has also been appropriate to consider the role of the media, including the evaluation of data and how to use it to communicate with others. It can be very important for managers to distinguish between their own agenda with regard to media presentation and that of media organisations.

Self-assessment questions

(If you wish to check the extent to which your answer to any of the following questions is appropriate, cross refer to the Table of Contents. The contents for this chapter are on pages xv–xvi.)

1 Identify eight examples of communication that you have been involved in during the last 24 hours.

2 Taking the examples given in your answer to question 1, identify the main obstacles there have been to that communication being effective.

3 How could you improve your own interpersonal oral communication?

4 Identify six key skills in effective oral presentation.

5 Identify four key skills in effective written communication.

6 Give examples of how differences in national culture can lead to misunderstanding.

7 If you had to give a presentation on radio or television, how would go about it?

References

(Works of particular interest are marked with a star.)

Airline Pilots Association (American)(1978), *Aircraft Accident Report: Engineering and Air Safety – Human Factors Report on the Tenerife Accident*.

*Argyle, Michael (1994), *The Psychology of Interpersonal Behaviour*, 5th ed., Penguin Books. (An excellent account of the dynamics of human interaction, including the communication dimension.)

Asch, S. E. (1964), summaries in P. F. Secord and C. W. Backman, *Social Psychology*, International Student Edition, McGraw-Hill Kogakusha Ltd.

Billen, Andrew (2000), *Banana Skins and a Bias Against Common Sense*, Evening Standard (London), 5 July.

Dixon, Norman F. (1976), *On the Psychology of Military Incompetence*, Cape.

Guy, V. and J. Mattock (1991), *The New International Manager – An Action Guide to Cross-Cultural Business*, Kogan Page.

Hall, Edward T. (1997), *Beyond Culture*, Anchor Books, US.

Hofstede, G. (2001), *Culture's Consequences*, Sage, 2nd ed.

Pascal, Blaise (1657), *Lettres Provinciales*.

Simpson, John (1991), *Why Saddam went to war*, Observer, Review Section, 21 July.

Singh, Simon (1998), *Fermat's Last Theorem*. BBC Horizon.

Stewart, Rosemary (1988), *Managers and Their Jobs*, 2nd ed., Macmillan.

The Guardian (2001), *Needless battle caused by uncommon language*. p. 3, 14 April.

The Sun (2007), statement attributed to Wing Commander Beaumont, 12 September.

The Sunday Times (2007), *Lonely of the Yard is 'off his trolley'*, 21 October.

The Times (2003), *Shevardnadze 'ready to flee to Germany'*, 21 November, p. 22.

The Times (2005), *Fat fingered typist costs traders bosses £285 million*, 9 December and *TSE President prepares to resign*, 20 December.

The Times (2006) Editorial, 17 June, and *Court fight over 'fat finger' trader blunder'*, Business Section, p. 67, 28 October.

The Times (2007)(a), *Socks, the Blue Peter cat who could cost BBC staff their jobs*, 20 September.

The Times (2007)(b), *Two BBC producers are forced out as more vote-rigging cases emerge*, 21 September.

The Times (2007)(c), *GMTV fined £2m for phone-in quizzes that deceived millions*, 27 September.

The Times (2007)(d), *Heads roll over corporation's cavalier treatment of Queen*, 6 October.

Further reading

Dickinson, Sarah (1990), *How to Take on the Media*, Weidenfeld Paperbacks.

Gowers, Sir Ernest (1986), *Plain Words*, revised by Sidney Greenbaum and Janet Whinart, HMSO, also Penguin (1987).

*Mead, Richard (2005), *International Management, Culture and Communication*, 3rd ed., Ch. 5, Blackwell. (An excellent account of the implications of the impact of cultural differences in communication for the manager.)

Payne, E. Kay (2002), *Different but Equal – Communication between the Sexes*, Westport, Praeger.

*Platt, Polly (2003), *French or Foe?, Getting the Most out of Visiting, Living and Working in France*, 3rd ed., Culture Crossings. (A very readable account of the cultural differences between France and the USA.)

Selection

Introduction

One of the most critical decisions that managers may have to make is the appointment of their staff. Managers may also be involved in the appointment of staff for other managers – for example, as members of interview panels. It is easier to exercise discretion at the appointment stage than later – it is much more difficult to remove staff once they have joined an organisation. The abilities of staff can have a critical effect on the performance of the manager concerned. Even though managers may only be involved in appointment decisions relatively infrequently, therefore, it is important that the selection decisions they take are the right ones. It is for this reason that a chapter has been devoted to selection.

One of the crucial issues in maximising the effectiveness of selection decisions is to adopt a systematic approach. Therefore, topics covered in this chapter are arranged in a particular order according to a systematic approach that managers may wish to consider adopting. This approach includes the need to identify carefully the nature of a job that has to be filled. The long-term nature of the job has to be considered as well as the immediate requirements. The next step is to identify appropriate selection criteria. Two methods are explained – developing a **person specification** and identifying the necessary **job competencies.** The ways in which information can be collected about candidates are identified. So too are the actual skills involved in selection interviewing, including the skills that may be required at panel interviews. When job criteria are established it may also be appropriate to reflect on the reasons why any previous holders of the job have left. There is no point in simply repeating any mistakes that were made about the job in the past.

This chapter includes a section on equal opportunities. This is important, because failure to have effective policies can lead to poor utilisation of the human resources available and feelings of inequity. Also there are an increasing number of legal protections against unjustified discrimination. These protections are particularly important in the areas of age, disability, gender, marital status, and race. Managers also need to be aware of their organisation's policies with regard to equal opportunities, as these policies may be more comprehensive than the statutory protections. The related topic of diversity, which takes a more proactive approach to making use of the variations and potential variations in the make-up of the workforce than simply avoiding illegal discrimination, is also covered.

The rather different skills that may be required if one is the person being interviewed for a job are also considered. A self-assessment form is included as an appendix to help readers see how they might develop their own, or other people's, selection interviewing skills.

Although this chapter is entitled 'Selection', recruitment will also be an important part of the process of recruiting a new member of staff. Broadly speaking, recruitment involves attracting a pool of candidates and selection is the process of choosing someone from that pool to be appointed. Very often specialist expertise will be available from the HR department to give advice on the process and on relevant legislation. Depending on organisational policies, the HR department will also be involved in drawing up and placing any advertisements, in attending selection interviews and administering any psychometric tests where these form part of the selection process.

The theory behind the following paragraphs is that for the effectiveness of the selection process to be maximised, a systematic process needs to be followed. The rest of this chapter suggests a process that managers should find to be effective.

Defining the job

Whether a job is new or old, considerable care needs to be taken initially in defining the exact objective and scope of the job. The material in Chapter 2 concerning the identification of objectives and key tasks may be relevant in this context. Even when jobs are well established it is important to remember that the requirements may have changed. The actual tasks that have historically been performed may not be appropriate in changed circumstances. A manager may be unaware of some of the adjustments that have taken place in a job since they perhaps occupied that position. A starting point for identifying the requirements of a job may be to get the existing job-holder to prepare an updated job description. Other information may, however, also be necessary. A job may have been tailored to take account of an individual's strengths and weaknesses. It may be necessary, therefore, to consider the extent to which such tailoring should remain if a new person is being appointed. An account given by an employee of their job may be inaccurate or may reflect what is done rather than what needs to be done. The manager concerned may need to consider what changes they and others think are necessary in a particular job. It may even be that the job does not need filling – either because there is no longer any purpose to it or because the individual tasks can more effectively be redistributed amongst other staff.

Is it necessary to fill the job?

For 20 years a large shipping company had difficulty filling one of its top jobs. It never had anyone really qualified for the position. And whoever filled it soon found themselves in trouble and conflict. But for 20 years the job was filled whenever it became vacant. In the 21st year a new president asked: 'What would happen if we did not fill it?' The answer came, 'Nothing'. It then turned out that the position had been created to perform a job that had long since become unnecessary.

(Drucker 1955, p. 320)

Sometimes a job may be necessary but not of the nature originally countenanced.

Identifying the job properly

At a panel selection interview, the clear purpose and content of a job was only completed after all the candidates had been interviewed. The original reasoning about the job in question was inadequate and the questions asked during the interviews led to a more accurate assessment of what was really required. This led to a redefined job being advertised and the whole process of selection being started again. The consolation in this example was that at least the initial error of inadequate assessment of the real job requirements was not compounded by an appointment based on an inadequate job definition.

SHORT-TERM AND LONG-TERM NEEDS

A potential problem area which is often overlooked is the distinction between the short-term and long-term needs in a job. A person may be recruited to fill a pressing but temporary need. The problem that may then arise is what to do with them when the need has passed.

Conflict between short-term and long-term needs

Someone with accountancy and computer skills was recruited to establish a computer-based accounts system. When the new system was running smoothly it was found that there was no longer any need for him and he was made redundant. Exactly the same thing happened to him in his next two jobs. Each employer appeared genuinely to think that they needed him for a permanent position. No-one had thought through what to do with the person in the medium to long term after the system had been established successfully.

The pace of technological and organisational change, in particular, means that the problem of conflict between short-term and long-term needs is likely to occur increasingly in the future. Historically jobs were, and still sometimes are, seen as positions that will remain substantially the same during the working life of the job-holders. This can cause people to try to freeze the activity of an organisation so that the demand for their existing skills is perpetuated. Once people join an organisation they become part of its political power structure. They are likely to take a lively interest in the prospects for security and promotion of people with their particular range of skills. Academic staff, for example, can take a ferocious interest in seeing that college departments run courses that provide the maximum prospects for maintaining or advancing their particular specialism. This can lead to a conflict between the short-term interests of the individual and the long-term interests of the organisation. It may, therefore, be necessary to anticipate the pressures that potential employees will put on the organisation to develop in a particular way or remain in a particular mould.

The length of manual worker apprenticeships has been gradually reduced and opportunities for apprentices and skilled workers to increase their range of skills improved. The concept of the multi-skilled worker has also made some headway. The advantages that these developments can bring include the possibility of reduced resistance to technological and organisational change because the employees are more able to adapt to changed circumstances.

Reconciling the need for specialist and generic skills

The dilemma of reconciling the need for specialist and generic skills was recognised by a multinational petrochemical company. The company recognised the dilemma of acquiring people with specialist skills for immediate problems, as well as needing people who would be prepared to adapt to the rapidly changing circumstances of their industry. The solution adopted was to recruit some graduate chemical engineers with specialised training to cope with immediate specialist needs. Other graduate engineers with a more general training were also recruited and were given either technical or managerial jobs. The latter were recruited with a view to being moved around the organisation so that they developed a range of technical and/or managerial skills. The reasoning was that as the organisation needed to adapt, so this group would be able to fill the emergent new jobs. Had only narrowly trained specialists been recruited, it seemed much less likely that the organisation would have been able to adapt to the rapidly changing circumstances of the petrochemical industry.

The distinction between short-term and long-term needs has to be considered whenever appointments are made. The pace of technological change, in particular, is such that one has to ask whether a person will be prepared and able to adapt to the radical changes in job content that are increasingly likely. Admittedly, in some cases one may say that the short-term problems are those that have to take priority and that, if necessary, future inability to cope may have to be dealt with by redundancy. It seems prudent, however, at least to consider taking on a person with a temperament and range of skills that would make adjustment an easier process compared with applicants who may be over-specialised. Alternative approaches for dealing with short-term problems are to use short-term contracts or buy in consultancy expertise.

Selection criteria

Having defined a job and balanced the short- and long-term needs, the next stage is to identify appropriate selection criteria. The problems in developing appropriate assessment criteria are more fully explained in the next chapter (on appraisal). It is necessary to also consider at this stage the main issues in implementing the selection criteria. These are likely to be:

- Validity – are we measuring what we think we are measuring?
- Reliability – are we using a reliable measurement that will produce the same results each time the measurement is made?
- Relevance – are the criteria used relevant to the actual job demands?
- Discrimination – can you distinguish between those who meet the criteria and those who do not?
- Comprehensiveness
- Assessability

Two specific approaches for identifying criteria are explained below – establishing a person specification and identifying the required job competencies. Other issues include the relevance of good and bad practice amongst existing job-holders, looking at the job as a whole, the dangers of choosing on the basis of historic performance, attitude and the particular importance of making valid selections in the case of those working abroad.

PERSON SPECIFICATION

A person specification identifies the personal attributes that the job-holder needs in order to do a job. The establishment of appropriate selection criteria can help with the recruitment and shortlisting stages of the selection process. Clear and valid selection criteria encourage those who potentially fit those criteria to apply and may discourage those who do not. The more relevant information that is given about jobs, the more that selection process can be assisted by advising potential applicants so that they do not pursue applications that would be inappropriate. Clear and appropriate criteria will also facilitate any short-listing process.

It is necessary however to beware of completing a specification in a way that gives a spurious impression of accuracy and certainty. An increasing number of applications are made online. This is increasingly associated with automated decision-making about who to shortlist and who to reject. This may particularly create a bias towards that which is easily quantifiable. Whether the 'matching' of applications to criteria is done automatically or by personal scrutiny, the accuracy will only at best be as good as the accuracy of the selection criteria. Inappropriate criteria can lead to good candidates being rejected and weaker candidates being shortlisted or even appointed. Inaccurate criteria can also contravene organisational equal opportunities policies and make an employer legally vulnerable to claims of discrimination. It may also be necessary for employers to ensure that their recruitment policies are not in contravention of equal opportunities policies and statutory safeguards. A policy issue is likely to be the extent to which jobs are advertised both internally and externally.

Follow-up and evaluation of the selection process

Decisions about the appropriateness of job selection criteria are subjective. However, the further guidance given in this chapter is designed to help managers establish appropriate and defensible criteria. A major advantage of establishing a person specification is that, provided it is done properly, it is relatively easy to explain to others involved in making selection decisions.

JOB COMPETENCIES

The alternative to drawing up a person specification is a competencies approach. This sidesteps the issue of personal characteristics and identifies instead the job skills and knowledge that a person needs to have in order to do a job adequately. Sometimes competencies are split into levels. These can be used to identify the minimum acceptable (threshold) level and that level which is desirable for a particular job. Potential advantages of identifying job competencies are:

- irrelevant requirements should be excluded – what will matter, for example, is whether a person has the technical ability or potential to do a job, not specific qualifications;
- the pool of candidates is likely to be increased;
- the approach is in keeping with equal opportunities policies;
- the established competencies may be useful in related areas – these include identifying training and development needs, performance management, and setting individual remuneration and pay grades.

Potential disadvantages of the competence approach are:

- it can be very complicated and therefore difficult to operate;
- the complexities can lead to inaccuracies and inconsistencies;
- it can be very time-consuming;
- there can be problems in applying generic competencies to specific jobs – important aspects can be missed, which can lead to important competencies being missed or unnecessary ones required;

- generic competencies can be difficult to alter in the light of changed circumstances, because, for example, of the time investment needed to change organisation-wide schemes;

- important factors that are not easily quantified or assessed, such as teamwork and attitude may be ignored;

- there may be too much focus on short-term needs;

- the ability of candidates to acquire relevant skills may be underestimated;

- the fact that a person has the required competencies does not guarantee that they will be motivated to do a job well or stay with an organisation.

OTHER ISSUES RELATED TO SELECTION
The relevance of good and bad practice amongst existing job-holders

A way of identifying appropriate selection criteria may be to consider the extent to which people, satisfactorily performing the same or a similar job, fit the specification or competencies that have been identified. Examples of both good and less appropriate practice in the job may also help.

Using standards of good performance to develop selection criteria

A soft drinks company identified the main factors that were linked to good performance in service engineers who maintained and repaired drink dispensers. They found that the key factors were social skills and organising ability. Customers liked service engineers who were polite and who kept them informed about when they were coming and of any changes in appointments. The company had previously recruited people mainly on the basis of their engineering skills. It found it had over-specified in that direction, particularly as the relevant technical skills could fairly easily be taught in-house. As a result of this investigation, the selection criteria for the job were radically altered.

Example

Differing selection criteria for internal and external candidates

In an unpublished survey of the selection of lecturing staff it was found that for some years different criteria had been used subconsciously regarding applicants who had not had previous contact with the department surveyed and those who had (e.g. as visiting lecturers or researchers). The former group had been primarily judged on their level of academic excellence, which was usually relatively easy to assess. Different criteria had, however, been applied to those applicants who were known to the panel members. This was because of the knowledge about the relative strengths and weaknesses of these applicants. The key attributes that emerged with this group were commitment, organising ability, teaching skills and motivation to do the job. It also emerged that the good performers in the department were mainly from those in this group and not in the group chosen primarily on the basis of academic excellence. However, previous knowledge of applicants did not always work in their favour. The different criteria used in their selection also often led to them being rejected.

Example

The totality of a job

Another aspect of selection may be to look at the totality of a job and of an applicant so that one sees the applicant as a whole person and does not get lost in the detail. Practice may vary, though, as to whether this approach is considered too judgemental or not. This approach may however enable those responsible for selection to take account of issues that should have been included.

Motivation

It is necessary to consider what constitutes a good match between a person and a job, as explained in Chapter 6. Someone of high ability may make a poor match for a routine job. A capable person may perform less well than a less able person who does not get bored with a routine job. The practice of discriminating against people because they are too able may vary, however, according to the organisational philosophy regarding access to jobs. Dangers of over-specification are job distortion (see Chapter 6) and being caught in the over-specification cycle. This phenomenon is explained in Figure 9.1.

It may also be necessary to try and identify 'job hoppers', i.e. those people who have a track record of moving quickly from one job to another and not showing commitment to any employer.

Over-reaction to previous failures

A current or former employee may have a particular failing which blinds those responsible for choosing a successor to the other ways in which a person can fail in a job. In their anxiety to avoid choosing someone with such a failing, those responsible for selection may not pay suffi-cient attention to other inappropriate attributes that candidates may have.

Figure 9.1	The over-specification cycle

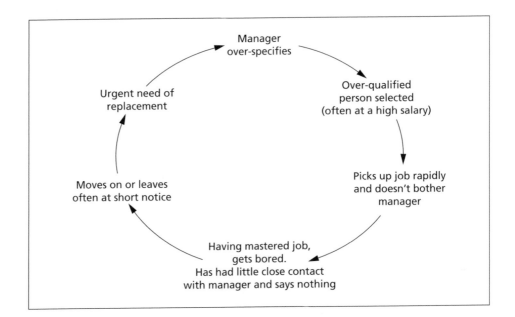

Choosing in one's own image

Particularly with senior positions, what may be needed is a person who complements, rather than replicates, the skills of the other team members. This fits with the findings of Belbin, explained in Chapter 4, on how effective teamwork is achieved.

Emotional intelligence

For some jobs **emotional intelligence** may be particularly necessary. Broadly speaking this is the maturity of an individual. However, it may be the product of innate characteristics as well as acquired behaviour. Most definitions also incorporate the concepts of self-awareness and awareness of others. It is distinct from cognitive reasoning ability. Unfortunately, the possession by an individual of high reasoning ability does not guarantee that they will be able to use it wisely. Emotional intelligence may be particularly important in jobs that are potentially very stressful, such as in management or in conflict situations such as many the military may have to face. What can be critical is the ability of people to use what reasoning ability they have sensibly rather than to simply reason in the abstract. The ability to handle other workers constructively in conditions of stress may be particularly important. Self-control can be a key feature. The possession of emotional intelligence may be very necessary for making sound judgements in difficult situations. Whilst emotional intelligence may be an important factor in many jobs, it may not be easy to assess. It may be useful, though, to look for evidence of maturity, or immaturity, particularly for those applying for potentially stressful jobs. (Goleman 1999, Dulewicz and Higgs 2002.)

Dangers of selecting on the basis of historic performance

Particular care has to be taken in identifying the differences between someone's previous work experience and the job for which they are applying. A person who has performed admirably in one job will not necessarily perform well in a different job, particularly if that different job necessitates work at a higher level of responsibility. There is more than a grain of truth in Lawrence Peter's (1970) concept of people passing through their threshold of competence, as previously explained in Chapter 1. His theory is that people are promoted on the basis of having done their last job well until they find themselves a job which they cannot do, which is when the basis for promotion ceases.

Historical experience of the dangers of selecting on the basis of past performance

Example

In reflecting on his experience as Minister of Munitions in 1915 during the First World War, David Lloyd George wrote:

> I cannot claim that my first choices were always the best. They were, I think, the best available at the time.

I found that some [people] were admirable workers provided they were under the control and direction of others, but not equal to the responsibility of a supreme position. It was then that I realised thoroughly for the first time that men ought to be marked like army lorries with their carrying capacity: 'Not to

▶

carry more than three tons'. The three-tonners are perfect so long as you do not overload them with burdens for which they are not constructed by Providence. I have seen that happen in Law and Politics. The barrister who acquired a great practice as a junior and failed completely when he took silk; the politician who showed great promise as an under-secretary and achieved nothing when promoted to the headship of a department.

(Lloyd George 1938, p. 149)

Attitude

Some organisations pay particular attention to attitude and try to ensure that those appointed 'fit' with the overall culture of the organisation. For example, Kirosingh (1984) reported that the electronics company Sony said they would prefer a person to have 100 per cent the right attitude and 90 per cent the right skills, never the other way around. However, reliable assessment of attitude may not always be easy at the selection stage.

Selection of employees to work abroad

As explained in Chapter 4, it is particularly important to make the most appropriate selection of those employees who will be working in a country other than their own. This is because of:

- the high cost of expatriate failure, i.e. the expatriate does not achieve the organisational objectives of the assignment (see Harzing and Christensen 2004 for a discussion on the concept of 'expatriate failure');
- the special problems that may be created by the impact on other members of a family, particularly a partner's career and children's education;
- the likely dependence of the success of the assignment on the ability of the selected candidate to operate in a different culture;
- the extra responsibilities, managerial or otherwise, compounded by geographic distance from superiors, that a person may have in a new job.

THE LINK BETWEEN RECRUITMENT AND SELECTION

Establishing appropriate selection is fundamental to the recruitment and short-listing stages of the selection process. Advertising clear and valid selection criteria will encourage those who potentially fit the criteria to apply and may discourage those who do not. The more relevant information that is given about jobs, the more that selection process will be assisted by people not pursuing applications that would be inappropriate. Clear and appropriate criteria can also facilitate any shortlisting process and provide a documentary base against any subsequent claims of illegal discrimination. Many employers issue their selection criteria to candidates in advance of interviews as part of their equal opportunities policies. Employers may also be prepared to give information to unsuccessful candidates about the reasons for their rejection.

FOLLOW-UP AND EVALUATION OF SELECTION PROCEDURES

To some extent the evaluation of selection procedures and the criteria used will always be speculative. Whatever follow-up investigations may reveal about the level of performance of people who join an organisation, one cannot really make judgements about how the people would have performed who were not selected. However, it would seem prudent to review selection procedures in the light of the performance of the people who are chosen to test the validity of those procedures. Even then, care has to be taken in coming to conclusions. Someone whose performance is poor may still have been the best of those candidates available at the time. There can be other explanations for poor performance, such as ineffective work arrangements. There is also the problem of whether you judge people by their contribution to short-term needs or by their long-term contribution to an organisation.

The systematic review of selection methods, whilst not leading to any magic answers, may reveal weaknesses that can be corrected in the future. One of the advantages of exit interviews is that recruitment officers in the HR department, in particular, can consider whether the pattern of people leaving indicates weaknesses in the selection procedure. The criteria for evaluating appraisal systems are also relevant to the selection process. These criteria are itemised in the next chapter on appraisal, in the section on rating and recording. However, the follow-up and evaluation of the effectiveness of the selection process is an integral part of ensuring that appropriate criteria have been used and sensibly checked out.

Consideration also needs to be given to the public relations aspects involved in selection. Quite apart from the considerations of natural justice, it would seem sensible for employers to leave unsuccessful candidates at least with the impression that their application has been considered fairly. A further issue is that the longer the selection process takes, the more likely it is that able candidates will find jobs elsewhere.

The collection of information about candidates

The identification of realistic and clear selection criteria can be of great value in determining what information is relevant to selection decisions. Information about candidates can be collected from a variety of sources. Scrutiny of job advertisements indicates which employers have worked out the sort of person they want and the information they require and which employers have not. A well-designed application form can present the relevant information to an employer in a way that they will find easy to follow. Examples of a person's work may help, as may references and testimonials from current or previous employers.

REFERENCES AND TESTIMONIALS

There is often confusion about the difference between the terms 'reference' and 'testimonial'. A testimonial is an open letter given by an employer to an employee to show to future prospective employers. As it is given to the person who is the subject of the testimonial, the writer may be reluctant to say anything detrimental about the person concerned. On the other hand, the fact that a person is prepared to praise a former employee in an open letter may be because the person deserves it. References, on the other hand, are communications made directly with a prospective employer. This may mean that the current or past employer may be more prepared to be frank about the person concerned. However, care has to be taken in the interpretation of written references. Someone writing a reference may feel reluctant to state the shortcomings of a person and mention just their good points. It is often the omissions that are the most important feature of a reference. Also developments in freedom of information legislation may mean that candidates can gain access to written references that former employers have provided about them.

Oral references may be the most accurate, but it is important to beware of the employer just in case they praise an employee they don't want to keep to increase the chance of them leaving. It may be appropriate to approach an employer for which a candidate has worked previously, rather than a current employer, so that the candidate's relationship with their existing employer is not compromised. In evaluating a reference, whether it be good or bad, it needs to be remembered that the information received is about a person's performance in a job which may be significantly different from the job for which they have applied. The past record, although often useful, should only be seen as a guide in making selection decisions.

ACCURACY OF INFORMATION

Care often has to be taken in checking the information provided by candidates. Misrepresentation can vary from the gentle massaging of employment histories to outright fraud. Checking for inconsistencies in the information provided, such as dates of previous employment, can help establish how accurate is the information provided. Minor inconsistencies can be signposts for greater misrepresentations. Some organisations ask to see original qualifications and retain copies of these documents.

INTERNAL CANDIDATES

If a candidate is applying for a transfer or promotion from within an organisation, there may be a wealth of information available about them. Care needs to be taken in evaluating the information, but the quantity and quality of the information may mean that any interview is much less important than may be the case with external appointments. It can have a devastating effect on an organisation to promote people who are recognised by colleagues as being incompetent, or to ignore the claims of those who are recognised as being competent. However, practice varies about the extent to which internal reports are admissible. Sometimes the view is taken that it is necessary to rely primarily on performance at selection panel interviews. This issue is considered further in the section on selection panels.

The development of the flexible workforce, explained in Chapter 3, means that people are increasingly likely to want to move from the peripheral to the core workforce, or in some cases, the other way around. Experience of employees in the peripheral workforce, and by them of the organisation, can provide invaluable information for both parties if there is ever the prospect of transfer to the core workforce. Another way in which relevant information can be obtained about internal candidates for promotion is to give them periods of acting up at a more senior level to see how they handle the increased responsibility.

WORKING INTERVIEWS

A practice has developed, particularly with office jobs, of sometimes asking candidates to attend for a day or so to undertake a paid 'working interview'. This may particularly fit with the job competence approach in establishing whether or not the candidate has the knowledge and skills to undertake a particular job. However, it is only appropriate if the candidate is able to undertake the tasks they are given without too much briefing and if there are not too many candidates. It may be particularly appropriate for a routine office job where there is only one candidate and the employer wants to check out if they are suitable or not.

ASSESSMENT CENTRES

A way of increasing the available information about internal and external applicants is the use of assessment centres. These have become increasingly popular in recent years. They can be used both for selection and staff development. The process of assessment often includes group exercises, job-related exercises and psychometric tests.

Dulewicz (1991, p. 50) claims that small increases in the validity of selection decisions made can generate a handsome return on the investment in assessment centres. He also claims that the following factors are key to the design of effective assessment centres:

- adequate specification of target competencies;
- the design of relevant and valid exercises;
- adequate integration of results of competence exercises and of any psychometric tests that are used;
- assessor training;
- careful selection and briefing of candidates;
- efficient programming and management of the process;
- adequate feedback to participants and follow up of recommendations;
- monitoring of the validity and benefits of the process.

However, according to Fletcher and Anderson (1998), such criteria are only likely to be met in half of the assessment centres that have been established.

Fallibility of assessment centres

One large company ran its assessment centre events for years before discovering that they had predicted nothing about future performance. Had the company done some monitoring it might have saved itself a lot of money. (Fletcher and Anderson, 1998, pp. 44–46)

The need for caution expressed both by Dulewicz and by Fletcher and Anderson was confirmed by the experience of a large bank in the UK. The bank found that the competence profiles it had developed of staff at assessment centres did not correlate at all with the subsequent performance assessments made of the same staff. It found that the competence requirements had been applied mechanistically in selection and simply did not fit many of the key requirements. It also found that staff complained of an air of unreality in many of the exercises conducted at the centre. There were far more variations in job requirements than had been allowed for in the standardised competence approach that had been used. Consequently, the standard competencies that had been laboriously developed and applied in selection and development were abandoned. The basic data that the assessment centre had been working on was simply too unreliable.

Examples of bad practice do not undermine a good concept. The basic point is that much more care may need to be taken with the establishment of assessment centres than is often the case. Even when considerable effort is put in, however, wrong assumptions can still undermine the whole process, as evidenced by the example of the bank given above. Conversely, sometimes basic exercises can enhance a conventional selection process. Appropriate case studies, for example, can prove particularly useful as one of the ways of identifying managerial potential.

PSYCHOMETRIC TESTS

Psychometric tests have also become increasingly popular over recent years, both within the context of assessment centres and independently of them. The term is often used interchangeably with 'psychological testing'. Whilst such tests can provide useful information to facilitate effective selection and development, like any technique they can be misapplied. Dangers include irrelevant tests, incompetent administration, cultural bias, a belief that the test results should determine the decision instead of facilitating decisions made in conjunction with other relevant information, and over-zealous sales promotion (CIPD 1997).

DATA PROTECTION AND SUBJECT ACCESS

In the context of considering information on employees it should be remembered that such information may be subject to legislative protection. There may be restrictions on the use to which it can be put, particularly without the permission of the person concerned. In addition there may be subject access provisions. This may cover unsuccessful candidates for employment, e.g. the right to see notes taken during a selection interview. A key piece of legislation within the EU is the European Data Protection Directive.

GOVERNMENT REQUIREMENTS

There may be some information that employers are required to collect by law. Increasing regulation relating to immigration may mean that proof of eligibility to work in a particular country may be required. In addition details of criminal history may be required if a person is applying for particular jobs, e.g. relating to sex offences if a person has applied to work with children.

The selection interview

Selection interview can be much more subjective and unreliable than people realise (Smith and Lister 2008). However, it is often an important – or the only – element in the process. Even if an employer were to dispense with the interview, they would need to consider how they were going to provide the candidates with information and answer their queries, so that the candidates could make their decisions of whether or not they should apply for or accept a job. The existence of clear selection criteria does enable an interview to be conducted systematically with the interviewer at least knowing what they are looking for. All too often the information collected at interviews is relatively worthless because the interviewer has not identified clearly enough what they wanted to know. Even when this has been done, a significant amount of skill may be needed to obtain the relevant information. The interviewer may have identified what they want to know, but a candidate may quite understandably be concerned with emphasising their strong points and with concealing their weaknesses.

There is a considerable amount of technique involved in obtaining information from a candidate. Readers are likely to have noticed the variation in skill demonstrated by people who have interviewed them for jobs. Appropriate training can improve the performance of interviewers both with regard to one-to-one interviews and selection panels.

PLANNING

The first stage in the interview is fairly obviously the prior preparation. Interviewers must not only have established the selection criteria but also studied any relevant information before the interview starts, including organisational policies and procedures regarding selection. They also need to consider what information should be given to a candidate before the interview. The location of an interview needs to be considered, so that it takes place in surroundings that are as congenial as possible for both the interviewer and the candidate. It is also necessary to arrange for the interview to be free from interruptions.

If more than one person is to interview candidates it is necessary to decide whether the interviewing is sequential or joint. Generally, it is easier to coax out information on a one-to-one basis. This may not involve any more organisational time as those involved in single interviewing do not have to sit through the questioning by other people. If more time is needed after the interviews to reconcile a variety of views about candidates this may be well worth the effort because the volume of data may be very valuable. However, the information so obtained may be

selectively interpreted and reported and this needs to be borne in mind if this approach is used. Often for political reasons, interviews need to be conducted by a panel of interviewers. The issues involved in joint interviewing are dealt with further in the section on selection panels.

Interviewers should have a good idea of what they want to find out during an interview. They may also want to identify the basic information that they will need to convey to a candidate. Checklists of information to be obtained and imparted can be very useful. It is also prudent to bear in mind that candidates are often understandably nervous and may not absorb much of what they are told. It is necessary to consider the structure and sequence of an interview so that the dialogue can be as effective as possible. If candidates are nervous it may be best to get them speaking as early as possible. It may only be when candidates have settled down that they are capable of absorbing important information.

One way of providing a clear and useful structure to the interview is to undertake a biographical interview. This involves the candidate being asked to explain their educational background and employment history in a chronological sequence. The interviewer can then concentrate on asking any supplementary questions that are needed to fill in any gaps. Such supplementary questioning may also need to focus on what the interviewee's actual achievements and skills are. Even if the biographical approach is not used, thought needs to be given to the structure of an interview and the agenda explained to the candidate. All too often interviews are conducted in a 'grasshopper' style, with questions being asked at random with little if any thought being given as to how to lead up to sensitive issues. This can be caused not just by lack of skill on the part of the interviewer but also by their nervousness. The development of selection interviewing skills can have the advantage of giving the interviewer sufficient confidence to conduct an interview in a relaxed and effective manner.

INTERVIEWING SKILLS
Questioning

Considerable thought may need to be given to the way that questions are asked in an interview. The interviewer will want to find out if there are any reasons why they should not appoint a particular person. Interviewers may need to ask questions in such a way that they do not reveal what they regard as an acceptable or unacceptable answer. To do this they will need to frame their questions in a neutral manner. Even if one were to convert a leading question such as 'Do you work hard?' into a neutral one, it would be fairly obvious what the interviewer was after. It may be more appropriate to ask what the tasks were that most interested a candidate in a previous job and which were the ones which least interested them, and why. It may also be appropriate to ask questions in an open-ended way so that the candidate may open up and talk freely. This is in contrast to closed questions which simply require a 'yes' or 'no' answer.

Asking the right questions in the right way can get a candidate talking freely. The more a candidate talks, the more the interviewer is likely to learn. The role of the interviewer may be to guide the interview gently, to look for leads that need to be followed up and to be on the watch for inconsistencies in the candidate's answers. Nervousness or lack of skill on the part of the interviewer may prevent this. The issues of questioning technique and getting people to talk are both dealt with further in Chapter 12 in the context of counselling.

Listening

One of the most common errors in interviews is for the interviewer to do most of the talking. This reduces the information that can be obtained from the candidate and on which the decision needs to be based. A useful rule of thumb is for the interviewer to spend no more than a quarter of the time talking, and to allow for the tendency to underestimate the amount of time that one speaks oneself. Listening carefully can require much more self-discipline and concentration than talking. If answers are unclear to the interviewer, it may be important to clarify just what an interviewee has meant. It may require considerable tact and patience to establish whether one has properly understood the point that a candidate is trying to make.

Interviewer confidence

A hidden agenda in interviews may be that the interviewer, in particular, is frightened of losing control and suffering embarrassment. This may be a reason why interviews are often played far too cautiously, with important issues remaining unexplored. The development of selection interviewing skills may be the most effective way of overcoming this obstacle. This may particularly affect the close of the interview and the explanation to the candidate of just what the position is with regard to their application.

Time allocation between candidates

Many selection decisions turn out to be fairly straightforward. This is most likely to be the case with people who are clearly unsuitable. Much more time may be needed to identify the possible weaknesses of a candidate who turns out to be suitable. The greatest time may need to be taken with those candidates who are genuinely marginal and where extra relevant information may justifiably tilt the balance one way or the other. However, time allocation may be constrained by equal opportunities policies, which are considered later in this chapter.

Feedback on interviewing skills

The development of one's interviewing technique may depend not just on practice but on getting feedback on one's performance and adjusting future performance in the light of such feedback. It may be possible for readers to do this for themselves, and for this reason a selection interviewing self-assessment questionnaire is included as an appendix to this chapter. Readers can complete the questionnaire and identify any weaknesses with a view to seeing if these have been eliminated or reduced when they do their next interview.

COMMON PROBLEMS
Freezing

One of the major problems in selection interviews is that both the interviewer and the candidate may freeze into a set pattern of question and answer, with the candidate feeling fairly restricted about the information that they can volunteer. One way of trying to unfreeze both interviewer and interviewee is to show the interviewee around the prospective work area. A dialogue can then develop under much more relaxed circumstances.

When the formal interview discussions have ended, much extra information is often volunteered which should have emerged during the interview but did not. The amount of extra information obtained in this way can sometimes be astonishing. It may be appropriate to deliberately build such a 'defreezing' process into the interview.

Choice of selectors

Ironically, it may well be that the higher up an organisation selection decisions are taken, the less appropriate they may be. The peer group may often be in the best position to judge, because of their close knowledge of the demands of the job, what is really required in a candidate. It may, therefore, be appropriate to consider whether the observations of the peer group should be sought, including their views on internal candidates. Factors such as seniority and length of experience tend to weigh heavily with selection panels in particular. This may be because they do not have the detailed knowledge of candidates and jobs that those closer to the situation have. Consequently, their decisions may be based on very superficial reasoning. More senior managers may not have to suffer the direct consequences of an inappropriate appointment. It is an understanding of this issue that has led some university medical schools to include a current student on the selection panels for prospective students.

The halo effect

Care also has to be taken to avoid the **'halo' effect,** where a particular strength in a candidate leads to over-generous assessments of their other attributes. A 'reverse halo' can also develop where a particular weakness leads to a candidate being unnecessarily marked down in all other areas. Obviously, employers also need to be aware of their own subjective views and biases and to allow for such factors in making decisions. A basic point is not placing too much emphasis on interview performance, whether before a single interviewer or a panel. This can unduly favour the fluent performer, whose subsequent actions on the job may not live up to their interview performance. This can be an important issue regarding selection panels. Their role and operation is considered next.

Selection panels

REASONS FOR PANELS

Selection panels are such a prominent feature of public sector appointments that they need examination and explanation. The presence of several people on a panel may be necessary because of the various interests that need to be represented at the selection stage. One of the historical reasons for the establishment of selection panels in the public sector was the need to see that jobs were not allocated on the basis of patronage. Subsequently, their structure and operation have often become key features of equal opportunities policies, especially in the public sector. Even when there is no formal requirement for selection panels, there may be a preference by the representatives of an employer to see a candidate together rather than separately. Thus, a line manager and recruitment officer may conduct a joint interview.

If there are clear policies and procedures about how selection panels are to operate, it is incumbent on panel members to understand and respect those policies and procedures. Basic issues concerning panel interviewing will now be explored. This is done to enable readers to understand the dynamics and to assist them with regard to any scope they have in their own organisations for interpreting or designing selection policies and procedures.

THE CONCEPT OF THE LEVEL PLAYING FIELD

In some organisations there is a strong belief that selection panels should be set up and operated in such a way that they provide a level playing field. This is to ensure that the selection process is operated so as not to favour any particular candidate. In these circumstances the selection decision may be based primarily on interview performance. An alternative approach to providing a level playing field is to rely on the established selection criteria and to allow information from a variety of sources to be tested against those criteria. This will involve making subjective judgements on a wider base of relevant data.

A basic issue is that however much effort is put into attempting to create a level playing field, selection decisions in the end are subjective and the limitations of the objective approach need to be recognised. If, for example, standard questions are asked of each candidate at a panel, subjective judgements still have to be made about what questions are asked, their relevance and the quality and the weighting given to individual responses. Judgements can be influenced by a variety of factors, including hidden interdepartmental rivalries. Questions may rightly or wrongly favour some candidates more than others. If questions are too rigidly standardised it may prevent members from following up leads about strengths and weaknesses that may be relevant to a candidate's application. There is also the danger that standardised questions may be anticipated, particularly by internal candidates, or even that prearranged questions are leaked to a favoured candidate.

POTENTIAL PROBLEMS

The problems of coaxing information out of candidates and probing for their strengths and weaknesses are likely to be much greater at panels compared with single interviewing. The amount of time available to each interviewer is much more restricted and the formality of the situation may inhibit candidates from making fluent responses. Sometimes it is argued that the ability to cope with panel-type situations is a critical aspect of the job. However, this is often not the case and this argument may be used as a rationalisation for a selection procedure which has been adopted for quite different reasons. Whatever method of selection is used, it is necessary to remember that the prime purpose is to discriminate in favour of those who are best fitted to perform particular work. As explained earlier in this chapter, because of the dangers of over-selection, this does not necessarily mean the most capable person. Selectors are likely to be looking for a combination of the person most likely to perform well and the person who will perform consistently to the highest standard.

Inappropriate or unlawful discrimination occurs when invalid criteria are used. Follow-up studies may be necessary to determine the validity of the process. If those involved with selection decisions then work with those appointed they will get regular feedback on the appropriateness of their decisions. Problems can arise if panel members make inappropriate decisions and fail to recognise what modifications in selection processes may be needed because of their ignorance of the consequences of past decisions.

THE ROLE OF THE PANEL CHAIR

The chances of effective decision-making at panels may be improved by careful chairing. If it is not possible to give training to panel members, the person chairing may be able to gently coach members in the skills of interviewing and selection – bearing in mind that often the worse interviewers are, the less they are likely to recognise their deficiencies. Where the information obtained by panel interviews is of little value at least it is best to recognise that and use what other valid information is available to panel members as a basis for decision-making.

"*Right, Mr Smith, just relax*"

Source: Private Eye, *8 May 1992, no. 783,* p. 12. Reproduced by kind permission of PRIVATE EYE/Foulds.

Equal opportunities

GENERAL FRAMEWORK

It is necessary to consider the impact of selection processes in terms of equality of opportunity and the legislative rights that prospective employees and those applying for promotion have to protect them against discriminatory employment practices.

However, the whole purpose of selection is to be discriminatory, in terms of choosing the person best fitted to do a particular job. Anti-discrimination law and policies are designed to prevent discrimination on an antisocial basis, not to oblige employers to choose people at random. Legal and contractual rights may be embraced in overall organisational policies for managing diversity.

The issue of discrimination needs to be viewed not just in the light of the minimum standards set by the law, but as organisational policies. It is sensible for employers to do so anyway: there is no merit or gain for organisations failing to make use of the talent and potential that is available by unjustified discrimination. A mix of backgrounds can also help with regard to creative thinking within an organisation. In addition, as explained in Chapter 3, employers may need to demonstrate that they take the issue of equal opportunities seriously in order, for example, to develop a positive image with their customers and to win public contracts. To do this they will need to look at the range of potentially inappropriate areas of discrimination and not just at selection.

SPECIFIC AREAS OF POTENTIALLY INAPPROPRIATE DISCRIMINATION

The areas of potential illegal discrimination are increasing. A particularly important piece of legislation in Europe is the EU's Equal Treatment Directive, as is the European Convention of Human Rights. Potential protections exist in the areas of:

- Sex
- Race
- Age
- Disability
- Religion
- Sexual orientation
- Trade union membership and/or activity

In the UK employers also have to comply with the terms of the Equality Act of 2006. This places an obligation on employers actively to promote equal treatment between the sexes. The Act also creates a special responsibility on public authorities not to discriminate on the grounds of religion, belief, or sexual orientation in the provision of goods, facilities, services and education.

The concept of **universal inclusion** takes the concept of inappropriate discrimination further. This involves avoiding any discrimination against personal attributes that can unreasonably affect employees' treatment and work performance.

It is perhaps easier for employers to fall into the trap of indirect discrimination than direct discrimination. Indirect discrimination occurs when an unnecessary selection criterion is used which has an adverse effect on applicants from a particular sex or group. This can happen, for example, when too much importance is given to experience in job selection which may work against women who have the skills and/or potential to do a job but not have had the same opportunities as men to gain years of experience. The use of job competencies in selection can reduce the chance of such indirect discrimination by focusing on the actual requirements of a job rather than conventional views about what length of experience and qualifications are required.

Example

Indirect discrimination

At one stage an upper age limit of 28 was applied for external candidates applying for positions as executive officers with the British Civil Service. This was held to be discriminatory against women because of the likelihood that family commitments would disproportionately reduce women's chances of applying for such positions.

(Price versus Civil Service Commissioner 1977)

REMEDIAL ACTION

It may be necessary for employers to demonstrate that they are really complying with legal requirements and not just paying 'lip service' to them. In order to monitor the situation, it may be necessary for employers to conduct a statistical analysis of their labour force and the reasons for a particular mix. In some cases it may necessary to undertake a pay audit to demonstrate the rationale for the distribution of earnings within an organisation. This can be particularly necessary with regard to **equal pay** or **equal value** claims, as explained in Chapter 6.

It may be appropriate for employers to take a proactive approach to ensure that any policies they have with regard to equal opportunities are actually working There is a basic distinction between **positive action** and **positive discrimination**. Positive action involves removing obstacles to equality of opportunity. One example of positive action is giving the option of part-time work, especially to mothers returning from maternity leave. Another example of positive action would be to provide training for individuals to enable them to develop the skills required for more senior jobs. A further example of positive action would be making reasonable adjustments to enable disabled people, who would otherwise be suitable, to take up employment. Positive action may also involve equality targets, but not equality quotas. Positive discrimination involves giving preferential treatment to under-represented groups. However, in many countries it is illegal, because it can be seen to conflict with the concept of equal opportunity.

There may be solid commercial advantages to having a proactive organisational policy on diversity.

An organisation diversifies its labour force for commercial reasons

There can be commercial reasons for taking action to increase the diversity in the workforce. This was the case with the computer firm IBM, whose aim was to use such a policy to raise an extra billion dollars in revenue in 5–10 years. It was felt that the labour force in the USA did not sufficiently reflect the population in the country. This was felt to be both an obstacle to the marketing of its products and services and an obstacle to creativity. Task forces were set up to uncover and understand differences among minority groups, such as Asians, Blacks, Hispanics, gays, lesbians, women and the disabled, to find ways of appealing to a broader set of employees and customers. Managing diversity became one of the core competencies on which the performance of managers was assessed.

(David A. Thomas 2004)

The creation of an equal opportunities policy may create dilemmas for some employers. One is the extent to which the policies are applied to subsidiaries in other countries where the law and culture may be very different. Another is whether or not to concentrate on the internal or external labour markets. In some countries and organisations there is a strong emphasis on the **internal labour market**, which involves developing staff and promoting from within. This contrasts with other countries and organisations where people are encouraged to apply from outside.

Applying for Jobs

This chapter has so far been written from the perspective of the employer selecting candidates for a job. Readers may also be applying for jobs at some stage. It is therefore appropriate to devote some time to considering the selection process from the perspective of the job applicant. As ever, it is necessary to be clear about the objectives of the process. The obvious objective is to secure a job, but there may need to be other objectives as well.

ANALYSIS OF THE PROCESS

As a way of encouraging an employer to make you a job offer it will help to understand the selection process and to get inside the mind of whoever will take the selection decision. It will be necessary to demonstrate that your application matches any specified selection criteria. This may be particularly important if there is an automated shortlisting procedure. The first stage is to demonstrate that you are worth shortlisting and should be granted an interview.

When completing any application forms you should work out what the organisation is likely to be looking for. Any job description should list the main tasks and responsibilities that the person appointed will be expected to perform. Some organisations, particularly those with an equal opportunities policy, may also state their selection criteria. If the employer does not send selection criteria, then it is advisable to try and identify them. Background research about the organisation will also help in getting a good approximation of this.

BEING INTERVIEWED

As first impressions tend to be disproportionately important, dress may need to be on the conservative side. In presenting oneself it is more important to concentrate on the content of what is being said than on peripheral issues like the positioning of one's hands or elimination of gestures. Having said that, prepared responses may sound too mechanistic, so it may be better to make notes on what you think you need to say and even consider leaving the notes at home on the day of the interview, rather than have a scripted response. The questions probably will not come up exactly as envisaged, anyway. You may also need to be aware of important new issues that may arise, such as selection criteria that were not included in any information that you have received, or may not have even been thought of before the interview.

In seeking to demonstrate how well you fit the selection criteria it is as well to be clear that your purpose will be to demonstrate the strengths in your case whilst the employer should be probing for weaknesses. In demonstrating your strengths, clear and interesting responses are to be preferred – convoluted statements may be boring. Samples of work or other relevant evidence may help in presenting your case. Many people undersell themselves by being too deferential to the interviewer(s) or by volunteering weaknesses in their case that may have been better left unsaid. If you feel that any important aspects have been missed out, you should raise such issues at the end of an interview. This may be made easier if you are asked if there is anything else you want to say. Steering the interviewer(s) to cover the key issues may cause them to be relaxed and feel that they have conducted a good interview.

Account also needs to be taken of the stress that can be present in job interviews. The stress inherent in such situations can be aggravated by problems involved in finding the location, being left waiting, changes in the arrangements and errors by the employer. The ability to cope with such stress before and during the interview can have a critical effect on the outcome. Particular reactions to avoid are talking too quickly and being aggressive. If testing questions are asked or sensitive issues raised these need to be dealt with diplomatically. Interviewers are more likely to appoint people with whom they feel at ease and with whom they think their colleagues will get along. The topics of aggressive, assertive and non-assertive behaviour were covered in some detail in Chapter 4.

POTENTIAL BARGAINING ISSUES

It may be counterproductive to concentrate only on how to persuade an employer to offer you a job if it leads to you being offered a job that you cannot do, starting a job you find you do not want or accepting an offer on unfavourable terms. Consequently, the interviewee, as well as planning how to present themselves, also needs to plan to extract the information that they need to determine whether a job is worth having or to find out if there are any areas where bargaining can be conducted. It may be useful to bear in mind that you can at least ask for time to make your mind up if you are unsure whether or not to accept an offer. Also, the time when your bargaining position will be strongest is when the employer has made an offer and you have not given your decision. If the offer is subject to conditions, such as a medical report or examination or satisfactory references, you may wish to delay resigning from a current job until it is confirmed that these conditions have been met.

LESSONS FOR NEXT TIME

If you are unsuccessful it may be appropriate to reflect on whether or not it was because you did not match the criteria as well as someone else. In the last analysis, all you can hope to do is to present yourself as well as possible. If one application fails there are likely to be other opportunities where one can successfully demonstrate that you provide the best fit to an employer's selection criteria. If you have a run of rejections it is important not to let it lead to you going into interviews with a defeatist attitude and thus under-selling yourself.

You may want to ask for feedback from the organisation as to why you did not get a job, but often people are too demoralised to do this. If you are perplexed as to why you have not got jobs you feel you should have, one further piece of preparation may be to get a friend to give you a simulated interview and feedback on your performance. If this can be done with the aid of closed-circuit television so that you can see how you perform, so much the better.

Summary

As with most things, the key to effective job selection is systematic and careful preparation. This is all the more so as selection decisions can critically affect the performance (or non-performance) of an organisation. It may also critically impact on whether one meets one's own work objectives. It is particularly important to work out the nature of a job and not to rely simply on historic and short-term needs. It is only when this is done that appropriate selection criteria can be identified. An alternative approach is to draw up a list of required job competencies. This is potentially a more rigorous approach but can be time-consuming and difficult for people not familiar with this method to handle accurately.

Selection is likely to be assisted by the careful collection and examination of information about candidates prior to an interview. It is also important to identify what information candidates need to have. Working to sensible selection criteria with the appropriate information available creates a framework for an effective interview. However, interviewers need to develop interviewing skills, which particularly involve good questioning and active listening.

The advantages and disadvantages of selection panels were also considered. These may form part of an equal opportunities policy. The volume of related law has steadily increased in many countries to ensure that the job selection process reduces or eliminates antisocial discrimination. These may be supplemented by further protections provided by individual employers. In addition employers are increasingly embracing the concept of **diversity management** to make use of the potential advantages of differences in the make-up of their workforce.

The chapter contained a final section on the skills of being interviewed, which have as a starting point understanding the selection process from the employer's perspective. An assessment questionnaire is attached as an appendix to this chapter to enable readers to review their own performance as an interviewer.

Self-assessment questions

(If you want to check the extent to which any of your answers to the following questions is appropriate, cross-refer to the Table of Contents. The contents for this chapter are on pages xvi–xvii.)

1 What criteria would you use for selecting a person for a particular job that you know about?

2 In the example given in question 1, what information would you try and collect about candidates in advance of the interview and how would you go about it?

3 How would you prepare for a job selection interview that you have to conduct?

4 What are the main potential advantages and disadvantages of selection panels?

5 What are the main areas of legal protection against illegal selection discrimination, in your circumstances?

6 What basic steps would you take to ensure that you presented yourself effectively at a job interview?

References

(Works of particular interest are marked with a star.)

*Daniels, Kathy and Macdonald, Lynda (2205), *Equality, Diversity and Discrimination – A Student Text.* (A useful account of the key issues in diversity management.)

Drucker, Peter (1955), *The Practice of Management*, Heinemann.

Dulewicz, Victor (1991), *Improving Assessment Centres*, Personnel Management, June.

Fletcher, C. and N. Anderson, (1998), *Assessment Centres: A Superficial Assessment.* People Management, 14 May, pp. 44–46.

Harzing, A.E. and C. Christensen (2004), *Expatriate failure: time to abandon the concept?* Career Development International, Vol. 9 No. 7, pp. 616–626.

Higgs, M.J. and V. Dulewicz (2002), *Making Sense of Emotional Intelligence*, 2nd ed., Windsor, NFER, Nelson.

Goleman, Daniel (1999), *Working with Emotional Intelligence*, Bloomsbury.

Kirosingh, M. (1984), *Changed Working Practices*, Allen & Unwin.

Lloyd George, David (1938), *War Memoirs of David Lloyd George*, Odhams Press, Vol. 1.

Peter, Lawrence and Raymond Hull (1970), *The Peter Principle*, Pan. (Alternatively, see the Souvenir Press edition (1969) reissued in 1992.)

*Smith, Paul and Julie Lister (2008), *Recruitment and Selection*, Ch. 7 in C. Porter, C. Bingham and D. Simmonds, *Exploring Human Resource Management*, McGraw-Hill. (A useful and practical account of the key elements in the recruitment and selection process.)

Thomas, David A. (2004), *Diversity as Strategy*, Harvard Business Review, September, pp. 98–108.

Case cited

Price versus the Civil Service Commission, IRLR, Industrial Relations Services, 1977, p. 291.

Further reading

Toplis, J. V. Dulcewicz and C.A. Fletcher (2004) *Psychological Testing*, 4th ed., CIPD.

Appendix to Chapter 9

INTERVIEW ASSESSMENT FORM

When making your judgements try to relate these to specific acts or omissions on your part. Be sure you understand why you rate each item as you do.

++ Very good
+   Largely satisfactory
0   Not so bad, could have been better
—   Not so good

++	+	0	—

1 *Preparation*: were you well prepared? Did you have clear and appropriate selection criteria? Were you aware of relevant organisational procedures and policies? Did you have a plan?

2 *The opening*: how successful were you in opening the interview?

3 *Putting the subject at ease*: was the subject very nervous? Could they talk freely?

4 *Facts*: did you collect the relevant facts? Did you find out why and how as well as what?

5 *Attitudes/feelings*: did you manage to discover these as well as the facts (if appropriate)?

6 *Questions*: did you ask open-ended questions and probe where necessary? Did you ask leading questions or answer your own questions?

7 *Listening*: did you listen enough? Did you talk too much?

8 *Giving information*: did you give all the information the candidate needed in a way that they could understand?

9 *Manner*: were you courteous, factual, tactful? Were you tense, abrupt, argumentative? Did you make value judgements?

10 *Discrimination*: was there any invalid or illegal discrimination?

11 *Closing*: in what frame of mind did the interviewee leave?

Appraisal

Introduction

In this chapter the various objectives of appraisal are identified and the point made that this is an area with many potential difficulties. One common problem is that, if schemes are not thought out properly, they may contain conflicting objectives. Another potential difficulty is the high level of interpersonal skills that can be needed in appraisal situations. National cultural factors may also need to affect the way that schemes are designed and operated. Consideration of the likely pitfalls is necessary in order to decide whether a formal appraisal scheme should be used or not. This is particularly necessary because of the high failure rate of such schemes. This means that if formal schemes are to be used knowledge of the potential problems is essential. One important distinction is between informal ongoing appraisal and formal appraisal. Ideally these two processes should complement one another.

After the general issue of employee appraisal has been covered, attention is given to performance management. Sometimes individual performance appraisal is part of an overall strategy for performance management. Performance may be improved both by focusing on corporate and individual objectives and the development of key **job competencies**. Sometimes performance-related pay is used as well. As with appraisal, considerable care is needed with the design, implementation and monitoring of performance-related pay schemes. It also needs to be remembered that pay is only one of the factors that determine the level of performance.

Objectives of employee appraisal schemes

There are a variety of reasons why managers may need to appraise their employees. The main reasons for carrying out appraisal are likely to be:

- probationary review,
- performance review,
- the identification of training needs,
- review of duties,
- pay review,
- determining upgradings,
- determining promotion,
- potential and succession planning.

The distinction between upgrading and promotion is that upgrading normally is, or will be, at the higher levels of responsibility within the existing job. Promotion, on the other hand, normally involves the employee transferring to a different job that is at a higher level of responsibility. Potential and succession planning is a longer term and less precise activity than determining promotion.

Potential problems with formal schemes

In an ideal world there would be many potential benefits of conducting an appraisal, giving a formal opportunity for managers and employees to discuss work in a reflective environment. Unfortunately, there are many factors that militate against the full potential of appraisal being achieved. Understanding these problems is necessary in order to decide whether or not to use a scheme and how a scheme might be designed. Appraisal can use up organisational time, so it is important that schemes are designed to maximise the benefits and, in some cases, to minimise the damage that they can cause.

THE FAILURE RATE OF SCHEMES

Fletcher (1993, p. 34) refers to a study where 80 per cent of respondents were dissatisfied with their appraisal schemes – mainly because of the multiplicity of objectives. This fits with substantial anecdotal evidence about how managers view their own organisational schemes.

The ritual of appraisal

'I get the impression that a lot of people are just going through the routine. Appraisal does not have the commitment of the directors. I have not been appraised in years. And nothing happens as a result of it and so employees regard it as a bit of a fag and the manager regards it as a bit of fag. So the two of them go though the sometimes embarrassing routine of something they know at the end of the day is . . . meaningless.'

Manager in a large UK electronics company: quoted in Watson 1994, p. 158.

Further evidence about the potential problems is given in Coens and Jenkins (2000). They claim that formal schemes are used in 80 per cent of workplaces in the USA but that 90 per cent of both appraisers and appraisees involved are dissatisfied with them.

UNCLEAR OR CONFLICTING OBJECTIVES

The objectives of formal appraisal schemes need to be clearly defined. There is little point in appraising just for the sake of it or because it is fashionable. This may not only be a waste of time but may actually be counterproductive. If judgements are made and communicated for no apparent purpose, the people who are judged may rightly feel resentful. Unfortunately, there is a great temptation for people in organisations, as in life in general, to make judgements about other people simply because they like doing it. Superficiality in the judgements and tactlessness in the way any views are communicated may compound this.

The compatibility of appraising with different but simultaneous objectives also needs to be considered. Often this point is overlooked and organisations adopt formal multipurpose appraisal schemes not realising that some of the objectives may be contradictory. Some employers even carry this to the extreme of formally including the maintenance of discipline as one of the objectives of a multipurpose scheme. Including such an objective would be likely to discredit the rest of a scheme. This is because of the negative connotations of discipline. Also, if a person being appraised sees their level of pay or future promotion influenced by the outcome of the exercise, they may be eager to demonstrate how good they are and to play down any shortcomings in their performance or training requirements. If the objectives of appraisal conflict in this way, it is much better to pursue the various objectives at different times rather than have the employee push in a single interview to achieve the objective they have singled out as being the most important.

The compatibility of appraisal with other organisational objectives also has to be considered. It may for example be counterproductive to introduce initiatives emphasising group performance alongside an individual performance scheme that stresses and may also reward people based on their individual performance.

OVER-OPTIMISM

Organisations may underestimate the resources needed for a scheme to operate effectively. The key cost is managerial time, but those being appraised also need to invest time, and the administrative expenses may also be significant. One of the reasons why multipurpose schemes with conflicting objectives are often established is to save on resources. Organisations may also be over-optimistic about the ability of their managers to handle a formal appraisal scheme. If the managerial structure and associated skills are undeveloped, appraisal may simply be too sophisticated to handle. In such circumstances, improvement in these other areas may need to be a higher priority anyway.

Explanations in textbooks about appraisal tend to suggest that formal schemes can be relatively easily implemented. Unfortunately this is often not the case. What is lacking in the literature is an appraisal of appraisal schemes explaining what actually happens in practice. A badly thought-out scheme, or one introduced in the wrong circumstances, can do much more harm than good.

CONFLICT

Considerable conflict can be built into appraisal situations, particularly performance appraisal. An employee will not automatically accept that the criteria by which they are being judged are appropriate, or that the judgements made about their level of performance are accurate. This may be because of misperception by the employee of what is appropriate or because, in some cases, the employee has the best appreciation of what is required. The deployment of people in organisations cannot reach that level of perfection where the manager is always more competent than the employee. There is the additional problem that the employee may appreciate what is required, as far as the organisation is concerned, but recognise that this is not necessarily in their own best interests. This was a point that was raised in Chapter 2, when considering management by objectives, and is sufficiently important to need reinforcing here. Organisational and personal objectives do not always neatly coincide. This can mean that at an appraisal interview a person finds themselves under pressure to do what they do not want to do. This could involve developing the job in a way they find inappropriate, or making cost savings that could affect their status, promotion prospects or even job security. The delicacy of these and the other issues that can arise during appraisal is such that the manager may require considerable skill and sensitivity to handle the situation.

CONFRONTATION

A danger of formal appraisal schemes is that managers may be precipitated into confrontations with their employees that they cannot handle. The simplistic answer to this is to train the managers in appraisal interviewing, but the reality is that many managers, however good they may be in other aspects of their job, will never have the interpersonal skills to handle sensitive appraisal interviews effectively. Many managers, in some cases wisely, just pay lip-service to formal appraisal and simply complete any necessary forms with as little embarrassment as possible. Others may simply upset their employees, often without realising it. Silence by the employee may be taken to mean agreement when the reality may be that the employee may just be managing to avoid losing their temper. Recognition of these problems does at least give the manager a chance of handling appraisal constructively, or of seeing when it is best to leave an issue alone. Sometimes confrontations may be quite unnecessary.

An appraisal ritual with no purpose

A government agency in the UK inherited a Civil Service practice of requiring employees to be assessed as suitable for promotion before they could be interviewed by a general promotion board. The practice of having general promotion boards was then stopped and employees were expected to apply for specific jobs if they wanted promotion. Although there was no longer any need formally to assess whether employees were fit for promotion or not, the practice still continued. Approximately half of the employees were stigmatised each year by being classified as not fit for promotion when there was no longer any purpose in such an assessment.

OVER-GENEROUS ASSESSMENT

As well as there being dangers of unproductive confrontation in appraisal schemes, there can also be the danger that there is a lack of critical comment.

Too much praise

A very senior civil servant in a Gulf state was in the habit of giving all his direct employees excellent performance ratings. As a result of reading a previous edition of this book he decided to base his assessments on actual performance and only a few people got an excellent rating. The feedback that was volunteered to him as a result of this change in his behaviour was that his assessments now meant something. Previously, people could get an excellent rating that they knew was not justified. After the change they felt that ratings were real. Excellence then became something to strive for and not an assessment that would be given automatically. The previous practice had actually been demotivating.

LACK OF ONGOING DIALOGUE

In many organisations managers are required to undertake appraisal of employees in their department as part of a formal scheme. However, whether or not there is a formal scheme, managers need to have an ongoing dialogue with their employees. A formal scheme should supplement and not replace this. The absence of a formal appraisal scheme does not remove the need for the manager to consider systematically, for example, the performance, training, payment or suitability for promotion of employees. A formal appraisal between the manager and an employee should not contain many surprises, rather the interview should review the ongoing dialogue that has taken place since the last formal meeting. Discussion is crucial, not only to check that any formal assessment is accurate, but also to enable any need for change to be talked through and hopefully agreed on by the two parties. For this to be productive, a manager needs to have clear ideas of what they are trying to assess and why, especially as this is an area where managerial thinking is often very muddled.

ILLEGAL DISCRIMINATION

It is necessary to monitor appraisal systems to ensure that they do not involve illegal discrimination. The criteria used in appraisal schemes need to be examined to see if they directly or indirectly unfairly discriminate. Performance, merit payment or promotion criteria could, for example unnecessarily place a premium on aspects that disadvantage a particular group. This could happen, for example, if experience was excessively weighted compared with the actual ability to do a job, which could disadvantage women applying for promotion.

Example

An illegal discriminatory performance pay scheme

In 1993 London Underground made a £60 000 settlement in a case taken by the Commission for Racial Equality on behalf of 20 black station managers who claimed that they had suffered indirect racial discrimination under a performance-related pay scheme between 1989 and 1992.

(Personnel Management 1993, p. 3)

NON-STANDARD CONTACTS

Consideration also needs to be given to need to appraise staff who are not employed on standard full-time contracts. This may include part-time staff, temporary workers and in some cases agency staff.

NATIONAL VARIATIONS

Particular care may be needed in using performance appraisal schemes in international organisations. Schemes designed in one country but used in another need as a minimum to be adapted to take into account local conditions. The very concept of appraisal, giving feedback and encouraging employees to respond may be much less acceptable in some countries than others, especially where power distances between managers and employees are high. The process of appraisal may also be complicated by tensions between different ethnic groups. Account also needs to be taken of whether the focus in a particular society is the individual or the group. Individually focused performance appraisal may be much more suited to North American organisations than those in Japan, where the focus is much more on the work group. The international manager conducting appraisal in a country other than their own will particularly need to acquire sensitivity to the norms and values of the country in which they are operating. They also need to take into account the different cultural backgrounds of people working in their own country.

There is also the question of how international managers should be judged compared with their counterparts operating in their home environment. In commercial organisations, trading conditions may be very different in other countries and the level of profitability may be considerably affected by factors such as internal transfer pricing. A job abroad may differ from a similar one filled by a manager operating in their home country. For example, the job-holder in another country may have to interact with governments and legislators in the host country but not at home. There may also be significant environmental constraints preventing the manager working abroad from operating as effectively as they might have done at home. Also, the host country may have a more turbulent economic or political environment.

Different cultural norms about acceptable criticism

Example

A Dutch doctor whose job was to evaluate a Chinese employee in a company clinic had a 'frank discussion' of the latter's shortcomings. In his view these could be easily remedied by attendance on the company's training course. Yet to the Chinese doctor, who had worked closely with the Dutch doctor and whom he regarded as a 'father figure', the criticism was a savage indictment, total rejection, and a betrayal of mutual confidence. The next morning he knifed his critic to death.

(Trompenaars, 1993)

A manager can be evaluated according to operational, managerial or strategic criteria. Strategic criteria may be particularly important when a manager is operating in another country because they will have a significant impact on the subsidiary's performance. A fuller account of operating formal appraisal systems in an international environment is given by Briscoe and Dowling (2004, Ch. 12, pp. 352–373).

Strategies for handling appraisal effectively

The rest of this section on appraisal is meant to show how schemes might be made to work effectively. The next chapter on training is also relevant. Effective training necessitates accurate diagnosis of training needs, and appraisal may play a critical part in the identification of these needs. Whatever purpose appraisal is used for and whether it be formal, informal or both, counselling skills are required by the managers handling the process. The skills involved in effective counselling are explained in Chapter 12.

ESTABLISHING THE RATIONALE OF A SCHEME

The need for clear and compatible objectives for appraisal schemes has already been stressed. What also needs to be stressed is that it is not enough to select one or more objectives and to assume that the logic of a scheme is self-evident. Care has to be taken to ensure that any objectives are realistically attainable and that the actual scheme devised will facilitate the achievement of objectives. It will be no good, for example, deciding to have a performance appraisal scheme that is based on unreliable, inconsistent and irrelevant judgements. Whatever the scheme, a considerable amount of intellectual effort is likely to be needed in identifying its precise objectives and the operational detail that is required if the objectives are to be accomplished. Specific objectives, and the circumstances in which schemes have to operate, are likely to vary widely from one organisation to another. It is unlikely that one can simply buy an 'off the shelf' scheme or copy someone else's. This may not stop people doing just that, which is no doubt one of the reasons why evidence of schemes actually working is so scarce. If schemes are to succeed, much patient effort is needed in developing appropriate in-house arrangements. The stages in the process include identifying and agreeing the objectives of a scheme with appropriate managers, the preparation of appropriate forms and briefing notes, and pilot runs to test the system. It is only then that the next essential step of training line managers in how to operate a system should be undertaken.

RATING AND RECORDING

A basic aspect of appraisal that needs to be explained is ratings – the method by which these are made and other material is recorded. The first step at this stage is to ensure that the criteria used to judge the employees are the appropriate ones. Ratings also need to meet the following criteria:

- validity: ratings must relate to actual job demands;
- reliability: ratings made by different raters should be comparable (i.e. produce closely similar results), as should ratings made by the same individual at different times;
- relevance: the behaviour or qualities rated should be important to success in the particular job concerned;
- discrimination: the ratings should genuinely discriminate between above average, average and below average individuals;
- comprehensiveness: ratings should cover all main aspects of behaviour relevant to the purpose of the scheme;
- assessability: some factors such as loyalty and a sense of humour mean different things to different people – criteria need to be defined as well as needing to be assessable;
- attainability: any set targets should be realistically attainable.

Particular care is needed to ensure that ratings really are reliable. The dangers of inconsistency are considerable and can easily bring a scheme into disrepute. The hazards include the **halo effect**, where there is a spin-off from one desirable quality in an employee which causes over-generous ratings on other factors. The reverse halo effect occurs when an undesirable quality causes other factors to be marked too harshly. Another phenomenon can be the 'favourite child' syndrome. This occurs when people are favoured for characteristics or behaviour unrelated to the job. It is concern over issues such as these that can arouse considerable trade union hostility to appraisal schemes. Another problem that can arise concerns the need to reconcile the ratings of managers who rate employees either consistently highly or consistently badly. Other managers may create another problem – that of rating nearly everyone as 'average'.

Sometimes managers are obliged to rate according to a normal statistical distribution to avoid such problems. However, this can create problems such as not discriminating between effective and ineffective departments.

Care has to be taken to ensure that any weighting of the various factors has the effect that the designers of a system intended.

Bias in ratings to that which is easily quantified

A merit rating scheme was operated in which the most important factor in practice was punctuality. This was not the intention of the designers of the scheme but was a consequence of the way the raters operated – it was much easier to assess punctuality than other more important but less tangible factors. As the dispersion of ratings for punctuality was therefore much wider than was the case with the other factors, the result in practice was that the differences in the total scores for individuals were accounted for more by punctuality than by any other single rating.

(Gill and Ungerson 1984, p. 47)

Various methods of recording ratings and other relevant information can be used – some of which are aimed at producing statistical reliability and consistency. The methods include:

● comparison with established standards,
● operating on a graded scale,
● comparative rating of employees,
● paired comparisons of employees,
● forced choice questions,
● forced distribution of marks or grades,
● critical incident recording,
● written reports.

Combinations of the above methods are likely to be used, the exact choice depending on the specific appraisal scheme.

Another issue that has to be resolved is whether or not appraisal reports are shown to the employees who have been appraised. One consequence of having open systems is that, not surprisingly, they are likely to lead to only mild criticisms being made by the manager. Employees may have rights of access to what is kept on file, particularly in Europe under the provisions of the European Data Protection Directive.

BALANCED SCORE CARDS

Sometimes organisations, especially private sector companies, use the **balanced score card** method to assess managers (Kaplan and Norton 1992). This involves identifying the four or so key factors that are necessary for overall organisational success. The factors used could include performance in the following areas:

- Financial
- Customer satisfaction
- Operational
- Innovation

One of the potential advantages is that the managers so assessed would consider their overall performance and not concentrate too much on one or two areas whilst neglecting others that are critical for organisational success. The key factors chosen would need to fit the needs of the organisation concerned. There may be advantages in such a system where the assessment requirements are similar for a significant number of managers. However, there is a danger of applying such a template where there are significant variations in the key performance requirements between managers. In addition, as ever, there is the danger that assessment and discussion is too skewed around quantitative measures and ignores important intangible factors.

APPRAISAL INTERVIEW PREPARATION

One of the critical contributions that line managers need to make in operating an appraisal scheme is spending an adequate amount of time in both preparing for and conducting interviews. Their preparation needs to include thorough understanding of a scheme and also being clear what it is they want to get out of an interview. All the managers involved require this commitment. The boss's boss (the organisational grandparent) may also need to be involved, and there may need to be inputs from other people with whom the appraisee interacts.

Preparation prior to an interview involves more than simply understanding the paperwork associated with a scheme. All relevant information should be assembled prior to an interview. There is no point in making judgements about, for example, levels of output or attendance patterns if objective data is available giving exact details. Judgement may be appropriate about the reason for a particular level of output or attendance pattern – but not to establish what the figures actually are. Care will be needed in deciding what judgements are relevant. Criteria also need to be established to ensure that the judgements are made systematically. Other relevant documentation that will need to be assembled includes details of any previous relevant appraisals – and particularly of any follow-up action that was planned. The job description and selection criteria are also likely to be needed.

Both the appraiser and the appraisee need time to prepare for the interview. The process should be seen as a two-way discussion and both parties need to think beforehand about how the interview can be constructively handled. It is hardly satisfactory if the appraisee is not given notice or, perhaps worse still, is told they have an interview but not told what it is to be about. A certain amount of tension and anxiety should also be anticipated which may affect both appraiser and appraisee. Appraisal interviews may reveal conflicts between the parties. This may well happen in performance appraisal interviews – as is explained later – but can happen in any type of appraisal situation. One implication of this is that the appraiser may need to consider what adjustments they need to make, either in their own behaviour or in organisational support, to help the appraisee accomplish their legitimate objectives. It is all too easy to see appraisal interviews as situations where adjustment just has to be made by the employee, but such a view is profoundly misconceived. A further way of endeavouring to secure a constructive outcome is to ensure that recent achievements by the appraisee are clearly acknowledged. All this means that a manager should not try and conduct too many appraisal interviews in one day. The interviews, as well as being likely to be time-consuming, may also be emotionally demanding. Time also has to be allowed for writing up and planning any appropriate action.

FEEDBACK

An extremely dangerous fallacy is that employees always want to know exactly where they stand and will always welcome feedback about their performance. The reality is that most people make a sharp distinction between receiving praise and receiving adverse criticism. Praise is invariably acceptable, but the extent to which people are prepared to accept criticism is limited.

Counterproductive feedback

A principal nursing officer failed to distinguish between a senior nursing officer's capacity for receiving praise and constructive criticism. This led to consid-

erable friction during the formal appraisal of the one by other. As a consequence the two people spoke to one another as little as possible after the interview.

Example

When feedback does have to be given, to decide what information should be given and in what way, it may help to use the following checklist:

- presenting data rather than judgements,
- being specific,
- considering the needs of the person being appraised,
- praising strengths and achievements,
- offering appropriate support and recognising the need for appropriate adjustment by yourself as well as the appraisee,
- generally only giving feedback to people about issues, including their own personality, that they can do something about.

SELF-APPRAISAL

If one is to embark on the performance appraisal of employees, whether formally or informally, it is likely that the best results will be achieved by encouraging the employee, as far as possible, to engage in self-appraisal. This may necessitate the use of counselling techniques, which are explained in Chapter 12. Self-appraisal involves asking the employee to identify the appropriate criteria, the extent to which they have met the criteria and areas of possible improvement. Employees may welcome the involvement this offers and may be more prepared to criticise themselves than have it done by others. People often tend to be their own harshest critics. Employees may also tend to over-criticise themselves for fear of seeming immodest. If this approach is taken, the manager may ironically find that they are in the position of telling employees that they are being too harsh on themselves and explaining that their assessment is more favourable. However, there may be aspects of an employee's performance where the employee does not appreciate the need to change their behaviour. The manager is in a far stronger position, psychologically, to try to draw such aspects tactfully to the attention of the employee if they have previously been building them up than if they had made such observations cold.

Careful judgement has to be made as to the extent to which an employee is able to benefit from criticism. If a person is simply going to reject it there may be little point in pursuing discussion. Often, however, someone may be able to take a certain amount of adverse comment – the skill lies in recognising how much the individual can take. If someone has volunteered three ways in which they will try to improve their performance and is able to accept direct comment about one out of the three areas in which they need to improve, it may be best simply to forget about the other two areas. If their attention is drawn to these other areas, they may become so defensive and demoralised that they refuse to accept the case for any improvement whatsoever.

INFORMAL GUIDANCE

The general philosophy of self-appraisal can be used when giving people informal guidance about how to improve their performance. It may be best to help people see for themselves how they can improve, but only to do this when it seems likely that the person will be able to benefit from such steering. The timing of discussion can be critical as well, with the manager needing to distinguish between when the time is right to help people improve and when such advice will be resisted. Often this will be best handled as problems actually occur. One of the further dangers of formal schemes is that they may be seen as a mechanism for bringing up old issues which are best forgotten. This practice has led some people to refer to the 'annual reprisal interview'. When problems do arise, a counselling technique may still be appropriate. If an employee has a problem, it may be best to start by asking how *they* think it should be handled. This may not only give the required result, but may develop the employee's capacity to work things out for themselves.

PEER AUDIT

A development related to self-appraisal is that of **peer audit**. This involves colleagues being assessed by each other. This has been used particularly in medicine and university teaching. The main benefit is that it can create a formal structure for critical self-appraisal and discussion where none existed before. It may also be more politically acceptable to professionals who often prefer to see themselves more as independent subcontractors than managed employees. Colleagues may be left to choose their partners. Alternatively, some people may be designated as auditors and employees choose which auditor evaluates their performance. This could involve some people carrying out several audits and others none. In the case of university lecturers, the audit would normally include sitting in on a teaching session with the person being audited. The technique is particularly appropriate for performance appraisal, maintaining quality standards and identifying training needs.

The technique of peer audit has interestingly been developed to assess the economic performance of countries. Examples are the African Peer Review Mechanism (APRM) and use within the Organisation for European Cooperation and Development (OECD). A peer audit by one African country of another can be a useful mechanism in presenting a case for development aid or inward investment by an outside company. It may also be more politically acceptable to have the review done by another African country that may have a good understanding of the local economic situation.

360-DEGREE APPRAISAL

The concept of **360-degree appraisal** has increasingly attracted interest (Huggett 1998, pp. 128–130). It involves the assessment of a person's performance by the parties particularly affected by it. The assessors may include not just the immediate boss but also other managers, immediate employees, internal and even external clients or customers. Sometimes information is collected by questionnaire. The theory is that this method will give a literally much more rounded assessment of a person's performance. Employees, for example, often have critical insights and information about a manager's strengths and weaknesses that the manager's boss does not have. However, although this form of appraisal has the potential to give a very thorough assessment, there can be considerable practical difficulties in implementing it. More traditional forms of appraisal can be difficult enough but particular attention has to be paid in 360-degree appraisal to the following:

- the time and resource investment required;
- colleagues may be in competition with one another for promotion or other rewards and this may distort the feedback;
- it may be inappropriate to ask even internal clients to formally assess a person's performance;
- a manager's ability to control and, where necessary, discipline staff may be undermined if they also are under pressure to get good appraisal ratings from them.

The related concept of **upward appraisal** is often used to gain feedback about the performance of lecturers and trainers. Forms are completed anonymously and analysed either just by the person involved, their boss or the client organisation as well. This can provide a useful source of information relatively easily. It is important, though, to carefully evaluate what has been reported. In the case of lecturers and trainers, it may be necessary to focus both on the responsibilities of the person who has taken a session, and also on those who have been receiving instruction, who need to play their part in order to benefit from the instruction.

Specific types of appraisal

Many of the points already made concerning appraisal generally apply to the range of appraisal situations. Performance appraisal is covered specifically in the next section of this chapter in the context of performance management. The appraisal of training needs is covered in the next chapter, and promotion was covered in Chapter 9. However, it is appropriate to look at some of the specific issues involved in upgrading appraisals, the review of probationary employment and the review of duties.

UPGRADINGS

A particular issue that needs careful thought is the choice of the criteria by which upgradings are given or withheld. These criteria need to fit with organisational objectives and enable consistent and defensible decisions to be made. Upgrading arrangements should also motivate employees to acquire any extra knowledge and skills that are needed so that they can cope with their new pattern of work. Sometimes this is done by rewarding people for the acquisition of new and relevant **job competencies**. However, care also has to be taken to ensure that there is an appropriate balance of employees at the higher and lower grades, otherwise there may be a mismatch between the numbers of employees in a certain grade and the work available at that level. It would be somewhat counterproductive, for example, to upgrade everyone in a particular section, leaving no one to do the routine work.

PROBATION

A particular point about probation appraisal is that arrangements for handling this often seem to be more honoured in the breach than the observance. Employees are frequently left to infer that their probation has been completed successfully by the absence of any comment whatsoever. It may even be that their performance has not been satisfactory, but the manager concerned has indicated otherwise by default, i.e. by not saying anything at the end of the stipulated period. Apart from anything else this may create difficulties in terminating the employment of an unsatisfactory employee. Even if a person does not have sufficient service to take legal action for unfair dismissal, organisational procedures for dismissal are usually much more comprehensive for the person who has completed their probation. One useful device that can be used in the case of marginal performers is to extend their probationary period. This can give the probationer more time to improve whilst retaining the relative freedom of the employer to terminate if the required improvement does not materialise. However, the extra time may mean a person has been employed long enough to challenge a dismissal at law. In the case of someone who has been moved into a new job within an organisation, e.g. through promotion, their overall length of service may also be such that they can legally challenge the grounds for dismissal, or even challenge a downgrading.

REVIEW OF DUTIES

Another appraisal situation that requires specific comment is where the duties of an employee are reviewed. Regular reviews of job content may be needed for a variety of reasons. Misunderstandings can easily arise about what actually is required in a job. Additionally, job demands change, and the capacity of employees to undertake particular tasks can also change. The motivational needs of employees also need to be considered, as was explained in Chapter 6, as does the danger of employees wanting to do, or actually doing, work that is not in the best interests of the organisation. It is particularly necessary to remember the propensity of people to neglect managerial work in favour of specialist activity, as explained in Chapter 1, and the pressures for job distortion, as explained in Chapter 6.

Performance management

In the context of performance management is necessary to examine appraisal in relation to setting objectives, key competencies and performance-related pay. The term 'performance management', imported from the USA, has become increasingly fashionable, and it is important to identify its meaning. One definition of performance management is that it is :

> A strategic and integrated approach to increasing the effectiveness of organisations by improving the performance of people who work in them and by developing the capabilities of teams and individual contributors.
>
> (Armstrong and Barron 1998, pp. 38–39)

Identifying training needs and appropriate pay arrangements are also usually an integral part of the performance management process. An integral part of performance management may be setting performance standards. However, as explained in Chapter 2, this can lead to an undue emphasis being placed on quantifiable measures of performance. Also performance statistics may be manipulated to show as favourable a picture as possible. For example, schools may use open or covert means of selection in order to have the best available pupils to teach in order to maintain or boost the school's performance standards. Hospital waiting lists may be reduced by giving a higher priority to minor conditions instead of more severe and resource-consuming treatments. This means that performance criteria have to be selected carefully and performance results closely examined.

Whatever the problems may be in operating performance management, however, the concept is vital to the success of any organisation. The emphasis on aspects such as organisational objectives, integration of activities and employee development are critical ingredients for success under whatever banner they feature.

CRITERIA FOR EFFECTIVE PERFORMANCE MANAGEMENT

The process of improving performance by trying to integrate individual employee objectives with the organisation's strategic plan can be achieved via the appraisal process. To try and do this it is essential to have clear and preferably agreed-upon criteria for judging performance. A methodology for doing this was explained in the context of management by objectives in Chapter 2. Performance management has many similarities with management by objectives. However, performance management is a looser term than management by objectives and is not a brand name associated with one particular firm of consultants. According to Fowler (1990), performance management generally involves more emphasis on the definition of organisational mission statements aims and objectives, and places less emphasis on quantification of performance and more on ownership by line management, particularly by the senior management team (Fowler 1990, pp. 47–51).

Because of the overlap between management by objectives and performance management it is as well to remember the main reasons for the collapse of formal management by objectives schemes. They were:

- their mechanistic nature,
- the lack of genuine involvement by line management,
- the ritualistic way in which schemes were often introduced and applied,
- failure to recognise conflicts of interest between individual and organisational objectives,
- failure to recognise the conflicts of interest that change can create.

SETTING OBJECTIVES

Objectives may be best specified in accordance with the SMART acronym:

- Specific
- Measurable
- Achievable
- Realistic
- Time-related

Ideally objectives and any specific targets should be established at the start of the appraisal period. There should, however, be periodic dialogue about this. This is necessary because of any changes in circumstances. Also, if corrective action is necessary, it needs to be taken as soon as is practicable and not at the end of the appraisal period, when it may be far too late. Even if everything is going smoothly, job-holders should be told so rather than left guessing whether they are seen to be performing effectively.

When performance is assessed it is important to distinguish between work behaviour and personalities. There is no point in making judgements about people unless such judgements are a necessary part of the assessment of performance. Any shortfall needs to be identified in objective terms relating to job demands and not in terms of personal failings.

The person who is normally best able to assess performance is the immediate supervisor or manager. It is prudent, though, to have someone review the assessment by the person making the appraisal. However, in the event of disagreement, care needs to be taken not to override the judgement of the immediate boss, who may be best placed to assess performance. In the event of an appeal against a performance assessment those who hear the appeal must also be wary about imposing their own judgement. They may be well advised to concentrate on verifying that the appropriate procedures were carried out. A way of handling performance appraisal is for the person conducting the appraisal to show draft reports to both the person being appraised and their own boss before the appraisal process is completed. This offers an opportunity to eliminate or minimise any disagreement by discussion before the process is finalised.

IDENTIFYING AND DEVELOPING KEY COMPETENCIES

Armstrong and Barron (1998) comment on the importance of the development of job competencies in performance management:

> What is now emerging is a fully rounded view of performance that embraces how people get things done as well as what they have done. Inputs such as competencies, approaches and understanding have become as important as outputs such as products, goals attained and objectives achieved.
>
> (Armstrong and Barron 1998, p. 39)

The job competence approach can be combined with objective setting by assessing the extent to which employees have developed both their job competencies and achieved their objectives. If job competencies have already been developed for selection purposes it will be logical to cross-check their validity with competencies required for performance management. However, there can be methodological problems in identifying and assessing them. These can include matching generic competencies with the key elements of a job. Also a certain amount of bargaining may take place about the extent to which competencies have been achieved or the levels of achievement.

Inconsistency in minimum job standards

Example

One employee insisted that high competence levels were essential in his job. His boss responded by saying he would agree to these high minimum levels but would take this into account when assessing the extent to which the employee met these high minimum levels. A knock-on effect of this was inconsistency in the minimum competencies that were set for similar jobs.

The issue of job competencies was also considered in the context of job evaluation in Chapter 7 and with regard to selection in Chapter 9. The topic is also examined in the next chapter in the context of training.

PERFORMANCE-RELATED PAY

Consideration of **performance related pay** (PRP) was held over from Chapter 7, on payment systems, because of the need for such schemes to be grounded in an effective appraisal scheme. The distinction between general performance appraisal and performance-related pay is that with the latter there is a formal link between performance and pay. Merit payment can be viewed as a generic term that subsumes performance-related pay.

There are a number of reasons why performance-related pay has become popular in many organisations. These are:

- budgetary pressures combined with low inflation – this has caused some employers to question whether they should give both annual pay increases and automatic incremental increases within salary scales;
- the attempt to create more of a performance culture, especially in the public sector;
- a greater stress on individual as opposed to collective terms of employment, particularly with regard to pay;
- greater fluidity and flexibility in jobs, which has made the nature of many jobs more personalised;
- greater use of job competencies so that people are encouraged to develop their competencies within a job.

As with most management schemes, careful analysis is needed about both the wisdom of having performance-related pay schemes and the way in which schemes are actually operated. Important issues to consider are:

- The need for a management structure that is strong enough to operate a performance-related pay scheme – schemes place considerable responsibility on line managers.
- The need for clear and defensible criteria for awarding differential pay increases to people doing the same or comparable jobs.
- A sound appraisal scheme.
- Whether increases should be given to the majority or a minority. Rewarding just the minority can have the effect of also punishing the majority. This can be exacerbated if the fixed distribution method for allocating increases is used, particularly in small departments.
- Whether or not there should be a fixed budget for performance increases. If there is, this can have the effect of only giving increases to those who increase their performance most, whatever the overall increase in performance may be.
- Whether increases are one-off or permanent increases. Also, whether increases are to be consolidated into the basic salary or not.
- Whether the introduction of a scheme is to be preceded by a pilot scheme.
- Identification of linkages with the identification of training needs and promotion.

- Mechanisms for dealing with market shortages of particular skills. Schemes can be easily distorted by using them to increase the pay for people with skills that are in short supply.
- The danger that staff will give too much priority to securing a pay increase at the expense of other necessary objectives such as long-term aims and individual and organisational development.

The decision as to whether or not a person is to receive an increase, and how much, needs to be taken in private after an informed discussion between the manager and employee. The discussion itself, or the subsequent communication of the decision, should not be allowed to degenerate into a bargaining session about payment. Performance-related pay is not a substitute for effective management but an aid to it. As explained in the context of performance appraisal appeals, procedures need to be worked out, but one needs to beware of removing ultimate pay decisions from the immediate manager. The judgement of others remote from the situation could easily be less accurate. Consequently, appeals are best restricted to procedural issues, with decisions referred back for review if the immediate manager has not handled the process adequately.

Trade unions tend to be unhappy about performance-related pay because of its emphasis on the individual employment contract as opposed to collective negotiation, and the potential for divisiveness within a workforce. However, they may not be in a position actually to prevent their members from having an opportunity to receive more money.

The use of performance-related pay involves risks as well as opportunities. It is likely to sharpen the interest in discussions about performance. Also, the case for trying to improve performance in organisations is self-evident. However, schemes need careful monitoring as well as design and implementation. The increasing volume of evidence is that initiatives to introduce performance-related pay in the public sector in the UK have generally not been very successful. A key factor accounting for failure is organisational culture. Success criteria are not so easy to define. The concept of generating surplus or profit is alien to many public-sector employees. Also, management structures and management skills in the public sector are not usually as well developed or as acceptable as in the private sector.

Performance-related pay in the UK Inland Revenue

Example

The effect of a performance-related pay scheme introduced in the Inland Revenue in the UK was found to have the general effect of reducing motivation and teamwork (Marsden and French 1998). An investigation by the Treasury's public services productivity panel reported that:

... the bonus scheme in four agencies failed to increase either the commitment of staff or the quality of the work ... [They are] ineffective and discredited ... almost all individuals in the national office networks of the four agencies work as integrated team members, and their individual contributions are difficult to distinguish from that of the team as a whole.

(Cooper 2000, p. 13)

Another particular problem in the public sector is that the performance-related pay element is often such a small part of total pay that it has not had much motivational impact. However, part of the appeal to the Treasury regarding performance-related pay in the public sector is that giving increases related to performance can reduce the size of annual pay awards. However, the budgetary implications of performance-related pay need to be properly planned.

Example

Lack of a budget for performance pay increases

In one publicly funded social work agency in the USA a performance pay scheme was introduced but there was no budgetary provision to finance pay increases. There was the potential to improve the level of service provided, but not on a self-financing basis. As a result, no staff were given high commendations for their performance because of the cost implications.

Whilst performance-related pay schemes can work and in some cases are very necessary, there is a danger that employers concentrate either exclusively or too much on the pay element regarding performance. As explained in Chapter 6 in the context of motivation, there can be many reasons for poor performance. What is needed is an integrated and strategic approach to performance improvement that may or may not include performance-related pay.

Summary

Staff appraisal occurs for a variety of purposes. Unfortunately, despite the need for effective appraisal arrangements, the failure rate of formal schemes is high. Reasons include having conflicting objectives in schemes, the level of resourcing needed and the problems of giving constructive criticism as opposed to praise to those being appraised. Formal schemes need also to be supplemented by regular informal discussion and not be a substitute for ongoing dialogue.

The way in which individual performance appraisal may be incorporated into an organisational strategy for performance management was examined. Performance management schemes increasingly involve focusing on employee development and organisational processes as well as achieving objectives and targets. Performance-related pay might be part of a performance management scheme. However, remuneration is only one variable affecting performance and the other variables need to be examined as well.

As with appraisal schemes, performance-related pay can have unintended effects and examples of such effects were given. Performance-related pay schemes may operate more successfully in the private than the public sector. This is particularly because of the generally different culture in the public sector.

Self-assessment questions

(If you want to check the extent to which your answer to any of the following questions is appropriate, cross-refer to the Table of Contents. The contents for this chapter are on pages xvii–xviii.)

1 For what main purposes are appraisal schemes used?

2 Why do formal appraisal schemes fail so often?

3 Give two examples of how national culture can affect the appraisal process.

4 How would you prepare for an informal appraisal interview that you need to initiate? If necessary choose a situation outside of work.

5 What do you understand by the concept of performance management?

6 What basic conditions need to be met in order for performance-related pay to be likely to succeed?

References

(Works of particular interest are marked with a star.)

Armstrong, Michael and Angela Barron (1998), *Performance Management – Out of the Tick Box*, People Management, 23 July.

Briscoe, D.R. and R.S. Dowling (2004), *International Human Resources Management*, Routledge.

CIPD (2005), Survey Report, *Performance Management*, September.

Coens, Tom and Mary Jenkins (2000), *Abolishing Performance Appraisals – Why they backfire and what to do instead,* Barrett-Koehler Publishers, Inc., San Francisco.

Cooper, Cathy (2000), *Civil Service Forced to Axe 'Ineffective' Pay Systems*, People Management, 17 February.

Fletcher, Clive (1993), *An Idea Whose Time Has Gone?*, Personnel Management, September.

Fowler, Alan (1990), *Performance Management: The MBO of the '90s?*, Personnel Management, July.

Gill, Deirdre and Ungerson, Bernard (1984), *Equal Pay: The Challenge of Equal Value*, Institute of Personnel Management.

Huggett, Marianne (1998), *360-degree Feedback – Great Expectations?*, Industrial and Commercial Training, MCB University Press, 30 (4).

Incomes Data Services (2005), HR Study 796, *Performance Management*.

Kaplan, Robert S. and David F. Norton (1992), *The Balanced Scorecard – Measures that Drive up Performance*, Harvard Business Review, January–February.

Marsden, D. W. and S. French (1998), *What a Performance: Performance-Related Pay in the Public Services*, Centre for Economic Performance special report, London School of Economics.

Personnel Management (1993), *Merit pay scheme was discriminatory*, News section, May.

Pickard, J. (2006), *Scorecard might not be so balanced, says research*, People Management, April, p. 5.

Trompenaars, Fons (1993), *Riding the Waves of Culture – Understanding Cultural Diversity in Business*, Nicholas Brealey Publishing, London.

Watson, A. J. (1994), *In Search of Management – Culture, Chaos and Control in Managerial Work*, ITBS.

Further reading

Fletcher, Clive (2004), *Appraisal and Feedback: Making Performance Review Work*, 3rd ed., Chartered Institute of Personnel and Development.

Armstrong, Michael and Angela Barron (2004), *Managing Performance: Performance Management in Action*, London: Chartered Institute of Personnel and Development.

Training and Development

Learning outcomes

By the end of this chapter you will be able to:

- Diagnose your own training and development needs and those of others
- Assess the main ways in which training and development needs can be met
- Assess developments in training and development
- Assess the need for and ways in which managers can be trained and developed
- Conduct a basic evaluation of the effectiveness of a training activity
- Establish a career plan for yourself over the next five years
- Establish a personal development plan for yourself over the next year

Introduction

It is becoming increasingly important to have a well-trained and developed work force. The key reasons for this include the increased pace of change and greater competition. The various ways in which training and development needs can be identified are covered in this chapter. These include performance assessment, training and development appraisal interviews, ongoing supervision, analysis of changes in the external environment, including the law, the identification of the training implications of organisational change and identification of problem areas where training might secure an improvement.

There is often confusion and overlap between the terms 'training' and 'development'. The distinction used in this chapter between the two terms is that training is specific and formally planned. The overlapping concept of development is a wider one which involves exposing people to situations and giving them responsibilities where they can develop their work skills in a much more general and often more fundamental way.

After a discussion of the identification of training and development needs, attention is paid in this chapter to the effective implementation of any planned training or development. This involves considering the ways in which people learn and the options in the delivery of training and development. There has been a shift to identifying training needs in particular in terms of required outcomes or **job competencies** rather than inputs. This can help ensure that training is effectively targeted and monitored. Learning is seen as occurring in a variety of ways including that which occurs on the job. This approach is having an increasingly important impact on the whole range of occupational and professional training and on the education provided in schools, colleges and universities. Another important development is the concept of the **learning organisation**. Whilst this can be more general aspiration than solid achievement, it is increasingly necessary for organisations to compete on the basis of their **intellectual capital**. This involves ensuring that organisations are open and flexible enough to adapt and adopt new ideas. The concept is also appropriate in the public and not-for-profit sectors to see that they address the needs of the communities they serve in the most appropriate way.

Specific attention is paid in this chapter to the need for effective management training and development. The potential obstacles to effectiveness in this area are identified, with a view to ensuring that activity is effective.

The ways in which training activities can be evaluated are considered. The key element in this is to try and identify what changes in behaviour have occurred as a result of training and to assess how appropriate they are. If training has not resulted in changes in behaviour it is necessary to question what the point of it has been. It can be methodologically more difficult to evaluate the impact of development activities, but these may still be so strategically important that they still have to be undertaken.

Individuals need increasingly to take responsibility for their own training and development needs. The pace of economic, organisational and technological change is such that many people will face unexpected and significant changes in their career plans and prospects. Whilst organisations may be able to help with some of this adjustment, it cannot be taken for granted that organisations will continue to exist in their present form or even at all. Consequently, the final section of this chapter is about career planning and **personal development plans**. Readers of this book may also need to pay particular attention to the need to develop their managerial expertise because of the likelihood of them being propelled up the **managerial escalator**, as explained in Chapter 1.

Identification of training and development needs

IMPORTANCE OF TRAINING AND DEVELOPMENT

Training and development has always been an issue that organisations need to take seriously and, if organised effectively, should be viewed as an essential investment and not an avoidable cost. The return on the investment involved should be such that as a result of the training employees reach an acceptable standard of performance more quickly than would otherwise have been the case. It is also a way of ensuring that employees perform to approved standards and avoid bad working practices. The standards achieved if training and development are properly organised are also likely to be higher than in organisations where training is neglected. Training and development have become even more important as a result of recent developments such as the accelerating rate of change and increased competitive pressures brought about by factors such as **globalisation** and the increasing development and application of information technology. The very ability of commercial organisations strategically to position themselves in the marketplace is likely to depend on them having the right permutation of often very sophisticated expertise in order to meet market needs. The existence of expertise, or the potential to develop it, can also create strategic options.

Public sector and non-governmental organisations have to take the identification of training needs seriously too. They are increasingly expected to learn from commercial organisations and to obtain value for money in their operations. They also need to be able to interact effectively with other organisations by, for example, being abreast of recent developments in information technology. Related developments include the concepts of continuous learning and the learning organisation. Both of these issues are examined later in this chapter. Another important factor is the increasing amount of capital equipment at the disposal of employees. There is little point in buying expensive equipment and then not having it used properly because employees do not have the skills to operate it. An even greater danger is that employees will misuse equipment or facilities so that expensive mistakes are made. Another basic issue is that the willingness, and the ability, of employees to cooperate in implementing change may be considerably influenced by the extent to which they have been equipped to handle such change.

The cumulative effect of the above developments is that both individuals and organisations have to increase their investment in training, including retraining, in order to remain effective. For this to happen it is crucial that managers regularly review their own training needs and those of their staff. Increasingly individuals may need to take responsibility for identifying their own needs. The rate of technological change and the reduced predictability of career paths make it increasingly difficult to judge what the needs are and individual employees may increasingly be the ones best placed to make an informed guess about the nature of their training needs. This may involve them in identifying how they retain or develop their marketability in case they lose their jobs, for example in a restructuring exercise.

METHODOLOGY

There are a variety of ways in which training needs can be identified. The methods used may overlap with one another. Key methods are:

- Establishing the training needs of newcomers to an organisation. Newcomers will normally need some induction training so that they are made aware of the context in which they work. Consideration may also need to be given to the remedial training that they may need to be able to perform the basic tasks in their job.

- Identifying the gap between actual and potential performance. This may be done by a process of formal performance appraisal and/or ongoing informal managerial assessment of how training might improve performance. Such activities may be conducted on an individual or departmental basis or both.

- Training needs assessment. Again this may be by a formal process of appraisal and/or ongoing informal managerial assessment of training needs. The focus may include the long-term developmental needs of individuals and groups to prepare them for the future. This may include preparing people for promotion and to be able to handle future organisational changes. Sometimes assessment centres are used as an element in this process. The way in which assessment centres operate was explained in Chapter 9 in the context of selection.

- Self-assessment. Given the increasing pace of change, individuals may be far better placed than their organisation to map the career paths that may be available and the direction in which they want to go. They may also need to demonstrate that they are developing their knowledge and skills in order to retain membership of a professional body.

- Peer audit. Professional level employees may be dependent on colleagues rather than managers for constructive comment about how they can develop their specialist skills. Such comment may also be more acceptable from peers, especially if the professionals concerned are resistant to a managerial culture.

- Identification of problem areas. Problems often centre around low levels of throughput and failure to meet quality standards. Many of these problem areas may be susceptible to training.

- Identifying the training implications of organisational change. Any organisational change has potential training implications that need to be identified. The greater the pace of change, the greater the potential training need. Such needs may arise from organisational restructuring, specific initiatives, new working arrangements, including the introduction of new equipment and changes in the law. Unfortunately, training needs are often overlooked or inadequately met, as illustrated in the following example:

Example

An organisation fails to identify the training implications of change

A national bank in the UK launched a major advertising campaign for a new financial product. However, many of the branch staff had not had the details of the new product properly explained to them. Consequently, many potential accounts were lost because of failures by staff to handle the customer enquires generated by the advertising campaign effectively.

Great care has to be taken to ensure that training needs are realistically identified. The need for training can all too easily be used as a spurious alibi for explaining all shortcomings in performance. Furthermore, performance problems are not always the fault of the individual concerned. What at first sight may seem to be a training requirement may, on closer examination, prove to be a case for changing work arrangements, amending policy or even buying in particular skills. The problems of diagnosing the real issues can sometimes be so complex that the initial diagnosis has to be changed. Organisational weaknesses may emerge that need correction instead of, or as well as, having a training intervention. Even if there is a training intervention, it may need to be with a different group of people.

A supervisory training need is ignored

It was decided to arrange training for employee representatives in employment law at a food processing plant in the UK. The training was particularly about disciplinary and dismissal procedures. The question was then asked about the need to first of all train the supervisors who would have to implement the revised procedures. It was then realised that it was necessary to train them first of all.

Realism has to be used in judging whether a particular person will benefit from training – some individuals have a remarkable talent for emerging unscathed after the most rigorous of training. Training is not always about the acquisition of new knowledge or skills. Sometimes changes in attitude are needed. However, realism may also be needed in this area, as employees may need to be convinced of both the need for and personal advantage to them of developing a different attitude. There may also be limits to the extent to which people can change.

An unrealistic training and development assignment

A departmental head working in local government in London had poor working relationships with the other members of his management team. His director decided that a training workshop on teamwork, involving all the members of the management team, might improve matters. Unfortunately, it soon emerged that the abrasive management style of the department head was so entrenched that no significant improvement was possible. If anything, the workshop made matters worse by making the head even more defensive and dashing the hopes of the rest of the management team that the workshop would have positive results. The realistic options were for the director to move the head out of his job; for the people concerned, including the director, to come to terms with the head's managerial style; or for people to leave.

The development of the flexible organisation means that it is increasingly important to consider the training and development needs of the peripheral workforce. Cost issues that need to be worked out include the marginal costs of releasing an employee, the other things the employee could be doing in that time (opportunity cost) and the time it will take for there to be a return on the training investment. Training should be geared to the major problems and issues facing an organisation; that way it is more likely to be seen as a necessary investment rather than an expendable cost. It also needs to be recognised that some needs can disappear, for example when skills are transferred from production operators and are handled automatically by new equipment.

Meeting training and development needs

RESOURCE OPTIONS

There are a variety of ways in which training and developmental needs can be met. These include on-the-job coaching and planned job rotation and progression. Formal training arranged either externally or internally may also be appropriate. The better managers are likely systematically to identify opportunities to help subordinates improve themselves. If they do this managers may find that, when the performance of those subordinates is assessed, there is often relatively little need for further improvement.

THE MANAGER AS COACH

Managers vary widely in their ability and willingness to undertake a coaching role. However, given the need for generally greater training investment, it is increasingly necessary for them to play this role. Sometimes it may be more effective for managers to coach an employee on the job than for such training to be provided off the job. Coaching may be necessary not just because of the need for staff to develop, but also to enable a manager to delegate.

The role of the coach also needs to be considered in the context of managerial style. Some managers may have a working relationship with their staff such that staff are encouraged to discuss work problems with their manager and in that way learn from them. The managers may also be able to treat mistakes more as learning opportunities than occasions for censure. As explained below it is necessary for managers to see that formal training dovetails with on-the-job learning and is not an unrelated activity. The topic of coaching people so that they develop their managerial expertise is considered later in this chapter in the section on management training and development.

FORMAL TRAINING

Sometimes managers see training as something to be handled entirely by external providers, including an organisation's training department. However, there is only so much that can be handled externally, and even that may not be appropriate. Whilst it would be a dangerously parochial view to ignore what external training providers can offer, one must also be clear about the potential conflict of interests between an organisation selling training services and one considering buying those services. Standardised packages may be inappropriate for particular buyers, as can consultancy services generally. Also one has to beware of entering into dependency relationships with outside organisations that discourage client organisations from working out their own strategies for salvation. Other problems include the lack of responsibility of consultants for implementation and the lack of ownership of their recommendations by the client organisation. Care has to be taken too about buying in programmes that are related to the latest fashion rather than the needs of an organisation. One sales technique can be to 'bounce' a senior manager into a commitment before those with the internal expertise to judge the appropriateness of what is on offer have had an opportunity to comment. However, external providers may have useful or even vital access to expertise and resources. Potential customers simply need to beware that what is on offer is not always aligned to their needs.

Employees sometimes offer themselves for training that is not related to their needs. This can be for a variety of reasons, including an inflated view of the level at which they require training. A person may opt for a seminar on corporate strategy when their needs may be much more basic, such as the need to develop supervisory skills. External training may also be sought because of its prestige, enjoyment or the prospects it offers for getting a job with a competitor. Not all external training is well handled anyway.

One way of checking the relevance of the courses on offer is to examine the objectives, or intended outcomes, and to compare these with the actual, as opposed to imagined, needs of subordinates. If the objectives or outcomes of courses are not clearly stated, that in itself may tell you something about the care or lack of it with which the course has been designed. The statement of objectives or outcomes can also help in checking if a person has benefited from a course. It is this, rather than just asking a person what they thought about a particular course, that is the acid test. When external training is appropriate the manager needs also to help staff to apply any relevant lessons, rather than let them suffer the frustration of seeing what needs to be done but being unable to do anything about it. A disciplined approach such as this should enable a judgement to be made as to whether the training activity has resulted in a worthwhile return on the investment made.

STRATEGIES FOR EFFECTIVE LEARNING

Whatever method of learning is used, it is necessary to consider the ways in which people actually learn. This may vary from person to person and according to the nature of the knowledge to be acquired or skill to be developed. There may also be cultural differences in learning. People from authoritarian and collectivist countries may be more comfortable with prescriptive approaches whilst those from individualistic cultures may prefer to have a significant amount of experiential learning where they work things out for themselves. Whoever is responsible for organising learning for others needs to examine the fit between their training style and the learning style of the people concerned. This is illustrated by the following example.

Example of a mismatch between training delivery and student needs

Example

A newly appointed lecturer in a UK business school conscientiously prepared his lecture material for the sessions that he took for a whole academic year. Towards the end of the year, one of his students, who had attended regularly, explained that he would not be taking the examination. The lecturer was surprised at this as he felt that the student had been thoroughly prepared for the examination. After considerable private discussion the student eventu-ally explained that it was because he had hardly understood a word the lecturer had said all year! This did, however, cause the lecturer to pay serious attention to his teaching methods in the future so that at least he learned from the error of his ways. It also caused him to question whether the term 'lecturer' was a helpful one, as it carried an implica-tion that the primary way in which people learn is from lectures.

The previous example illustrates the need for checks to be made about the effectiveness of training whilst it is in progress. The example also demonstrates the dangers of assuming that information that is imparted is actually absorbed, as was explained in Chapter 8 on communication. If the learning process is ineffective, remedial action needs to be taken quickly. Early feedback on performance is necessary both for the instructor as well as those receiving training. Unfortunately, the authority system in many learning relationships is such that the blame for failure is automatically placed on those receiving the training.

Example

It's all the students' fault!

A student on a Master's programme in the Fine Arts in the UK, who had had teaching experience, complained about the lack of any obvious learning strategies for those on the programme. The response she got from the teaching staff was that the institution had a policy of 'high ability intake' and those who could not cope with the programme as it was had no business being on it!

Strategies for ensuring that learning activities are effective include the following:

- Specifying realistic learning outcomes that are clear to both the trainer and trainee. If standards are too high, less learning will occur compared with the establishment of lower but attainable targets. However, if standards are set too low this can also create problems with regard to achievement and motivation.

- Ensuring that learning inputs are aligned to the specified learning outcomes. Unfortunately, people responsible for learning inputs sometimes concentrate on 'telling' rather than identifying and then explaining what students need to learn.

- Trying to ensure that those responsible for the learning of others pay attention to the manner in which learning is likely to be most effective. Many people automatically assume that the level, manner and language that come naturally to them are equally convenient to others. Learning is much more likely to be effective if trainers identify the starting point of trainees and make regular checks to see how they are progressing.

- Trainers need to evaluate the effectiveness of their presentation skills. This was a topic that was covered in Chapter 8 in the section on presentational skills, which includes a comprehensive check list.

- Account needs to be taken of the **learning curve**. People may take a long time getting started but then accelerate. Learning targets need to be aligned to where people are on the learning curve.

- Many routine tasks simply involve getting people to do things in a specified sequence. It is necessary for those responsible for the training to invest time in identifying the most logical sequence before trying to explain it to trainees. Doing this may reveal illogicalities in existing work methods. Speed generally comes from people avoiding unnecessary movements rather than deliberate attempts to work quickly, which can create errors. When a routine sequence has been mastered by trainees, however, performance may fall because of boredom.

- Consideration needs to be given to the motivation of trainees to learn. They may need to be convinced of the benefits to them as well as to the organisation.

- Care needs to be taken to ensure that the explanation of theory is at a level and pace in line with the ability of people to absorb it. Checks need to be taken on the effectiveness of the process. Theory may need to be interspersed with opportunities for practical application, which may also create theoretical insights.

The need for regular feedback on progress

Example

A lecturer in photography used to give students feedback on their performance after every few photographs they took. However, it was found administratively convenient to get the students to do their 'field work' over much longer periods. Unfortunately this had the effect of each student often repeating basic errors in a hundred or more photographs instead of being shown how to correct these errors early on.

The link between theory and practice and the timing of feedback on performance are issues that may need to be addressed in many programmes. The training of medical students and nurses in the UK may suffer, for example, because of the long periods of theoretical college training before they see a patient!

Consideration may also need to be given to the sequence in which theoretical explanation and practical application take place. The traditional approach is to explain the theory and then give those being trained the opportunity to apply it. However, this does not always work.

Where practice needed to come before theory

Example

A series of courses were run on disciplinary handling in a large manufacturing company in the UK. Relevant law was carefully explained in as clear and interesting a way as possible. However, when the managers were asked to apply the law in a case study they were generally unable to apply even basic concepts. This was because they had not absorbed the legal information in a meaningful way. Consequently, the sequence was reversed and the case study given first. This focused the managers' minds on what was really relevant and motivated them to ask appropriate questions of the tutor during syndicate discussions. They were also more receptive to a presentation of basic legal issues after the case study exercise. The reversal of sequence also made it a much more interesting experience for them.

Sometimes therefore it may be appropriate to reverse the process of theoretical explanation followed by practical application. This is because some people learn more after exposure to practical issues. This reversed sequence may be particularly suitable for some subject areas and is often appropriate in management training.

Some training may involve changing attitudes. This may be more difficult than the development of new skills. Trainees may need to be convinced of the legitimacy of the recommended attitudes before reviewing their own. The problems in doing this are often underestimated when attempts are made to change organisational culture, particularly if the benefits of the change to the actual employees are not obvious. Attitude change may be more easily accomplished in countries that have a high power distance and collectivist orientation such as Japan than in low power distance and individualistic national cultures such as the UK and Australia. However, such training may be much more likely to be effective if it involves group discussion and not just exhortation. This is because it will give the people concerned more chance to reason through the issues and develop a sense of involvement and commitment.

Cultural change in organisations may sometimes need to be accomplished by a significant amount of pressure, as in the following example.

Example

An imposed culture change

Home Depot is a US company that sold items such as do-it-yourself equipment and materials for home improvements. Founded in 1978, it achieved a revenue of $46 billion by 2000. However, progress then faltered as competition increased and the company failed to make effective use of its huge buying power. There needed to be a change from an organic structure, where local managers had considerable autonomy, to a centralised structure. Top management changed and the culture was changed to one with a much greater emphasis on financial performance and strict accountability. Much more standardisation was also introduced in the stores. Appraisal and promotions were based much more on financial performance. Training too was much more geared to sales performance. This culture change was not to the liking of many of the senior management team and many left in the first year of the new regime, in some cases because they simply had a different management style. A key player in the culture change was the recently hired Human Resources Director.

(Ram Charan 2006)

Bob Nardelli, the CEO, was so successful in implementing cultural change that he left the organisation in 2007 with a pay-out of $210 million.

(http://ir.homedepot.com/releasedetail.cfm?releaseid=224078)

Consideration needs to be given to organisational support and the reinforcement of learning. Good training practice needs to be reinforced by actual working practices within the organisation and not undermined by them.

Example

Undermining of training by bad work practices

In one police station in the UK new members of staff were told by some long-established employees to forget what they had learned at the police training college and live in the 'real world'. Unfortunately, the 'real world' included corrupt practices, which led to the prosecution of some of the police officers concerned.

EFFECTIVENESS OF TRAINING DEPARTMENTS

An issue that managers may need carefully to consider is the competence of their own training department, if they have one. Effective training is literally disturbing, as the whole point of it is to alter existing patterns of behaviour. Some training departments help identify and facilitate such change, whilst others either opt out of mainstream activity or are never allowed near it. This can result in the activity of a training department being anaesthetised.

An indication of this phenomenon is the preoccupation of a training department with 'soft' options that do not contain a workshop element. Training may instead be focused on prescriptive packages involving skills, such as report-writing and time management, that may be marginally useful to some of the individuals attending courses. A further feature may be that such activities are easily administered. However, such options are not likely to be part of a coherent strategy to address the key issues facing the organisation that require significant changes in individual behaviour. Other indications are whether the training department is working in relative isolation from line management and engaging in training that is merely fashionable, random or token – or perhaps all three. Hopefully, managers who want a genuine contribution from their training department will encourage them to become involved with real issues that are relevant to the needs of the organisation and not connive in their relegation to dealing only with peripheral issues. Genuine training and development also involves those in senior positions considering what adjustments they may need to make in their behaviour and support, as illustrated by the following example.

The need for the involvement and support of top management

Example

The Chief Executive of a financial services organisation that was experiencing trading difficulties arranged for all his managers to attend a two-day residential management training workshop. However, he saw no need to stay after his introductory comments, nor to meet the managers afterwards to identify what they had learned and to listen to what suggestions they had for organisational improvement. He believed that the only people who needed to change their behaviour were the managers. This is similar to one partner in a troubled marriage expecting the other partner to be the only one to receive marriage guidance counselling.

THE LEARNING ORGANISATION

A number of developments have led to the concept of the **learning organisation**. Pedler, Burgoyne and Boydell (1991, p. 1) defined the 'learning company' as an organisation which facilitates the learning of all its members and continuously transforms itself. The term 'learning organisation', as opposed to 'learning company' is used in this book because continuous learning needs to apply to all organisations, not just those that are designated 'company'. The concept overlaps with the concept of individual continuous development. However, it can be difficult to distinguish between good intentions and practical achievement. Some of the factors that have contributed to the practical and theoretical development of the concept have already been examined. These include the increasing rate of change, the greater need for flexible organisational structures, the concept of continuous improvement and the need to structure the pattern of interactions within an organisation so that there can be optimum interaction between its members. The concept of the learning organisation overlaps with that of **intellectual capital**, which was explained in Chapter 3. If organisations need to survive by the high value added content in their products and services, they need to develop processes whereby their intellectual capital is developed and maintained. The example was given in Chapter 3 of how Procter and Gamble restructured their research and development activity so as to be more receptive to relevant external developments. The concepts of intellectual capital and **knowledge management**, covered in Chapter 3, also have increasing relevance to that of the learning organisation.

The objective of the learning organisation is to enable those involved in an organisation to learn and thereby adapt in line with external changes and internal developments. This is meant to involve structuring the whole organisation so that such learning is facilitated, particularly in an experiential manner. This makes the approach qualitatively different from discrete 'bolted-on' training activities. The process ideally involves all key **stakeholders**, including customers and suppliers. The successful creation of a learning organisation is seen as the key to organisational survival and development. Other aspects are the importance of learning from those engaged in other functions so that a 'holistic' approach can be developed. Human resources are seen as 'elastic' and in need of effective motivation and development. The learning organisation also creates a learning climate that in turn creates and is reinforced by a social system that values and encourages learning.

The learning organisation also needs to fit with organisational culture and managerial style. It is much more likely to flourish in organic adaptive organisations than in mechanistic bureaucratic ones. Another basic requirement is that managers have an open style of management and are receptive to new ideas rather than adopt a prescriptive and secretive style.

The objectives of the learning organisation are praiseworthy. However, it is important that its practical implementation is thought through rather than create a climate where 'anything goes'. Not all development opportunities can or should be followed up – otherwise organisational activity may lack coherence. There is the danger too that individuals may assume that personal developmental opportunities are automatically beneficial for the organisation. Employers need to be clear what the benefits of developmental activities are to the organisation as well as to the individuals concerned. In stable situations, or ones where risks need to be carefully controlled, strong central direction may be entirely appropriate. It may also be very difficult to create an experiential learning climate when an organisation is restructuring or 'downsizing'.

Relevant developments

THE COMPETENCE APPROACH

The competence approach was explained in Chapter 9 in the context of selection. Selection criteria can be defined in terms of the key specific behaviours that people need to have mastered in order to be able to do a job. Similarly, training programmes can be organised around the outcomes that are expected at the end of the activity. This can lead to effective targeting of what is needed. Specification of the required outcomes can also help with monitoring and assessment of training. Readers of this book will have noted that learning outcomes have been specified at the start of each chapter. The self-assessment questions at the end of each chapter are linked to these expected outcomes. This approach has increasingly been used within organisations and with educational institutions.

Historically, in both craft trades and in the professions, the length and complexity of training was sometimes used as a means of restricting entry to an occupation in order to manipulate the labour market to the advantage of those employed in those areas. The competence approach challenges such restrictive arrangements. Even in those professions where there has been no covert policy of restricting entry, some of them have yet to undertake a fundamental appraisal of their arrangements for training and membership. The competence approach is having a significant impact on the job design, occupational standards, syllabus structure and content and methods of training delivery of many professions.

The competence approach can facilitate speedier progression than traditional training by providing for recognition of existing competencies, however acquired, and by excluding irrelevant knowledge. With some occupations, in some countries, there are national standards of required competencies which are not geared just to the needs of individual employers. Skills are therefore more easily transferred between employing organisations. Training, where required, takes place in a number of ways. It is likely to include coaching, supplemented by formal off the job training as and when necessary.

The competence approach to training is more easily applied to demonstrable physical and observable skills than to more intangible areas such as management. Consequently, it is likely to be more applicable to training rather than development activities. However, the approach can lead to a much more disciplined method of establishing syllabus content, strategies for learning and means of assessment. Such developments are increasingly making training providers the coordinators of training and information services rather than simply trainers.

LEARNING CONTRACTS

An adaptation of the competence approach is that of **learning contracts**. Under this arrangement the trainer and trainee or trainees agree what outcomes are expected from the trainee. What is also agreed are the inputs that the trainer will give. This should create both more involvement and commitment by trainees and also any necessary re-examination of what it is appropriate to expect from trainees and the support that they need.

TECHNOLOGICAL DEVELOPMENTS

Developments in technology have helped with the delivery of training. This has been fortunate because of the greater amount of information that mangers have to be able to access as economies develop. Within the EU, for example, employers in member countries also have to comply with increased regulation in the form of European detailed minimum standards and protections with regard to consumers, the public, the environment and employees. This increase in regulation has often coincided with a reduction in the number of specialist advisers available because of organisational de-layering. A way for managers to cope with the extra responsibilities placed on them is by having access to packages and Internet services explaining government regulations and how to comply with them.

The use of new technology as an aid to learning has been described as **e-learning**. This has been defined as 'learning that is delivered, enabled, or mediated by electronic technology' (Sloman and Rolph 2003, p. 1). For it to be effective it may be necessary to allocate time for staff to familiarise themselves with material that is electronically available. This may need to be done away from the work station. It may also be necessary to provide training so that staff know how to use the electronic processes that can be so useful them. E-learning can be particularly useful in organisations where the staff are dispersed in time and place, such as airlines.

CONTINUOUS PROFESSIONAL DEVELOPMENT

The concept of continuous professional development (CPD) is being gradually but unevenly applied to membership and training arrangements by professional bodies. Some now make CPD a condition of continuing membership. This involves members being able to demonstrate that they are maintaining and developing their skills, particularly in core areas. A coherent strategy for self-development is also required. There is also a need for educational institutions to place increasing emphasis on teaching people to 'learn how to learn' and to help them manage such ongoing development. The pace of change is such that on formal programmes a significant amount of material covered early on may be out of date before the programme is completed. Judgements about learning priorities and access to reference material are increasingly important because of the ongoing explosion in the quantity of information.

THE NATIONAL PICTURE

Training and development needs need to be looked at on a national level as well as at the level of the individual organisation. If countries are to be competitive and have effective public services a comparison needs to be made between the skills and expertise that are available and those that are actually needed. Such 'matching' needs to take into account the likely future pattern as well as the current one. Overall there may need to be an increase in the total amount of investment. One way of encouraging this in the UK has been the development of the **Investors in People** (IIP) scheme.

Example

The IIP scheme in the UK

The central organisation is Investors in People UK. To gain accreditation employers must demonstrate that they have a coherent training policy and plan which is adequately resourced and which delivers appropriate results. Organisations must also have an explicit commitment to equal employment opportunities. To retain accreditation employers need either to have an annual external audit or reapply every three years. Ideally organisations use the scheme as a framework for identifying and meeting important training needs and not simply as a public relations kite mark to help attract more customers or clients. The IIP framework is best integrated with existing training arrangements, not as a separate set of policies and procedures.

It is also important to see that whatever vocational output a nation's education system is expected to deliver is in line with the actual qualitative and quantitative needs of a country.

Mismatch between supply and demand

In the UK a combination of an increase in the level of medical training facilities and budget difficulties at the level of hospital trusts led to a major mismatch emerging in 2007 between in the number of junior hospital doctors wanting further training and the places available. A total of 30 000 junior doctors were competing for 22 000 hospital positions. Those unable to find new training placements would be without hospital jobs. A complication with the planning process is that although the number of years needed to train a medical consultant had been reduced by two years, it still takes 11 years.

(The Times 2007)

Switch from command to market economies

A further example of the need to look at the national picture regarding the match between and supply and demand of vocational expertise concerns former Eastern European countries that were part of the Soviet bloc. The switch from command, producer-orientated economies to market economies revealed great gaps in marketing expertise and customer handling skills. This gap is not likely to be quickly filled because of the magnitude of the change in thinking and behaviour that is required.

Management training and development

ITS IMPORTANCE

As explained in Chapter 1, the effectiveness of organisations can critically depend on their level of managerial expertise. As also explained in that chapter, the biggest problem often facing organisations is the preference of those with managerial responsibilities to neglect these duties in favour of specialist activity. Effective management training and development can do much to rectify this. However, it is necessary to recognise and avoid the ways in which such activity can be undermined.

POTENTIAL OBSTACLES TO EFFECTIVE MANAGEMENT TRAINING AND DEVELOPMENT

The list below identifies some of the potential obstacles to effective management development. A key feature of this chapter is consideration of the extent to which these problems can be overcome.

- Management training and development can be costly and the results difficult to verify. When there is pressure on budgets, long-term and speculative investments like management training are not likely to receive favour and training and development budgets are particularly vulnerable when short-term economies are required. However, if management training is carefully planned and targeted it is likely to be seen much more as an essential investment than an avoidable cost. Also some interventions, like senior managers taking responsibility for coaching junior managers, may not be that costly.

- Investment in management training and development may fail because people lacking managerial potential have been appointed as managers.
- Training and development is not geared to organisational needs and developments.
- The organisational culture is not supportive of training and development.
- Inadequate attention is paid to both organisational and national culture. These factors may affect the environment in which people have to operate and the ways in which they learn.
- Training and development may be offered too early or too late in people's careers for them to make effective use of it.
- The diagnosis of needs may be correct but the training delivery may be ineffective. Many training contractors, for example, provide programmes that are based around standard prescriptive packages, not around carefully diagnosed organisational needs.
- A wide range of topics can be passed off as falling within the definition of management education and training. Training can switch to being about management instead of being for managers, and be taught as a set of unrelated theoretical disciplines which can aggravate the problem of the over-compartmentalisation of management activity.
- Undergraduate and other pre-experience management training needs to be reinforced by further training once those concerned have had greater exposure to management problems. Such exposure is likely to lead to an increased awareness of what the problems really are and the concepts and skills that may assist in their resolution.
- The expectations of what management training can do are often unrealistic. Sponsors and managers may believe that there are prescriptive solutions to most management problems that can easily be learned and applied. Development in managerial expertise is often much more complicated than that.
- The skills of effective teaching are sophisticated and in short supply and the effectiveness of teaching in this area is difficult to validate.
- Management training and development, unlike purely technical training, has to be integrated with personal behaviour. This is a particularly sensitive area and egos can easily get bruised if people feel that their job performance is being criticised. Consequently, lessons that people need to learn may be 'blocked' because they are too personally threatening. Also the mere acquisition of knowledge does not mean that people become better managers unless they are willing and able to apply that knowledge.
- Even if training is effective, one needs to ensure that the result has been achieved in the most cost-effective way.

Example of an effective management development programme

It emerged at a London local authority that whilst senior officers were generally well qualified technically there was a need to develop their managerial expertise. Consequently, a series of management development workshops were arranged within each directorate run by an external consultant and each director. Tailor-made teaching material was prepared, particularly case studies. The workshops were designed to identify and address management problems within the various workshops and this was combined with relevant inputs by the external consultant and relevant management topics. The workshops concluded with action plans being drawn up both for the individuals who attended and each directorate. A feature of this approach was that there was a culture change within each directorate with regard to the need for and development of managerial expertise. The fact that each directorate was involved in this process meant that the effect of the workshops was reinforced throughout the authority.

There are elements of the **action learning** approach in the above example so it is appropriate to consider that topic next.

ACTION LEARNING

One potentially useful approach to management training and development is 'action learning' (Revans 1987). This can combine problem-solving with management development so that organisations gain a double benefit. It also ensures that development is focused on an organisation's real problems. A further advantage is that if it is conducted in-house on a group basis it overcomes the problem of managers being sent on external programmes and returning to a working environment that may be unsympathetic or unsupportive to any new ideas they have developed. Use of the technique of role set analysis in this context, explained in Chapter 2, can prove particularly useful.

Some followers of the concept of action learning maintain that working in almost any other management area is likely to bring useful insights into one's existing job. Whilst there may be an element of truth in this, resource constraints mean that action learning needs to be focused on the issues most likely to yield benefit and not on a random basis. Consequently, it may or may not need to include the secondment of individuals into other management functions.

MANAGEMENT COACHING

As has previously been explained in this chapter, managers need to accept responsibility for the development of their subordinates. This may be particularly appropriate for the development of managerial expertise. Coaching is usually about the development of specific areas of expertise and the improvement of performance. It normally involves feedback from the person giving the coaching. Whilst not all senior managers give their coaching role a high priority, the following is an example of one who did, at least for newly appointed executives.

Example

Example of management coaching

The Chief Executive of a London engineering factory told newly appointed senior executives to make a note each day of the issues they would like to discuss with him. He then arranged to see them at the end of the day and spent an hour discussing their queries and related issues with them. After a few weeks he began to reduce the length of the sessions until they stopped completely. He then only expected to spend the same amount of time discussing matters with the new executives as he did with the others, although this could vary according to job demands.

MENTORING

The concept of mentoring has become increasingly popular. Whilst some mentoring may be conducted by the immediate boss, formal mentoring involves the appointment of a more senior manager in a different, if related, department. The organisational distance this creates can reduce the political problems in the relationship. It can also bring detachment to the role and widen the experience of the person being mentored. Much though will depend on the enthusiasm of the parties and the process skills of the mentor.

Sometimes it may be appropriate to appoint an external mentor (Rees 1992, pp. 20–21). Although this will normally cost more, it can bring several advantages, which may include:

- Increasing the pool of possible mentors.
- An external mentor need not be involved in internal organisational politics.
- A suitable internal mentor may not be available. The more senior the manager, the more this is likely to be the case.
- Appointment of an external mentor may enable a person to be developed when they cannot be released from their job.
- An external mentor may be able develop a more confidential relationship with the person they are mentoring than would be possible with an internal mentor. This can assist with the development of a constructive counselling relationship. The skills of workplace counselling are covered in the next chapter.

A concept related to that of mentoring is **shadowing**. This involves development by the programmed observation of a more senior manager in your own organisation. It can also be affected by observing the behaviour of a manager doing a similar job to the 'shadower' in another organisation.

PREPARATION FOR WORKING ABROAD

If managers are to work abroad, either on a short-term or long-term basis, it can be very necessary to see that they have adequate pre-departure training. As was explained in Chapters 4 and

9 it can also be very important to see that an appropriate person is appointed who is able and willing to adapt to the possibly very different conditions of an overseas assignment. It is no good having a person with the right technical skills if they are not able to adapt to the local culture. Hurn (2007) indicates that failure to adapt to the culture is a more frequent cause of overseas assignment failure than lack of professional or technical competence. The greater the difference between their own and the host country's culture, the greater the adjustment that will be necessary. Family issues may also be of critical importance. Pre-departure training will also need to include briefing about the terms and conditions on which a person is being posted. As Dowling and Welch (2004) point out, this may include a brief visit for the employee and their partner to the host country. They also discuss the necessity for language training – 'disregarding the importance of foreign language skills (even given the role of English as the language of business) may reflect a degree of ethnocentrism' (Dowling and Welch 2004 p. 125). It is also necessary for careful thought to be given to the re-entry process if and when the person concerned returns home.

Evaluation

COST-BENEFIT ANALYSIS

Whatever pattern of training and development is adopted in an organisation, it is important that it be monitored to ensure that it is meeting the appropriate needs and giving value for money. As has already been stated, the identification of training needs in terms of objectives and/or expected outcomes makes it easier to judge whether training has been worthwhile. This is not just an activity that should be undertaken at the end of a learning activity – interim evaluation may be needed so that adjustments can be made in time for those on a programme to benefit before the activity is completed. Follow-up studies may also be needed, though, to estimate the long-term impact of training particularly in areas such as management development. Such studies can be very useful as a means of improving future activity. The studies may also need to consider alternative ways of achieving required results. Line managers need to be involved in evaluation and follow-up activity in order to ensure that money spent on their behalf is achieving the desired results. Ways of doing this include interviewing people after they have completed formal programmes to discuss what can be applied in the workplace and reviewing the effectiveness of training during formal appraisal interviews.

Training costs are often relatively easily identified, e.g. by aggregating the costs of releasing a person with the cost of the training provision. This can then be compared with the benefits, i.e. the effect of the training on actual performance, which may be more difficult. However, this can provide the framework for a cost-benefit analysis to assess whether or not there has been a net benefit to the organisation. It can be particularly difficult to undertake a cost benefit analysis with management training and development. The 'opportunity cost' of releasing managers has to be considered. Also it may be particularly difficult to measure changes in performance and to isolate those which have resulted from training. Estimates of whether a person is likely to stay, or be needed, in an organisation may also be necessary. Feedback forms can be used to obtain the views of those who have participated in training activities. However, the key issue is to find out what changes in behaviour have occurred as a result of the training activity.

FOLLOW-UP ANALYSIS

One way of trying to overcome some of the above problems is to build in a follow-up session in a training activity. This may be particularly appropriate with management training. As well as asking people to comment on what has happened as a result of their training, they may also be asked to report on a project designed to demonstrate the application of their learning. As well as helping assess the effectiveness of training this can also have considerable learning value. It may also further motivate people to apply their learning. Participants may also learn from one another's presentations at a follow-up event. However, one methodological problem is disentangling what people have done as a result of the training and what they may have done anyway. The follow-up of formal training activities may also reveal that people vary widely in their ability to benefit from the same programme. In some cases the methodological problems of assessing what benefits have derived from training and development activities may be insuperable. However, it may also be the case that activities such as management training and development are too important to be ignored and some investment is necessary as an 'act of faith'.

Example

Evaluation of a management development programme at a national oil company

An attempt was made to evaluate the effectiveness of a major management programme, spread over some years, in the national oil company of a developing country. The company's activities included oil and gas exploration, production and distribution of oil and gas and increasingly the production of petrochemical products. There were so many variables, imponderable issues and methodological problems that the conclusion was reached that it was not possible to make a valid assessment of the programme's effectiveness. The conclusion was also reached, however, that given the increasingly sophistication and competitiveness of the markets in which the company was now operating, and the political need to develop local expertise, the only option was to continue to try and develop local managerial talent sensibly.

RETENTION OF TRAINED STAFF

It may also be necessary to check on the extent to which organisations retain the people that they have trained and developed. This is more necessary in countries such as the UK where job mobility is generally higher than in countries such as Japan. Sometimes organisations make the mistake of having a considerable training investment in people that they then lose to other employers because they have not provided them with adequate opportunities to use their new-found skills. This can also happen if pay levels get out of line with organisations that are competing for the same skills. It may be particularly necessary to review both the opportunities and pay levels in comparison with 'poacher' organisations who invest little in training themselves but rely instead on recruiting people who have been trained elsewhere.

Responsibility for one's own development

As explained in the earlier section on the identification of training and development needs, individuals need increasingly to take responsibility for managing this themselves. An individual may be the best person to judge their own needs anyway. In addition, however, they can hardly expect their employer to take a keen interest in helping them to develop if their objective is to move to another organisation. As has also previously explained in this chapter, continuing membership of professional bodies may also depend on individuals demonstrating that they have made adequate attempts to maintain and develop their expertise.

MANAGING ONE'S OWN CAREER

The management of one's own career is made increasingly difficult by the pace of economic and organisational change. Even if one stays within the same occupation there may be fundamental changes in the knowledge and skills required to meet a changing pattern of job demands. This means that however carefully one plans one's own career it will be necessary to build an element of flexibility into it to account for significant and unexpected change. Individuals will normally want to develop employment security as well as to have work that they find interesting. The best form of security may be to try to ensure that you have expertise that is going to be in demand in the marketplace whoever the employer may be.

PERSONAL DEVELOPMENT PLANS (PDPs)

Having stated that flexibility needs to be built into one's career plans, a sensible first step in career planning is to try to identify the progression that is realistically available over the next few years. This may identify a gap in skills and expertise that you need to fill. This leads on to the next step – how you propose to fill that gap. This methodology can be applied both to students who have not yet had a full-time job and people already in jobs. Closing the gap means combining what organisational assistance you can get with arrangements that you may need to make for yourself. For people in jobs this may involve going on external courses even if this is not with the blessing of an employer. In addition, it will be necessary to see that you keep up to date with any current job that you have, so that your expertise does not get out of date. Keeping up to date with your current expertise may also reduce the prospects of your work being declared unnecessary. A recurring theme of this book is that you also need to consider where you plan to be on the managerial escalator.

Constructing a PDP may necessitate recording achievements, identifying strengths and weaknesses, setting goals and action plans and reviewing progress. People in management or supervisory positions may want to encourage their employees to use PDPs as well as considering using them for themselves. It is suggested in the self-assessment questions at the end of this chapter that readers complete a PDP for the coming year.

Summary

The increasing importance of training and development has been explained in this chapter. Factors accounting for this increasing importance include the accelerating rate of change, growing competitive pressures, partly because of globalisation and the greater capital intensive nature of much employment. Consequently, increased organisational resources need to be spent in identifying and meeting training and development needs. Developments in information technology both generate new training needs and provide new ways of meeting them. Developments that have been examined include an emphasis on learning outcomes and the development of specific competencies. Initiatives may also be necessary at a macro level so that there is a reasonable match between a country's human resources and the economic needs of the country.

Traditional career paths are often disappearing and individuals need to maintain and develop their expertise so that they retain their marketability. They may also need to be able to demonstrate their continuous professional development if they are to retain membership of a professional organisation. The construction of a personal development plan can aid the individual in managing their own career.

The concept of the learning organisation is important because of the need for organisations to adjust their stock of human capital to market and community needs. This overlaps with the concepts of intellectual capital and knowledge management.

Management training and development is particularly important because of the need for managers capable of exploiting the potential opportunities for an organisation. This is likely to be particularly important for readers of this book, especially in ensuring they get the right balance between specialist and management activities as they move up the managerial escalator.

Another important area is the evaluation of training and development. The establishment of clear learning outcomes can create a logical framework both for the implementation and evaluation of training. Follow-up studies can also be instructive in helping determine if the training investment has been worthwhile.

It is important that readers apply the lessons of this chapter to themselves, as well as others. This is particularly so with regard to their own career planning and personal development plans.

Self-assessment questions

(If you want to check the extent to which your answer to any of the following questions is appropriate, cross-refer to the Table of Contents. The contents for this chapter are on pages xviii–xix.)

1 How would you assess the training needs of an employee, known to yourself, in an organisation?

2 What are the main ways in which job training needs can be met?

3 Why has there been a trend to organise training around outcomes rather than inputs?

4 Identify and comment on the ways in which those with managerial responsibilities can be trained and developed.

5 How would you evaluate the effectiveness of a training activity?

6 Identify your own likely career path over the next five years.

7 Construct your own personal development plan over the coming year.

References

(Works of particular interest are marked with a star.)

Charan, Ram (2006), *Home Depot's Blueprint for Culture Change,* Harvard Business Review, April, pp. 61–70.

*Hurn, Brian (2007), *Pre-departure training for international business managers*, Industrial and Commercial Training, Vol. 39, No 1. (A very useful account of what training may be necessary and how it might be delivered for managers going on international assignments.)

Pedler, Mike, John Burgoyne and Tom Boydell (1991), *The Learning Company, A Strategy for Sustainable Development,* McGraw-Hill.

Rees, W. David (1992), *Someone to Watch Over Me – An Experiment in Mentoring in Hackney,* Local Government Management, Autumn.

Sloman, Martyn and Jesssica Rolph (2003), *The Change Agenda – E Learning,* CIPD.

The Times (2007), *Health chiefs retreat,* March 7.

Further reading

Bennett, Roger (1990), *Choosing and Using Management Consultants*, Kogan Page.

Clutterbuck, David and David Megginson (2004), *Techniques for Coaching and Mentoring*, Butterworth-Heinemann.

Clutterbuck, David (2007), *Coaching the Team at Work*, Nicholas Brearley Publishing.

Cottrell, S. (2003), *Skills for Success: The Personal Development Planning Handbook*, Palgrave Macmillan.

Dowling, Peter and Denise Welch (2004), *International Human Resource Management: Managing People in a Multinational Context*. 4th edn., Thomson Learning.

Easterby-Smith, Mark, John Burgoyne and Luis Arajo (eds)(1999), *Organisational Learning and the Learning Organisation*, Sage Publications.

Garvey, Robert, David Megginson and Paul Stokes (2007), *Mentoring and Coaching – Theory and Practice*, Sage.

*Harrison, Rosemary (2005), *Learning and Development*, 4th ed., CIPD. (A comprehensive, sound and useful account of the organisation of the training and development function.)

Megginson, David and Vivien Whitaker (2007), *Continuing Professional Development*, CIPD.

Mumford, Alan and Jeff Gold (2004), *Management Development – Strategy for Action*, McGraw-Hill.

Reid, Margaret, Harry Barrington and Mary Brown (2004), *Human Resource Development: Beyond Training Interventions*, 4th ed., CIPD.

Revans, Reg (1987), *The ABC of Action Learning*, Chartwell Brett, UK.

Stroh, Linda, J. Stewart Black, Mark Mendenhall and Hal B. Gregersen (2004) *International Assignments: An Integration of Research, Theory and Practice*, Lawrence Erlbaum Associates.

Counselling

Introduction

Some reference was made to the need for counselling in the previous chapter on appraisal. It is now appropriate, however, to deal with the subject in greater detail. The nature of counselling is explained, as are the range of work situations in which it may be needed. These situations include discussing work-related problems, personal problems that affect work, handling grievances and some disciplinary situations. The skills may be needed with colleagues, subordinates and customers. The basic skills of counselling are explained. These include recognising the various stages of counselling, identification of the actual problem and active listening. Counselling in this context particularly involves helping people work out their own solutions to problems rather than telling them what to do. This can be very time-consuming and managers may need to take a conscious decision over whether they wish to or should get involved in particular situations. Counselling skills can be particularly useful and necessary when handling grievances and dealing with some disciplinary situations. Consequently, specific sections are included in the chapter on these areas.

The nature and need for counselling

THE NATURE OF COUNSELLING

Counselling can be defined as a purposeful relationship in which one person helps another to help themselves. It is a way of relating and responding to another person so that that person is helped to explore their thoughts, feelings and behaviour with the aim of reaching a clearer understanding. The clearer understanding may be of themselves or of a problem, or of the one in relation to the other. The point of all this is to enable people to work out how they will handle issues, problems or decisions that have to be made for themselves. The technique is necessary because it may be that it is only by this process that an issue can be understood and/or the commitment created that will lead to an appropriate course of action being taken by the person concerned.

THE NEED FOR WORKPLACE COUNSELLING

The need for counselling can arise in a wide range of situations. Appraisal has already been mentioned, and the requirement for these skills in grievance and some disciplinary situations is explained later in this chapter. Counselling may also be particularly necessary, when employees are experiencing work-related stress (see Chapter 6). The need for counselling skills can arise whenever a subordinate or colleague has a work-related problem. Sometimes it may be necessary to use these skills with clients as well. As well as managers needing counselling skills themselves, they also have to consider the extent to which their staff need these skills. It may be particularly important that any employee who has direct contact with clients or the public is trained in how to handle such contacts.

Given that managers spend most of their time in some form of communication and that much of it is oral communication, as explained in Chapter 8, the need for counselling techniques can arise very frequently. The skills may not have the glamour of more high-status management activities, but can nevertheless be one of the most critical of all management skills. The skills may also constructively be applied in one's personal life.

Usually, counselling discussions are initiated by the person who needs the help. However, there will be occasions when managers need to take the initiative and encourage employees to face up to issues that are having an adverse effect on their work. Whoever initiates discussion, some interpretation of an employee's responses will be necessary. Care needs to be taken about the level of discussion and analysis that is attempted. In-depth Freudian probing and analysis, for example, is better handled by those qualified to do it than by amateur psychiatrists. The requirement for counselling in work situations is usually for work-related rather than personal problems anyway. Obviously, personal problems can affect behaviour at work, and counselling may be given by one person to another in the capacity of personal friend. There may well be situations, though, where it is not appropriate for a manager to get involved or where the best help that can be given is to refer a person to an appropriate agency or service.

Specific skills

Having explained the general nature and purpose of counselling, it is now appropriate to explain the skills in more detail. A particular feature of counselling skills is that managers will often have no advance notice of when they are going to need them. Consequently, if they are to act as counsellors they need to have sufficient mastery of the skills involved to be able to deploy them at a moment's notice.

CHOICE OF COUNSELLOR

The choice of who counsels and when is much more in the hands of the person wanting this type of help than with the potential counsellor. A person may choose not to speak about their problems to some people and may refuse offers of help that are made. The opportunity for counselling is likely to be determined by the person wanting help, but it is up to the manager, if invited, to decide whether or not to respond. The counselling that is required may be easily dealt with in a few moments or may involve several lengthy discussions. Those who have the opportunity to provide this type of help have to judge whether it is appropriate for them to give it and to assess whether they are really likely to help, if they have the time to spare and whether there are other more appropriate ways of helping. A complication is that decisions on whether or not to counsel may have to be taken very quickly. If a person is rebuffed they may not ask again or, if counselling-type help is offered, it may be very difficult to stop once it has started.

STAGES IN THE PROCESS

There are normally several stages in a counselling interview. Part of the skill of counselling effectively is to identify the pattern an interview may take. The main stages are likely to be:

- identification of the problem,
- collection and exchange of information,
- checking that all the necessary statements have been made,
- establishing the criteria for a satisfactory solution,
- deciding on the appropriate solution,
- subsequently checking whether or not the solution has worked,
- evaluating any outstanding problems.

The issue of the different stages in a counselling interview is not quite the same as the different styles of counselling. Each person who counsels may have their own style, which may vary from that of other people involved in intervention (or non-intervention) and the specific skills that are used. However, whatever basic style is used, it will need to be varied according to the personality of the subject, the issue under discussion and the stage of the counselling process. See the appendix to this chapter for further explanation of this and a sample continuum of counselling styles.

IDENTIFICATION OF THE PROBLEM

The problem that a person raises may just be a lead-in or a pretext for going on to discuss much more serious issues. Often the stated problem is rather like the tip of an iceberg. The subject may want to check that they are going to get a sympathetic response before being prepared to reveal the next part of a problem. Sometimes a person may not even be aware that the problem is much deeper than that indicated by them initially. This shows the danger of trying to deal with just the tip. The help that a person may need is to reason through the whole of a problem in such a way that they can cope with it, allowing for their own personality. It may be that there are also issues of which they are aware but which they deliberately keep secret. This is yet another reason for the counsellor to beware of seeking to impose a solution, as it may be based on an incomplete knowledge of the facts.

In order to discover the rest of the iceberg and to get the person to speak freely, the counsellor will find it useful to pay attention to their questioning technique. Open questions (i.e. those that start with an interrogative such as 'how', 'what', 'why', 'where') are more likely to help widen the conversation and explore the issues involved in a particular problem than closed questions. Closed questions are often phrased in such a way that they start with a verb: 'Do you enjoy your work?' If the interviewee is reluctant to talk, the 'yes' or 'no' given in answer to such a question may only help in a marginal way. There will, though, be situations when a straight 'yes' or 'no' answer is what is appropriate. Other skills that may be useful in building up rapport and encouraging the employee to talk include the processes of summarising, clarifying and reflecting back saying, for example, 'So that made you feel rather annoyed?'. Premature intervention by the counsellor can prevent further disclosure by the subject.

ACTIVE LISTENING
Appearance of counsellor

Active listening skills, which are necessary in a counselling situation, involve two aspects. The first is to be listening as well as actually hearing what is being said. Non-verbal skills in this situation include eye contact, leaning forward, not shuffling papers or making notes. The counsellor needs to be aware of the need for eye contact when appropriate throughout a counselling interview. That is not to say that they should spend all their time staring at the subject, but eye contact can be helpful in showing that the counsellor is taking an interest in what is being said. It is also necessary to be aware of signals that are being given by a person's body language. This concept has already been explained in Chapter 8.

Barriers to communication

The second aspect of listening skills which is important includes being aware of the source of barriers to hearing exactly what is being said. These barriers include some obvious ones like language differences, day-dreaming and environmental noise, but also selective perception (hearing what we want to hear), self-consciousness (the counsellor is more aware of the impression they are making) and behaviour rehearsal (the counsellor is busy working out what they are going to say next). There may also be a barrier when the counsellor has problems of their own which occupy their thoughts or where the content of what the employee is saying arouses anger or hostility in the counsellor. In many instances, simply being aware of the likely barriers can help the counsellor to make a conscious effort to eradicate them. These points on listening skills will also be relevant in other types of interview, as will the idea of open and closed questions. Some further points on questioning technique were made in Chapter 9 on selection.

The pressure that people are often under before they speak needs to be kept in mind.

The build up of pressure

An apocryphal story that demonstrates how worked-up people can get before they speak concerns someone who had moved into a new house and knocked at a neighbour's door to ask if they could borrow their lawn mower. The newcomer had worked himself up into such a state about the legitimacy of his request to someone he hadn't yet met that when the neighbour opened the door he shouted 'you can keep your lawn-mower – I know you won't lend it to me!' before the neighbour even had a chance to speak.

Example

LEVEL OF DIRECTION

The amount of direction given by the counsellor will vary according to the situation and the personalities involved. It is the essence of counselling, though, that the person is helped to work the problem out for themselves. Not only may value judgements be inappropriate if made by the counsellor but, if they vary from the value judgements of the person requiring help, that person may see the counsellor as unsympathetic and consequently terminate any discussion. Nevertheless, even given all this, there can be a range of counselling styles (see the appendix to this chapter). At the one extreme a person may be totally non-directive and just give sufficient response, perhaps by way of grunts, to let the other person know that they are actually listening. In other cases it may be appropriate for the counsellor to be rather more interventionist, whilst at the same time avoiding imposing their own views. This can be done in a neutral but friendly manner by positively encouraging a person to elaborate on an issue. Further interventions can be made to clarify what has been said and questions can be asked that are designed to get the person to talk more.

It may be necessary for the counsellor to add information in such a way that the person being counselled feels free to make use of the information or ignore it. This represents a further stage in counselling intervention without sacrificing the neutrality of the counsellor. Another stage is to help the person concerned identify the options available to them – the critical point being that the choice has to be made by the person being counselled and not by the counsellor. This can involve a person taking a decision that is not necessarily in the interests of the organisation – for example, to leave (or in some cases not to leave). There is little point, however, in the counsellor seeking to impose the decision that is in the organisation's interests, as the person would probably ignore it. If someone is going to decide to leave, for example, it may be just as well to help them come to that decision relatively quickly rather than to let the issue drag on.

One problem may lead to another and perhaps much bigger area, and the counsellor needs to be aware that the closing of discussion on a particular topic is by no means necessarily the end of a counselling interview.

The use of non-directive counselling

A newly qualified human resources officer was appointed to his first job. Unfortunately, his formal training had not included counselling. Line managers and others, however, frequently asked his advice about human relations problems. Anxious to help, he made all sorts of suggestions about how these problems might be handled. However, he invariably found that for some reason his ideas were not practicable or acceptable. After a while he realised that the problem was that he was being too directive. He then encouraged people to talk through their problems with him. This enabled colleagues to frame solutions that took account not only of the facts that they had not disclosed and but also of their own personality. They were also more committed to the solutions that they themselves developed. The human resources officer then found that people were often thanking him for helping solve problems that he sometimes had not even understood, far less had a solution for.

CONFIDENTIALITY

Normally, the whole basis on which counselling takes place is one of complete confidence. Sometimes, however, the counsellor will need to warn the subject that information that may emerge, or already has, cannot be treated confidentially. If an accountant is told that their cashier has been systematically embezzling money, for example it is hardly likely that they can, or should want to, keep this a private matter between the parties.

Grievance handling

A grievance can be about either an action that has already been taken, is proposed or is merely feared. Grievances may be raised by colleagues, subordinates, clients or members of the public. Commercial organisations increasingly promote customer complaints (or grievance) procedures in order to demonstrate their concern for their customers. An increasing volume of statutory protection and provisions for processing complaints reinforces this. Grievance and complaints procedures can provide very useful corrective mechanisms for organisations. There is a danger that, if grievances and complaints are not taken seriously, such procedures will decay.

Counselling may be needed in handling grievance situations. Before we look at the specific skills involved it is necessary to look at the framework within which grievances need to be handled.

RIGHTS OF THOSE RAISING GRIEVANCES

Employers may have written grievance procedures explaining the procedure employees should use if they want to raise a complaint against their employer. In some countries, including the

UK, there is a general statutory requirement for employers to have such a procedure. There is also a requirement for employees to try and resolve grievances internally before taking them to an employment tribunal. It may also, as explained in the next chapter on disciplinary handling, be appropriate to use a grievance procedure as an appeals mechanism against minor disciplinary warnings.

Other parties may also have contractual or statutory rights to raise grievances with organisations. Such rights can derive from commercial contracts, consumer protection legislation, or legislation protecting the public. In some cases there is the right of appeal to an ombudsman, either appointed by statute or voluntarily. Trading standards departments are increasingly active in responding to complaints by aggrieved customers. The increase in grievance and complaints procedures has been reinforced by the growth of a litigation culture so that people are more likely to use these procedures. A related development is the promotion of 'no win, no fee' legal services.

LEVELS FOR HANDLING GRIEVANCES

Counselling skills may be most useful in handling informal grievances, which constitute the great majority of grievances. Most issues should be settled at the informal level, and the chances of this happening are increased if front-line staff are selected and trained to handle grievances effectively. With formal procedures the various stages will be specified. Normally the first stage will be informal discussion, but if this stage is inappropriate the further stages will involve increasingly senior levels of management. These will be used if there is no resolution at an earlier stage.

It is important to examine carefully what is said when grievances are raised in order to examine whether there is any aspect of the grievance that can be addressed. If this is not done, it can mean that the grievance festers and may become larger as time goes on. Other grievances can then arise and become linked to the original grievance.

IDENTIFICATION OF WHO NEEDS GRIEVANCE HANDLING SKILLS

Grievance handling skills may be needed by many levels of people within an organisation. It is not enough for managers to have the skills to handle grievances effectively themselves. They need to ensure that those people who work for them and who need the skills are also effective in this area. An audit may be needed of those who need grievance handling skills. This may include all those with managerial or supervisory responsibilities, sales staff and other front-line staff such as receptionists and switchboard operators. Airline staff, traditionally at least, compare favourably with railway staff in their customer handling. This is because of the effort put into customer handling including dealing with grievances. The same soft drinks company mentioned in Chapter 9, for example, came to recognise that their delivery drivers needed to be selected and trained so that they acted as ambassadors for the company and not just as people who delivered goods. Often aggrieved clients or customers vent their frustrations on the first representative of an organisation that they come into contact with. In fairness to the front-line staff and those making complaints, representatives of the organisation need to be trained in how to handle such situations. Such training needs to include details of organisational policies and procedures so that representatives of an organisation are well briefed, which in turn helps to develop their confidence when dealing with employee grievances or customer complaints.

THE FALLIBILITY OF GRIEVANCE PROCEDURES

Unfortunately, the formal stages of grievance procedures covering employees tend to be little used, as the immediate boss is usually designated for the task of hearing the grievance but is normally also the cause of it! Consequently, the grievance procedure may only have a cosmetic effect.

Example

Cosmetic procedures

Recruits at an engineering company were given a standard letter informing them of their right to take a grievance up with the managing director if necessary. On the one occasion that this right was taken up, it turned out the managing director was quite unaware of this arrangement – the undertaking had been given by one of his predecessors.

Another example concerns the way in which information about a grievance procedure was given in a manner designed to prevent its use. British Royal Air Force recruits were told the details of the grievance procedure that they could use if they felt they were being victimised. This was by their senior non-commissioned officer during their basic training. He also advised them that the last person to use the procedure was a recent recruit whom they could observe doing punishment drill around the camp – thus making it clear that the procedure was not a genuine opportunity for recruits to complain.

People are generally averse to receiving no response whatsoever if they have raised a grievance. It would seem better, even if the answer is negative from the employee's or customer's point of view, to have the courtesy to at least tell them that. The problem with ineffective grievance or complaints procedures is that the opportunity is not taken to see if corrective action is necessary, both from the point of the person who may have been aggrieved and the organisation which may be failing in a particular respect.

Example

The need for grievances to be addressed

A local government officer asked for two years why he was not being paid an acting up allowance. After receiving no reply during that period he resorted to using the formal grievance procedure. Unfortunately, by the time the grievance was heard, relationships had deteriorated so much that he ended up being sacked and instituted proceedings against the organisation for unfair dismissal. Even if the employer felt justified in not paying the allowance, a patient explanation of the reasons at the outset may have prevented this breakdown in working relationships.

A misconception that some managers have is that they must support their junior managers. However, if this is done automatically there is no point in having a grievance procedure. There needs to be a sensible balance between the merits of the respective cases. If the employee's complaint is justified, it needs to be rectified with the employer taking corrective action in such a way that those responsible lose as little face as is possible. Even if this does cause some embarrassment, at least the grievances should not recur. It is also necessary, though, to make sure that the management or supervisory case is properly heard.

Example

The need to hear the evidence from the parties involved at the appropriate level

In some organisations there is a failure to hear both the employee's case and those of the people they are complaining about. In one instance the Chief Executive would deal with grievances himself if they were addressed to him. He regularly failed to check whether or not it would have been appropriate to have had grievances dealt with at a lower level. This created a pattern of staff raising grievances directly with him instead of systematically going through the various stages of the procedure. The problem was sometimes compounded by him not ensuring that subordinate managers were given an opportunity to state their side of the story before he decided on the outcome.

THE ROLE OF COUNSELLING IN GRIEVANCE HANDLING

There can be a variety of ways of handling grievances, including having a first-class row, ignoring it, referring it to someone else or giving the person what they want. Often grievances cannot, and should not, be ignored. It may be that a person has a perfectly justifiable grievance, but nothing concrete can be done about it. It is in situations like this that counselling may be not only desirable, but is the only course of action that can be taken. This makes it all the more important that those who are likely to handle grievances are given some basic instruction in the skills of counselling. In some grievance situations the answer may be simply to let people talk themselves out of their fury. Their frustration may require an outlet, and counselling techniques may enable them gradually to dissipate their anger.

At the end of the discussion, an aggrieved person may actually thank the person at whom they have directed their anger, for their help and go away reconciled to the situation. The dilemma for the person who has to handle the grievance is that, if they openly agree with the complaints, they may compromise their employer, but if they rebut the complaints, they may infuriate the complainant. Neutral yet sympathetic listening in many cases is not merely the only option but may be a complete answer. It may even be appropriate for the person at the receiving end of the grievance to take the initiative as the anger subsides and probe to see if there is any more anger that needs ventilation.

Sometimes the counselling of a person with a grievance will simply mark the end of the first stage of the discussion. It may then be necessary to see what, if anything, can be done about the person's complaint. It may be that a decision has to be deferred or the answer given that, whilst you are sympathetic, nothing can be done. It is crucial, however, that where feelings run high, this is only attempted after the counselling stage has been completed. It may only be then that a person can participate in a rational discussion of what can or cannot be done. Even if they still expect some action, a hearing of their case may have gone some way, if not the whole way, to providing psychological restitution. It may also emerge that their anger has prevented them from properly explaining their grievance and that the cause of their dissatisfaction is rather different from that which first seemed to be the case. Clarification of the nature of the grievance may be crucial, as otherwise decisions cannot be sensibly taken about what action should, or should not, follow – yet sometimes it may only be at a relatively late stage in the proceedings that this is possible.

When customers complain, organisations can sometimes seize the initiative by empowering front-line staff to make routine decisions regarding compensation and thus convert dissatisfied customers into people who praise the organisation instead. Enlightened organisations will also see that taking employee grievances and customer complaints seriously can be essential part of good employee relations, quality control and good customer relations. Sometimes organisations take a more proactive approach and conduct surveys of staff and customers.

The processes described above can be very necessary in confrontations between managers and union representatives, or with other special interest groups for that matter. It may be impossible to communicate effectively with representatives until they have ventilated their feelings about a particular issue. It may only be then that representatives are able to listen to the organisational side of a case. The problem for whoever is chairing such joint meetings is to prevent anyone on the organisation's side from retaliating and so inflaming a situation. This may be particularly necessary as the opposing interest group may have actually moderated their position after saying their piece.

Counselling in disciplinary situations

Counselling may also be applicable in disciplinary situations. As with grievance handling, counselling can be a necessary first stage and sometimes the only stage in resolving disciplinary problems. The best form of discipline is usually self-discipline, and an attempt to impose a pattern of behaviour on an employee should normally only be considered if the employee is unable to show the appropriate self-discipline. If it is appropriate for them to change their behaviour, one should normally seek to do this with the minimum amount of pressure consistent with that objective. If an employee's performance or conduct is inappropriate, it would generally seem sensible to encourage the employee to see this and work out for themselves the required change in their behaviour. As was stated during the section on performance appraisal in Chapter 10, people can often be their own harshest critics. It would seem far better, therefore, to give an employee the opportunity to mend their ways voluntarily rather than to try to impose one's authority. Apart from the greater commitment that this may create, it may also save the employee's face if they are allowed to work out their own salvation. Again, as with grievance handling, even if counselling does not prove to be a complete answer, it may clear the way for appropriate action on any residual disagreement. The counselling stage may also be necessary to clarify the exact nature of the shortcomings, if indeed there are any. One of the problems of disciplinary handling is that there may need to be a considerable amount of discussion before it can be clarified whether there is a disciplinary problem or not. Counselling may, however, be just the first stage in the disciplinary process. The handling of further stages in that process is the subject of the next chapter.

Summary

Managers may often need to or be invited to counsel other people about their problems. These may be work-related or personal ones that may affect work. Many will be about minor operational issues that are dealt with quite informally. The essence of counselling is helping people work out their own solution to a problem rather than simply telling them what to do. Counselling techniques may be particularly necessary when appraising staff or dealing with grievances, customer complaints or many disciplinary issues. As managers often get little or no notice of when they may need to use counselling skills, they need to master the basic skills so that they can deploy immediately if necessary. However, they will also need to judge when it is appropriate for them to get involved in counselling situations and what style of behaviour to adopt at any particular point in the proceedings (see the appendix to this chapter).

It is also necessary to consider which subordinate staff and colleagues also need to have basic counselling skills. It is likely to be particularly important that front-line staff in direct contact with customers or members of the public have basic counselling skills so that complaints are dealt with promptly and effectively. Even when counselling is not the complete answer, it can help further discussion by defusing a situation and clarifying what the options are.

Effective grievance-handling strategies are important as a way of identifying when corrective action needs to be taken both with regard to the person who is aggrieved and ensuring that an organisation is functioning effectively. They are also increasingly important because of increased employee and customer rights. Counselling may also be important as a technique for helping employees change their behaviour in disciplinary situations.

Self-assessment questions

(If you want to check the extent to which your answer to any of the following questions is appropriate, cross-refer to the Table of Contents. The contents for this chapter are on page xix.)

1 What do you understand by the term 'counselling'?

2 In what work situations might counselling be appropriate?

3 What are the key skills involved in counselling?

4 How might counselling be of use in dealing with grievances, whether in the workplace or in another relevant situation?

5 How might counselling be of use in dealing with disciplinary problems, whether in the workplace or another relevant situation?

Further reading

(Works of particular interest are marked with a star.)

* Advisory Conciliation and Arbitration Service (2004), *Discipline and grievances at work,* ACAS. (Particularly important for its treatment of grievance handling and related statutory rights in the UK.)

Coles, Adrian (2003), *Counselling in the Workplace (Counselling in Context)*, Open University Press.

*MacLennan, Nigel (1996), *Counselling for Managers*, Gower. (A comprehensive, practical and useful guide to workplace counselling.)

Summerfield, Jenny and Lyn Oudshoorn (1997), *Counselling in the Workplace, Chartered Institute of Personnel and Development.*

Appendix to Chapter 12

CONTINUUM OF COUNSELLING STYLES

The following diagram shows the range of styles of counselling behaviour. The skilful counsellor may need to operate over a range of the continuum, and will decide which kind of behaviour will be most effective in each phase of any counselling situation.

OTHER-FOCUSED

Behaviour style	Examples
Refuses to become involved	'Why don't you try to cope on your own first?' 'I'm too busy to help.' 'That is your problem to sort out.'
Listens	Remains silent, occasionally encouraging the other by eye contact, nods or saying 'uh huh'. 'Could you say more?'
Reflects or clarifies	'As I understand it, you're saying . . .' 'You seem to feel . . . (e.g. encouraged, unfairly treated, confused, etc.)'.
Probes/questions	'Could you tell me more about it?' 'Why do you think so?' 'Have you tried to do anything to improve the situation?'
Interprets	'It seems to me that . . . (e.g. you feel insecure about the future, there is a status problem, etc.)'
Adds new data	'I will tell you some of the background to . . . (e.g. the decision, the problem, etc.)' 'There are several alternative courses of action you could take . . .'
Identifies options	'It seems to me that you could do . . . or possibly . . .' 'You could talk to Mr X before going ahead.'
Proposes criteria for evaluating alternatives	'It seems to me that your choice should be guided by . . . (e.g. what is acceptable to the employee, the likely effect on the employee's work, the likely reaction from staff).'
Recommends/proposes solution	'I think you should do . . .'

SELF-FOCUSED

Disciplinary handling and dismissal

Learning outcomes

By the end of this chapter you will be able to:

- Understand the objectives of discipline in an organisation, including preventative policies
- Understand and advise on basic law relating to dismissal, including European redundancy protection
- Identify and assess the responsibilities of individual line managers regarding discipline
- Handle disciplinary issues informally and effectively when appropriate
- Know how to present a case at a formal disciplinary hearing and also at the appeal stage, and do so if appropriate
- Advise and/or chair a formal disciplinary or appeal hearing

In achieving the above outcomes, readers will not only be able to manage situations at work, but also be able to protect their own rights if they are ever threatened with disciplinary action or redundancy.

Introduction

In this chapter attention is paid to the objectives of disciplinary policies. Preventative policies are important to try and ensure that disciplinary problems are kept to a minimum. When problems nevertheless arise it is important that they are dealt with effectively and fairly. Often the term 'discipline' is seen as synonymous with dismissal, but discipline is a generic term, and dismissal is simply the severest penalty that an employer may enforce. Also, some dismissals, for example on grounds of redundancy or ill-health, are not for disciplinary reasons.

Some explanation of dismissal law in the UK is given. This is not just for the benefit of British readers, but also because it may provide a framework for understanding the legal protections in other countries. Much of this law is simply what amounts to good managerial practice anyway. A basic explanation is also given of European legal protections for redundancy. However, it has to be remembered that national law in individual EU member countries may exceed the European minimum requirements.

The consequences of legal actions by former employees alleging unfair dismissal have to be considered. However, most disciplinary action will involve less severe penalties or be best handled informally. This is explained by way of the 'disciplinary pyramid'. This demonstrates that the greatest volume of activity is at an informal level at the base of the pyramid. It is crucial that line managers accept their responsibilities for maintaining discipline. Reasons why they might not are explained, as are strategies for encouraging managers to act effectively in this area. Consideration of these issues is important whatever the framework of national law.

The skills involved in formal disciplinary and appeal hearings are also examined. The need for clear role identification and separation at hearings are explained. Key roles are those of the case presenter, chair and employee representative. Important issues are the need for a logical sequence of events at a hearing and for an open mind on the part of those who adjudicate on disciplinary issues.

Two appendices are included in the chapter. Appendix 1 is a model sequence of events at a formal disciplinary hearing. Appendix 2 is a checklist of the items that should be considered when writing disciplinary letters.

The objectives of discipline

KEY OBJECTIVES

The primary objective of discipline is to prevent or, failing that, to deal with inappropriate behaviour by employees that has an adverse effect on their work or the work of colleagues. The preventative aspect involves educating employees about the behaviour that is expected of them and reinforcing that with effective management control. Unless a person is dismissed, the aim needs to be to change their behaviour so that it becomes acceptable. Another important objective is to demonstrate that discipline is administered fairly. It is necessary to try to do this, not only to the person who may be the subject of disciplinary action, but also to their colleagues, whose attitudes can be considerably influenced by the action taken.

Example

The connection between disciplinary issues and preventative action

In a large UK health care trust responsible for providing ambulance services, some recurring problems emerged during disciplinary and appeal hearings regarding the level of service provided. This pattern was reported to the clinical governance committee. This led to a review of training and monitoring arrangements so that these recurring failures could either be eliminated or at least be substantially reduced.

EVALUATION OF DISCIPLINARY EFFECTIVENESS

Just as with appraisal, so with disciplinary situations: managers need to work out quite carefully just what they are trying to achieve. Too often consideration of this topic simply consists of a discussion of an employer's track record when legal cases are brought against them. It may be that an employer has never lost a case, or has never even had to defend a case, but that may prove very little. The easiest way not to lose a case is never to dismiss anyone or to only do so when there is an over-whelming case. There is not much point in an employer always winning legal cases if, in the mean-time, their line managers have opted out of their disciplinary role, possibly with a marked adverse effect on standards of performance. It is also necessary to look at basic performance criteria and check if any shortfalls are because of poor control. The areas that may need to be examined include:

- levels of cost-effective performance in an organisation,
- quality standards, including levels of customer service,
- the extent to which important disciplinary rules are observed, particularly in the area of health and safety,
- absence and timekeeping levels.

Weaknesses in disciplinary effectiveness may be a symptom of the wider issue of managerial effectiveness and control in an organisation. A wide range of factors other than discipline can also cause performance problems.

CIRCUMSTANCES WHEN DISCIPLINARY ACTION MAY BE APPROPRIATE

Dismissal may be necessary only if other more appropriate means of dealing with a disciplinary problem, including attempts to change a person's behaviour, have failed or are clearly pointless. Any formal intervention can to some extent be regarded as a sign of failure in that the more sat-isfactory approach of self-discipline may have failed. Disciplinary action may also only be appropriate if someone's behaviour is having a detrimental effect on their or other people's work. The objective is normally to try to get a person to mend their ways so that their behaviour is improved. If this is likely to prove impossible, then a manager has to make a judgement about whether to put up with it or to consider following the avenue that could lead to dismissal.

Judgements about when to intervene, and over what issues, may need considerable thought. People may have many irritating habits that they cannot or will not change, and it may be point-less trying to make them. Conversely, if managers are too lenient, they may find that events get seriously out of hand – the adage of 'a stitch in time saves nine' can be highly appropriate with regard to discipline. A small issue discreetly checked at the right time can prevent escalation into something that is far more difficult to contain.

DETERMINATION OF STANDARDS

There is a tendency for some managers to overestimate the extent to which standards in the disci-plinary area are decided externally. It can be very convenient to assume that the responsibility for establishing and maintaining disciplinary standards lies elsewhere – either within the organisation or outside it. Organisations invariably have overall policies and procedures concerning discipline, but these provide a framework within which a manager should operate rather than devices for managers to avoid responsibility. It is only the manager in an individual department who can monitor and interpret the policies and procedures. If a person is not doing their job properly, it would seem to be a fundamental part of the manager's job to consider bringing the matter to the individual's attention. The definition of standards within a department has to be undertaken, communicated and, when appropriate, enforced by the manager concerned.

The existence of overall policies and procedures does not take away the individual manager's responsibility in this area, however much some managers would like to pretend that it does. Often employees prefer a stricter discipline than actually exists and may resent seeing colleagues being able to behave in an inappropriate way. This tends to devalue their own job and may lead to them leaving or deciding that they may as well follow the lead that is given. Inconsistencies in treatment, especially within a department, can create considerable resentment. Standards of attendance and punctuality can vary widely from department to department, even within the same organisation, according to the lead given by the managers concerned. Employees can also object to too harsh a regime, which is why managers need to think carefully about what standards are appropriate and how they should be achieved, rather than avoid thinking about the issue at all.

The political judgements that managers have to make may be particularly difficult when dealing with professional-level employees. Some of them may find any concept of external control unacceptable, yet develop their work in a way that does not fit with the needs of the organisation. It is useful to distinguish between the professional's technical competence and their accountability for achieving objectives. It may be more effective, and acceptable, to make the point that discussion about accountability does not necessarily reflect on the professional employee's specialist competence.

The legal rights of an ex-employee to pursue a case for unfair dismissal are likely to have an impact on the disciplinary policies and procedures in an organisation. Consequently, it is appropriate to explain the legal position in the UK before considering the skills involved in disciplinary handling. This may also serve as a basis for considering good practice and law in other countries.

The law relating to dismissal

GENERAL FRAMEWORK

The current legal framework regarding unfair dismissal is contained in the UK Employment Rights Act 1996. However, there have been some amendments as a result of other later statutes. The key additions are incorporated in this section. Before statutory protection against unfair dismissal was first implemented in 1972, the only significant right of employees who had been dismissed was to take an action in the civil courts under common law if they had not received their proper entitlement to notice. Such actions alleging wrongful dismissal were, and are, restricted to considering the amount of notice, or money in lieu of notice, to which the ex-employee is entitled.

The grounds on which an employer can establish that a dismissal was fair are quite broad. The three main grounds that constitute fair dismissal are:

- Capacity,
- Conduct,
- Redundancy.

Dismissal can also be for 'other substantial reasons'. This is when the employee has broken their contract of employment in a fundamental way which is not necessarily covered by these three main headings.

For dismissal to be fair it also has to be reasonable in the circumstances. Judgement is on the balance of probabilities.

EXCLUSIONS

Not all dismissed employees can allege unfair dismissal at an employment tribunal. They have to have had a year's employment with the employer concerned unless they are claiming that they have been dismissed because of illegal discrimination, or for exercising a statutory right. There is no minimum hours requirement, e.g. over the course of a week, for an employee to have to work in order to take a claim.

The situation regarding employees who have reached an organisation's retirement age in the UK is affected by the Employment Equality (Age) Regulations of 2006, which were introduced to comply with a European Framework Directive establishing the right to equal treatment in employment matters, introduced in 2000. Under these regulations employers generally have the option of retiring staff at age 65 (the default age). It is possible that default ages for retirement might be regarded as illegal under European law. However, the UK Government has argued that it is able to claim exemption from any such interpretation in the national interest. This is to be reviewed in 2011 by the UK Government, by which time that government hopes (particularly because of the pension implications) that more employers will have moved to flexible policies with regard to retirement. In the meantime, employers in the UK may be able to retire staff at the normal retirement age, usually 65, provided they do not discriminate between employees in a way that is illegal, for example on grounds of sex. Employers, though, have to allow employees to at least make a case for continuing to work beyond the normal retirement age. It is in any case open to employers to argue that, in individual cases, a particular employee aged 65 or over no longer has the capacity to continue doing a particular job. Case law developments within the EU will be particularly important with regard to the issue of standard retirement ages, especially decisions of the European Court of Justice.

CONSTRUCTIVE DISMISSAL

Normally the act of dismissal is not contested. However, there can be cases where it is unclear whether the employee resigned or was dismissed. The sooner the employee clarifies the position, the stronger their case. If an employer breaches a basic element of the contract, the employee has the option of treating such action as a contract repudiation and therefore a dismissal. Such action can include severely unreasonable behaviour on the part of the employer. If the employee does not leave immediately, they need to make it clear that they regard the contract as having been broken. The longer an employee continues with their employer, the more difficult it is for them to succeed in a claim that their position had become intolerable. One way of maintaining their position could be to institute an action for breach of contract whilst continuing in their job (Hogg versus Dover College, 1990).

It may also be possible for an employee to withdraw notice if it was given in the 'heat of the moment' and after provocation. Relevant issues may be the extent of any provocation and the psychological make-up of the employee (Kwik-Fit GB versus Lineham, 1992).

In the event of a case going to an employment tribunal, the issue arises of whether or not there has been a dismissal: this would need to be decided first. In the event of there having been a dismissal, it would then have to be determined whether or not the dismissal was fair. The weakness in an employer's case would be likely to be that no procedure had been followed before the dismissal occurred. This is a particular danger if employers try to circumvent the whole disciplinary process by putting pressure on an employee to leave.

CAPACITY

Dismissal on grounds of lack of capacity may be justified because of a person's poor performance. There are, unfortunately, occasions when people can be trying their best but nevertheless still fail to meet minimum job standards. Such situations are not really disciplinary situations, although they may still result in dismissal. Medical cases might also be dealt with as 'capacity' cases or under 'other substantial reasons'. Again, dismissal may result even though the person concerned may not be to blame. In some organisations separate procedures are established to deal with such cases, whilst in others the cases are handled within the disciplinary procedure. Guidance on this and related issues is contained in the **ACAS** handbook, Discipline and Grievances at Work (2004).

Whatever procedure is used, it is important that the manager investigates such cases carefully to see what help the employer can reasonably give. In the case of sickness absence it is important to check on the prospects of an early return to work and to consider seeking medical advice. It may also be necessary to warn employees of the consequences of their not being able to resume normal work, or appropriate alternative work. Another important issue is the impact of the Disability Discrimination Act 1995. Case law decisions have resulted in a widening range of illnesses, such as schizophrenia, being classified as disabilities. Employers need to be careful in demonstrating that they have taken all reasonable steps to help an employee who may be classified as disabled before considering dismissal.

CONDUCT

Dismissal on grounds of misconduct may be either because of a single instance of gross misconduct, which can entitle an employer to summarily dismiss (without notice), or because of cumulative misconduct, in which case the appropriate notice, or money in lieu, has to be given.

Gross misconduct is not easy to define but legally occurs when an employee's (mis)behaviour goes to the root of the contract. It is prudent for an employer to clarify the position by giving predictable and accessible written examples of what is considered to be gross misconduct. These might well include theft or fraud perpetrated against the organisation and physical assault in the course of employment. This may have both an educative effect and make it easier to establish that particular behaviour constitutes gross misconduct. However, lack of such advance publicity will not automatically prevent employers from treating other behaviour as gross misconduct if it is sufficiently serious.

The basic expectations the employer has of employees should also be an integral part of induction training for newcomers. Also, if new rules are introduced, or if there are other changes in the expectations that employers have of employees, these should be communicated in advance. It is important that employees do not learn of the existence of rules or new expectations by being disciplined. Employers also need to demonstrate that they have systematically and fairly sought to enforce any such rules. Their position at a tribunal would be weak if a former employee was able to demonstrate uneven application of any such rules. Erratic attendance and timekeeping are particularly common examples of cumulative misconduct, and in cases like this the employer needs to be able to demonstrate to a tribunal that they have tried to operate policies fairly and in such a way that the pressure on an employee was gradually stepped up before any consideration of dismissal.

REDUNDANCY

Employers are able to fairly dismiss on grounds of redundancy, provided that it is genuine, that the selection is fair and that there is appropriate consultation.

Selection

A crucial test in establishing a redundancy is whether or not the dismissed employee was replaced. Selection for redundancy may be in accordance with a previously established policy which may also have been agreed with recognised trade unions. Length of service is an important criterion in deciding who should be retained and who should be dismissed, but other criteria, including capability, may need to be considered as well. Objective data may be necessary to demonstrate that selection criteria have been fairly applied.

It is necessary to ensure that redundancy selection does not unfairly disadvantage a particular group. This could happen, for example, if all part-timers were dismissed but a majority were women.

An employer may offer an employee an alternative job in lieu of redundancy. Employees are entitled to four weeks' trial in the alternative job without forfeiting any of their legal rights. An appeal procedure is necessary both to consider appeals against redundancy and against offers of alternative work within the organisation. In the event of the redundancy selection being deemed unfair by an employment tribunal, the former employee would be entitled to compensation for unfair dismissal as well as their redundancy entitlement.

Consultation

Employees are entitled to be consulted about redundancy on an individual basis. This should be done as early as is practicable if they are likely to be made redundant. Such consultation should include ways of avoiding the redundancy and also examination of the opportunity for alternative work within the organisation.

Redundancy consultation is also affected by the European Collective Redundancies Directive. The minimum requirements are that employers planning a redundancy of 20 or more employees are required to consult with relevant trade union representatives, or in the absence of a trade union with elected employee representatives, with a view to reaching agreement. Consultation is necessary even if the redundancies are all voluntary. Such consultation would also need to include ways of avoiding or minimising proposed redundancy. The consultation has to take place 'in good time' – at least 30 days before dismissal with redundancies of between 20 and 99 employees, and 90 days before dismissal if the redundancies are expected to be 100 or over. Dismissal notices cannot be issued until that consultation process has been completed.

There are also financial penalties for breach of the provisions for collective redundancy consultation. A protective award of a normal week's pay for a maximum period of 90 days can be awarded if an employer is in breach of this requirement. The award can be in respect of every employee where it is held that there has been such a breach.

Employers acquiring new businesses, or even sometimes winning contracts for economic entities, must consult with employee representatives if the acquisition or the contract involves the potential or actual redundancy of acquired or existing employees. This is in addition to the European-wide legislation regarding the transfer of undertakings, which creates a further potential liability for employers. These regulations also necessitate collective consultation even if only one person is threatened with redundancy or if existing employees are likely to be significantly affected by the transfer.

Employers are also affected by the European Directive on Information and Consultation. This requires them to consult with employees about the current and future business economic situation, particularly developments that may affect employment arrangements. From 2008 this Directive covers all businesses employing 50 or more.

Redundancy compensation

The statutory minimum payments that employers have to make in the UK to employees with a minimum of two years' service with them are:

- for each year of service under the age of 22 – half a week's pay;
- for each year of service at age 22 but under 41 – one week's pay;
- for each year of service at age 41 or over – one and a half week's pay.

These limits are subject, however, to an earnings cap which is reviewed annually. The cap in 2007 was £310 per week. This means that the compensation is calculated on the basis of regular weekly earnings or the cap, whichever is the lower. The statutory entitlement is also limited to a maximum of 20 years' service. Redundant employees are also entitled to a week's notice, or money in lieu, for every year of service up to a maximum of 12 weeks. Employees may be entitled to higher payments under their contract of employment. The first £30 000 of redundancy compensation is tax-free. Employees faced with redundancy are also statutorily entitled to reasonable paid time off to look for another job and for training during the notice period.

Redundancy compensation may be higher under the terms of the contracts of employment staff have with their employers. The arrangements for statutory minimum payments vary from country to country, even within the EU, and are significantly higher in some EU countries than others.

PROCEDURAL REQUIREMENTS

In the UK minimum procedural requirements regarding discipline and dismissal are specified in the Dispute Resolution Regulations of 2004, which form part of the Employment Act of 2002. There is no exemption for small organisations. Employers must normally observe a three-step procedure if there is a formal disciplinary hearing. Even if the statutory basis for these requirements is altered the basic three steps are likely to remain:

- A statement about the reasons for the hearing. The basis for the grounds needs to be set out in the statement.
- The hearing must be held before a decision is taken. The outcome must be explained as well as any appeal rights if the outcome results in formal disciplinary action.
- The employer must hold an appeal hearing if the employee makes a written request for one.

Employees are also entitled to be represented at a formal disciplinary hearing. In the event of a person being dismissed and the above steps not being observed, the dismissal will at present automatically be deemed to be unfair. The financial penalties for unfair dismissal are explained in the later section in this chapter dealing with compensation. Employers also need to observe the provisions of any internal disciplinary procedure that they have established, which may well be more comprehensive than the statutory minimum three-step process. However, if the employer can establish that the decision would have been the same if the internal procedures had been followed, currently the dismissal will not be unfair provided that the employer has met the minimum statutory procedural requirements.

In addition to the legal and internal procedural requirements that have already been explained for the UK, regard also has to be paid to the ACAS Code of Practice on Disciplinary Procedures if an employee is dismissed (ACAS 2004). The guidelines contained in this document are rather like the Highway Code – a breach in itself is not actionable but, in the circumstances of a dismissal, a breach of the guidelines can lead to an application for unfair dismissal being successful.

THE NEED FOR EFFECTIVE PROCEDURES

The weakness of employers at tribunals often turns out to be their failure to follow a systematic procedure, even though there may be a clearly defined procedure within the organisation that the employer should follow. Individual managers may fail to deal with a disciplinary issue and then, when their frustration builds up, dismiss an employee in a moment of anger. The legal requirements are not so much aimed at preventing dismissal but at ensuring that, when it does take place, it is done for appropriate reasons and in a manner which preserves the rights of the individual concerned to natural justice. These requirements do not seem too difficult to follow but, as with so many areas of management, the problem is one of the application of existing knowledge rather than having some magic wand for dealing with problems that could have been avoided if only dealt with properly in the first place.

Example

The penalty for procedural shortcomings

In a study of unfair dismissal decisions by tribunals, 69 out of 165 cases were found in favour of the applicant. 'Where employees won their claims, their success related almost without exception to procedural short-comings on the part of the employer, whether the dismissal was for reasons of conduct, redundancy or incapacity.'

(Earnshaw 1997, p. 35)

The observance of appropriate procedures is not just a technical matter but one which can affect the actual decision that is taken. The decision to dismiss a person before they have, for example, had the opportunity to state their case is wrong, not just because it is a breach of justice but also because the fact-finding process is incomplete. However, employers also need to beware of overcompensating in this area and having procedures that are unduly elaborate. In some organisations, especially with some public sector employers, this has led to the procedures being too complex for many of their managers to handle. This in turn may lead to managers opting out of discipline and/or the organisation repeatedly losing tribunal cases because they have not kept to their self-imposed elaborate requirements.

It is not sufficient for employers to have good procedures; it is also necessary for their managers to have the skills to operate the procedures appropriately. This is necessary for the handling of all disciplinary cases, not just the small proportion that result in dismissal. Consequently, the skills involved in disciplinary handling are considered in detail later in this chapter.

THE RELATIONSHIP BETWEEN DISMISSAL AND CRIMINAL LAW

A further issue that has to be considered is if a person has apparently committed a criminal action. It is a fallacy to assume that such action can only be handled by the police. If, for example, someone has apparently stolen something, it may be appropriate for the employer to institute disciplinary proceedings about the employee's apparent unauthorised possession of property belonging to the employer. This will initially involve investigation and hearings. Any decisions about whether or not there should be a prosecution should be handled separately. This is assuming that evidence does not rely solely on that which will be presented to a court.

The option of letting such an issue be handled just by the police may not be as easy as it seems. The burden of proof in criminal law has to be established 'beyond reasonable doubt', as opposed to 'on the balance of probabilities' in civil law. The procedural rules are also much stricter in the criminal courts and it may be necessary to establish that a felony was committed or attempted. Added to this is the problem that, if no action is taken pending a court hearing, an employee may have to be suspended on pay for several months. In any case, the employer may find that, if the case is substantiated, the primary remedy they want is to be able to dismiss the person concerned. The point that needs to be stressed is that apparent criminal activity by an employee against their employer does not automatically remove the employer's rights to handle an issue as a disciplinary matter.

Example of the difference between criminal and civil law

The much higher standards needed to secure a criminal conviction compared with success in a civil action were dramatically illustrated by the O. J. Simpson case.

O.J. Simpson had been a particularly famous American football star. In 1995 he was acquitted by a Californian court of the murder of his former wife, Nicole Simpson and her partner, Ronald Goldman, who had both been killed the previous year. However, in 1997 in a civil action for damages he was unanimously held to have caused both deaths. Initial damages were awarded against him of $8.5 million, followed by a later punitive award of $25 million in damages.

Provided there is no specific procedural requirement that a prosecution should be resolved before disciplinary proceedings are taken, it is normally better for the employer to resolve the disciplinary issue in advance of a prosecution being resolved. Amongst other things, this avoids the dilemma of what to do if a person has already been acquitted in the criminal courts. Subsequent acquittal does not invalidate disciplinary action previously taken, because the disciplinary action should be based on the rather separate issue of the extent to which the employee, or ex-employee, fulfilled their employment contract. If the employee is not prepared to state their case because it may reveal issues they prefer were only raised at subsequent criminal proceedings, this does not of itself prevent the employer from going ahead with a disciplinary hearing. Documentation, including statements by those accused, may need to be prepared separately and to different standards in any subsequent criminal case. People may raise the issue of 'double jeopardy', arguing that a person cannot be tried twice for the same offence. However, this argument is fallacious as the law simply prevents people being tried twice under criminal law for the same offence.

Employers may want carefully to consider the timing of any disciplinary action so that they do not jeopardise any covert police surveillance that is in progress. They should also not automatically assume that conviction for a criminal offence justifies dismissal. Much will depend on the circumstances of a case, including the relevance of the conviction to a person's job. In the event of a custodial sentence being awarded by the courts, employers might decide to dismiss the employee concerned, if only because of their non-availability for work.

REMEDIES FOR UNFAIR DISMISSAL

Employers have freedom to dismiss. Any action for unfair dismissal will normally be made only after the employee has been given notice of dismissal. However, the employer needs to be aware of the consequences of being judged to have dismissed an employee unfairly. If the decision is in favour of the former employee there are three potential legal remedies.

Reinstatement

Employment tribunals are obliged to consider reinstatement (or re-engagement) as a remedy if an application alleging unfair dismissal is upheld, but this can only be recommended and not enforced. Although tribunals can award extra compensation if a recommendation to reinstate is resisted by the employer, the normal remedy is financial compensation and not reinstatement.

Basic award

The basic award, to be made if a dismissal is found to be unfair, is equivalent to an employee's statutory redundancy entitlement. This is based on age and length of service and subject to a weekly earnings cap (£310 in 2007). There is a minimum award of four weeks' pay if the employer has been in serious breach of the minimum statutory procedural requirements regarding dismissal, introduced in 2004.

Compensatory award

The compensatory award is designed to cover any further loss suffered by the applicant. It will include loss of earnings suffered since the dismissal, loss of pension rights and an estimate of future earnings loss. The maximum award was £60 600 in 2007 and is reviewed annually. Enhanced compensation for specified reasons are not subsumed within the maximum figure. The grounds for enhanced compensation are failure to implement a reinstatement order, dismissal for membership or non-membership of a trade union, legitimate trade union activity and legitimate health and safety activity.

In a range of cases involving illegal discrimination there is no limit on the compensatory award. The range includes cases involving discrimination on the basis of sex, race, age or disability. However, people who have been dismissed have a duty to mitigate their loss by looking for other work. Also, compensation can be reduced by the proportion by which people contributed to their own dismissal. Additionally, if the employee has not used the internal procedures, including any rights of appeal before proceeding to a tribunal, any compensation awarded would normally be reduced however, by between 10 per cent and 50 per cent. However, in the case of a significant procedural breach by the employer, compensation would normally be increased by between 10 per cent and 50 per cent. The arrangements for varying compensation up or down were introduced by the dispute regulations of 2004. As these regulations were under review at the time of writing, it is always possible that these arrangements will be modified.

General pattern of compensation

The median compensation awarded by tribunals for unfair dismissal claims in 2005–6 was £4 228. However, the legal costs and managerial time involved may be substantial whether a case is won or lost. Because of these factors, employers often make conciliated settlements which may be above the level of the median tribunal award. This avoids the need to appear at a tribunal. In 2005–6, 35 per cent of cases referred to tribunals resulted in conciliated settlements (Employment Tribunals Service Annual Report 2005–6).

Conciliation settlements are arranged by ACAS conciliation officers after a claim has been made to an employment tribunal. As explained later in the chapter, compromise agreements can also be negotiated directly between the parties whereby a settlement is reached without a case necessarily having been lodged with a tribunal.

EMPLOYMENT TRIBUNALS

Employment tribunals currently have three members – a person with an employer background, one with an employee background (normally from a trade union), and a lawyer who acts as judge. In some circumstances, when the issue is essentially a point of law, there is provision for the judge to sit alone. Appeals can be made against tribunal decisions, but only on points of law or where the decision is claimed to be perverse.

Tribunals have proved to be more formal and legalistic than was originally intended. This has been an almost inevitable development given the right of appeal through the legal system against the decisions of employment tribunals. The volume of case law has contributed to the increased use of lawyers. Applicants are not allowed to apply for legal aid at tribunals – although they can apply for aid with regard to case preparation and appeals to the Employment Appeals Tribunal. Costs do not go 'with the action' as in other civil cases, but in some circumstances an award can be made against unsuccessful applicants for frivolous cases or if a case is conducted in an unreasonable manner. In some cases a preliminary hearing is held to determine whether a case is substantial enough or eligible to proceed to a full hearing.

The main costs to an employer can be the time spent in defending a case and any fees paid to professional representatives. Former employees can be deterred by the formality and legal complexity, although if they are a member of a trade union they may have free representation. Even if evidence available after the dismissal (and after any internal appeal hearing) proves that the employer was wrong, the dismissal may still be judged to have been 'reasonable' on the basis of the information available to the employer at the time.

Only 21 per cent of unfair dismissal cases that were initiated in 2005–6 actually resulted in a full tribunal hearing; 35 per cent were withdrawn and, as previously explained, 35 per cent, resulted in conciliated settlements. Of the 21 per cent of cases that proceeded to a full hearing, 54 per cent were won by the employer and 46 per cent by the employee. Employers are more likely to be defending the defensible rather than the indefensible if they appear before a tribunal (Employment Tribunals Service Annual Report 2005–6).

The freedom of action of the employer to dismiss is often greatly underestimated. This may be because of misunderstandings about the legal position or because it may be a convenient alibi to maintain that the employer has much less discretion than is really the case.

In some cases even where employers have suffered losses and been unable to identify the culprit, their actions in dismissing those who could have been responsible have been upheld (e.g. Monie versus Coral Racing, 1980). Much will depend on the circumstances in such cases, but this emphasises the point that it is the employer's reasonableness that is the issue rather than the employee's. In defining reasonable behaviour it is necessary to consider what a reasonable (not a perfect) employer might have done, the size and administrative resources of the employer, how genuine the belief was, the basis for the suspicion of wrongdoing and the norms in the particular industry. Tribunals are obliged to accept that there can be a number of different ways of handling a situation, all of which can be regarded as reasonable. An employer's judgement does not necessarily have to coincide with the judgement that the tribunal members would have made in the same situation for it to be regarded as reasonable. The employer's behaviour needs to be 'within the range of reasonable options'.

Any well-organised employer should, almost by definition, be able to have a much better track record at tribunals than the national average. Successful claims against the employer occur particularly in the less well-organised sectors of the economy where managerial resources are limited. A convenient rule of thumb is for an employer to expect to win at least four out of every five cases taken against them. A lower success rate may indicate weaknesses that need attention. A very high success rate raises the possibility that the employer is being too cautious and only dismissing when they feel certain they will win. There will be some differences of opinion between employers and tribunals. Employers can always consider reinstating an employee if they lose a case at a tribunal. It is important to recognise that, if employers are seen to opt out of dismissing employees, unless the reasons are overwhelming, this can create a climate where nobody tries to tell anybody what to do on the basis that nothing is likely to be done if the person refuses. The impact of decisions concerning dismissal needs to be seen in relation to the signals it is sending within an organisation and not in isolation, or just in terms of the track record at tribunals.

COMPROMISE AGREEMENTS

As was explained earlier in this chapter in the context of financial compensation, employees who have made a claim to a tribunal for unfair dismissal often reach a conciliated settlement with the employer instead of proceeding to a tribunal hearing. However, there is also provision for compromise agreements to be made before an application is made to an employment tribunal under which claimants waive their right to take a case to a tribunal. For such an agreement to be valid, it is necessary for the former employee to receive independent advice from a lawyer or other specialist who has professional indemnity insurance. The other specialist could be a full-time trade union official.

THE ARBITRATION OPTION

Under the terms of the Employment Rights (Dispute Resolution) Act of 1998, many unfair dismissal cases can be resolved by binding arbitration instead of being referred to an employment tribunal. This option requires the agreement of both the employer and former employee. Access to this arrangement would normally be via a conciliation officer of ACAS. The remit of arbitrators, who sit alone, is to decide whether or not a dismissal was fair on the basis of the facts and not the law. This distinction will determine whether cases are appropriate for arbitration or not. The only way in which a decision can be challenged is by a formal judicial review.

OTHER IMPLICATIONS OF DISMISSAL PROCEEDINGS
Industrial

Employers also have to consider the industrial repercussions of a dismissal. Irrespective of whether a tribunal judges a dismissal to be fair or unfair or if a tribunal even hears a case, sanctions may be applied by the remaining workers to try to secure the reinstatement of a colleague. Changed economic circumstances and access to tribunals have, however, greatly reduced industrial action on dismissal. However, a dismissal may still have an effect on other employees and may have to be organisationally acceptable. This will particularly be the case where the employer is heavily dependent on employee goodwill.

Public relations

There may also be public relations implications involved in tribunal cases. Organisations with a high public profile might be particularly sensitive, for example, to discrimination cases. Even if they win a case at a tribunal, some of the publicity they receive may be unfavourable.

Personal

Tribunal cases can be stressful and time-consuming. There may also be a temptation on the part of employers to look for scapegoats if any fault is found with the way they handled a case. However, witch-hunts are likely to have the effect of discouraging managers from taking disciplinary action when it may be needed in the future. The checks and balances in internal procedures, particularly of separating the chairing of a hearing from case presentation and the right of internal appeal, should in any case mean that responsibility for dismissal is shared.

Precedent

Some issues may involve important matters of principle and employers may feel that they need to defend a case in order to demonstrate that they have behaved correctly. Employers may also want to demonstrate to their managers that they will back them when they have behaved correctly. A further issue is not to unduly encourage former employees to pursue weak cases in order to get a conciliated cash settlement. Former employees may use this tactic hoping that employers will find it cheaper to make a financial settlement rather than have the expense of successfully defending a case at a tribunal. The danger is that this could become common practice even when employees have very little chance of winning.

The responsibility of the individual manager

THE DISCIPLINARY PYRAMID

The introduction of unfair dismissal law has tended to concentrate attention on dismissal. Discipline is a generic term, and dismissal is just one aspect of the disciplinary process. Ideally, policies and practices should be such that disciplinary issues are contained, so that it is rare for a dismissal to be necessary. If there is effective supervisory and managerial control, disciplinary issues should be generally so handled. If this is not the case, too many issues may be allowed to spiral upwards before being dealt with. The main volume of activity should be in encouraging self-discipline, containment and low level penalties (see Figure 13.1). However, there will be occasions when the nature of an employee's behaviour will require formal disciplinary action.

When more formality was needed than was given

An employer explained at a tribunal hearing that:
   [He] did not give the applicant a serious reprimand, although he did mention that he would kill him if such a thing occurred again.

(IDS 1976, p. 13)

A heavy emphasis on severe penalties may be indicative of ineffective control at the lower levels of the pyramid. This can happen all too frequently and what can emerge is that 'disciplinary problems' are a symptom of much deeper organisational problems, such as the lack of

Figure 13.1 | The disciplinary pyramid

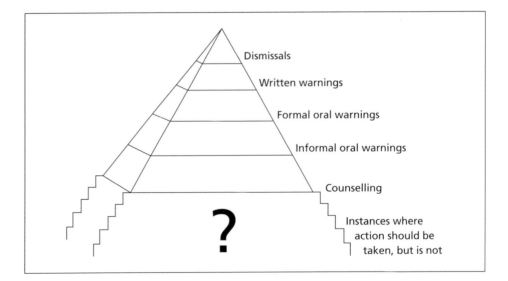

effective supervision and poor organisational structure. Contributory factors to this can be a general opting out of the management process and poor selection and training of supervisors and managers.

Sometimes supervisors either see themselves as not having any disciplinary responsibility at all, or are extremely vague about just what those responsibilities are. It may be particularly important to clarify exactly what the disciplinary responsibilities and powers are of the various levels of management. This is likely to be most needed with regard to the penalties that can be awarded at the base of the disciplinary pyramid where most action needs to take place and where the opportunity for confusion is greatest. The need to discipline staff is often an embarrassing and unpopular, if necessary, activity. The area where greatest organisational attention and clarification is often needed is the responsibility for investigation and follow-up of minor issues and the administering, where appropriate, of low-level penalties. This involves not just the drawing up of a clear procedure but also the training of supervisors and managers in how to handle their responsibilities. If these steps are not taken one is likely to have supervisors and managers intervening and getting it wrong, or getting away with the potentially disastrous attitude that disciplinary control of their own subordinates is nothing to do with them but is some other mystery person's responsibility.

Even when responsibilities are clarified, it is common for disciplinary issues to be referred upwards. It is important that managers do not get sucked into handling disciplinary issues that should be handled at a lower level. Instead they should coach those at a lower level in the managerial hierarchy in how to handle their responsibilities. This may involve junior managers keeping a diary note of informal warnings when appropriate. This may be useful if an employee later claims that they had not been told about a particular issue. However, such notes may be best kept in a general diary and not a diary or local file specifically about the person concerned. This is to avoid complications under the data protection legislation. To make such entries on a central personnel file would also contradict the concept of an informal oral warning. The operation of discipline at this level is likely to overlap with general managerial control and the giving of work instructions.

A further reason for generally handling issues low down the pyramid is that any required change might as well be achieved with the minimum amount of pressure that will have the desired effect. If a quiet word will do the trick, there is little point in antagonising employees by using more pressure than is necessary. The informal oral warning may be the most important sanction in the disciplinary process. It may be convenient for people to argue that the only penalty is dismissal, but the reality is that most people do not like being corrected and that, psychologically, the informal oral warning is a sanction that managers may find they can use effectively. Only if this does not lead to the required change in behaviour does a manager need to consider more formal measures. In some cases employees may not even need reprimanding to change their behaviour.

Is there a need for disciplinary action?

A technician wrecked a particularly expensive piece of equipment in a chemical works. The manager concerned took the view that that was one mistake the technician would never make again and that there was no need to take disciplinary action.

However, sometimes employees do need to have the error of their ways pointed out to them – either because they do not realise that they are in error or because they think that they can behave in a particular way with impunity.

THE ROLE OF THE HUMAN RESOURCES (HR) DEPARTMENT

Encouraging and helping junior managers to handle their responsibilities for discipline also leaves more senior managers free to be involved in more serious issues or in hearing appeals. A danger is that disciplinary issues are referred to the HR department for executive action. However, such involvement encourages managers to opt out of their responsibilities. The general role of the human resources department should be to advise on the operation of disciplinary procedures rather than take a crucial element of management away from line managers. One of the ways in which this can be done is by having an HR specialist as a member of a disciplinary panel, if only in an advisory capacity. Another HR specialist will then need to be assigned to give general procedural advice to the managers involved in presenting a case.

An issue where advice is often particularly needed is the level of penalty to be awarded when cases are upheld. This is often a grey area and it may be necessary to encourage managers to work through the implications of awarding particular penalties and the concept of the 'range of reasonable options'. The precedent effect of decisions and their impact on managers who are trying to maintain performance standards also have to be considered. The psychological aspects of discipline may also need to be taken into account. In many cases the very fact that a person has been called to account for their actions creates a considerable pressure. Also, the way in which an oral warning can be administered may make a marked impression on the person receiving it. It may also be necessary to encourage managers to focus on ways of getting employees to change their behaviour, rather than simply establishing guilt or innocence. It may also be appropriate for an HR department to arrange disciplinary skills training for line managers, particularly as this can be both necessary and very effective (Rees and Lee 1983, pp. 42–45).

It may be necessary for an employer to dispel myths about the operation of the disciplinary process.

Example

Establishing the facts about the operation of a disciplinary procedure

In one health authority there was a generally held belief amongst managers that there was no point in taking disciplinary action against employees because such action would only be reversed on appeal. On investigation it emerged that, of the ten internal appeals against dismissal in the previous 12 months, nine had failed and the one that had been allowed was generally felt to be the correction of an inappropriate previous decision. This simple statistic had not previously been established, and what people believed was a myth, not the reality. People may actually want to believe such myths, which is why it may be necessary to communicate what really does happen, as opposed to what people may prefer to think happens.

THE IMPACT OF OTHER MANAGEMENT ACTIVITIES

It may be necessary to probe into other management activities to see what impact they are having on discipline.

The need for effective selection procedures and management structure

Example

In the Social Services department of a local authority, there was a particularly high need to employ staff who would take proper care of their clients, especially those in full-time care. Unfortunately, the screening process regarding the selection of staff was not very rigorous.

As a consequence avoidable selection errors were made. The disciplinary problems that ensued, including the abuse of vulnerable people in care, were too great to be handled effectively by a weak management structure.

Disciplinary procedures and procedural skills

Any form of action needs to be preceded by careful diagnosis. There can be many reasons for inappropriate behaviour, including an inaccurate definition of what is appropriate. It is only when the facts have been checked out that one can begin to consider if disciplinary action may be necessary. This may need to be done by a specially appointed investigating officer. When formal disciplinary proceedings appear to be needed, managers need to refer to the disciplinary procedures which their organisations should have or, failing that, the guidelines contained in the ACAS Code of Practice (2004). It may also be necessary to refer to any disciplinary rules that exist or the need for such rules.

SUSPENSION

A predicament which employers can face is behaviour by an employee which necessitates them leaving the employer's premises immediately. This could be for a variety of reasons, including fighting, apparent drunkenness or apparent theft. The appropriate course of action in such situations is to suspend the employee on pay pending an investigation. Even if it appears that the employee has committed gross misconduct that justifies summary dismissal, such a decision should not be taken without there being a disciplinary hearing. If the case against an employee is established at a hearing, then dismissal may be given without notice from that point in time. If there is no such hearing, the employer will have fallen into the trap of prejudging the issue. Apart from giving an employee time to prepare their case, an interval between an incident and a decision can lead to a cooling of tempers all round and increase the prospects of a rational decision.

Suspension from duty is quite distinct from suspension without pay, which is sometimes used as a penalty after a hearing has been completed. The imposition of such a penalty would have to be provided for in the contract of employment. This distinction may need to be made to employees who are being suspended, together with an explanation that nothing is decided until the hearing is completed and that there is no loss of pay involved. The important point is that managers faced with the problem of needing to get somebody off the premises immediately should do this by paid suspension and not instant dismissal. A related point is that employees who are suspended with pay pending an investigation may nevertheless face embarrassment at being suspended and not welcome the suspicions about their behaviour that may arise. If paid suspension is nevertheless necessary, it is up to management to see that the accompanying investigation and associated disciplinary proceedings are conducted within a reasonable period of time.

DISCIPLINARY HEARINGS

Perhaps the most crucial of all the distinctions that need to be made is that between a 'disciplinary hearing' and 'disciplinary action'. A common failing, revealed by a Department of Employment survey (1975, pp. 33–34), is for managers to assume that the outcome of proceedings is a foregone conclusion and to sentence the employee early in such proceedings. The word 'hearing' is as important as the word 'disciplinary', and one cannot be sure that disciplinary action is appropriate until the hearing has been completed. A formal hearing may not be necessary if relatively minor action is likely, but whatever the level of formality it is important that the employee is given the opportunity to state their case before any action is taken. At a formal hearing, it is appropriate for whoever is conducting the hearing to recess before communicating any decision. This gives the chair time to consider the position carefully or, if a panel is involved, to consider any differences of view before any action is determined. Even if an employee's conduct seems quite inexcusable, there will be occasions when it turns out that an issue was not as straightforward as it first appeared. In any case, justice needs to be seen to be done, not just for the benefit of the employee concerned, but for their colleagues as well. Although these points are obvious enough, unfortunately they are often neglected.

Example

Demonstrating that a decision has not been prejudged

At one disciplinary hearing an employee was listened to carefully, only to be handed a letter of dismissal which must have been typed before the hearing started.

On another occasion an employee was asked to sit outside the room to await the decision of a disciplinary panel and was then given a letter of dismissal that could have been typed during the recess – apart from the fact that it was dated a week previously!

THE ROLE OF THE CHAIR

When formal disciplinary hearings are held, consideration should be given to one of the managers acting as chair. A manager obviously will not be viewed as a totally independent person, but proper chairing can help ensure that proceedings are conducted as impartially as possible.

The chair should not be directly involved in the case before a hearing; it is often appropriate for the chair to be the boss's boss. One of the dangers of the senior manager present putting the case is that they may then be seen as judge, prosecutor, jury, executioner and possibly witness all rolled into one. A further problem is that if the senior manager gets involved in an argument, which would not be surprising given so many conflicting roles, then it will be difficult for anyone else to keep the proceedings in order. A more satisfactory procedure is for the senior manager to concentrate on chairing, leaving other people to present any case and evidence. This is not only necessary for form's sake, but to see that the proceedings are conducted in a systematic manner, so that no decision is taken until all the arguments have been properly considered. The role of chair should continue during a recess. Consideration also has to be given as to who should participate in the discussions during the recess. Managers who have been involved in presenting the case against an employee need to be excluded at this stage. This is in order to reduce the possibility of collusion between those playing the roles of judge and prosecutor.

Perhaps the most awkward part of the whole disciplinary process for the chair and/or panel is handling disagreements either about what happened or about what action should be taken. It is a fallacy that management is impotent unless an employee agrees to be disciplined, or that irrefutable proof has to be produced to substantiate any difference of opinion. As with tribunals, the standard of proof, or the strictness of procedure, does not have to match criminal proceedings. The parties are in fact considering a civil issue – concerning the degree to which an employee has fulfilled their contract of employment – and not a criminal trial.

For proceedings to be handled effectively, a clear and preferably agreed sequence of events needs to be established. This should include arrangements for the exchange of any written documents and explanations of when each side should state their case, produce witnesses, cross-examine and sum up. The framework is essentially judicial, but sometimes the parties can mistakenly adopt a negotiating approach. If that happens, proceedings can degenerate into an unsystematic attempt by each side to browbeat the other, which can aggravate an already delicate situation instead of defusing it. The chair will also need to be aware of one or other party trying to take over the chair's role by, for example, giving procedural rulings (as opposed to raising points for the chair to rule on). Other dangers include the use of leading questions to the party's own witnesses, and attempts to intimidate witnesses produced by the other side. An example of a procedural sequence that will help a chair maintain control and facilitate a systematic hearing is given in Appendix 1 to this chapter. The general skills of chairing are explained in the final chapter of this book.

Sometimes it is best to give any decision later in writing to let tempers cool and allow the parties to come to terms with the fact that they might not win their case. Also the emotion involved in hearing a case and assembly of the parties involved in a case can create a potentially explosive environment. However, if the chair does give the decision orally it is essential that there should not be any further argument. If the proceedings have been conducted properly all the relevant points should have been made and considered anyway. If an employee disagrees with a decision, the appropriate way of handling the situation is simply to explain the rights of appeal. Sometimes heated arguments break out at this stage simply because it is not made clear to an employee that there is an appeals procedure that they are entitled to use.

PRESENTING OFFICER

Managerial representatives presenting a case need to prepare carefully beforehand. They may combine their role with that of investigating officer, or assign someone else to fill that role. A person's guilt may be self-evident, but the whole point of a quasi-judicial hearing is to enable the person or people sitting in judgement to decide solely on the basis of the evidence and argument that is openly presented. Consequently, patient work has to be undertaken in developing logical arguments and collecting relevant evidence. Consideration also has to be given to the presentational skills involved. All this is particularly important, as the skills of advocacy are often much more part of the 'stock in trade' of union representatives than of managers. This means that if managers fail to do their homework they may needlessly lose cases, and their confidence. Some of the basic issues concerning preparation and presentation are listed below (Evans 1992).

Preparation

- Investigate and gather evidence;
- if appropriate, select charge(s) carefully – pick the important one or ones you can sustain, and don't use a scatter-gun approach;
- copy documents to the chair and employee's representative;
- organise witnesses.

Presentation

- Use an aide-memoire if it helps;
- speak clearly and to the chair or panel (you have to convince them rather than the opposing party);
- use logical argument and avoid 'purple prose';
- identify and see if you can destroy the main argument in your opponent's case – if you can do that the rest of the issues may fall into place;
- be assertive, not aggressive, and show conviction in your case;
- do not let yourself get riled by the other side;
- ask one question at a time;
- beware of asking questions to which you do not know the answer;
- keep cool under pressure.

If the presenting officer is making a case at an employment tribunal, they will need to do it primarily by putting questions to their witnesses.

THE ROLE OF THE REPRESENTATIVE

In practice the person who accompanies an employee is likely to act as a representative. It is difficult to see how a hearing can be fairly conducted otherwise. The representative can be a colleague or a union official of the employee's choice (even if the employer does not recognise unions). Employers may want, however, to consider restricting the rights of representation to colleagues or trade union officials. If there is no restriction, they may find that an employee is accompanied by a lawyer who may introduce a greater level of formality and legalism into the proceedings than they wish to have.

There is a need for employees (and workers) to be represented regardless of any statutory rights. A representative's function is to help a person put their case so that any decision is taken only after all the relevant arguments have been considered. The representative may have heard only the employee's version of events. A formal hearing can provide an employer with the opportunity to put over their version of events. This may influence the representative, whose views may be crucial if an issue is sensitive and could lead to industrial action. If an employer has a good case, it is appropriate that it should be explained; if the case is weak, then perhaps it should be dropped. Often managers fail to realise that the really critical audience in disciplinary proceedings can be the employee's colleagues.

The position of the representative also has to be considered. They may well feel that, whatever an employee has done, they have the right to have their case argued strongly, even if privately the representative does not condone the employee's behaviour. At the end of a hearing at least the representative can explain that they have done what they can for the employee concerned. If the representative does not agree with the action that an employer eventually takes, at least any subsequent disagreement need not be compounded by arguments about whether the person had a fair hearing. The crucial distinction is that, whatever an employee has or has not done, this should not affect their right to a fair hearing. Care should be taken to ensure that employees know their procedural rights and it is preferable that they have a copy of any relevant disciplinary rules and procedures. They also need to have copies of any written evidence that is to be used.

COMMUNICATING THE RESULT

Before any decision is taken after a hearing, there needs to be a careful review of the options and of the need to communicate accurately what has been decided. The options include stating that the employee has been cleared. In cases of cumulative misconduct it is appropriate to step up the pressure on an employee gradually, so that they either mend their ways or are made perfectly aware that failure to change will result in more serious action next time. Care needs to be taken in deciding just what a person is to be warned about. If the grounds of the warning are narrow, for 'lateness' for example, an employee may be able to maintain that their lateness record cannot be taken into account if they are subsequently disciplined for absence. Thus it may be appropriate to broaden the base of a warning from lateness to general attendance. Warnings about other matters may need to include a proviso that repetition of a particular action or related misconduct can result in further disciplinary action. Too narrow a definition of what the warning is about can lead to the possibility of a person getting a number of 'final' warnings, all for different offences.

Consideration also needs to be given as to whether or not there should be automatic time limits for any penalties imposed. These are recommended in the ACAS advisory handbook (ACAS 2004, p. 41). However, one needs to be aware of the rigidities that specific time limits can create. Holidays, sickness, staff changes and other work commitments can cause procedural delays, causing a warning to be spent before it can be used as a platform for further disciplinary action. If fixed time limits are not used, consideration will have to be given when a penalty is imposed as to how long it is reasonable to take into account previous warnings. It is also necessary to consider just what previous warnings can be taken into account. There may be some semantic issues with regard to formal oral warnings. They differ from informal oral warnings in that they are a higher-level penalty which was considered sufficiently serious to be confirmed in writing. However, they are one stage below written warnings. The authority for giving these differing levels of penalties may also be vested in different levels of management or supervision. If the distinction between an informal and a formal oral warning is seen as too obscure it may be best to eliminate the stage of a formal oral warning and have a written warning instead.

An advantage of having formal warnings in writing is to ensure that a person realises what is happening. It is possible for disciplinary interviews to be handled with so light a touch that a person comes away with the impression that they have been commended rather than rebuked.

Ambiguities and carelessness in communicating just what has happened as a consequence of a disciplinary hearing can result not only in failure to achieve the desired effect but also in confrontation, if a person is disciplined again, about what really was decided the last time. The representative of an employee should be given a copy of any written warning so that it is also clear to them what has happened. This may also help to prevent subsequent argument about whether or not an employee has received their copy. A further way of avoiding argument on that score may be to ask an employee to acknowledge receipt of a warning, making it clear that this is only an acknowledgement, and not meant to commit the employee either to agreeing or to disagreeing with a written warning.

The importance and number of points to be considered in drafting written warnings is such that a checklist of the potential issues is necessary. Such a checklist is produced as Appendix 2 to this chapter.

APPEALS

Thought has to be given to the stage at which appeals can be lodged. It may not be necessary to provide for appeals against informal warnings, for example, especially as an employee can always use the grievance procedure if there is no formal procedure for handling appeals against minor penalties. It would seem appropriate, though, to build an appeals procedure into a disciplinary procedure when warnings get to the stage of indicating that dismissal is becoming a possibility. Appeals should be to managers not previously involved in the case. The grounds for an appeal should be clarified – they should not involve a total rehearing of a case unless that is clearly appropriate. It may be appropriate to let the employee speak first and let the agenda be set, at least initially, by their written grounds of appeal. If an appeal is just against the disciplinary action that has been imposed, for example, it is just the level of penalty that needs to be considered. Another important issue concerns the admissibility of fresh evidence by either party. If it is relevant to the original charge it must be taken into account with internal appeals (West Midlands Co-operative Society versus Tipton, 1986).

In the UK it used to be thought that the only way in which significant procedural defects at a hearing could be rectified was by a rehearing at the appeal stage (Whitbread and Company versus Mills, 1988). However, that position was changed by the Court of Appeal judgement in Taylor versus OCS group (2006). The view was then taken that what mattered was whether or not the procedure overall was fair. It may be possible, therefore, to put right earlier procedural defects at the appeal stage without starting again with a rehearing of the full case.

An employee's right of appeal should always be made clear, regardless of whether or not they argue about the decision when they are told about it. Time limits need to be imposed, so that if an appeal is not lodged within a certain period of time it lapses. This can avoid subsequent disagreement about whether or not the employee accepted the decision. It may also be appropriate to specify the time within which appeals are to be heard. In cases where employees are dismissed, consideration also has to be given as to whether or not they stay on the payroll pending the hearing of their appeal. A danger of keeping people on the payroll pending appeal is that some people may appeal simply as a means of securing further pay. If, however, an appeal is successful, it will normally be appropriate to give a person back pay for any period that they have been off the payroll, though consideration may need to be given to any other income they have had in the meantime.

Summary

The importance of effective disciplinary handling has been examined, as has the need for preventative policies and procedures. Sound management and education about what behaviour is expected of employees can do much to contain or prevent problems in this area. Relevant law has been examined, including the related area of redundancy dismissal. This is because of the statutory protections of employees regarding unfair dismissal and redundancy. Separate procedures may be necessary for handling cases of ill health and poor performance.

Where appropriate law has been considered an explanation of the law regarding dismissal in the UK has also been given. This is of particular relevance to British readers. However, the main aspects of law in the UK may be of interest to readers from other countries. This is because there may be similarities with their law, and dismissal law incorporates much that is simply good management practice anyway.

As has been stressed, most disciplinary handling needs to be at the lower level of the disciplinary pyramid in terms of the level of sanction. Unfortunately, those with managerial responsibility often opt out of their responsibilities in this area. This can be for a variety of reasons. These include a general reluctance to manage, a lack of clarity about who has responsibility for control and discipline and the unpopularity that managers can fear from taking disciplinary action. This can lead to a general loss of control and to issues having to be dealt with more seriously than would otherwise have been necessary. On-the-job coaching and formal training can do much to train people about their responsibilities in this area and how to handle them.

The need for an adequate investigation into potential disciplinary issues was explained. It is necessary to properly investigate the facts and to give any employee concerned the opportunity to state their case before any decision is taken. This not only helps to ensure decisions are correct, but is likely to protect an employer from a successful action for unfair dismissal at an employment tribunal. In formal hearings it is advisable to separate out the roles of presenting officer and the person who has to chair the proceedings. Employees have the legal right to be accompanied in such proceedings. If a major penalty is imposed it is necessary for the employee concerned to have a right of appeal. Where practicable, this should be to a higher level of management and to people not previously involved in a case.

Self-assessment questions

(If you want to check the extent to which your answer to any of the following questions is appropriate, cross-refer to the Table of Contents. The contents for this chapter are on page xx.)

1 How would you assess whether or not disciplinary policies in an organisation were effective?

2 What are the three main grounds for fair dismissal in the UK?

3 Explain the concept of the disciplinary pyramid.

4 How would you handle a disciplinary issue at the informal level?

5 How would you set out to present a case at a formal disciplinary hearing?

6 What are the basic requirements for seeing that a formal disciplinary hearing is chaired properly?

References

(Works of particular interest are marked with a star.)

*ACAS: Advisory, Conciliation and Arbitration Service (2004), *Discipline and grievances at work*. (An essential reference and a comprehensive guide to disciplinary handling and related law in the UK. It includes the code on disciplinary and grievance procedures.) (For web access, see http://www.acas.org.uk.)

Department of Employment (1975), Manpower paper no. 14, HMSO.

Earnshaw, Jill (1997), *Tribunals and Tribulations*, People Management, 29 May.

Employment Tribunals Service, Appendix to Annual Report 2005–6 (giving details of Employment Tribunal decisions).

Evans, Keith (1992), *Advocacy at the Bar: A Beginner's Guide*, Blackstone Press.

Incomes Data Services (IDS) (1976), Brief 99.

Rees, David and Bob Lee (1983), *Disciplinary Skills Training at Canada Dry Rawlings*, Personnel Executive, February.

Cases cited

Hogg versus Dover College (1998) IRLIB 374, EAT.

Kwik-Fit (GB) Ltd versus Lineham (1992) IRLR 156, EAT.

Monie versus Coral Racing (1980) IRLR 464 CA.

Taylor versus OCS Group (2006) LRLR CA.

West Midlands Co-operative Society versus Tipton (1986) ICR 192, House of Lords.

Whitbread and Company plc versus Mills (1988) ICR 716, EAT.

Further reading

*Advisory Conciliation and Arbitration Service (2004), *Redundancy Handling*, Booklet, ACAS. (An essential reference and comprehensive guide to redundancy handling in the UK – for web access, see http://www.acas.org.uk.)

Gould, Tony (2007), *Unfair Dismissal: A Guide to Relevant Case Law.* 25th edition, LexusNexus.

Appendix 1 to Chapter 13

EXAMPLE OF PROCEDURAL SEQUENCE AT A DISCIPLINARY HEARING

1 Introduction(s) by chair
Explanation of charge(s)
Check that the parties have received any relevant documentation
Explanation of sequence of events at hearing

2 Presentation of case against the employee by the appropriate line manager
Management witnesses
Questioning of management witnesses, via the chair

3 Response on behalf of the employee
Witnesses on behalf of the employee
Questioning of employee witnesses, via the chair

4 Further points by management
Further points on behalf of the employee
Questions by chair/panel

5 Management summing up
Employee summing up

6 Recess

7 Decision – orally and/or in writing later

Appendix 2 to Chapter 13

CHECK LIST FOR DISCIPLINARY LETTERS

Item	Comments
1. *Requesting attendance at disciplinary hearing.*	
Specify charges.	The charges are allegations. They may or may not be proved as a result of a hearing.
Suggest the employee brings a representative if they wish and relevant witnesses, if appropriate.	If a representative comes it will give you the opportunity to put your case over to them, as well as ensuring that the arguments are properly examined.
Give appropriate information and time for the employee to prepare their defence adequately.	Failure to do this may invalidate the proceedings.
Refer to the disciplinary procedure.	The employee should have a copy. If there is any doubt, send them one.
Indicate that disciplinary action could be imposed according to the outcome of the hearing.	
2. *Disciplinary letter (after the hearing).*	
State the nature of the offence(s).	You may wish to incorporate general terms, such as misconduct, in any warning letter. This may make it easier in the future to refer back to earlier offences.
State what disciplinary action, if any, is to be taken.	
Specify any conditions about future behaviour. This may include any help you are prepared to give.	You may warn an employee about future conduct and state that any repetition or related offence may/will render them liable to further action.
Specify any time limits.	Sometimes procedures provide for warnings to lapse after a specified period of good behaviour. You do not have to put in time limits though – they can be rather rigid.
Specify the appeal procedure and the time limit for using it.	The more serious the penalty the more important it is to specify the right of appeal.
State whether you want the employee to: (i) acknowledge receipt of the letter; (ii) register any dissent about any part of the letter they consider inaccurate.	
If suspension is involved, state whether it is with or without pay.	If suspension is without pay, check that you have the contractual right to do this.
Send a copy of the letter to the employee's representative and to any managers concerned.	

The manager and employee relations

Learning outcomes

By the end of this chapter you will be able to:

- Identify the objectives of both management and employees in organisations
- Locate the employee relations function within an organisation
- Explain the interrelationship between employee relations and human resource management
- Identify the key variables in the labour market in which employee relations activity takes place
- Evaluate the role of trade unions in employee relations
- Identify and assess the causes of problems in the employee relations area and develop strategies for dealing with these issues
- Identify the role conflict involved in managers being members of trade unions and establish a way of coping with this if necessary

Introduction

In this chapter the objectives of both employers and employees are examined. Whilst there can be overlap in these objectives, there can also be conflicts of interest. Conflicts can arise whether an employee is a member of a trade union or not. Employers need to have strategies for handling such key issues as pay and performance standards for all their employees, not just those in trade unions. That is why the term 'employee relations' is used rather than industrial relations. The term has become increasingly appropriate because of the decline in many countries and industries of the number of employees who are members of trade unions. The factors shaping employee relations activity are increasingly of a global nature; this chapter focuses therefore on general international developments.

Employee relations activity in an organisation can be widely distributed and is an important activity whether trade unions are recognised or not. Maintaining cost-effective production or service is a key responsibility of line management. Personnel or human resource management specialists may also play a key role. The employee relations activity is significantly influenced by the labour market in which it operates. It is also influenced by the national legal framework and in the case of countries who are within the European Union, EU directives. The role of trade unions is also examined. An international perspective is taken, as the role of trade unions can vary considerably, particularly between liberal democracies and authoritarian regimes. An important feature of employee relations within EU member countries has been the increases in statutory rights. This to some extent has compensated for the reduction in the scope and power of collective bargaining. It has also meant that unions are now often more concerned with the enforcement of statutory rights and less with collective bargaining and related industrial action.

Identifying the causes of employee relations problems is not always easy. This is because weaknesses in other areas of organisational activity can have a knock-on effect into the employee relations area. An understanding of how this can happen can be essential to developing appropriate remedial strategies. Finally, the potential for conflict is examined if managers are also trade union members. Strategies for coping with any such conflict are explained. The related area of negotiating skills is covered in the next chapter.

Objectives in employee relations

MANAGERIAL VERSUS EMPLOYEE OBJECTIVES

The primary aim of managers in the employee relations area is likely to be to obtain the cooperation of the workforce in achieving organisational objectives, such as:

- cost-effective performance (resulting in low unit labour costs);
- control of change;
- the avoidance of stoppages and other sanctions.

The pursuit of these objectives needs to be balanced as they may conflict with one another. This can also be the case with the objectives of trade unions (and/or individual employees) which are likely to be:

- the maintenance and possible improvement of the terms and conditions of employment;
- job security;
- control of change;
- the avoidance of stoppages and other sanctions.

The terms under which people work are negotiated either individually or between union representatives and the employer, or sometimes a combination of these two processes. The negotiated agreements represent a balance that provides sufficient incentive for both parties to come together. The parties will, however, take a continuing interest in the extent to which their concerns are being met. This may be done quite amicably – the resolution of areas of conflict through negotiation does not mean that sanctions have to be applied. Often the term 'conflict' is used synonymously with the term 'strike', ignoring the point that the application of sanctions is a way of trying to resolve conflict only when negotiations have broken down.

One has to be wary of the term 'good employee relations', as it begs the question, 'Good from whose point of view?' Each party will need to assess success according to whether or not they have adequately achieved their objectives. There can be win–win situations when, for example, an organisation is flourishing, wages are generous and there is job security. However, there will be occasions when this is not possible, and one needs to beware of adopting an unrealistic **unitarist** view of organisations which ignores the potential for genuine conflicts of interests. This issue has been previously discussed, particularly in Chapter 2, but is so essential to employee relations it needs further explanation in this chapter. It is also referred to in the next chapter in the context of negotiation.

FRAMES OF REFERENCE

Fox (1965) used the concepts of **unitary** and **pluralistic** frames of reference to classify managers into two groups. Unitarists view the organisation as having one common purpose with sectional interests needing to be subordinated to overall organisational objectives. Activity that detracts from this is seen as being illegitimate. Attempts to pursue sectional interests are seen as irrational because they damage the organisation overall. A relevant analogy is that of a sports team which has the overriding aim of winning. This view is in contrast with the pluralistic frame of reference which recognises that the objectives of the organisation and the various interest groups within it do not always coincide. An example of this is if there is a need for redundancy. The pluralist perspective provides a framework both for identifying potential conflict and dealing with it.

The unitary and pluralistic frames of reference can be a very useful way of analysing the way people approach employee relations. The two approaches highlight the fact that managers have to manage groups and people whose interests will not always coincide with organisational objectives. Sometimes employees or their representatives have a reverse unitarist approach which leads them to believe that anything that is for the benefit of the employee is automatically beneficial for the organisation. Managers generally don't make a choice of a particular frame of reference; it is likely to be an inherent part of their personality and value system and not easily changed. Those with a unitary frame of reference may have difficulty in identifying the reasons for conflict generally, not just in the employee relations area.

The importance of managers having a frame of reference that enables them to recognise the causes and rationality of conflict is illustrated by the following example.

Example

Limitations of a consensus model

An engineering company in London had carefully built up a **consensus** model for decision-making with its employees. This meant that all policies with an employee relations dimension were meant to be agreed with union representatives. There were many areas of common interest where productive discussions took place. However, the model was not able to cope with significant areas of conflict. During a time of labour scarcity, management proposed that operations be relocated to the West of England where labour was more plentiful and cheaper. However, employee representatives were understandably reluctant to agree to their members being made redundant or having to move to an area where wages were lower. Problems involving the transfer of council housing were another issue. The move did not take place. Similar difficulties had been experienced in getting the employee representatives to agree to progressive equal opportunities policies. This case illustrates the limitations of the consensus model, attractive as that model may seem.

Failure to recognise conflicts of interest can also make schemes of self-regulation ineffective. Examples of where it could be argued that the interests of members should not override those of the public, but often do, include disciplinary action against medical doctors, lawyers, newspapers and stock exchanges. The problems faced by front-line managers in dealing with conflicts of interest between managerial and employee objectives are dealt with later in this chapter. Strategies for supporting the position of the first-line manager are also considered. The problems of trying to achieve consensus in employee participation schemes are also examined.

Employee relations in the context of the organisation

RANGE OF ACTIVITIES

Employee relations activity is likely to be widely distributed within an organisation. Activities in this area include:

- the determination of pay and benefits,
- work performance,
- disciplinary handling,
- individual and collective grievances,
- collective representation, including employee participation,
- health and safety,
- redundancy,
- other statutory rights of employees.

The involvement of a human resources department, if there is one, is often necessary to ensure that decisions form an integrated pattern and not a set of conflicting precedents. However, the individual manager is bound to have some responsibility within this framework, often at increasing levels. Even if all the financial and other formal agreements are determined outside their department, as a minimum line managers have to control labour costs and standards of performance.

HUMAN RESOURCE MANAGEMENT

Employee relations activity is usually part of a wider set of activities that fall within the **human resource management (HRM)** function. The term 'HRM' is subject to a variety of interpretations. It is sometimes subdivided into hard (quantifiable) and soft (intangible) areas. Examples of hard HRM areas include employee costs and head-counts. Soft areas include issues such as organisational capability, motivation, and training and development. Effective HRM should involve a genuine attempt to integrate the various aspects of personnel (or human resource) management with one another as well as with corporate and other policy decision-making. The term HRM is generally meant to imply such a link with corporate policy. It has generally replaced the term 'personnel management'. However, the use of the term HRM does not always guarantee that there is a proactive link with corporate policy. Conversely, effective personnel management departments historically did have such a link with corporate policy. This demonstrates the variety of interpretations that there are in actual practice regarding activity that goes under the label of HRM.

The generally reduced bargaining power of trade unions, together with cost and competitive pressures, have created an impetus for more proactive policies in the personnel/human resource (HR) area. In the employee relations area this has often led to a change of emphasis by managers from trouble-shooting to an examination of ways in which more cost-effective working practices can be introduced. The more turbulent context in which employee relations now needs to operate is demonstrated in particular by the growth of **private equity** organisations. These organisations seek to take over public companies, mainly with borrowed money, and run them more profitably. This may well involve significant changes in working methods and reduced staffing and/or an element of asset stripping. Such takeovers are often attempted with a view to later selling on the organisation concerned at a profit. Even if public companies are not taken over by private equity organisations, they need to ensure that they are cost-effective to avoid being taken over.

HRM should involve a tailoring of policies to fit the specific needs of an organisation rather than the use of a set of standard prescriptive remedies. As well as facilitating change, HR specialists should specify both the organisational objectives and the constraints that exist before strategic decisions are taken, rather than be expected to simply implement strategic decisions in which they have not been involved. Both the options and the constraints may revolve around the capacity of the organisation and its staff to successfully undertake certain activities. An example was given in Chapter 2 of the national charity that seriously overextended itself by an expansion programme and ignored its lack of managerial expertise and the legal obligation to retain 'acquired' staff. It follows that HR specialists may need to be involved in developing the organisational capability to handle potential new developments.

Specific ways in which HRM has been developed in the UK include:

- The use of management information systems to facilitate staff planning and cost control.
- The development of individual rather than collective employment contracts.
- Direct communication with the workforce rather than just through trade unions.
- Gearing of employment policies to increase customer or client orientation – this may involve attempts to change organisational culture and commitment.
- Increased emphasis on the value added by individuals and activities – sometimes this has involved the use of performance-related pay.
- Ensuring that training and development activities are closely aligned to corporate objectives.
- The development of internal consultancy skills and acting as a change agent.
- Contracting out or sharing discrete activities such as payroll administration.
- Internal surveys and benchmarking to help evaluate effectiveness.
- The adoption of flexible working practices, either in terms of flexibility of function, flexibility of location or numerical flexibility. The concept of the flexible organisation was examined in Chapter 3.

Strategic HRM is often part of management philosophy and practice, particularly in some Japanese and North American companies. Some critics argue that the concept is unitarist and that it ignores the potential conflict of interests between employers and employees. There is also potential conflict between the hard and soft variants of HRM. For example, it may be difficult to expect commitment from employees who are on short-term contracts to suit the organisation's need for numerical flexibility. The alternative point of view is that sound strategies take account of such potential conflicts. Inevitably, strategic HRM requires the close involvement of senior management, and it is a process that is essentially driven by line management. Often, however, what may be described as HRM is no more than routine personnel administration. There can also be huge variations in its practice between countries and between organisations. In some cases too it can unfortunately be based on the concept that labour is expendable and not capable of more effective utilisation through better management. This may be exacerbated by a lack of any effective legal protection for employees in some countries.

SUPERVISORY CONTROL

A crucial aspect of employee relations in any organisation is the extent to which managerial interests are safeguarded at the level of first-line supervision. This is the most junior level of management but also forms the largest part of the managerial pyramid. The term 'supervision' is used in this context to include managers with first-line responsibility for managing people. Managing at this level can often involve trying to reconcile the sometimes differing aspirations of the organisation and the employees with regard to issues such as work roles, working methods, and quantity and quality of production or service delivered. The problem of trying to reconcile conflicts can be intensified if the person in charge is also a member of the work group.

Unfortunately, senior managers may not understand the difficulties that first-line managers or supervisors have. This is particularly likely to be the case if senior managers have a unitary frame of reference. A potential consequence is that first-line managers or supervisors may give way to work group pressures and, in order to protect themselves, conceal this as far as possible from their superiors. Some people may not even want to accept or discharge their managerial responsibilities, as was explained in Chapter 1. Also, the advantages of being a supervisor in some organisations have been reduced by developments such as the harmonisation of staff terms and conditions of employment with those of manual workers. Strategies to counter these issues include:

- Judicious monitoring of what is really happening at the critical level of first-line managers (including supervisors).

- Examination of the impact of financial incentives on the role of the supervisor. As was explained in Chapter 7, such schemes can undermine the position of the supervisor. This danger also needs to be taken into account when the use of such schemes is proposed.

- Careful identification of the role of supervisors – e.g. what is the role of a supervisor if a separate team leader has been appointed?

- Careful selection, training and development of supervisors.

- Well-developed two-way communication between first-line supervisors and their work groups.

- The development of lateral relationships between supervisors as a means of mutual support.

- The delegation of appropriate authority to supervisors and care in seeing that this is not eroded, e.g. by unnecessarily overruling them, forgetting to consult with them and letting employee representatives bypass them.

- Building up the position of supervisors by enabling them to give rewards as well as penalties. If any organisational favours are to be given, e.g. upgradings, merit increases and promotions, supervisors need to be seen to be influential in this process.

EMPLOYEE PARTICIPATION

Another dimension of employee relations is employee participation. This can be defined as a way of involving the workforce in organisational issues that affect them. It is different from the concept of worker control where control is vested with the employees. There are few examples of worker control, if only because of the reluctance of investors to forfeit control of their investment. In employee participation, the final decision rests with management.

The issue of ultimate control can create problems with joint regulatory mechanisms such as supervisory boards. If the employer does not have the final say, major problems can be created. These include the financing of organisations, accountability to the general public and the veto that the employees can have on any change that is to their disadvantage. This can create major problems for employee representatives, who may have to handle conflicts of interest between the organisations and employees. These difficulties are often ignored by advocates of joint control, who may focus on the constitutional arrangements for resolving such problems without actually examining what happens in practice. The problem may be compounded by those with a unitary frame of reference not being able to understand the potential for conflict between different interest groups.

Employee participation also needs to be seen in the context of organisational and national culture as a whole. Participatory schemes are not going to be very effective if the overall culture is autocratic and secretive. In Chapter 4 reference was made to the study in which it was found that the success or failure of joint consultative schemes depended not on the constitutional mechanisms but on the style of individual managers. Those who were proactive in making their committees work were successful. Those who did not invest much time and thought in the scheme were predictably unsuccessful (Rees and Porter 1998, pp. 165–170).

There are a number of different participative mechanisms. The main categories are direct, indirect and financial.

Direct participation

A basic characteristic of direct schemes of employee participation is that employees are directly involved rather than indirectly via a representative. Common arrangements include:

- Self-managed work groups, where the group is left to determine its own way of working within parameters set by management. These parameters include quantitative and qualitative performance standards.
- Briefing groups – but note the emphasis on downward communication which is a unitary model; also in-house magazines.
- Attitude surveys of employees, particularly in non-unionised environments, and facilities for employees to submit anonymous letters about their organisation.
- Job enrichment (explained in Chapter 6).
- Discussions with line management – this can be the most important factor of all. However, formal employee participation schemes can do little to compensate for the problems of working for an autocratic boss, particularly if the boss is incompetent as well.

Indirect participation

Indirect employee participation schemes may include:

- Collective bargaining with a trade union or staff association – these arrangements may include discussion with representatives over a wide range of issues.
- Joint consultative committees.
- Health and safety representatives and committees.
- Suggestion schemes – these are a combination of direct and indirect participation; suggestions are made directly by employees, but employee representatives may sit on the committee that considers them.

- Works councils – there is a statutory requirement for European Works Councils to be established if a company has 1000 employees in two member states. This would be with a minimum threshold of 150 employees in each country. In addition, under the terms of the Information and Consultation European Directive, employers are obliged to establish local works councils if just 10 per cent of the workforce support such a claim if they employ 100 or more staff (reducing to 50 staff in 2008). The requirement is to consult rather than negotiate but, as explained in the previous chapter, in the case of proposed collective redundancies there is a requirement to consult with a view to reaching agreement.

- Partnership agreements – these are formal agreements by employers and unions designed to increase cooperation between them on an ongoing basis in areas of common interest. The common interest areas normally include the success of individual enterprises, the encouragement of union membership and the need both for employment flexibility and job security.

Financial participation

Financial employee participation schemes may include:

- performance-related pay,
- profit-sharing,
- share options.

The above examples of financial participation are all covered in Chapter 7. A further example is the case of the John Lewis Partnership in Britain. This example is interesting as it involves all the net profits being distributed to the workforce. The workforce are classified as partners and actually own the organisation, there being no shareholders. The strong management hierarchy in this organisation though makes it more an example of financial involvement in the organisation than an example of employee participation (Flanders et al. 1968). The benevolence of the former owner was behind this arrangement.

A concept that overlaps with employee participation is that of stakeholding. **Stakeholders** have an interest in and some responsibility for the success of an organisation and are distinct from external pressure groups which are simply trying to influence the organisation concerned. Thus external groups such as Friends of the Earth and Greenpeace, which have general environmental aims, would not be classified as an organisational stakeholder. However, it is not always clear what stakeholding means in practice. Representational arrangements may involve employee consultation, union recognition, employee directors, and mechanisms for involving suppliers and consumers or clients.

The labour market

KEY CHARACTERISTICS

There have been major changes in the nature of the employment markets in many countries in recent years. This has mirrored changes in economies in general, including the impact of

globalisation. The state of the labour market has a great impact on employee relations, especially whether the demand for particular occupational skills is high or low. The state of the market will vary not only from country to country, but within countries.

Key factors determining the state of labour markets are as follows:

- The level of manufacturing output. Employment in manufacturing is in decline in most Western countries because of global competition. Employment in areas such as services in general and computer services in particular are often increasing, however.

- An aspect of increased globalisation is the growth of multinational and **transnational** corporations. This can enable production to be more easily outsourced or switched to other countries. This may affect production of components, complete products or both, and also gives international companies leverage in negotiations with trade unions about wage claims and working practices. Employee or union representatives may also have difficulty in getting access to the real decision-makers.

- **Outsourcing** will not only affect the pattern of employment within an organisation, but often creates pressures internal to the organisation for more efficient work practices to prevent outsourcing.

- Developments such as the flexible organisation have created more peripheral and part-time jobs. Sometimes employees are disadvantaged by this, particularly, for example, if they have **zero hours contracts**, which mean that there is no minimum number of guaranteed hours of work. In other cases, these changes mean that employees need to develop a portfolio of economic activities or find part-time work as a convenient way of balancing work and domestic commitments.

- The increased rate of economic and technological change has meant that jobs have a shorter shelf-life and the nature of jobs that remain changes more quickly. This creates economic insecurity for many even if the national economy is generally strong. The increased pace of change also increases the need for retraining and continuous professional development.

- Employment is often more capital-intensive, thus reducing the number of staff that are needed. An aspect of this is the increased computer technology available to a wide range of employees. This increases the need to see that capital is utilised effectively. This and the development of large capital installations such as supermarkets and call centres has led to an increase in continuous working, with associated shift-working patterns.

- As Western economies have fragmented, so has the power and coverage of trade unions generally diminished. Days lost through industrial action have generally declined dramatically. The ability of trade unions to control changes in work practices is also greatly reduced. This is partly because of competitive pressures and the generally increased ability of employers to find other sources of supply. The pace of change also threatens jobs in their existing form.

- Changes in organisational structures have often had significant effects on pay determination. Devolution of authority to managers in semi-autonomous business units has given them greater control over wages and working arrangements.

- The **alternative economy** has developed in many Western countries. Some people work, do not pay tax but claim state benefits. There is also a stratum of unemployed people who receive minimum state benefits and who are not easily employable.

- The free movement of labour within an enlarged EU has increased labour mobility within Europe, though there are significant barriers because of housing, social factors and language. Additionally, illegal immigration from a range of countries has often increased the availability of labour within the alternative economy. This is despite attempts by governments to stem illegal immigration.

- The general decline in trade union power has been partly offset in Europe by the increase in statutory rights, particularly with regard to individual employment protection.

- People with scarce skills are likely to exploit their market position by moving to more highly paid jobs. Alternatively, employers may raise pay in order to stop this happening. They also need to avoid abrasive management styles with employees with scarce skills and to consider positive means of gaining commitment. Skills shortages are exacerbated by a general lack of training investment.

- There is an increasing tendency for pay to be partly determined by individual performance. Sometimes this is by formal performance-related pay schemes even though, as explained in Chapter 7, the results in the public sector in the U.K. have not been encouraging.

- Complex job evaluation schemes are less in evidence. This is partly because such schemes are generally not responsive enough to quickly changing labour market conditions. However, jobs are increasingly defined in terms of required competencies. They also tend to be defined in generic terms to assist flexibility at work.

- Executive remuneration has tended to increase as competition for executive talent in a results-orientated labour market has increased. Also shareholder and legal controls on executive remuneration and **golden handshakes** are weak. Some executives are more likely to look for jobs in other countries because of the rewards, their language skills and their ability to cope with the housing market.

- Pension provision has become an increasingly key issue for governments, employers and employees. Governments and employers are increasingly concerned about the cost, particularly given the increases in life expectancy. Final salary schemes are increasingly not available to new employees and are sometimes amended for existing staff. There is an increasing reluctance on the part of employers to get involved in pension provision, which can cause governments to have to insist that they do contribute financially. Conversely, employees are increasingly concerned about pension provision and sometimes this may make them reluctant to change employers if this means moving to a less favourable pension scheme.

- An issue that is linked to that of pension provision is that in most developed countries the workforce is ageing. This means that as people leave the labour force there are fewer people to replace them and to support those who have retired. To some extent this gap may be met by immigration.

● In Western economies nearly half of the workforce is female. Many women return to work after maternity leave. The dual income couple is often a powerful economic unit. However, this means couples placing limits on work involvement to improve work–life balance.

● Women are tending to break through **glass ceilings** at work and increasingly achieve positions of responsibility. Both legal protections and cultural changes have facilitated this. To a lesser extent this has also happened in the UK with members of ethnic minority groups.

THE IMPACT OF LABOUR MARKET REGULATION

A major issue is the extent to which the labour market in any particular country or economic area is regulated. The pattern in developing countries is for a low level of market regulation. By Western standards the USA also has a low level of labour market regulation. The UK labour market, although more regulated than the US, has a low level of regulation and employment protection compared with many other members countries within the EU. However, the UK market is affected by the minimum standards within the EU. This contrasts with the culture and arrangements in many of the other EU countries, particularly older members. However, they are increasingly finding it hard to finance the level of employee benefits provided both by the state and individual employers.

The application of EU minimum standards of employment protection to new members of the EU will have a variety of effects. It will improve the protection of employees (which may be particularly important if trade unions are weak) and reduce a source of 'unfair labour competition' within Europe. However, it will also increase the cost base of employers in new member countries. This in turn will affect the ability of employers to compete with countries outside the EU, which will often involve competition with neighbouring countries.

THE IMPACT OF INWARD INVESTMENT

Another aspect of the labour market that merits consideration is the impact of **inward investment**. Companies that have inwardly invested are often sophisticated multinational organisations in capital-intensive industries. There may be a significant difference between the organisational cultures of the companies that inwardly invest and the host countries. These differences may in part be because of the national culture that influenced a multi-national company before it expanded its activities into other countries.

There can be considerable benefits from inward investment. Sometimes governments offer subsidies to companies based overseas to invest in their country because of the employment that such investment generates, especially if the investment can be made in area of high unemployment. There can also be gains in terms of the expertise that is acquired within the host country by learning how to produce or deliver particular goods or services. Sometimes, though, investing companies are reluctant to share too much expertise. This can happen in the case of 'screwdriver assembly plants' where the local input, though quantitatively high, may involve little design work. Another issue is the extent to which local staff are allowed to occupy senior positions.

A further important dimension of inward investment is the way both local staff and the organisation need to adapt to one another. The employer will have to operate within a different legal framework. In addition, whilst it may both need and want to change some local working practices, there may be limits to the extent to which this is practicable or even desirable. These issues were covered in some detail in both Chapters 3 and 4.

Legal framework

EU LAW ALREADY COVERED

The legal framework of countries within the EU is greatly influenced by various EU directives. These in turn have had a large impact on HR departments because of the need to develop policies and procedures in line with these directives as well as any extra legal requirements under individual national law. Various aspects of European law have already been considered in previous chapters, as follows:

- Protection of employees when organisations are taken over (Chapter 3)
- Sex discrimination with regard to pay (Chapter 7)
- Data protection (Chapter 9)
- Protection against discrimination on grounds of disability, sex race, religion and sexual orientation (Chapter 9)
- Protection against age discrimination (Chapters 9 and 12)
- Human rights protection (Chapter 12)
- Consultation about collective redundancy (Chapter 12)
- Arrangements for informing and consulting with the workforce on matters that may effect them (Chapter 12)
- The establishment of works councils (Chapter 14)

OTHER RELEVANT EU LAW

Other aspects of European employment protection include:

- Maximum working hours
- Maternity and paternity leave
- Protection for employees on fixed-term contracts
- Equal treatment for part-time workers compared with full-time workers
- Health and safety, including provision for the appointment of workplace safety representatives

The role of trade unions

The role of trade unions varies from country to country. In liberal democracies trade unions are largely independent of the state. The concept of **pluralism** applies to having independent sources of power within a country as well as the recognition of conflicts of interest within organisations. However, in unitarist states trade unions may only be expected to exist as long as they do not challenge the authority of the state. In the former Soviet bloc, trade unions had to act more as agents of the state, with hierarchical control being exercised by the communist governments. The welfare aspects of trade unions were often prominent in such unions. This is still the case in some authoritarian regimes, both within former Soviet bloc countries and elsewhere. In such situations any change to create genuinely independent trade unions can require a great alteration in behaviour by trade union leaders, assuming that these leaders have not been replaced by people who behave more as representatives of their members' wishes.

Trade unions have often been important as a means and an outlet of political dissent. In many British colonies they served such a purpose and when independence was granted the new political leaders were often people who had achieved prominence within the trade union movement.

Example

From trade union activist to President

Lech Walesa was an active trade unionist in Poland in the 1970s and 1980s. From being the leader of an unofficial strike committee at the Gdansk shipyard, he progressed to become the leader of the national union organisation, Solidarity, which was eventually grudgingly tolerated by the (Communist) Polish government. When the country regained political independence in 1990, he became the new President.

Because of historic links, trade unions often have links with political parties. An example of this is in the UK where the trade unions actually established the Labour Party in 1902. However, complications can arise when such political parties form the government, because they then have to be responsible to the community as a whole. There is also the problem of how they handle their employer role and have to negotiate with their former colleagues. However, whatever government is in power, unions may want to maintain and develop contacts with them so that they can influence legislation and economic and social policy affecting their members. Trade unions may also find it increasingly important to influence international organisations such as the EU.

Another aspect of trade union activity is often their increasing ability and motivation to attract and retain members by obtaining discounts for their members for goods and services provided by a range of commercial organisations.

MEMBERSHIP PATTERN

As explained in the earlier section in this chapter, changes in the labour market have had a considerable impact both on the pattern of trade union membership in some countries and their power. As economies have fragmented, so it has usually become both more difficult to organise employees into unions and for a union to exert a labour monopoly pressure on employers. In other words, both customers and employers may find it increasingly easy to find alternative supplies of goods and services (or even alternative supplies of labour). There are a few exceptions to this, which are covered shortly.

In the UK in 2005 only 29 per cent of employees were union members (DTI 2006). The general decline in numbers employed in manufacturing (a traditional area of high trade union membership) in Western countries has increased the proportion of the total of trade union members employed in the public sector. However, even in the public sector, union membership is usually falling because of developments such as privatisation and contracting out of services. The overall scale of public services may also be in decline. A decline in the public sector is particularly marked in counties that were formerly part of the Soviet bloc. In such countries the state has become just one employer. The move to a market economy has also meant that activities such as manufacture have often dramatically declined. Those that remain in existence are often now in private ownership and have had to change their financial and working practices substantially in order to survive in a competitive market. Those employees remaining in the public sector have to bargain with a state that often has great difficulty matching income with expenditure.

The general decline in trade union membership has reduced union income. This has given a boost to the pressure for amalgamations and mergers between trade unions. Ironically the logic for joining unions may have increased in recent years. This is because of an increasing rate of change and its impact on patterns of employment. Even in healthy economies there is likely to be more enforced change than in previous years. The opportunity for trade unions to enforce statutory employment rights has also increased. This has made it even more appropriate for unions to have employees join them so that they can represent them on such issues. A further important argument for joining unions is the legal representation they can provide in health and safety cases. Such a service can be important for managers as well as non-managerial staff. This is demonstrated, for example, in Chapter 6 by the danger of staff becoming victims of stress.

TRADE UNION RECOGNITION

When employers agree to consult and/or negotiate with trade union representatives of employees on a formal basis about either individual or collective matters affecting employment, they are said to be granting trade union recognition. In some countries, including the USA and the UK, there are statutory provisions for trade unions to obtain recognition if they can demonstrate sufficient support in a ballot. Within the EU various directives require workplace representation. These include directives relating to works councils, information and consultation, collective redundancy and health and safety.

Account has to be taken of the fact that negotiated agreements can determine the terms and conditions of non-union members as well as union members. Collective agreements are discussed in the next section. However, these issues do not alter the fact that trade unions generally have less coverage and impact than they used to. There is also often an element of creeping derecognition in many organisations, with some grades being excluded from collective bargaining arrangements, the range of issues reduced, non-recognition of trade unions in many new organisations and less notice taken of what unions have to say anyway. Another example of this erosion is the increase in the number of personal contracts and performance-related pay. Flexible working and generic job titles also reduce the opportunity of unions to make cases for upgrading. The increased tendency of employers to engage in direct communication with their workforce is also significant.

Sometimes employers have a positive attitude to union recognition. They may find mechanisms for discussing matters of mutual interest with representatives of the workforce convenient and productive. The advantages may outweigh any problems caused when the parties disagree. Recognising trade unions may not alter the power relationships between the parties. In any case, if a union is strong the employer may have to recognise it anyway. As was stated at the start of this chapter, even where an employer decides not to recognise trade unions, there will still be issues of common concern that management and employees will need to discuss, and therefore some thought needs to be given to how these discussions are going to take place and on what basis. In other words, all employers will need an employee relations policy.

COLLECTIVE AGREEMENTS

Relationships between employers and employees may to some extent be regulated by joint agreements. There are two main types of collective agreement. Collective agreements can be either:

- procedural, stipulating the manner in which differences will be resolved; or
- substantive, containing the outcome of agreements negotiated via the appropriate procedure. Such agreements will normally cover matter such as wages and terms and conditions of employment.

Procedural agreements can be likened to the Queensberry rules for boxing – there should at least be rules regulating the manner in which arguments about substantive issues are conducted. Sometimes there may be disagreement about the nature of the procedural agreement, as one party may feel that it will unduly help the other party achieve their substantive aims. If agreement about the procedure cannot be reached, the management may need to issue a procedure and say that this is the basis on which they propose to proceed.

The following issues are often covered by procedural agreements:

Individual

- Discipline and dismissal.
- Grievances.

Collective

- Disputes: these are for dealing with grievances affecting more than one person. Examples of such grievances could include the interpretation of collective agreements and changes in work arrangements.

- Pay claims: there may be a standing procedure for handling annual pay claims. Such claims are likely to cover a range of fringe benefits, such as holidays, sick pay and pensions, as well as rates of pay.

- Redundancy: agreements may cover consultation about redundancy, selection for redundancy and compensation.

- Health and safety: the arrangements for the maintenance of safe working conditions and for representatives and safety committees.

Sometimes employers enter into voluntary agreements according to the level of union membership. They may require a higher level of union membership or support for collective compared with individual issues. This is because of the range of issues covered by collective issues. Employers may be anxious to keep to a minimum the number of unions they deal with to avoid inter-union competition and friction. Japanese companies investing in new sites often set up 'beauty competitions' to give potential unions the chance to tender for recognition before anyone is employed.

Procedural arrangements can provide a very useful framework for handling differences when they emerge. Managers and employee representatives can both be somewhat at a loss as to what to do when discussions end in failure. They can though have a common interest in defining the area in dispute and agreeing on the next step and what, if anything, is to happen in the meantime. In this way a dispute can be processed without either party having had to give way, with the issue normally being referred to the next level so that it can be tackled afresh. The definition of the area of disagreement and time bought for fresh thought may help in the subsequent resolution of a dispute. If nothing else, procedures can gain time for the immediate parties to consider their positions. Ultimately, if discussion at higher levels does not produce agreement, the thorny issue of what happens next has to be considered. Either side may give way or consider imposing their will, which in a way is the final stage of procedure. Managers will have to weigh up carefully the disadvantages of risking union resistance and the impact on employee morale against the disadvantages of giving way. This needs to be a consciously taken decision.

Although the handling of differences via an agreed procedure will not guarantee a satisfactory resolution, it does at least provide an alternative to an immediate 'shoot-out' and gives the parties the opportunity to explore the possibilities for an agreed solution. Knowledge that, if there is no agreement, there may be resort to other means can in itself have a sobering effect on the parties.

Sometimes arbitration is seen as the answer to unresolved differences, but if it is too readily available it may relieve the parties of the responsibility for settlement and lead to exaggerated claims and counter-claims with no movement towards a negotiated settlement. However, there is a general reluctance to use arbitration as the final stage of procedure. This is because usually the stronger party will not agree, believing that they can use their industrial muscle to get a better deal. A problem with compulsory, as opposed to voluntary arbitration, is how to enforce it on reluctant employees. As explained in Chapter 15, voluntary arbitration may be most useful in disagreements about the interpretation of collective agreements, rather than in determining what the agreements should be in the first place.

One of the advantages of agreed procedures is that the parties can at least limit the area of disagreement by agreeing on what is in dispute and how the difference should be resolved, even if resolution can ultimately mean that one side coerces the other. A further way of limiting the area of dispute can be the use of a **status quo** clause in a disputes procedure which provides for the continuation of work on the basis that existed before a dispute began. This can be a useful device, but there can be occasions when it is difficult to identify just when a dispute arose and therefore what the status quo position was. Sometimes, too, employers feel that they are conceding too much opportunity to unions to block changes that are not to the unions' liking if such a clause is part of a disputes procedure.

Example

Example of a procedure for introducing change

The solution one British engineering company adopted to resolve the dilemma of introducing disputed change was to introduce a ten-day rule. If management felt that discussions about changes in working practices were being unduly protracted they reserved the right to serve notice that in ten days the change would be introduced unless there was some other agreement in the meantime.

Employers may also find other advantages in using collective agreements. It may be much more time-effective to negotiate many issues with representatives than with each individual employee. This is particularly so if many of the fringe benefits are or need to be standard. Employers may also find that representative structures are very useful for a two-way flow of information about employee relations issues. Such structures may be constructively used for improving cooperation in areas of common interest.

Despite the existence of collective agreements, employers and employees may have to register a 'failure to agree', and this might entail the employees taking industrial action of some description in an effort to persuade employers to agree with employee demands.

INDUSTRIAL ACTION

Union bargaining power has declined greatly in many countries in recent years. In the UK only 157 400 days' work were lost through industrial action in the UK (in 116 separate disputes) in 2005. This was the lowest loss since records were first kept in 1881 (Labour Market Trends 2006). However, one area where unions can still have significant power is in relation to employment in the transport sector. Union power in the transport sector stems from the fact that these employees may provide an essential service which cannot be run effectively without them. This can be particularly so with railway drivers, including those employed on tube trains, and signal staff. This industrial power is also evident sometimes in the airline industry, where there is a noticeable tendency for staff to strike, or threaten to strike, during holiday seasons. A feature of industrial action in the transport sector is that it can cause considerable dislocation, especially with airlines, and a loss of revenue that cannot be replaced. Another feature of the airline business is the increasing competition between old established airlines and newer low-cost ones.

This is forcing the old established airlines to review their cost base, which means examining the effectiveness of existing working practices.

Industrial action is usually seen as being the same as strike action. However, there may be occasions when the action is short of withdrawal of labour. Other examples of industrial action may include not working overtime and/or not doing the work of absent colleagues. Sometimes such action is claimed to be 'working to rule'. This in turn raises the issue of whether the union interpretation of the employment contract is the same as that of the management and whether this interpretation is legal or not. Another tactic can be the 'sick-out': this is when employees collude to report sick together, and may also involve them claiming sickness benefit for their absence.

In assessing union power it is necessary to take into account the fact that it exists at the bottom of the organisation rather than at the top. The fact that unions have an organisational hierarchy can cause people to believe that they either do, or should, behave like organisations where power is much more at the top – as is generally the case with employers. Control in unions is ultimately in the hands of the trade union members who pay subscriptions and who elect the trade union leaders. Elected groups of members have the ultimate formal authority in unions but, in any case, unions have to move in line with their members' wishes. This reality is reinforced by any legislation requiring ballots before industrial action is taken. Sometimes, though, such ballots are simply used as a tactical device to encourage employers to be more generous in negotiations. The mistake that some people make is to see union officials as being akin to police officers with the responsibility and ability to instruct their members about what they should do. Even if union officials were to accept this debatable view of their role, they have little if anything in the way of sanctions to impose their will on their members.

Sometimes industrial action may be both unofficial and illegal. If unions disassociate themselves from such action there may be little that they can do to prevent it. Employers and governments may also find that taking legal action against the employees concerned is counterproductive. However, there have been cases where employers have carried out a threat to dismiss all strikers on the basis that they are breaking their contract of employment.

Diagnostic skills

It has been necessary to spend some time clarifying the framework within which managers operate in the employee relations area as the context has important implications regarding their behaviour. It is also necessary to spend some time examining the diagnostic skills that managers need. The nature of employee relations problems can often be easy enough to recognise – some of the most likely ones being interruptions to work, poor performance, resistance to change and restrictive practices. What can be much more difficult is establishing the actual causes of these problems and working out what, if anything, can be done about them. The emotional nature of the subject can hinder accurate diagnosis – if one has come to hate the sight of a particular employee representative it can be very tempting to go along with a stereotyped view to the effect that all troublemakers should be sacked. The reality is, of course, that whatever one's feelings, one usually has to live with particular representatives and they with their managers, about whom they may have equally strong views.

Bad personal relationships can exacerbate management–union relationships and in some cases conflicts may be no more than personality clashes. However, even if all the people involved are angels, they still have to resolve issues where the interests of the parties are in conflict. One of the skills that managers need in this area is the ability to identify the basic conflicts that lie behind any personal issues. It is important, too, for the manager to judge the extent to which a representative is reflecting the views of their colleagues. Getting rid of the representative, even if this is possible, may not do much good if they are replaced by someone else who behaves in a similar manner. This is because the behaviour is often dictated by the role. The issues remain the same, even if the individuals involved are different. The concept of role behaviour was explained in Chapter 3.

RECOGNISING CONFLICTS OF INTEREST

Perhaps the most critical ability needed by the manager with regard to employee relations is that of being able to recognise when managerial and employee interests come into conflict. Some people adopt a unitary perspective of the organisation and simply do not accept that this can happen. The line of argument can be that what is good for the organisation is automatically good for all its employees. Whilst this approach may present a simple and comforting philosophy for those who hold it, it does not help equip managers to deal with the genuine conflicts of interest that can and do arise, for example about wage levels, working arrangements and job security. Managers may be so preoccupied with the various pressures upon them that they neglect to consider the implications for their employees of particular decisions. If employees see their interests being threatened by changes, they are hardly likely to be enthusiastic about such changes. It may, for example, be highly inconvenient for an employer to find that employees don't cooperate with the introduction of new processes because they threaten their career opportunities and job security. This is not to say that employers should not be implementing changes that cut across employees' interests – sometimes this is very necessary – but these conflicts need to be recognised and taken into account even before the changes are mooted. Decision-making by managers on how to proceed needs to be based on an accurate assessment of the employees' views and not on wishful thinking.

Resistance to change can blandly be ascribed to the innate conservatism of the workforce, but such an analysis may miss the point that employees may resist a particular change because it represents a threat to their interests. Other changes, such as pay increases, may be eagerly accepted. It is the nature of the change and its impact on their interests that employees are likely to consider. In a study of restrictive practices carried out for the Royal Commission on Trade Unions and Employers Associations in the UK, it was concluded that 'there must be few restrictive labour practices which are not genuinely thought by at least one of the parties concerned to be defensible in terms of their own interests' (Royal Commission 1967, p. 52)

If problem diagnosis has been accurately undertaken, it is at least possible for managers to consider what, if anything, can be done. Acceptance that one just has to live with some problems may be much more constructive than wasting time, money and effort on false solutions that will not work because the diagnosis was faulty. With some problems remedial action can be taken. It may be that effective communication can remove misunderstanding, or that it can pave the way to a negotiated answer which gives sufficient concessions to both parties to make a deal worthwhile. Anticipation of problems can lead to their being avoided or reduced in scale. Much can be achieved simply by managers thinking through the implications of their decisions as far as the employees are concerned.

Managers may make apparently simple technical decisions blissfully unaware of the problems their decisions could create in other parts of the organisation. If production schedules, for example, are to be altered in such a way that people's earnings are affected, it is best to anticipate the likely reaction of employees, and to take that into account at the decision-making stage, rather than to take the decision in ignorance of its likely effects. Diagnosis also needs to take account of power relationships. If a clash of interests is identified, it is then necessary to calculate the extent to which the respective parties are able to impose their views. It may seem regrettable that conflicts are determined by power relationships as well as by intellectual, technical and moral criteria, but it is hardly prudent for a manager to try to impose a particular decision if it can easily be resisted. Conversely, the mere fact that employees protest about a proposal does not automatically mean that the employer is unable to implement it.

THE INTEGRATION OF EMPLOYEE RELATIONS WITH OTHER MANAGEMENT ACTIVITIES

The emphasis in this chapter so far has mainly been on looking at employee relations as a subject on its own. However, for there to be any real understanding of the area it is vital to see the way in which employee relations interrelates with other management functions. This can be a crucial diagnostic skill. This is because the causes of employee relations problems, and by implication any remedies, may lie in these other areas. This basic point is often missed because of departmental boundaries. This may be compounded by lack of knowledge of those inside the employee relations area of what goes on outside it and, conversely, lack of knowledge of those outside the area of what goes on within employee relations.

Example of the cause of a strike lying outside the employee relations area

Example

A sack manufacturing company in Guyana (South America) endured a strike of several weeks over a redundancy. The organisation had invested in extra equipment and labour to meet a large order from a sugar producer. The order was not met on time because it had not proved possible to increase production capacity quickly enough. This led to the order being cancelled and the extra staff employed to meet the order being dismissed. Subsequent investigations revealed that delivery of this order had been promised for a time of peak seasonal demand for sacks and there had never been any prospect that the order could be met on time. The cause of the redundancy and the subsequent strike had been the reckless acceptance of an order that had little or no prospect of being met on time.

Example of the knock-on effect of changes in production methods on employee relations

A children's clothing firm in the UK decided to widen its product range. This necessitated shorter runs of a wider range of fashion garments compared with the previous longer runs of a smaller range of standard products. This change failed because no account was taken of the learning problems this created for the assembly line employees, with a consequential reduction in their productivity and the related bonus earnings. (Legge 1978, pp. 45–46)

It is necessary to make the crucial point about the interrelationship of employee relations with other functions by way of examples because of their illustrative value and the lack of systematic study in this area. Unfortunately, employee relations is often seen as a self-contained activity, both by many industrialists and many academics. This is despite the potentially integrative approach involved in HRM.

The lesson for managers is clearly not to look for or expect progress in tackling employee relations problems to come just from initiatives in that area. Whilst effective procedures and employee relations expertise may be useful, they may not on their own enable basic causes of employee relations to be identified. Unfortunately, the training and background of those in employee relations is sometimes such that they may not understand that the causes of many of their problems lie outside their sphere. Conversely, those outside the employee relations area may know so little about the area that they do not appreciate the need to work out the employee relations implications of decisions they are taking. One answer to this problem is general management training for all managers. The case for this is all the more powerful when one realises that the way in which employee relations problems can be created by decisions or failures elsewhere is but one example of the way in which problems can be transmitted from one area of management into another. Managers need to see the implications of their decisions in all other areas and also to recognise that plain incompetence in one area can easily precipitate crises elsewhere.

A positive development, covered earlier in this chapter, is that genuine strategic HRM initiatives linked to corporate policy should embrace employee relations issues in the context of an integrated systems approach to organisational issues. However, not all corporate and HR initiatives are properly integrated and thought out. There are many examples of the human dimension being ignored or it being considered in a simplistic way without specialist advice at the design stage of policy. This topic was examined in Chapter 2 and relevant examples are given concerning the high failure rate of performance-related pay schemes (Chapter 10). This problem of narrowly based or superficially integrated initiatives unfortunately characterises the way many different types of organisational change are often handled.

The manager as a trade union member

REASONS FOR JOINING

Managers may have to give serious thought as to whether or not they join or remain in a trade union. Public sector unions have traditionally included senior levels of management amongst their members. This has partly been because of employer acceptance of this and also because of the size of the organisations concerned. People may retain membership when they are promoted and unions often offer specialist services of which employees may wish to continue to make use. The sheer size of some employer organisations may mean that union membership is the only way in which there can be proper discussions about a manager's terms and conditions of employment.

Whilst increases in the use of personal contracts and merit or performance-related pay has reduced the emphasis on collective negotiation, managers may still sometimes want the cover of a union to represent their interests. Concerns about job security and, in some cases, abrasive management styles are further reasons for joining unions. Legal insurance and legal representation services can also be selling points to the potential managerial recruit. Health and safety issues can also be a reason for managers joining unions. As was explained in Chapter 6, stress is just as likely, or even more so, to affect the manager than other workers. Union representation can be important in such cases, especially if they lead to litigation. Some managers may also join or stay in unions with the ulterior motive of using a membership as a means as of finding out what the union strategies and plans are.

CHOICE OF UNION

One of the decisions that a manager may have to make is just which union they should join. A specialist union, because of its specialised appeal, may not have many members and therefore lack comprehensive support services. Larger unions, whilst not perhaps offering the same degree of understanding about the individual manager's problems, may have a comprehensive range of services and specialists and the negotiating strength that can come from having a large membership, particularly if this membership includes large groups of key workers. Whilst some specialist unions thrive, others fail to last and merge with larger unions, often to the relief of the employer, for this reduces the number of different unions with which they have to deal.

CONFLICTS OF INTEREST

Whilst it may be to the advantage of the individual manager to join a trade union, membership can bring with it a fresh set of problems. Managers may find that it is not always easy to reconcile their union and managerial roles. Sometimes the accommodation is fairly easy. The manager may join a managerial union, or a managerial/administrative section of a manual workers' union. On the face of it there may be no problem in negotiating as a representative of the employer with employees who are in other unions, or even the same union but in a different section. However, sections of the same union can be bound by common policies, and also some union branches can take in a large vertical section of the white-collar workers with a particular employer. This can lead to role conflict, such as an employee wanting to pursue a grievance against a boss who may not only be in the same union branch but also one of its officers!

In the circumstances of industrial action, members may find that there is a conflict between the need to maintain production or services and a union desire to disrupt those services. Such conflicts have been most common in the public sector. The individual manager may find that they are damned by their employer if they do not keep services working and damned by their union if they do.

There is no easy answer to the conflicts that can arise for managers within unions. However, if the individual manager recognises the problems that can arise, this should help them make careful judgements about whether or not they should join a union, which union it should be, whether they should hold office within that union and the way in which role conflicts that occur for themselves and their colleagues within the union can be resolved. Many managers who are union members handle these potential problems by keeping a low profile within the union.

Summary

As has been demonstrated, the area of employee relations is potentially both complex and fluid. Globalisation and changes within national economies are causing more economic fragmentation, which is making it more difficult for trade unions to organise and to control change. However, in non-unionised environments there will still be conflicts of interest that need to be identified and managed. There may also be areas of common interest where cooperation can be constructively improved. Employee relations activities include pay, terms and conditions of employment, performance, working arrangements and job security. The greater pace of change means that working arrangements are changed with increasing frequency. It is essential that line management be actively involved in ensuring that working arrangements are effective and are reviewed in the light of changed circumstances. Employee relations interfaces with HRM and the overlapping relationship between these two activities has been examined.

Key parameters within which employee relations exist are the labour market and employment law and these have both been examined. However, some people are able to exploit skills and geographic shortages of labour. Also, in the case of EU member countries, there has been a significant increase in employment rights within member countries.

Difficulties can exist in diagnosing the causes of employee relations problems because such problems can be precipitated by decisions taken in other areas of managerial activity. Weaknesses in line management can have repercussive effects in employee relations. Effective general management is a basic requirement for effective employee relations.

Finally, the role of the manager as a trade union member was examined. The various ways of handling potential conflicts of interest include identifying the nature of the conflict that can arise with both the union and the manager's line manager. The manager may decide to absent themselves from union meetings where these conflicts are to be discussed. The related area of negotiation is the subject of the next chapter.

Self-assessment questions

(If you wish to check the extent to which your answer to any of the following questions is appropriate, cross-refer to the Table of Contents. The contents of this chapter are listed on page xxi.)

1 What are the objectives of both managers and employees in organisations?

2 What are likely to be the key employee relations issues in an organisation?

3 What is the difference between 'hard' and 'soft' HRM?

4 In what ways might the labour market affect your employment prospects?

5 Identify the role of trade unions. Why might you wish to be, or are you, a member of a trade union?

6 Explain how failings in other areas of management can have a knock-on effect on employee relations. (Cross-refer to the boxed examples in the section headed 'Diagnostic skills'.)

7 Can membership of a trade union be reconciled with also being a manager?

References

(Works of particular interest are marked with a star.)

Department of Trade and Industry (March 2006), Employment Analysis and Research, *Trade Union Membership, 2005*.

Flanders, A. et al. (1968), *Experiment in Industrial Democracy*, Faber.

*Fox, Alan (1965), Research Paper 3, *Industrial Sociology and Industrial Relations*, Royal Commission on Trade Unions and Employers' Associations, HMSO. (A masterful account of the concepts of unitary and pluralistic frames of reference.)

Labour Market Trends (2006), *Labour Disputes in 2005*, Vol. 114 , No. 6, pp. 174–190.

Legge, K. (1978), *Power, Innovation and Problem Solving*, McGraw-Hill.

Royal Commission on Trade Unions and Employers' Associations, The Donovan Commission (1967). *Productivity Bargaining and Restrictive Labour Practices*, Research Paper No. 4, HMSO.

Further reading

Gennard, John, and Judge Graham (2005), *Employee Relations*, CIPD.

*Harris, H., C Brewster, and P. Sparrow (2007), *International Human Resource Management*, 2nd ed., CIPD. (A very useful account of global trends in HRM.)

Legge, K. (1978), *Power, Innovation and Problem-solving in Personnel Management*, McGraw-Hill.

Legge, Karen (1995), *Human Resource Management – Rhetoric and Realities*, MacMillan Business.

*Porter, C., C. Bingham and D. Simmonds (2008), *Exploring Human Resource Management*, McGraw-Hill. (A useful and comprehensive account of HRM.)

*Rees, W. David and Christine Porter (1998), *Employee Participation and Managerial Style – the Key Variable*, Industrial and Commercial Training, 30 (5). (An explanation of why managerial style is likely to be the key factor in employee participation.)

Negotiating skills

Introduction

Negotiation is seen by many as a mystic art, with the corollary that negotiators are born with innate skills that are not easily transferable. However, whilst some people may have a natural aptitude for negotiation, the process of negotiation is capable of analysis. Once it has been analysed it is possible to consciously develop people's skills in the area just as it is possible to develop other skills. The accelerating pace of change means that this is an increasingly important part of a manager's job as commercial and working arrangements have to be renegotiated to meet changed circumstances.

The range of formal and informal negotiating situations in which managers are likely to be involved are identified in this chapter. Relevant theories are examined to help with both the analysis of the negotiating process and with skills development. The need to create a framework for negotiations

is explained. This framework will apply even in informal negotiations between two people. A key feature is the need for those involved in negotiations to understand the different roles that need to be played, sometimes by the same person. Often negotiations fail because people get so involved in the negotiations that they neglect to create a proper framework or allocate appropriate roles.

The various stages in the negotiating process are identified, including the concept of the negotiating ritual. The importance of effective chairing during negotiations is explained, as is the fact that this sometimes needs to be done on an informal and discreet basis. The process skills of the chair, in particular, can be crucial in determining whether there is a constructive outcome to negotiations or not. These skills are also necessary to avoid false agreements being reached, based on misunderstandings of the parties about what was agreed. This can all too easily happen because communications during negotiations are often very fragile. Often the best results are obtained by the parties behaving assertively rather than aggressively. By adopting assertive behaviour, the potential for agreement can be explored and confrontations which threaten the process avoided.

The importance of preparation is explained, as is the need to set realistic objectives. This is likely to involve an examination of the power realities and consideration of what to do if negotiations fail. Sometimes it is better to have no agreement than a bad one. In group negotiations, a considerable amount of time may be needed to resolve internal differences. Often such internal differences are harder to resolve than differences with whoever the group is trying to negotiate with.

Finally, attention is paid in this chapter to the need for agreements to be evaluated, implemented and monitored. For the negotiating process to be effective, formal and informal training may be necessary.

Negotiating roles and trends

ROLES

Negotiating is not something that is just the province of specialist negotiators. All managers are likely to be involved in some level of negotiations. Whilst most negotiations will be small-scale, their cumulative effect can be considerable. Much of the negotiation managers are involved in is likely to be about operational matters, e.g. the implementation and monitoring of existing commercial contracts. They are likely also to be involved in a considerable amount of negotiation about how they meet other managers' needs and how other managers meet their needs. Organisation of their own department may also involve much informal negotiation. This is likely to include allocation of work, logistical working arrangements and the quality control of what is done.

Negotiations do not cease when managers finish work. They will inevitably be involved with negotiations about, for example, their living arrangements and purchases. Social trends have created a much more egalitarian society which involves continuous negotiations about domestic arrangements. Some of the hardest negotiations can be with children about such issues as bedtime, homework and contributions to domestic chores.

A particular need is for managers to develop the habit of reflecting on the way that they, and others, negotiate. The increasing amount of time spent in negotiations creates a considerable opportunity to learn from the skills that are used and the mistakes made.

The stereotype of the effective negotiator is the person who drives a very hard bargain. Whilst this can sometimes be appropriate, it is not always a helpful image. Negotiators need to get the best that they can out of a given situation and often this may involve coming to a mutually satisfactory agreement. To try and drive too hard a bargain can sometimes mean no agreement at all. The key to effective negotiation is developing procedural and process skills so that the framework and conduct of negotiations is such that that which is potentially attainable is achieved.

TRENDS

The amount of negotiations that managers have to do seems to be increasing significantly. Whilst negotiations with trade unions are generally easier than they were when unions were generally more powerful, in many areas negotiations are becoming more difficult and more frequent. The increasing pace of change causes organisational arrangements to be reviewed more frequently. This can involve reviewing both commercial contracts and negotiations with employees about what they do, when and where. Failure to do this can affect the very survival of an organisation. A general excess of production capacity in the world, boosted by technological development and **globalisation**, has turned many industries and services into a buyer's market. This has created chronic pressures for producers and providers of services simultaneously to increase quality and reduce costs. The mismatch between expectations and available resources in the public sector has also created increasing pressure to improve value for money.

Relevant theories

The process of negotiation is so complex that there neither is, nor can be, one theory that embraces all its aspects. However, there are two particularly useful theories about negotiation that cover key aspects. These theories can create an analytical framework for examining and developing your own skills and examining the behaviour of others. As with all theories, they need to be applied in the right context. Unsurprisingly, the two theories are not recent. This is because the process of negotiation is so long-established that writers have had plenty of time to study it.

INTEGRATIVE AND DISTRIBUTIVE BARGAINING

The seminal work on the theory of negotiation was written by Walton and McKersie (1965). They distinguished between distributive and **integrative bargaining**. In **distributive bargaining** one party can only gain at the expense of the other. This can be described as a fixed-sum game, such as in the sale of an item by one party and its purchase by another party. In integrative bargaining there is the potential to increase the amount that can be distributed. This can be described as a varying-sum game. An example of integrative bargaining from the employee relations area is productivity bargaining. Productivity bargaining can enable the value added by a group of people to be increased. In return they would expect to have some reward for their increased contribution. However, if the parties don't cooperate effectively they may not only fail to generate a mutual gain, but they may actually undermine existing arrangements. In that event, the potential for a win–win outcome may not be achieved and instead there may be a lose–lose result.

Whilst the concepts of integrative and distributive bargaining are very clear in theory, in practice they may overlap. A negotiation can involve elements of both types of bargaining. Although the sale of a house, for example, is essentially a fixed-sum game, there may be some potential for integrative bargaining. This could arise, for example, by agreeing a mutually advantageous completion date. In conducting negotiations it can be useful to identify what elements of integrative and distributive bargaining potentially exist.

UNITARY AND PLURALISTIC FRAMES OF REFERENCE

A second relevant and important theory relates to the concepts of **unitary** and **pluralistic frames of reference** (Fox 1965). These concepts were examined in the previous chapter because of their particular significance to the understanding of employee relations. However, these concepts are also basic to an understanding of negotiations. This is because conflicts of interest are not always obvious. In internal organisation bargaining those with a unitary frame of reference may be unable to recognise conflicts of interest between different parts of the organisation. This is because they will apply a team concept and assume that everyone will or should subordinate their own objectives to those of the organisation overall. Those with a pluralistic frame of reference, however, will recognise that when sectional interests are threatened, people will not automatically cooperate for the common good. It is necessary to be able to recognise such conflicts of interest in order to develop a framework for dealing with them.

CONFLICTS OF RIGHT AND CONFLICTS OF INTEREST

A further useful concept is the difference between **conflicts of right** and **conflicts of interest**. Conflicts of right occur when there is a dispute about the interpretation of an existing agreement. Conflicts of interest occur when the parties dispute what an agreement should be, as opposed to what it is.

The framework of negotiations

Whenever people negotiate there needs to be a framework, however informal it may be. The framework relates to how an issue is being negotiated. The parties can be so involved in the substance of the negotiations that they can neglect to pay sufficient attention to the way in which the negotiations are being handled. This can reduce the chances of a positive outcome. This is particularly the case when the negotiations are complicated and/or a number of parties are involved. In team negotiations there may need to be a division of labour so that the different aspects of negotiation are handled effectively. Particular attention may need to be paid to internal differences between team members. As well as needing to structure negotiations effect-ively, it is also necessary for those involved to be clear about their objectives and tactics. Power realities also need to be carefully examined.

PROCEDURAL AND SUBSTANTIVE ISSUES

A basic distinction in negotiations is between the procedure that is used to negotiate and the actual substantive issues being negotiated about. If negotiations between the parties are part of an established pattern, the negotiations may have been formalised into a procedural agreement. If that is not the case, at least the historic pattern will probably represent the expectations of the par-ties as to the way they wish to proceed. Even in small informal negotiations the parties need to consider the way in which they need to proceed and may also want to come to a joint understand-ing about that. There can be so much conflict and tension in negotiations about substantive issues that it can be in the interests of both parties to try and remove any misunderstandings about how the negotiations are to be conducted beforehand. There is a strong argument therefore for having a procedure agreed well in advance of negotiations. It can be difficult enough trying to resolve the substantive issues without having to agree the procedure immediately beforehand, or having to make it up as you go along. To make an analogy with sport, the rules of the game are agreed well in advance of an actual game: great care is usually taken to ensure that the neutral parties in charge of sporting contests apply the rules in a consistent manner.

OBJECTIVES

Managers and others involved in negotiations need carefully to establish their objectives. Some-times objectives are self-evident. On other occasions they involve patient diagnostic work. If a reactive style is taken, it may be automatic to respond to a demand by saying 'no', prevaricating or making a less generous counter-offer. However, on some occasions it may be in both the par-ties' interests if a demand is accepted. If, for example, there is a shortage of a particular category of staff, it may be in management's interests to agree to a demand for a wage increase rather than reactively resist it. In identifying objectives it can be crucial that the parties look forward and do not dwell on perceived historic injustices. Another important issue can be that demands may only be the symptom of a deeper underlying problem.

Identifying the real problem

Example

In a former public utility there was high turnover of computer staff. When people left they said that they were leaving because they had been offered more money to work elsewhere. More money was given to the computer staff but the labour turnover remained high. The employer then asked people who were leaving what had caused them to look for another job.

The clear pattern with the responses to his question was the poor interpersonal and management skills of their technical supervisors. The primary solution was clearly to do with the selection, development and monitoring of the supervisors of computer staff and not increasing wages.

PREPARATION

Once the negotiating objectives have been defined, it is then necessary to work out how those objectives might be achieved. One useful framework is as follows:

- Define objectives and rank them in order of importance.

- Decide tactics to achieve objectives.

- Identify the maximum concessions you will make (the bottom line).

- Decide on the action you will take if you do not achieve your objectives. This may cause you to rethink the concessions you are prepared to give.

It is particularly important to examine the power relationships. These may have far more impact on the outcome of negotiations than the intellectual or moral quality of a case. It involves asking such blunt questions as, 'Who can do what to whom and when?' A man with a knife at your throat may have a poor intellectual and moral case for robbing you but is likely to succeed. The Prussian military theorist Karl von Clausewitz explained the nature of power realities with reference to international politics in the nineteenth century. He stated, 'War is nothing but the continuation of politics with a mixture of other means' (David 1997, p. 149).

Example

Example of the effective use of an understanding of power realities

A local community leader in Britain was involved in negotiations about the closure of a rural railway line. He realised that he would not be able to stop the closure, so he concentrated his attention on getting the maximum concessions with a replacement bus service. This enabled him to get a better result than by simply protesting about the closure.

Negotiations can take place at two levels. The surface element may be the intellectual presentation of a case supported by apparently relevant information. However, this can have a large element of charade about it. The parties may in reality be concentrating on what pressure they can bring on the others involved and how they might do it. However, whilst it is important to recognise and take into account the power realities, careful case preparation and presentation do sometimes significantly affect the outcome. Issues to consider including when constructing a case might be:

- economic impact,

- legal impact,

- precedents and practice elsewhere,

- the precedent effect of accepting a demand,

- ability of the parties to pay.

A further factor to consider is the nature of the relationship between the parties. Managers may be able to take much more on trust with a party if they have a long established relationship and a good reputation. They will need to be much more cautious in dealing with people they know little about, especially in a one-off negotiation. In a long-term relationship there is the factor of goodwill to be taken into account. It may also lead to the giving of face-saving compromises to the other side. If goodwill is not an issue there may be the temptation to use sharp practice to gain a better deal.

The confidentiality of information about bargaining positions can't always be taken for granted. Information can be leaked deliberately or accidentally. There is also often a grapevine by which people can gain information. However, care should be taken to try and avoid damaging leaks. Sometimes it is also necessary to beware of 'information' that is created or released to undermine the negotiating position of another party.

INTERNAL DIFFERENCES

Attention is often concentrated on the differences between the two 'sides' or parties in a negotiation. However, often the 'sides' represent coalitions of interest groups. Members of a negotiating team can assume that because they are all on the same side they have a common position. However, as well as differing personalities, there can be quite different pressures on different members of a side. Some team members may feel that other team members are being disloyal by not agreeing with their position. However, it is more profitable to try and understand the reasons why members of a team might disagree and explore what accommodations are possible. The worst thing to do is not to explore these issues beforehand and find that the internal differences only become obvious during negotiations with the other party.

The scale of the internal differences within a side can be greater and more difficult to resolve than the external differences between them and the other main party. This is not always obvious because of the much greater secrecy that may be involved in trying to resolve such differences. However, adequate time has to be given to establishing a party line. Sides can split into 'hawks' and 'doves'. Moderates are sometimes called doves because of the term 'doves of peace'. This is in contrast to hard-liners, who are sometimes called hawks, hawks being birds of prey. It may be counterproductive to exclude hawks from the negotiating team. They may need to be exposed to the negotiating pressures and involved in any proposals for settlement. They may cause far more trouble shouting their opposition from the sidelines.

There are many examples from the world of politics of the problems of reconciling internal differences. In Northern Ireland it became increasingly possible to get agreement between the moderates on both sides. This has also generally been the case in the dispute between the Palestinians and Israel. The problem is getting their hawks to agree. Too many concessions to the other side, however, can destabilise the position of leaders and even lead to their death; for example, the assassination of the Israeli Prime Minister Yitzhak Rabin by an Israeli fundamentalist in 1995 following the Oslo Accords. An earlier example is the assassination of Michael Collins by Irish nationalists in 1922. This followed his conclusion of a peace deal with the British Government which involved independence for the south of Ireland but not the north. Sometimes deals are made secretly between the leaders who then try to persuade their own side to accept them.

Political parties often have formal party meetings before meetings of national and local government assemblies to agree the party line. This is where the real decisions are usually taken, rather than in public debate. The relationship between internal and external differences is illustrated in Figure 15.1

| Figure 15.1 | **Handling of internal differences** |

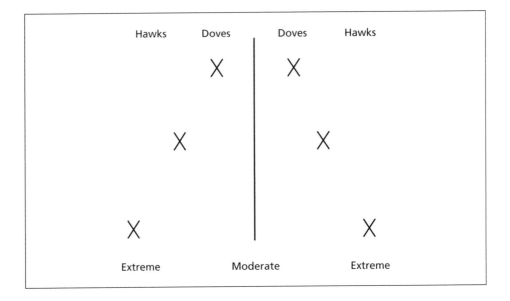

ROLE ALLOCATIONS

Even in one-to-one negotiations there can be a number of different roles that the parties have to handle according to the stage they are at in the negotiating process. A procedural framework needs to be established. This needs to include the time and place for negotiations, an agenda, and the preparation and presentation of any relevant documents. The parties will need to spend time both presenting and listening to one another during the substantive negotiations. It may be necessary to organise adjournments and further meetings. If a deal is concluded, attention then has to be paid to how it is implemented. Failure to pay adequate attention to these issues can jeopardise the negotiations. It may be necessary for one of the parties, even if informally, to assume a chairing role in identifying and dealing with these issues.

In team negotiations the need for a division of labour between different members is more obvious than the need for one person to switch roles when they are bargaining on their own. However, even in team negotiations the need to arrange a sensible role allocation is often sadly neglected. This can lead to one person being quite unnecessarily overloaded, whilst their colleagues don't have enough to do. Key roles that have to be handled in team negotiations are described below.

Chairing

There can be three dimensions to the chairing role: chairing a team in the negotiations with the other party, chairing internal discussions and chairing joint meetings. Sometimes there are formal arrangements for handling joint meetings, for example by rotation or by having an independent chair handle it. Often there is no such provision and the chair of a team may need to handle this in such a way that an effective frame-work is provided without irritating the other side at this exercise of control. The chairing roles can be of great importance and require significant skill and attention, as explained in Chapter 16 on meetings and chairing. It is up to the chair to see that negotiations stay on course and to intervene if there is a danger of the process breaking down. This is much more easily done if they are concentrating primarily on this aspect and are detached from the argument about substantive issues.

Case presentation

A common practice is for the most senior person on the management side to handle all the chairing roles and be the lead negotiator. However, given the danger of role overload and the damaging consequences this can have, it is often best to have a separate person act as the lead negotiator. The lead negotiator can then concentrate on just the negotiating issues and leave the procedural aspects to the chair. It also means that if there is a deadlock in discussions, or if they get too heated, the chair can intervene. This may also create valuable thinking time for the lead negotiator.

Recording

Another way of easing the burden on the chair and lead negotiator is to have someone else take notes. The case for someone doing this is even stronger if that person does not have any other formal responsibility in the negotiations. Verbatim notes of a whole meeting are not necessary, but great care may be necessary to get an accurate record of key issues. The person taking notes will normally need to sit next to the chair so that they can liaise about note-taking. The chair may to need to have the lead negotiator on their other side.

Observing

Much may be learnt about the other side's real intentions and internal differences by a careful study of their demeanour during negotiations. Points to watch can be:

- who people defer to within a team,
- body language, including facial expressions,
- signs of tension, e.g. in rate of talking, language used and pitch of voice,
- the issues on which negotiators seem to need to refer back to their principals,
- cross-talk,
- contradictions in what is said.

It can be time well spent to have someone concentrate on observing. If necessary, this can be combined with another role, e.g. recording.

Consideration may also be given to the need for expert witnesses during negotiations, who may stay for the whole meeting or just the relevant part.

SPECIALIST REPRESENTATION

Sometimes managers need to consider the case for appointing a specialist to lead negotiations. This will be logical if the costs of such representation are less than the potential gain in the negotiations. The specialist may be internally or externally appointed. Human Resource (HR) managers often need to lead internal negotiations with employee representatives because of the dangers of line managers getting a poor or flawed deal. However, there are dangers of the HR function taking over too much executive authority and in so doing preventing line managers from developing negotiating skills in the employee relations area. One option is to have line managers lead negotiations with a personnel representative present as an adviser.

Trade unions have long understood the need for specialist representation. The expertise of some employee representatives and of full-time union officials generally is such that they can often outmanoeuvre an inexperienced line manager. Also, union representatives may be appointed because of their negotiating ability, whilst this may be a peripheral skill and issue for the line manager. The negotiating ability of managers is an issue that may justify selection and training, a topic that is addressed later in this chapter.

Sometimes organisations need to consider the use of external specialists to represent them. This often happens with employment tribunal cases, although this is a judicial and not a negotiating process. Organisations that belong to employers' associations may get a specialist negotiator from the association to represent them on some issues. On commercial issues it may be necessary to consider using a commercial agent.

Advantages that specialist negotiators can bring include emotional detachment, knowledge of the substantive area, market trends and practice elsewhere, and contacts. Managers may be at a disadvantage if the person they are dealing with has specialist knowledge or specialist representation and they do not. However, conflicts of interests can sometimes emerge between the specialist negotiator and their client, such as the length of negotiations and fee arrangements. Also, agreements can sometimes be more satisfactorily struck by direct contact with the other side. This is because specialist representatives may strive too hard to get the best possible deal and ignore the need for ongoing relationships to be maintained between the parties. Dangers can arise though if you negotiate without a specialist representative.

Example

The need for specialist representation

Four young musicians who had formed their own group were offered a contract by a medium-sized recording studio. They were invited to travel to London to sign a contract. They told their accountant of this, and he advised them to take a lawyer with them. When the musicians entered the conference room they found that four printed standard contracts had been placed on the table for them to sign. The secretary who had showed them into the room asked the members of the group who the fifth person was. When they introduced their lawyer the secretary responded by saying 'you won't be needing these contracts then'. She returned with four different printed contracts. It emerged that the original contract forms contained an open-ended cost clause, which would have enabled the recording company to offset costs against the income generated by the contract, so that the musicians might not have received any money. The contract that the musicians eventually did sign had a fixed level of costs.

Negotiating processes

As well as a need for attention to be paid to the procedural framework for negotiations, care is also needed in managing the way in which people interact with one another during negotiations. Whoever is chairing a meeting or a team has a particular responsibility to manage these processes constructively. There can be considerable emotion and tension during negotiations, and careful management of the processes can make all the difference as to whether agreement is reached or not. Particular attention needs to be paid to the sequence in which events are handled, the many communication problems that can arise and the ways in which deadlock may be overcome.

SEQUENCE OF EVENTS

There are three particularly important aspects to consider in relation to the sequence of events during negotiations. These are the need for a **negotiating ritual**, including the issue of who should make the first bid, the need for the chair to stay in role and see that the other parties do the same, and the need to focus on the important issues.

The negotiating ritual

It is probably best to try and agree the sequence of events with the other party before negotiations begin. If there is a procedural agreement, this may specify the sequence. Invariably there is a ritual to negotiations. This usually consists of a series of offers and counter-offers and eventual compromise agreement. This ritual can fulfil a necessary function. This is particularly so if the parties negotiating have interest groups to whom they are responsible. The negotiators will need to demonstrate that they have got the best offer available in order to 'sell' any deal to whomever they represent. Consequently it is important to avoid public displays of triumph if a good deal is obtained, as this can undermine the position of the negotiators for the other side. Even in cases in which the principals are negotiating directly with one another, they will also need to feel that they have achieved a good deal.

Thought needs to be given as to whether it is better to make the first offer yourself or to try and get the other party to make the first bid. The pitching of an initial offer can have a crucial effect on the ultimate outcome. In the case of trying to buy something, too low an offer may mean that you are not taken seriously. Too high an offer can create the expectation that you can be persuaded to improve your offer significantly.

Parties to negotiations may have a recognisable historic pattern in the way they handle the ritual. It may help a manager in handling the ritual to try and identify that pattern. It may be necessary to take account of past patterns altering if a new and important person joins a negotiating team. The negotiating ritual needs to be handled with some skill. Sometimes mistakes can be elementary.

The need for skill in handling the negotiating ritual

Example

At the start of annual railway pay negotiations the lead management negotiator referred to management proposals as 'the first offer'. This drew a swift response from the union spokesperson: 'We don't like the first offer – what about the second one?'

There is also a need to consider who makes their case first. Often it makes sense for the person who is trying to change a situation to be allowed to go first. If one side is particularly emotional about an issue it may be best to let them present first so that they can dissipate some of their anger. Having done that they may be more able to listen to the response and also may have even moderated their position through being given the chance to be heard. It is particularly important for the chair of the opposing side to prevent retaliatory comment from hawks on their own side at this stage, as this could undo all the good work that may have already been accomplished. A further point is the need to consider what you should ask for in return whenever you make an offer. Opposing negotiators may be much more likely to make concessions if a trade-off is involved.

Keeping in role

The chair needs to ensure that the agreed procedure and sequence of negotiations are followed and that the parties keep to their allotted roles. It is all too easy for 'tennis matches' to develop whereby each side refutes what the other says and the discussions not only do not progress but get increasingly acrimonious (Rees and Porter 1997, p. 67). Understandably, both sides will want to concentrate on the strong and not the weak points in their case. It is up to the chair to let both sides make their case and then move on. Sometimes it may be necessary to agree to differ on a particular point and agree to return to it later. In order to navigate through these difficulties it is essential that the chair stays in role and doesn't get unnecessarily involved in argument about the substantive issues. If the chair is for some reason involved in the substantive negotiations, e.g. if the negotiations are conducted between just two people, they may need to be adept at signalling when they are bargaining and when they are trying to manage the procedure and processes. This situation is akin to refereeing a sports match in which one is also playing and is a topic given further detailed attention in Chapter 16 on meetings and chairing.

Tunnel vision

A further issue is the need for the parties to avoid **tunnel vision**. This can happen when the parties focus their attention on one aspect of negotiations and ignore other issues which may be far more important. Sometimes one or both of the parties may fail to see that the issue with which they are dealing is a symptom of something more fundamental. This reinforces the need to think carefully about objectives, as explained in the section on the framework of negotiations earlier in this chapter.

Example

Identifying the real issue

The managers in a manufacturing company became preoccupied with the earnings drift of a particular group of production workers who were receiving the benefit of a 'loose' group bonus scheme. These workers were benefiting because of changes in production methods that were enabling them to receive more money without any extra effort on their part. However, the real problem was not in limiting their increases, but in getting rid of the bonus scheme altogether. It was no longer acting as an incentive for extra effort (as intended), but had become just a way of paying more money, and thereby distorting the overall pay structure.

COMMUNICATION ISSUES

Communication processes can be fragile at the best of times. However, they can be particularly vulnerable during negotiations. This is because of the presence of factors such as conflict and emotion and the complexities that can arise during negotiations. Also, distortion is possible at each stage of the chain of communication. There is a need for people in chairing roles to pay particular attention to the potential for misunderstandings and to take preventative action to avoid them and the often very serious consequences that can flow from them. Key communication areas in negotiating will involve listening and observing, taking account of any cultural differences and avoiding ambiguity.

Listening and observing

One of the dangers in negotiating meetings is that people get so involved in presenting their case that they do not listen carefully enough to what the other side has to say and then reflect on it. People in chairing roles need to give the other side adequate opportunity to present their case and ensure that it is listened to. A common problem is for people to use the time when the other side is presenting their case simply to rehearse the arguments they are going to use instead of listening to what is actually being said (this is called 'behaviour rehearsal'). Listening and observing are all the more important because a certain amount of posturing takes place during negotiations and it is necessary to get behind that to try and discover the other side's true intentions.

The style used in the negotiations can also be very important. There can be complications enough without the differences being personalised. The parties should generally try and behave assertively and not aggressively. The distinction between these two styles of behaviour was explained in Chapter 4. If a person is nevertheless aggressive, it is best to remain assertive and not make matters worse by responding aggressively. The tactic of remaining assertive can have the effect of calming the other person down. If it doesn't, it may lead to the other person losing the thread of their argument, making mistakes and losing sympathy with their colleagues.

Particular attention may need to be paid to the language that is used. Sometimes coded messages are sent between lead negotiators to indicate whether they are taking a hard or a soft line on a particular issue. On other occasions parties may unintentionally reveal their intentions by the use of particular words or by carelessness. Words such as 'review', if used in the context of pay negotiations, are likely to be interpreted as meaning an increase.

The need for the careful use of words

Example

At a consultative meeting about the possible merger of two units, the chief executive of an organisation unwittingly revealed that the logistical arrangements to effect the merger had already been set in motion, and that the consultation was meaningless.

Body language

Body language was covered in a general manner in Chapter 8 in the context of communication. The concept of body language can be of particular importance in negotiation. People can give away their intentions by accidental gestures. However, other gestures may be deliberate signals to indicate how well or badly a particular suggestion has been received.

Example

How to benefit from recognising body language

The famous American international sports agent, Mark McCormack, explained in his book how:

> When I am meeting at someone else's office I have often noticed that people will sort of 'lean in' to the situation when they are ready to get serious, even unconsciously using their hands to push everything on their desk a couple of inches forward. Yet almost as often I have seen people at this point lean back in their chairs and feign a totally relaxed position. (McCormack 1984, pp. 24–24)

McCormack also explained in a British radio interview how one negotiator would unwittingly reveal his intentions by moving his chair back before making his final offer. The advantage of recognising such a cue is obviously to keep asking for more until the person moves their chair back!

Cultural differences

Attention will need to be paid to any potential cultural barriers to understanding during negotiations, especially given increasing cultural diversity within nations and globalisation (Mead 2005). It may be important to have a person to advise on how to handle the different negotiating conventions of those from other cultures. The impact of culture on communication is also considered in both Chapter 4 on managerial style and in Chapter 8 on communication.

The rituals that people are used to from other countries may be different and in some countries much more prolonged than in others. In countries such as the USA, communications are likely to be direct and often reinforced by written contracts. In some Asian countries, in contrast, much more attention will have to be paid to the context in which negotiations take place. More may have to be taken on trust, as to ask for too much written clarification could be taken as insulting, with the implication that the other party is not to be trusted. In such cultures there also may be a higher need to save the face of the weaker party. Deference to elders can vary from culture to culture. In dealing with the Japanese, for example, it may be important to recognise the deference shown to elder members on their team and to show politeness yourself. It may also be important to work out the effect that culture can have on power realities within a team.

The nature and importance of body language may also differ considerably from one culture to another. People from some cultures may be much more impassive than those from other cultural backgrounds. If a manager causes offence to people from some cultures, they be much less likely to realise it, however damaging it may be. The meaning of gestures can vary critically from one culture to another.

Variation of the meaning of body gestures in different countries

Negotiations involving an international organisation in India were hampered at one stage by the habit of the people with whom they were trying to do business shaking their heads from side to side as if in disagreement. It then emerged that in this particular part of the country that gesture meant agreement and not disagreement.

Avoiding ambiguity

It is crucial for negotiators to avoid unintended ambiguity during negotiations, especially in any agreement that is reached. Unfortunately, this can all too easily happen. Negotiators may remember the concessions that they have gained during negotiations far more readily than the concessions they have made to the other party. Such selective perception may be compounded by the use of words that can have more than one meaning. Words such as 'may' can be interpreted as 'must', 'probably', or 'possibly'. Those involved in negotiating are apt to make the interpretation most convenient to them, unaware that the other party may be doing the same thing in reverse. To make matters worse, when the difference in interpretations emerges, the parties may think that there has been deliberate deceit rather than genuine misunderstanding.

The frequency of ambiguity

In a series of experiments with simulated negotiating exercises with managers it was found that it was more common than not to have significant misunderstandings about what the parties thought they had agreed. This emerged when, at the conclusion of negotiations, each individual was asked to record the main items of agreement. The people involved were not allowed to confer with one another when recording their perception of the outcome. The managers concerned tended to misperceive the outcomes in their favour, i.e. managers would all tend to think that they had conceded less than other managers playing the part of employee representatives, thought they had. (Rees and Porter 1997, pp. 68–69)

To avoid unintended ambiguity it is necessary for the chair and lead negotiator in particular to keep on checking during negotiations that misunderstanding has not occurred. Careful listening and observing is a way of helping to see if misunderstanding has developed or not. Frequent summarising of what has or has not been agreed may be necessary during a meeting. It may be necessary to repeat the same point a number of times to make sure that there is genuine agreement and understanding. The following example shows how serious misunderstandings can easily and innocently arise.

An important but avoidable misunderstanding

The payroll computer at a factory crashed on pay-day at a time when most manual employees were still paid in cash. Employee representatives demanded that each employee affected be given a cash payment because of this. The company refused to do this, and a three-day strike ensued. It was then discovered that the employees had simply wanted a cash advance which could later be deducted from whatever wages were due to them. The company had thought that the employees were asking for a cash payment to compensate for inconvenience as well as their wages. The problem then arose as to whether the men should receive any payment for the three days they had been on strike because of this misunderstanding. The nature of the confusion was only identified during talks convened to try and resolve the dispute when the two parties were asked to explain just what their differences were.

Recording the outcome of negotiations is a further way of preventing misunderstanding. However, the damage may be done by the time a written document is issued. It is necessary to ensure that ambiguity does not arise during negotiations so that a written record confirms what was really agreed, not just what the person writing the document thought was agreed.

Sometimes there is a need for deliberate ambiguity. This can be the case when neither party wants to concede a particular issue but they don't want to contest it at that point in time. Providing there are no problems about implementing ambiguous wording, this can be a necessary device for getting agreement.

Reporting back

Particular problems can arise when negotiators report back to the groups they represent. This can be because of the pressure that negotiators may come under to say that they have obtained a better deal than they really have. If this is happening on both sides of a negotiation, the perceptions of those in the interest groups of what was really agreed upon can become even more distorted. It is therefore important that those who receive reports from negotiators coax out of them what really happened at the negotiations. If there is a danger of distortion in reporting back from employee representatives to employees, managers may need to distribute written details to employees on the outcome of negotiations.

HANDLING DEADLOCKS

Handling deadlocks can be a key skill for negotiators. There are a number of ways of trying to prevent or resolve deadlock.

Agree on what can be agreed

It may be best to identify what can be agreed on and what cannot. Finding some areas of agreement can create an element of mutual trust and become a platform for later agreement on more difficult issues. If necessary, more difficult issues may have to be left for another occasion.

Dealing with conflicting principles

Particular difficulties can emerge if the parties are pursuing different and conflicting points of principle. This may appear to rule out room for manoeuvre. Ways of trying to resolve this are to:

- Make value judgements about the respective importance of the principles involved. In some cases it is necessary to let one principle override another because of its greater importance. This may involve giving way or standing firm.

- Consider whether the other party has simply run out of arguments and is clinging to a principle in order to save face. If so, it will then be necessary to try and find ways of saving the face of the other party so that they can discreetly withdraw from the issue of principle.

- Examine whether the principle involved has practical significance or is actually hampering the party that is clinging to it.

- Devise a compromise deal that appears to leave conflicting principles intact, even though in practice that may not be the case.

Appointing a devil's advocate

It may help to have someone act as devil's advocate. This involves one of your team examining the negotiating position of your opponent, which may generate insights into the position of the other party. These may include an understanding of the concessions the other party may be able to make and the points that they will not be able to concede.

Identifying convergence and divergence

There is often a pattern in negotiations of the parties sometimes converging towards agreement and sometimes diverging. If the convergence is bringing the parties close to agreement, further small concessions may result in a deal. Once divergence sets in, the opportunity may be lost. There may be no point in making concessions when parties are moving apart – they may have to wait until there are prospects of convergence again before getting a constructive response to concessions.

Deadlines

Sometimes deadlines are set for agreement to be reached. If agreement is not reached, an offer may be withdrawn, change implemented or some other action taken. This can work provided that the party setting the deadline has a viable plan of what to implement if there is no agreement.

Adjournments

If negotiations become acrimonious or if fresh ideas are needed, it may be best to seek an adjournment. Adjournments may also be necessary if one or other party needs to consider a fresh point or to resolve internal differences within their team. It may also be necessary for one of the parties to report back to its interest group to receive fresh instructions. Sometimes parties need time to come to terms with what concessions have to be made. Delicate issues of timing can be involved in judging when it can be productive or counterproductive to arrange an adjournment.

Keeping the parties together

If agreement seems possible, it may be best to try and keep the parties together and clinch a deal. In marginal situations, factors such as fatigue may help to encourage people to agree. If the negotiations are adjourned, people may have second thoughts or be urged to take a harder line by the interest groups they represent. Once the parties have separated it may be difficult to bring them back together. This why a former chief conciliation officer of the UK Advisory Conciliation and Arbitration Service (ACAS) said that it may be necessary to provide 'cold fish and chips and warm lager' to keep the parties together. However, any deal has to be realistic and not one that will be repudiated afterwards.

Example

Problems of negotiating when one of the parties will not meet with the other

In the case of a six-week brewery strike in Britain, the management found that they were unable to negotiate with the people they desperately wanted to talk to because they had stated that they would not '**negotiate under duress**'.

Separating interests and positions

An example of the constructive distinction between interests and positions occurred in the Israeli–Egyptian peace negotiations in 1978.

Example

Separating interests from positions

It emerged that Israel's interests were centred upon security rather than its position on the continued occupation of the Sinai peninsula. Egypt wanted to regain sovereignty of the Sinai but did not have military objectives. When this was realised, it enabled a deal to be struck that satisfied the interests of both parties. This involved Egypt regaining the Sinai on the understanding that it would not base tanks there. (Fisher, Ury and Patton 1997)

Back channels

Deadlock can sometimes be resolved by the use of 'back channels'. These are secret contacts between some of the negotiators on each side. They may or may not involve the use of a third party. Back channels can be used to explore the possibility of agreement. If agreement is found to be possible, then the proposals can be presented to the respective negotiating teams. If the secret talks indicate that agreement is not possible, then they remain secret to protect the position of the parties involved.

The use of a back channel

Example

An example of the use of back channels is the secret discussions between representatives of the Israeli government and the Palestine Liberation Organisation (PLO) in Oslo in 1993. These discussions took place whilst official talks were taking place in Washington. When it emerged in Oslo that agreement was possible the main political leaders got officially involved and later signed a formal agreement.

Secret deals

Some issues may be so important and yet so sensitive that the parties may reach secret agreements about them. These may involve mutual understandings or formal secret protocols. There are dangers in this, particularly if a key negotiator is replaced or one party fails to honour their side of the bargain.

A secret deal

Example

During the Cuban missile crisis in 1962, President Kennedy secretly agreed to withdraw nuclear missiles from Turkey. This was in exchange for the Russian public withdrawal of nuclear missiles from Cuba. President Kennedy needed secrecy about his concession because of his greater dependence on public opinion than the Russian leader, Nikita Khrushchev.

Third parties

Sometimes third parties may be able to help resolve deadlock. Independent parties include lawyers and commercial arbitrators In the case of employment disputes in the UK, the services of the Advisory, Conciliation and Arbitration Service (**ACAS**) are available free of charge. ACAS has considerable experience and expertise in providing conciliation, mediation and arbitration services in disputes between employers and trade unions. Many other countries have similar arrangements. Arbitration is often on a voluntary basis. This means that both parties need to agree to the process, unlike the case of compulsory arbitration. However, the party in the more powerful position in a dispute may be reluctant to accept arbitration if they think that this will give them a less favourable outcome than using their negotiating power. Arbitration awards in trade disputes in the UK are not legally binding, but are invariably accepted.

If recourse is made to arbitration, it is essential to have clear terms of reference.

The need for clear terms of arbitration reference

A privately arranged arbitration panel was appointed to resolve a dispute between a central London-based company and its employees. The issue concerned the car mileage rate to be paid to employees who had to drive to work during train strikes. The company wanted to pay a different and lower rate than that given when employees had to use their cars for company business. The terms of reference were to confirm that the company practice of paying the lower mileage rate during train strikes was correct. Once proceedings had started it emerged that the company's interpretation of the terms of reference was such that the panel could only rule in its favour. The panel had no authority to vary the company practice! When this became apparent, the union side promptly withdrew from the proceedings.

Accepting failure

Not all deadlocks can or even should be broken. Managers need to consider their bottom line, as explained in the section on objectives earlier in this chapter. No deal may be better than a bad deal. However, the consequences of not having agreement may need to be reconsidered before breaking off negotiations. If agreement is not reached there is always the possibility that the matter can be reconsidered in the future. In that respect, a 'no' is not as final as a 'yes'. Also, other opportunities for progress may arise in other directions.

Even if a negotiator fails to achieve their objectives, it can be possible to put up markers for the future. This can be about issues to be raised at a later date. If negotiators make predictions that are ignored but which later turn out to have been correct, this is likely to enhance their personal reputation. They are also likely to enhance their reputation by the dignity with which they accept failure.

Negotiating outcomes

COMMUNICATING THE RESULT

Once an agreement is made it may need to be written up and communicated to all the parties concerned. Employers may want to see that each employee is given details of any agreements affecting them. Care needs to be taken to see that there are no misunderstandings about the content and interpretation of an agreement. In some cases it may be appropriate to issue press releases or hold press conferences.

EVALUATION

It may help to do a cost–benefit analysis of an agreement to see what lessons there are for the future. This can help decide whether there should be further negotiations in the area concerned or if it should be left alone.

IMPLEMENTATION

The terms of an agreement need to be achieved in practice. The practicability of being able to implement the terms of an agreement need to be considered very early on in the negotiating process. Historically there are many cases in the UK of productivity deals between trade unions and employers at a national level which were not implemented locally. Consequently, employers were paying for productivity gains they were not getting. Attention needs to be paid to arrangements for monitoring and control and the need for safeguards if promised concessions are not implemented. Sometimes phased payments are made in accordance with progress made.

INTERPRETATIVE DISPUTES

It may be necessary to provide a mechanism for resolving disputes about the interpretation of an agreement. This may be handled by internal procedures. If internal procedures do not result in agreement there is sometimes provision for reference to an outside party. In the UK there is increasing use of an ombudsman, for example in national and local government and in the banking and travel industries. As previously explained, in the case of disputes between employers and trade unions there can be reference to ACAS for voluntary arbitration.

The way in which disputes about the interpretation of agreements are to be resolved needs to be taken into account when agreements are written. In collective employee relations agreements in the UK the tradition has been to abide by the spirit rather than the letter of the agreement. This is in contrast to the USA, where such documents are legally binding between the parties and interpreted according to the letter of the agreement. Agreements that are binding in spirit may be difficult to interpret by outsiders because of ambiguities and mutual unwritten understandings. However, there is always a case for expressing agreements as clearly as is practicable. The ease with which disputes can arise about what was agreed and the difficulties that can arise in settling such disputes underlines the need to ensure that negotiations are conducted and concluded in such a way that there is little or no room for subsequent disagreement.

VARIATION OF AGREEMENTS

Provision may need to be made for the variation of an agreement. The duration of an agreement may need to be specified, as well as the procedure for seeking to vary it. There may also need to be provision for inflation and escape clauses in the event of specified circumstances. Building and construction contracts usually allow for renegotiation of the price if extra work is requested. It is necessary to beware of open-ended commitments, especially if they can be manipulated by one of the parties. An example of how this can happen was given earlier in the chapter: the open-ended costs clause in a contract offered by a recording studio to four young musicians which could have enabled the studio to offset whatever costs they liked against the revenue generated.

TRAINING

In evaluating negotiating outcomes attention may need to be paid to the skill with which the negotiations were handled. This may reveal training needs. Training needs may also be created by reorganisation, particularly if that involves giving more responsibility to line managers for negotiation. This often happens when business units are created and the authority of central functional departments, such as HR, is reduced.

The development of negotiating skills can be achieved by the gradual exposure of managers to negotiating situations. They may learn much by watching experienced negotiators in action. Skills can also be developed on formal training courses. Participants can develop their diagnostic skills by identifying objectives and tactics in a graded series of exercises. Simulation exercises involving role-playing can provide the opportunity for people to practice their negotiating skills and gain feedback on their performance in a risk-free environment. Feedback can be given by other participants, observers and, if appropriate, closed-circuit television replays of critical incidents. It can be particularly useful for participants to identify misunderstandings that arise during simulated negotiations and the causes of these misunderstandings. It can also be very useful for participants to experiment with different role allocations during team negotiations (Rees and Porter 1997, pp. 65–68, 153–157).

Summary

Managers spend much of their time in negotiation over a wide range of topics, much of it informal. The pace of change is such that negotiation and renegotiation is becoming ever more important. A key theoretical distinction is between integrative and distributive bargaining. In integrative bargaining the parties may be able to co-operate in such a way that they make their objectives complementary to one another. In distributive bargaining one party can only gain at the expense of the other. The importance of the frames of reference of the negotiators was also considered in this chapter. Managers with a unitarist perspective may be handicapped by failing to understand the rationale of those with whom they are negotiating. Those with a pluralist perspective are more able to understand the rationale and even the legitimacy of the claims of other parties.

The need for managers to develop a framework for negotiation even in informal situations was explained. This involves preparation, identification of objectives and a rational sequence of events during the bargaining process. Often the internal differences within a team can be more difficult to resolve than those with the external party with whom negotiations need to be conducted. Consequently, considerable time may need to be taken to try and resolve internal differences before negotiations can start. It is also important to examine the power relationships in a bargaining relationship. Power relationships are likely to have much more influence on the outcome of negotiations than the debating skills of the parties involved.

The need for clear roles to be allocated to those involved in team negotiations was stressed. The complexity and pressures involved in negotiations can be such that misunderstandings easily arise. Anticipation of communication problems is important to ensure that real agreement is reached. Division of labour within negotiating teams is one way of avoiding such problems. Key roles are chairing, case presentation, recording and observing. In one-to-one negotiations these activities will all need to be covered by the same person. Sometimes the cost of hiring a specialist negotiator may be a sound investment.

Consideration may need to be given to how deadlock is handled. One way of doing this is by the involvement of a third party. Acceptance of the need for a negotiating ritual, including a series of offers and counter-offers, may be necessary if agreement is to be reached. However, no agreement may be better than a bad agreement. Consideration was also given to the effective implementation and monitoring of agreements. It may also be necessary to make arrangements for variations of agreements and resolving disputes about the interpretation of agreements.

The way in which negotiating skills can be developed was also covered. The skills of negotiation can be systematically identified. Managers can develop their ability to apply these skills by observation, practice, reflection on their own negotiating behaviour, coaching and formal training. The use of simulation exercises can be a useful way of developing negotiating skills in a risk-free environment.

Self-assessment questions

(If you want to check on the extent to which your answer to any of the following questions is appropriate, cross-refer to the Table of Contents. The contents for this chapter are on pages xxi–xxii.)

1 Identify issues you recently had to negotiate both at work and/or elsewhere.

2 Explain one theory relevant to negotiation.

3 Why is it necessary to have a procedural framework for negotiations?

4 What are the different roles that people may need to play during team negotiations?

5 Why is it necessary to identify the power realities of the parties involved in negotiations?

6 Explain the term 'negotiating ritual' and its potential importance.

7 Why are misunderstandings likely during negotiations?

8 How can you try and ensure that agreements are kept?

References

(Works of particular interest are marked with a star.)

David, Saul (1997), *Military Blunders – The How and Why of Military Failure*, Robinson Publishing Ltd.

McCormack, Mark H. (1986), *What They Don't Teach You at Harvard Business School*, Harper Collins.

*Mead, Richard (2005), *International Management, Cross-Cultural Dimensions,* 3rd ed., Blackwell Business. See Ch. 7 *Dispute Resolution and Negotiation* (Mead is invariably good value and Chapter 7 deals with the cross-cultural dimension of negotiation).

*Rees, W. David and C. Porter (1997), *Negotiation – Mystic Art or Identifiable Process?, Parts 1–2,* Industrial and Commercial Training (29: 3, 5). (Part 1 of the article gives a useful account of the value of running training workshops in negotiating skills and how they can be organised. Both articles received a highly commended award by the Emerald Literati club and are available on the book's companion website).

Walton, R. E. and R. B. McKersie (1965), *A Behavioral Theory of Labor Negotiations,* McGraw-Hill, New York.

Further reading

Cohen, Raymond (1998), *Negotiating Across Cultures: International Communication in an Interdependent World,* United States Institute of Peace.

*Fisher, R., W. Ury and B. Patton (1997), *Getting to Yes, Negotiating an Agreement Without Giving In,* 2nd ed., Arrow. (A popular, informative, easy to read and useful account of the negotiating process.)

*Fox, A. (1965), *Industrial Sociology and Industrial Relations*, Research paper no. 3, Royal Commission on Trade Unions and Employers Associations, HMSO. (It may be difficult to access the original paper. Fox's explanation of the concept of unitary and pluralistic frames of reference is classic though and even summaries of his work are well worth reading.)

Meetings and chairing

Introduction

In this chapter the role of meetings in organisations and the associated skills in seeing that they are conducted effectively are examined. Meetings, whether formal or informal, are an integral part of organisational activity and attendance at them can occupy a considerable part of a manager's time. The different types of meetings are explained and the need stressed for those attending a meeting to be clear about their objectives and any decision-making arrangements involved. It is particularly important that the chair and secretary of formal meetings prepare beforehand to ensure that the time at meetings is used effectively. Other members may also need to prepare beforehand, particularly if they want to influence any outcomes. Prior preparation may also be necessary for informal meetings.

The differences between procedures, processes and tasks are explained. Attention is given to the way in which conflict at a meeting may need to be handled and the need for the chair to avoid getting over-involved in discussion. The importance of follow-up action, including implementation and monitoring, is covered. The appendix to this chapter explains the main rules relating to formal committee procedure.

The term 'chair' is used throughout the chapter rather than the alternative expression 'chairman' to emphasise the point that the chair can be a man or a woman.

The need for meetings

PLACE IN ORGANISATIONAL STRUCTURE

Meetings can be an indispensable part of an organisation's structure. In some organisations, such as local government, policy decisions must be taken by a committee-type structure with various committees or subcommittees reporting to the council as a whole. In commercial organisations the need for meetings below the level of shareholders' and directors' meetings may not be obligatory but will still be very necessary.

Meetings may be necessary as an aid to the running of departments. They can also be vital in promoting interdepartmental cooperation which otherwise might not be achieved. The growing complexity of decision-making, caused partly by the diffusion of knowledge within organisations, means that very often decisions can only be taken effectively by groups of people coming together and pooling their knowledge and expertise. **Globalisation** and developments in information technology mean that some meetings involve simultaneous multilingual translation and/or electronic conferencing. If meetings are ineffective it can mean that a vital aspect of organisational structure is failing.

CONSEQUENCES OF INEFFECTIVENESS

There are many reasons why attention needs to be paid to the effective conduct of meetings. The decisions that are taken in meetings can be very important. The quality of decision-making may correlate with the skill with which meetings are conducted. Small improvements in the effectiveness of meetings can also lead to considerable savings in time because of the multiplication of the time saved by the number of people present. Meetings can also have functions other than decision-making, such as providing briefing for those present or ensuring that decisions are taken in an open way.

The quality of decision-making and the efficiency with which business is conducted can affect working relationships outside meetings and the credibility of the role of meetings for future occasions. Managers should also be aware that they are in the spotlight when chairing meetings and that the effectiveness of their performance is likely to enhance or damage their reputation, often before critical audiences. However, if others are responsible for the poor conduct of meetings, at least managers can learn by their mistakes. By contrast, effective chairing is not so obvious as bad chairing simply because things go so smoothly. It is for that reason that the best sports referees are often the ones who are least noticed.

Activities in meetings

LEVEL OF FORMALITY

Meetings can vary in importance and formality, from the proceedings of Parliament to the informal discussion of a temporary problem between colleagues. Whatever the type of meeting, it is necessary for the participants to be aware of the methods by which the business is conducted. These methods fall broadly into the categories listed below.

SUBSTANTIVE CONTENT OR TASK

Substantive content or the task can be defined as the business of the meeting. For the business to be conducted effectively there needs to be a sound procedural and process framework.

PROCEDURAL ARRANGEMENTS

These are the rules that govern the conduct of the meeting. They may be formally embodied in the constitution or terms of reference of a committee, agreed by the parties present or, in some cases, imposed by one party on another.

PROCESS CONTROL

This is the interpersonal interaction between those present. For meetings to be effectively handled there needs to be constructive management of these interactions. Even in very informal situations there is always a process aspect to the discussions, and the skill with which this is handled can affect the quality and acceptability of any outcome. It may be very necessary for someone to discretly take the lead in managing the process in informal situations, thus creating a framework within which discussions can take place. Once the other people involved realise that the lead is being taken by someone simply to facilitate matters rather than to impose their own decision, they may relax and welcome the lead that has been taken.

PURPOSES OF MEETINGS

Meetings can be for a variety of purposes. Important types of meetings are:

- decision-making (which may be part of a constitutional decision-making process),
- negotiating,
- consultation,
- briefing,
- fact-finding,
- exchange of views (which sometimes may involve brainstorming),
- problem-solving,
- bonding – this may be between individuals or a group and other parts of an organisation.

The above classification is a very broad one, and there can be subdivisions within the general headings. Also, some meetings may involve a number or even all of the above activities.

DECISION-MAKING

In the case of decision-making meetings, there are a number of ways in which decisions may be taken. Decisions can be taken by:

- the most senior person present,
- voting,
- consensus,
- negotiation,
- recommendation to another body.

It is important for people to be able to distinguish between the different decision-making arrangements of meetings. If the members of a meeting fail to see the distinction it can lead to confusion; if the chair does not see the differences it can lead to chaos. This can happen if people have a stereotyped view of meetings and start applying the wrong conventions in a particular situation. Managers may assume that they have to operate by consensus or majority vote, when the reality may be that an organisation has vested them ultimately with the sole decision-making responsibility within a particular area. Management chairs at joint consultative meetings can, and sometimes do, use voting procedures and short-circuit established management structures because the chair has not appreciated that a consultative meeting literally means just that. It is an aid to decision-making via established management procedures, not a substitute for those procedures. During formal negotiations there can be three different centres of decision-making: at the pre-meetings of two separate groups, before a joint meeting and during a joint meeting. All three discussions require effective chairing.

Roles in meetings

Even in small informal meetings it may be necessary to identify the roles that members need to play and have an appropriate division of labour. In some cases people can change roles in a meeting, for example from presenting a case to acting as a chair so that others can put their case. Particularly important roles are those of chair and secretary.

THE ROLE OF THE CHAIR

A chair needs to understand the substantive issue under discussion but also needs to devote some time to a consideration of how the meeting is to be handled effectively. A common error is for the chair to be so immersed in the substantive issues that they neglect the procedural arrangements and the issue of process control. An appropriate division of labour in formal meetings is that the chair spends perhaps most of their time on procedural matters and process control, someone else takes the minutes and the other members concentrate on the substantive issues. A meeting where no one concentrates or even bothers about the procedural and process aspects is the one most likely to be ineffective. The role of the chair is examined later in the chapter with particular regard to resolving conflict during meetings and the danger of the chair's overinvolvement in discussion.

The need for process leadership may exist even in informal discussions between relatively few people. Sometimes the level of informality, the competitive nature of relationships or the sensitivity of the issues being discussed is such that it is inappropriate for a formal chair to be appointed. It may nevertheless be both useful and necessary if one person, perhaps quite informally, deals with the process aspects of discussion. This may involve taking a purely neutral role and asking such questions as 'What is the problem?' or 'What are everyone's views?'. The other parties may be quite prepared to let one person emerge as the informal chair, particularly if it is seen that they are confining themselves to a neutral role. It may later be possible for that person to enter into the substantive discussions – but only so long as they demonstrate that this is not going to endanger the process control arrangements that have evolved. Otherwise, the person may find that their substantive contributions are not welcome or that their process leadership is challenged.

THE ROLE OF THE SECRETARY

If a meeting is of any size it may be necessary to have a secretary. This can be a very influential role. This may be a legal or other formal requirement. The secretary can take much of the load off the chair. This may be particularly important if the chair has other extensive commitments. It will also enable the chair to concentrate on the important issues that need attention. Much of the preparatory, administrative and follow-up work may need to be handled by the secretary, including preparation of the draft agenda and distribution of relevant papers, including the agreed agenda. The chair and secretary should spend time together before a meeting to plan how it can be most effectively handled. This can increase the influence of the secretary, but one should beware of the business of a meeting being pre-empted by such discussions. A preliminary meeting should be in order to facilitate the smooth running of the main meeting, not to ensure that it acts as a rubber-stamp for the chair and secretary.

The secretary will also take responsibility for keeping a record of a meeting. They may do this themselves or alternatively have another person operating under their control taking notes. The minutes will need to be checked by both the secretary and chair. Even in small informal meetings it may be best if one of the parties identifies and carries on whatever secretarial activity is necessary. This may include a note of any significant outcomes, including what follow-up action is needed and by whom. This topic is considered further in the section on recording the outcome of meetings later in this chapter.

Preparation before meetings

The amount of preparation required before meetings will vary according to the type of meeting – its formality, importance, predictability and the role that the individual who is attending the meeting is going to take. There can be few meetings, however, to which people do not need to give some prior thought. Perhaps the most important issue to consider is what your own objectives are going to be at a meeting. It is only when these have been clarified that it is possible to establish what other prior preparation is required. It is also necessary to consider what is likely to be expected of you at a meeting. This may indicate the preparation you need to make so that other people's needs can be taken into account.

Any procedural rules or constitutional statement about the powers of a meeting not only need to be to hand but also thoroughly understood, so that such issues can be dealt with immediately and reassuringly if they emerge during a meeting. One would not be reassured by a football referee who had continually to refer to a book on the rules of football whilst a game was being played. The more formal the meeting, the more a chair may rely on the secretary to handle procedural matters before a meeting and to be a source of information during it. It may be expected that the meeting will be run not just in accordance with its constitution but also by the normal conventions of committee procedure. Consequently, a list of these conventions is included as an appendix to this chapter. The chair will also need to understand the substantive issues and their history sufficiently to guide the discussion effectively.

THE AGENDA AND ITS MANAGEMENT

Clearly, meetings need a structure for the consideration of substantive items. This structure is normally provided by an agenda. However, it is necessary to be proactive in thinking about an agenda and not simply list the items in the order that they are received. Both the chair and the secretary may have to think carefully about what items need to be considered. If decisions are to be taken at a meeting, the degrees of freedom available need to be identified and explained.

The frequency of meetings and their duration need to be related to the volume of business. The volume of business may also need to be managed by combining items. Thought should also be given to logical sequence of items. A further issue is the need to allocate time for discussion of individual items. It is all too easy to spend an inordinate amount of time on easy and relatively minor items with key issues being left to the end when people may be in a hurry, tired and a meeting not even **quorate**. Approval may be needed from the meeting as a whole about issues such as sequence, time allocations and deferment of items. Exceptionally, the order of business may need to be varied because, for example, a key person has to leave. Other items may be introduced under 'any other business', but not if they are controversial and should have been identified on the original agenda. The chair also needs to beware of the agenda being hijacked by a member or members raising items 'on the back of' other items instead of tabling these issues beforehand with written reports if necessary. Another issue for the chair to beware of is a meeting being used as a dumping ground for issues where responsibilities lie elsewhere or for problems that simply cannot be resolved.

Sometimes it is appropriate to have reports under standard headings, e.g. from the heads of the various departments, at a meeting. However, there is a danger that this can descend into a defensive ritual.

Reporting by exception

In a British manufacturing company most of the time in meetings was spent in receiving and considering reports from departments within the company. These tended to be both detailed and defensive and led to little productive outcome. As result it was decided to institute reporting by exception, i.e. reports were only received from individual departments if there was something exceptional that needed to be discussed. This had the advantage of freeing up considerable time for the issues that really did need discussion.

WHO SHOULD ATTEND MEETINGS?

Thought may have to be given to who should be invited to a meeting. This may be totally prescribed by the constitution of a committee but, when the constitution is first established, the matter has to be examined. In any case, constitutions sometimes need amendment, people may need to be specially invited to attend meetings and, on occasions, people may need to be excluded from meetings or part of the proceedings because of conflicts of interest. A balance usually has to be struck between having the interested parties present and not involving too many people because of the varying levels of interest and the costs involved, particularly in terms of time. A system of subcommittees can be a way of getting the optimum balance between differing interests and economy of time. Sometimes it will be appropriate to establish **ad hoc** subcommittees that can enable the detail of a particular issue to be examined without holding up the main business of a meeting.

It can be particularly dangerous to exclude a person from a meeting primarily because they are likely to take a controversial position, or at least one that is considered to be controversial as far as the chair is concerned. To exclude someone on this basis may lead to charges of unfair chairing, which may then mean that the chair is under procedural challenge as well as being challenged on a substantive issue. Controversial issues tend to surface anyway, and it may be best to see that this happens via the established machinery for resolving conflict rather than in another way, particularly if the chair would otherwise lose respect in the process.

OTHER PREPARATION

Other issues that may require forethought include the exact nature of information that people attending meetings need to have beforehand so that they can contribute effectively and the seating arrangements at a meeting. The type of room and layout can affect discussion, as can seating arrangements. Seating arrangements can be controlled by providing place names, which has the added advantage of identifying those present.

There may be pre-meetings before the main meeting. In national and local government it is customary for political parties to meet to agree on a party line before engaging in public debate at the formal decision-making body. It is usually the case that the real decisions are taken by the majority party in their pre-meeting. Other pre-meetings may be of groups of people forming a **caucus** to try to agree the line that they will take during a meeting. A small minority who prepare in this way can have a powerful influence on the outcome of any discussions. They will be primed and create a certain amount of momentum for the views that they express during a meeting. If they vote together at a meeting, they may find that the natural divisions amongst the other people present make it relatively easy to get a majority in favour of their point of view. This may lead other sub-groups to have pre-meetings as well, in an attempt to counter such tactics. One way of dealing with an attempt to force a minority point of view through a committee or other meeting is simply to alert other members as to what is happening beforehand. The chair or any member of a committee may wish to forestall a particular proposal. It may be a matter not so much of converting others, which may be difficult, but of alerting people as to what is happening so that they are on their guard as far as their own interests are concerned. This may also be necessary when there is an attempt to conceal information.

The importance of preparation before meetings was illustrated by the example given in Chapter 4 concerning the former Wales Gas Board. Those managers who prepared for the consultative committee meetings with employee representatives found that the committees played a constructive role. Those who did not prepare and who perhaps also did not take the committees seriously found that the employee representatives simply stopped attending, causing the committees to collapse.

Conduct by the chair during meetings

THE CHAIR AS A FACILITATOR

Several problems can arise during a meeting. A key job of the chair is to see that they actually use the knowledge of the people who are present. It is up to the chair to see that appropriate issues are identified for discussion and then ensure that the collective knowledge and skills of the members are used to resolve the issues. If further information would help, the chair needs to consider releasing or obtaining it.

The chair may contribute to the substantive discussions, but should only do so when the issues have been properly identified. In practice chairs vary considerably in the skill with which they use the abilities of the people present. Good and bad examples are obvious on radio and television programmes, just as there will be good and bad examples of chairing in most organisations. It can be instructive to identify the differences between effective and ineffective chairs on public display in the media. Some chairs are very adept at drawing out the views of those who have been invited to speak and at controlling subsequent media discussion. Others lacking this skill, or just wishing to be the centre of attention themselves, may invite people to contribute to programmes and then use their procedural position and studio confidence to talk too much themselves, and in so doing wreck any discussion.

THE CHAIR'S ROLE IN RESOLVING CONFLICT

One of the key roles of meetings can be as a way of resolving conflict. Ironically, the role of a chair can be to identify what the conflict is in the first place. Unless this is done, agreement may be reached before the basic issues have been adequately considered. Another general problem is the need to handle conflict in such a way that the mechanism for resolving it is not destroyed in the process. Sometimes there is little or no conflict and the exchange of specialist information leads to a decision to which all contributors are equally committed. On other occasions the conflicts can be so bitter that the decision-making process collapses. The range of potential conflict within national government assemblies is such that members do not risk having a chair who is not neutral: the Speaker, who chairs the proceedings, has a neutral procedural role. Non-executive mayors fulfil the same function in meetings of local government councils. Many trade unions appoint a president who fulfils a similar function. One of the advantages of having separate people as Chairman of the Board of Directors and Chief Executive, covered in Chapter 3, is that the Chairman can concentrate on the procedural and process issues, leaving the Chief Executive to take the lead on substantive matters.

In the absence of a specially appointed and generally neutral chair, it will normally be the most senior person present who will chair a meeting. If they are in conflict with other people at a meeting it will often be appropriate to simply try and talk the issue through. Often other members of a meeting may be able to challenge inappropriate ideas more strongly than the chair because they are not hampered by the need to control discussion in an equitable way at the same time. Members of a meeting may also find that it is more acceptable to have the flaws in their logic exposed by other members rather than the chair. Often the members will resolve controversial issues without the chair having to get involved. Even if that is the case it may be easier for the chair to resolve some controversial issues later rather than sooner. In addition some of the conflict may have been resolved, leaving the chair only having to deal with residual issues. However, that does not mean that the chair should not, when appropriate, take the lead and explain why a particular course of discussion is likely to be unproductive. This may be particularly necessary because often the chair is also the person who may know most about the substantive issues that are being discussed.

What members of a meeting may take particular exception to is not being allowed to air their views when appropriate. It is one thing to have the reasons why your views are not acceptable explained, but quite another thing not to be given an opportunity to express them at all. In situations in which the final decision rests with the chair it may be quite appropriate and acceptable for the chair to say at the end of discussion 'I have heard all that you have had to say and this is what I am going to do.' If disagreement has to be resolved in some other way, for example, by a vote, that is the time when the chair should ask for one of the members to put the issue to a vote.

A further cause of irritation, particularly where the final decision rests with the chair, can be if members are invited to discuss issues that the chair has secretly already decided. It may then emerge that the members have complete freedom to come to the decision that the chair has already determined! A chair can avoid or reduce such irritation by saying that they are disposed to take a particular course of action but want to check if there are any objections that they had not anticipated. It may also be appropriate to say that a decision has been taken and the discussion is only about implementation. What a chair should avoid is the pretence that the members of a meeting can influence a decision when it has already been made.

The ability of chairs to handle a discussion where they have an interest in the outcome varies considerably. It can be likened to trying to referee a football match in which you are also playing. Some people will be able to handle such potential conflict better than others. Sometimes it may be appropriate to have someone else chair discussion on an issue where the chair is particularly involved or where there is a conflict with their personal interests. However, it is not always practicable or desirable to keep asking to have a neutral chair. This means that chairing skills are one of the key skills that managers need to develop.

DANGERS OF OVERINVOLVEMENT BY THE CHAIR

It is very easy for the person chairing a meeting to underestimate the extent to which they get involved in discussion and to overestimate the extent to which other people are involved. This is also a problem that can confront lecturers who have responsibility for leading discussions. One system for training lecturers in the technique of discussion-leading is to chart the pattern of contributions during a discussion. The resultant chart or '**sociogram**' can reveal a pattern of which the discussion leader was unaware. A typical pattern is shown in Figure 16.1.

An examination of the flow of discussion in Figure 16.1 shows that most of the discussion was centred upon the chair or discussion leader. There was little cross-discussion, and one person did not contribute at all. If this was appropriate, and the chair was aware of what was really happening, it may have been perfectly satisfactory. However, it is very easy for a chair to assume that, because they are involved and interested, so is everyone else. This is not automatically the

| **Figure 16.1** | **Chair-centred discussion** |

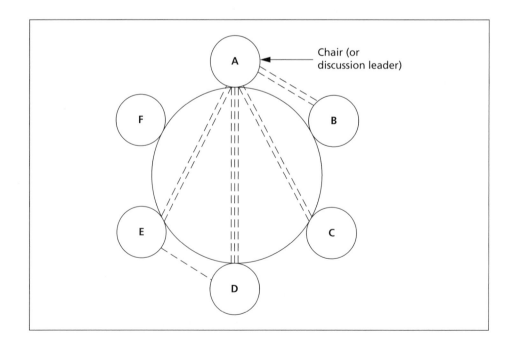

case. It is possible for a person to sit through a meeting, seething with frustration, but not contributing. Others may remain passively silent though able to contribute. Meanwhile, the chair may be quite unaware of all this. It can be instructive for a chair to be shown a flow chart (or sociogram) of a meeting they have chaired and mentally try to build up a picture of the actual pattern of discussion during their next meeting. Regular checks on the body language of those present can provide important clues as to their feelings about particular topics and about the conduct of the meeting generally. It can also be instructive for one's self development to draw a sociogram of a meeting you have attended.

The chair who talked too much

Example

A story is told about a brand new judge who took his place on the bench determined to achieve standards of self-restraint. At the end of his first day he thought he had done remarkably well and went round to his old chambers to see a friend who had been appearing in front of him all day. 'How did I do?' asked the new judge confidently. 'Not bad at all dear boy,' said the other. 'But you really must stop talking so much.'

(Evans 1983 p. 87)

INVOLVING MEMBERS

Often the flow of discussion that is actually needed is more like that shown in Figure 16.2. In this second chart it is much less obvious who is the chair. Everyone has contributed and there is more cross-discussion than was the case in the previous chart. The flow of discussion may need to be routed more through the chair in large formal meetings, but even in that situation it may be appropriate to allow some cross-discussion provided it is not disruptive. In large formal meetings it may still be necessary for the chair to check out the attitudes of members to the way meetings are handled. There may be major misperceptions of the dynamics of meetings.

Inadequate involvement of members

Example

The attitudes of the various members of a hospital management committee towards the way in which meetings were handled were established by observation of the meetings and interviews with key participants. There were some surprising differences in perception. The chair and secretary appeared convinced that everyone had ample opportunity to contribute. This was in marked contrast to the senior member of the nursing staff in particular, who was clearly of the opinion that she was only permitted to speak when invited to do so. In this particular case, open discussion was not helped by the fact that meetings were conducted in a long rectangular room. The higher the status of a person, the closer they sat to the head of the table. Discussion was confined to those sitting close to the chair. The nursing representative sat at the far end of the table, away from the chair and secretary.

Figure 16.2	Group-centred discussion

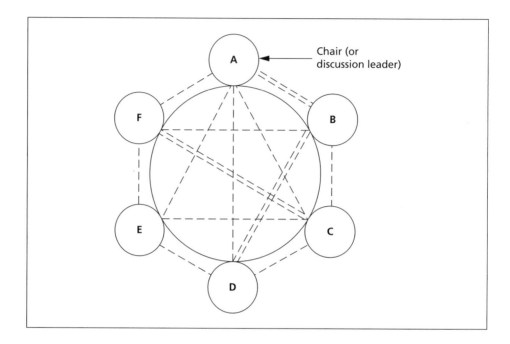

Appropriate involvement of members

At another hospital in the same group as in the previous example, management committee meetings were held in a room which permitted seating arrangements to be in the form of a semi-circle, which seemed to permit a more genuinely open discussion. The different seating arrangements, whether by accident or design, reflected the very different managerial styles of those organising the meetings.

OTHER ISSUES
Control by the chair

There are other important points to note. These include the need for the chair to protect the position of a member if they are being ridiculed, particularly if they have a potential contribution to make. The routing of all contributions through the chair may only be necessary when the group lacks the self-discipline to evolve a means of taking it in turns to speak. If the chair is ignored, or if people talk whilst the chair is speaking, the pointed silence may be a more appropriate way of re-establishing control than by the raising of one's voice. The use of humour may also be an effective way of relieving tension and progressing a meeting.

Pace of discussion

Chairs need to strike the right balance concerning the pace of discussion. People may be very concerned to state their own views but impatient of the right of others to do the same. Too quick a pace may leave many people with the feeling that they have not had adequate opportunity to state their views, whilst too slow a pace may leave many people with the view that their time has been unnecessarily wasted. The ease with which points at issue can simply be misunderstood should never be underestimated. It is important that the chair clarifies and summarises whenever there appears to be any doubt or whenever decisions are taken.

Cultural issues

It is increasingly necessary to take account of any cultural diversity within meetings. This is more common because of globalisation, ease of international travel, greater cultural diversity within countries and developments in technology. It is also more likely because of organisational developments such as multi- and transnational companies, joint ventures, greater inter-government cooperation on a regional and national basis and developments such as European Works Councils. Sometimes such developments necessitate simultaneous translation into a number of different languages.

Videoconferencing

Meetings can now take place without all members being physically present by video link-up. Whilst videoconferencing can have many advantages, it is also necessary to be aware of its limitations. Considerable technological resources are needed to set it up. The quality of interaction cannot be as great as if members are physically together. Also, a key aspect of meetings can be the informal exchanges between members that often take place before, during and after meetings.

RECORDING THE OUTCOME

The possibility of confusion about the content and outcome of a meeting will be reduced if there are adequate minutes or whatever other record is appropriate. However, for this to be undertaken effectively, meetings need to have been conducted properly in the first place. One does not, for example, want misunderstandings about what was really decided to be left to surface when the minutes are distributed. As was explained in the previous chapter in the context of negotiation, there are many factors which can cause confusion. These include selective perception, poor listening skills and the use of ambiguous language.

Recording can take a variety of forms, but verbatim records are rarely necessary or useful. A circulated minute is the most common type of record but, if this is inappropriate, as a minimum the chair should make an 'aide-mémoire' even in many informal situations. Other parties involved may also find it prudent to record an aide-mémoire where there is no formal minute.

A record of the outcomes of a meeting is what is crucial. A record of the whole course of discussion may be counterproductive. In the heat of discussion people may say things that it is in no-one's interest to record. Consequently, considerable tact may be needed in writing up minutes so that the outcomes are accurately recorded without rekindling arguments that have been settled. The responsibility for action also needs to be carefully identified to help ensure that action that is agreed is actually implemented. Where the scale and importance justifies it, one may need a note-taker who is separate from the person advising the chair on procedural matters.

Summary

Informal and formal meetings are an integral part of organisational activity. Consequently, managers need to know the various purposes of meetings and how they are or should be structured. As managers are often likely to chair meetings it is particularly important that they develop effective chairing skills. The effects of badly organised meetings were examined. These effects include poor communication and decision-making. Badly conducted meetings can also waste a lot of people's time and damage the reputation of those responsible for their organisation. The need for prior preparation was explained, even with informal meetings. This affects all those involved in a meeting, but particularly the chair and any secretary. The preparation for formal meetings involves the drawing up of an agenda and arranging a division of labour at a meeting so that the chair in particular is not overloaded.

The role of conflict at meetings was examined, as was a strategy for handling it. Usually it is best for chairs to facilitate a fair discussion about the issues and then use whatever mechanism is appropriate (e.g. voting, negotiation, unilateral decision-making) for resolving it. Members may be far more likely to be upset about not having had the chance to raise legitimate concerns than by having a decision go against them. Decisions are in any case likely to be more balanced if they are taken after a full examination of the issues.

The need for chairs not to get over-involved in substantive discussion at meetings was stressed, as this can damage the procedural framework within which discussions need to take place. Their overinvolvement can also lead to inadequate process control during a meeting. The need for effective recording was also considered. It is important that responsibility for any action is clearly identified and that implementation is monitored.

Self-assessment questions

(If you want to check on the extent to which your answer to any of the following questions is appropriate, cross-refer to the Table of Contents. The contents for this chapter are on pages xxi–xxii.)

1 Identify the range of meetings in which you are likely to be involved in any one day or week, both formal and informal.

2 Identify the purpose of these meetings and any decision-making mechanisms.

3 Select a meeting that you have recently attended and consider whether roles were properly allocated and kept to or not.

4 Draw a sociogram (or flow chart) of the discussion at the meeting you attended.

5 Practise using chairing skills at an informal meeting you attend.

6 How might the chair of a meeting best handle conflict? If possible, answer with reference to a meeting you have attended.

7 What follow-up action may be necessary to ensure that meetings are effective? Answer with reference to a meeting you have attended.

References

Evans, Keith (1983), *Advocacy at the Bar: A Beginner's Guide*, Financial Training Publications.

Further reading

Evans, Keith (1992), *Advocacy at the Bar: A Beginner's Guide*, 2nd ed., Blackstone Press.
Forsyth, P. (1998), *Making Meetings Work*, Institute of Personnel and Development: London.
Tropman, J. E. (1996), *Making Meetings Work: Achieving High Quality Business Decisions*, Sage.

Appendix to chapter 16

DEFINITIONS AND EXPLANATIONS OF SOME TERMS USED IN FORMAL MEETINGS

Ad hoc: this Latin phrase literally means 'to this'. Its meaning has been extended to 'set up to serve a particular purpose'. Thus, an *ad hoc* committee is one which has been set up to serve a particular purpose and which will cease to exist as soon as this purpose has been served.

Agenda: Latin meaning 'things requiring or deserving to be done'. It is really plural in form but is now used as a singular word and means simply 'a list of the items of business to be dealt with at a meeting'.

Amendment: when someone moves that a proposition should be altered in some way, they are moving an amendment. It should be noted that an amendment proposes an alteration of a proposition, not a direct negation of it or a completely different proposition.

Ballot: a secret vote. Members register their votes on paper and not by a show of hands.

Casting vote: the chair is allowed an ordinary vote as a member of the meeting. Sometimes, however, the standing orders allow them an extra vote, which is called a casting vote, because they may, if they so wish, use it to decide on an issue on which the voting is equal.

Co-opt: if a committee feels that it would benefit from the services of some person possessing special qualifications or experience, it may decide (if it has been given such powers) to co-opt that person, i.e. to make them an additional member of the committee. The committee has exercised power of co-option and the person has been co-opted.

Ex officio: a person may claim to be a member of a committee, not because they have been elected, but *ex officio*, that is 'by virtue of their office'.

Minutes: a brief but accurate record of what took place at a meeting.

Motion: anything that is moved or proposed at a meeting. Thus, a proposition is a motion but an amendment is also a motion.

Nem. con.: an abbreviation for the Latin phrase *nemine contradicente* which means 'no-one speaking against'. Thus an item 'carried *nem. con.*' may have people abstaining from voting and therefore does not mean the same as 'carried unanimously', which means that everyone present voted for the motion.

Next business: when a motion is being debated it may appear to some member or members that it would be unfortunate for the meeting to reach a decision on the matter in question or that it would be a waste of time to continue the debate. One device to stop the debate is for a member who has not already spoken to stand up and say 'Chair, I move next business'. If this motion is seconded, it is put to the vote immediately, without discussion, and if it is carried the meeting does in fact move on to the next business. If the motion is defeated, the meeting then resumes the debate on which it was already engaged.

Nominate: to propose someone for election to an office. A nomination does not necessarily need to be seconded.

Other business: this may appear on the agenda of a meeting to allow members to raise items which have come to light after the agenda has been prepared. However, any items the chair allows under this heading must be agreed by the meeting to be urgent and to have come to notice so recently that there was no time to have them included in the agenda.

Point of information: sometimes a member who does not wish to take part in a discussion, or who is preparing to speak later, may wish to ask a question on relevant facts. They may do this by saying 'Chair, on a point of information, can you tell me, etc.'

Point of order: a member may rise at any time and say something on a point of order, but they should soon be told to sit down if what they say is not in fact on a point of order. The member must be able to prove, or reasonably to question whether, another member has spoken or acted, or something has been done, or is going to be done that is not in accordance with the rules, standing orders or terms of reference or other regulations which govern the conduct of the meeting. A point of order relates only to procedure – if the point raised is really part of the subject under discussion, it is not a point of order.

Previous question: that the question be not now put. If the motion is carried, no more discussion of the main question can occur, and it is shelved. If it is not carried, then the original motion must be put to the vote at once. Previous question can only be moved for an original or substantive motion.

Quorum: this is a Latin word meaning simply 'of whom'. Its meaning in meeting procedure is extended to the number of members who must be present before the proceedings can be valid. The quorum for a meeting is usually laid down in the rules or standing orders which apply, but if it is not laid down it is generally taken to mean a minimum of approximately one-third of the membership and never less than three.

Reference: when a task has been delegated by a meeting to a committee or by a committee to a subcommittee, the committee or subcommittee will eventually report to the main body and will probably recommend some action. If a member of the main body does not agree with any action reported or recommendation made, they should move the reference back to the report. This motion is discussed and if it is carried it means that the committee or subcommittee must reconsider the subject in question and report again later.

Resolution: it is wrong to talk of moving or proposing a resolution. One can move or propose a motion or proposition and either of these becomes a resolution if it is passed. In other words, a resolution is something that a meeting has resolved to do.

Right to reply: it is customary to allow the mover of a proposition (but not of an amendment), who will have spoken first in the debate, the right to speak again at the end of the debate. In the second speech, however, they must not introduce any new material, but merely reply to points already raised by other speakers.

Standing orders: organisations which hold regular formal meetings (e.g., trade unions, councils, clubs) often have rules which stipulate the manner in which the business of their meetings shall be conducted. These are called standing orders, and they deal with such things as the length of time for which speakers may speak, the order in which speakers shall speak, the manner of conducting elections of officers, the order in which items shall be taken. Standing orders may be in addition to, or may even override, the general rules of meeting procedure. If there are any standing orders, the chair and the secretary should be very familiar with them. A member may at any time move suspension of standing orders and have this motion debated. For instance, if standing orders stipulate that a speaker may speak for only five minutes, it may occasionally be desirable to allow someone to exceed this limit in order to complete an important statement. Suspension of standing orders, if carried, will allow them to do this.

Substantive motion: when any amendments to a motion have been passed, the motion has its wording altered accordingly and is then called the substantive motion.

Teller: this means a member who has been appointed to count the number of votes cast on any question.

Terms of reference: these are instructions given, generally to a committee, defining clearly the nature and the limits of the task which it has been set.

That the question be now put: this may be moved at any time during the debate on a motion but must be moved by someone who has not already spoken. If it is carried, the matter under debate is immediately put to the vote; if it is not carried, the debate is resumed. Clearly this is a useful device to stop unnecessary or useless discussion (see also **next business**).

Glossary

The terms below are printed in bold in the text the first time they are used in a chapter.

ACAS: Advisory Arbitration and Conciliation Service (UK).

Act down: undertaking tasks that are normally or more appropriately undertaken by subordinates.

Act up: undertaking tasks normally done by one's boss when the boss (or bosses) are unavailable.

Action learning: management development via problem-solving with others, conceived as a formal methodology by Reg Revans.

Ad hoc: this Latin phrase literally means 'to this'. Its meaning has been extended to 'set up to serve a particular purpose'. Thus, an *ad hoc* committee is one which has been set up to serve a particular purpose and which will cease to exist as soon as this purpose has been served.

Added value: the value added to a product or service by an organisation.

Alternative economy: the unofficial economy in a country that operates outside state control.

Assertiveness: putting one's point politely but firmly while recognising the right of others to do the same.

Balanced score card: a means of staff appraisal to assess the profile of a person in key areas.

CA: Court of Appeal

Caucus: a sub-group of people who meet privately to try and influence the decision of a larger group or meeting.

Charisma: charm combined with force of personality.

Conflicts of interest: (in the context of employee relations) a difference about what an agreement should be, e.g. the amount of an annual pay award.

Conflicts of right: (in the context of employee relations) a difference about the interpretation of an agreement.

Consensus: by agreement of all the parties directly concerned.

Contingency approach: the adaptation of behaviour (or choice of management techniques) according to the needs of the situation.

Corporate governance: the system of policy-making, control and ethics in any organisation, including governments.

Corporate and social responsibility: acceptance by an organisation of its wider responsibilities towards those affected by its decisions, such as customers, suppliers, the community and the environment, as well as to those who finance it and its employees.

Critical path analysis (CPA): a method for determining the most logical sequence of scheduling a project.

Digital divide: the division between those who are computer literate and those who are not.

Discretionary authority: a situation in which the person making a decision is able to use their judgement.

Discretionary content: that part of a job where the manner of execution is left to the job-holder, as long as the execution is conducted in a reasonable manner and the overall objectives are achieved.

Disposable workforce: the employment of staff so that they can be released with the minimum of notice and payment when the need for them has reduced or ended.

Distributive bargaining: a situation in which one person or group can only gain at the expense of another.

Diversity management: a way of managing that capitalises on a diverse workforce by using the mix of talent, values and points of view to business advantage.

Dotted line relationship: the relationship of a person who reports to, or gives advice to, another, but only on an advisory basis.

E-commerce: trade carried out by electronic means.

E-learning: the use of information technology to facilitate learning.

EAT: Employment Appeal Tribunal.

ECJ: Eropean Court of Justice.

Electronic data interchange (EDI): A set of standards for the electronic exchange of data for business purposes.

Emotional intelligence: being able, for example, to rein in an emotional impulse, to handle relationships smoothly, to motivate oneself and to persist in the face of conflict and frustrations.

Empowerment: the authority of a person or group to take decisions without prior authorisation by a higher level.

Equal pay: equal payment for same or similar work. Generally there is a legal right to this between the sexes under European law.

Equal value: equal pay for work which though different is equally demanding. There is a general legal right to this between the sexes under European law.

Ethnocentric: attention, concern and values based around a particular national group.

Explicit knowledge: important know-how in an organisation that is clear and probably recorded (the converse of tacit knowledge).

Flexible organisation: an organisation with only a core group of workers but many peripheral ones, which may be very reliant on outsourcing as well. Where there are very few core workers, such an organisation may be described as a virtual organisation.

Fordism: mass production based on division of labour and strict control, as practised by Henry Ford and the Ford Motor Company.

Frames of reference: whether a person adopts a unitary or pluralistic perspective to conflicts of interest within an organisation. See also **pluralistic** and/or **unitary**.

Functional control: where those in charge of functional areas of management have line authority over others in the same function, wherever they are located. Examples of the standard functions in organisations are Production, Finance, Sales, Human Resources and Quallity Control. An extreme version of functional control is where the head of a function also controls those elements of their functional area performed by people working in other areas.

Glass ceiling: an invisible barrier that prevents people from being promoted. May particularly apply to minority groups.

Globlisation: the increasing internationalisation of market forces, technology and social interaction.

Golden handshake: an arrangement for an employee to leave an organisation on terms that are financially advantageous to them.

Halo effect: a perceived favoured aspect of an individual's behaviours or a favoured personal characteristic that is assumed to be representative of an individual's total ability or behaviour. The opposite is 'reverse halo effect' or 'horns effect'.

Human capital management: protecting, consolidating and developing the intellectual assets of an organisation.

Human resource management (HRM): the effective utilisation of employees. Usually facilitated by, but not directly controlled by, an HRM department.

Instrumentality: in the case of employees this means the minimisation of input so that work objectives can be achieved with least effort. It can also involve the distrortion of organisational objectives to suit the employee.

Integrative bargaining: where constructive bargaining can lead to gain on the part of both or all the parties involved.

Intellectual capital: the accumulation of intellectual assets of an organisation.

Intellectual property: the legal rights to the intellectual assets of an organisation, e.g. patents and copyright.

Internal labour market: the staff resources available within an organisation.

Investors in People (IIP): a British government accreditation scheme recognising organisations that manage their training and development needs appropriately.

Inward investment: capital investment in a country by an organisation or organisations in other countries.

Job competences/competencies: defining job demands in terms of the outputs that are required. Potentially useful in selection, training and pay.

Job distortion: when a job has been rearranged so that the appropriate objectives and activities are not being met either in full or in part. Can particularly happen when a job is rearranged to meet individual rather than organisational needs.

Job instrumentality: taking a very calculating and material approach to one's job and carefully limiting what is given in return.

Just-in-time employment: the deployment (and disposal) of staff only at the point in time when they are needed.

Kaizen: discussion groups designed to secure continuous improvements in quality and efficiency, used particularly in Japanese business organisations.

(Key) performance indicators (K)PI: measures of effectiveness of an organisation, potentially particularly appropriate in the public and other not-for-profit sectors.

Knock-on effect: the repercussive consequences of decisions.

Knowledge management: systematic review of an organisation's intellectual assets with a view to their maintenance, protection, development and utilisation.

Learning contract: an agreement under which the trainer and the trainee specify their respective inputs and the desired learning outcomes they expect to be achieved.

Learning curve: graphical representation of the rate at which people acquire new skills and/or knowledge.

Learning organisation: an open type of organisation that facilitates the exchange of ideas both internally and externally with a view to developing both staff and the organisation.

Line and staff relationship: organisational arrangement where authority is vested in line managers and advice given by functional staff.

Management by objectives (MBO): a formal scheme of management direction and control centred upon interlocking objectives.

Managerial escalator: the progression from specialist to managerial activity.

Managerial gap: the extent to which managerial activities are neglected in favour of specialist activities.

Managerial grid: a measure of how managers allocate their time between task and employee needs. A concept developed by Blake and Mouton.

Managerial hybrid: a person with significant managerial and specialist responsibilities.

Matrix structure: an organisational arrangement under which people have both a line manager and a project leader.

Mechanistic systems: a clear if rigid set of arrangements for structuring an organisation based in particular on hierarchy, specialisation and unity of command.

Micromanagement: involvement in the detailed control of the activities in one's area of responsibility.

Mission statement: a statement of the overall aims, objectives and values of an organisation.

Monochronic: concentrating on one task at a time.

Negotiating ritual: a series of offers and counter-offers made with a view to obtaining eventual agreement.

Negotiating under duress: pressure being applied during negotiations, e.g. strike action.

Non-government entity (NGE): a not-for-profit organisation that is not controlled by the government, e.g. a charity. If international, e.g. OXFAM, it is known as an INGE.

Non-governmental organisation (NGO): similar to NGE.

Offshoring: contracting out production or services to overseas suppliers.

Opportunity cost: the alternative use that could have been made of resources.

Organic systems: a fluid approach to organisational structure based on market needs with authority and reporting relationships arranged to fit those needs.

Outsourcing: contracting out of production or services, not necessarily overseas.

Peer audit: review of performance by colleagues.

Performance-related pay: a formal link between pay and performance. Usually dependent on the achievement of specified tasks and/or objectives.

Personal development plan (PDP): a programme for improving one's performance and capability.

Person specification: the main personal attributes, education and experience that a person needs in order to be able to do a particular job.

Pluralist/pluralistic: a recognition that whilst there will be common aims in an organisation, there will also be competing sectional interests.

Polychronic: dealing with several tasks at once.

Positive action: employment policies designed to improve the representation of minority groups within the workforce in general and/or specific grades e.g. by the provision of developmental training. It does not involve positive discrimination.

Positive discrimination: preferential treatment of minority groups within the workforce to improve their representation in general and/or specific grades.

Power distance: the hierarchical gap between people in an organisation – may also involve the extent of the deference by one person to another.

Prescribed content: that part of a job that must be carried out in a particular way, e.g. in order to conform to organisational policies and the law.

Private equity: used in a specific sense to describe a group of private investors who seek to take over a company with a view to increasing its profitability.

Private finance initiative (PFI): public sector organisations borrowing from the private sector to finance capital projects.

Psychological contract: the expectations that an employee will have of their employer and vice versa. These expectations will not necessarily be written down or enforceable in law, but will influence the state of the relationship between an employer and their employees.

Quorate: having the constitutional minimum number of people at a meeting to make it valid.

Referent power: the ability to influence others by virtue of personal liking, charisma or reputation.

Role set analysis (RSA): a technique for prioritising work.

Sapiential authority: influence by virtue of one's job expertise and facilitation skills.

Serial entrepreneur: an entrepreneur who starts up a series of successful businesses.

Shadowing: learning by observing the behaviour of a senior manager or colleague.

Sociogram: a chart of the pattern of discussion at a meeting.

Socio-technical systems: an organisation structure or substructure caused by the interaction between technical and social factors.

Span of control: the number of people reporting to a particular manager.

Stakeholders: individuals or groups who contribute to the performance of an organisation and/or who have an interest in its success. Examples are shareholders, financial backers, employees, suppliers and customers.

Status quo: arrangements as they are before an actual or planned change.

Subsidiarity: allowing decisions to be taken at the lowest appropriate level.

Synergy: where the whole is greater than the sum of parts.

Systems theory: a view of organisations as a dynamic set of interconnecting activities which also interact with the external environment.

SWOT analysis: estimate of the strengths, weaknesses, opportunities and threats facing an organisation.

Tacit knowledge: implicit 'know-how' in organisations that may be held by groups and/or individuals which, though important, may not be recorded (the converse of explicit knowledge).

360-degree appraisal: performance assessment of a person by the key people or groups with whom they interact. May include external people or groups such as customers.

Total quality management (TQM)**:** a formal method of ensuring that appropriate standards are built into the process whereby products or services are provided.

Transnational corporation: an international commercial organisation with its roots in no particular country.

Triple I organisation: an organisation based on intelligence, information and ideas.

Tunnel vision: over-concentration on a particular task or job.

Uncertainty avoidance: the desire to avoid ambiguity.

Universal inclusion: an employer that takes a positive approach to all sections of the workforce and their potential contribution.

Unitary/unitarist: viewing an organisation as having common aims to which all should or do subscribe.

Unity of command: an organisational structure in which each member of staff has only one boss.

Upward appraisal: assessment from below, particularly by subordinates.

Zero-hours contracts: an arrangement by an employer to provide work but without actually guaranteeing any.

Index